Prophetic warnings to modern America

Duane S. Crowther

INTERNATIONAL STANDARD BOOK NUMBER
0-88290-016-1

LIBRARY OF CONGRESS CATALOG CARD NUMBER
77-87431

Second Printing, November 1979

Printed in the
United States of America
by

Horizon Publishers
& Distributors
P.O. Box 490
50 South 500 West
Bountiful, Utah 84010

Dedication

To my family,
whose love and companionship I cherish
and desire for the eternities.
May this book
strengthen them, guide them, and
stabilize their faith
during the trials of the last days.

Back row, left to right: Duane, Don, Scott, David, William. *Front row:* Sharon, Jean, Bethany (on lap), Lisa. Not shown is Laura (deceased).

Acknowledgements

Deep appreciation is felt for the staff of Horizon Publishers, who rendered effective service in helping this book towards completion. Anyone acquainted with publishing will readily acknowledge that this book would present a major challenge to any typesetter. Norma Lund rose to that challenge and met it well, devoting many weeks to the task and doing so with patience and painstaking effort. Anna Marie Bollschweiler and Pat Horton worked cheerfully and accurately to paste up, strip negatives, and make bluelines and plates to prepare for the press runs.

Naaman Buckmiller, production foreman, supervised the entire manufacturing effort with care. His keen eye for detail, his ability to manage a variety of projects simultaneously, and his kind and loyal spirit are valued assets to the company and the basis of my deep respect and friendship. Final production of the book was performed by Horizon's bindery staff. Their efforts are appreciated on this project, as on every task they undertake.

Horizon's office staff, shipping department, and salesman were poised and ready to send the book on its way as it was completed, which I greatly appreciated also.

All of these individuals, plus others not involved in the production of this book, are my co-workers at Horizon Publishers and Distributors. They are good people, who maintain the spirit of the gospel in their lives from day to day. I deem it a real privilege to be able to work with them and to count them as friends.

During all the many months in which this book was being written, my wife, Jean, gave encouragement, read proofs, made constructive suggestions, and maintained a spirit of harmony in the home. She supported me in the effort, as she does in all things. How blessed I am to have her! And how blessed I have been, also, to have had the love and support of my family. I was strengthened by all of them, and even the youngest ones prayed to their Heavenly Father, asking Him to "please help Daddy finish his book!"

Prophetic Warnings to Modern America was not easily written. It required many months of work and effort, with time taken from a schedule which was already full to overflowing. Much was written beginning at four o'clock in the morning. Yet I often felt the promptings and guidance of that Being in whom I have placed my trust and love, and I *know* His influence has been manifested in much of what I have written. I readily confess His hand in all things, and express my deepest gratitude for His guidance, direction, and protection. May His blessings be upon us all.

Table of Contents

Section I

America—God's Chosen Land

Section II

The Prophetic Warnings

Section III

Famine, Sword and Pestilence—
Instruments of God's Judgments

Section IV

Personal Preparation for the Last Days

Explanation of
Reference Symbols

Most references have been cited in full, giving full bibliographical data. Scriptural references have been cited in standard form, giving the accepted abbreviation for the book followed by chapter and verse(s). Certain well-known sources, however, have been referred to in abbreviated form, as follows:

CR — *Conference Reports* of The Church of Jesus Christ of Latter-day Saints. Issued semi-annually, these are near-verbatim reports of the proceedings of April and October General Conferences. Items cited are identified by date.

DEN — *Deseret Evening News*, a newspaper which circulated in Utah during the early pioneer period.

DN — *Deseret News*, a daily newspaper in current circulation in Utah and surrounding states. Most items cited from this source are actually national news releases from the various wire news services.

HC — *History of the Church*, a seven volume Latter-day Saint history covering the Joseph Smith era and including the western exodus of the Mormon pioneers. It was written by and under the direction of Joseph Smith, edited by B. H. Roberts, and is sometimes called the *Documentary History of the Church*.

IE — *The Improvement Era*, a monthly periodical published by the LDS Church beginning shortly after the turn of the century. It was recently discontinued and replaced by the *Ensign* and the *New Era*.

JD — *Journal of Discourses*, a twenty-six volume collection of discourses by LDS Church leaders from approximately the first three decades of the Utah period.

TPJS — *Teachings of the Prophet Joseph Smith*, a one volume compilation of doctrinal writings and discourses of the prophet Joseph, extracted primarily from the *History of the Church*.

Preface

I love America! It is my home, my native land. It has been great and good—a bastion of freedom and liberty. America has enjoyed the blessings and guidance of God, and her people have been protected through divine providence.

I have partaken of the liberties which she has granted to her citizens—privileges which are denied to people in many other lands. These liberties I value highly, and I regard them as priceless gems to be preserved at all costs. In the shadow of her freedoms I work, I plan, I dream, I hope, I build for the future. I seek America's well-being, her progress, and her protection, for my future is inseparably connected with hers. If she grows and prospers, I may progress also; if she endures trauma and agony, I also must suffer. I am an American citizen. Like every American—my future and fate is inextricably related to the future of this great country.

Seven Reasons Why This Book Was Written

During the past several years, as this book has moved from creative idea to researched notes to finished pages, I have carefully defined my motives for writing it. So that they may be clearly understood by those who read this volume, I have chosen to list those motives. They are as follows:

1. **I love America, and seek the preservation of this land and of her liberties.** There are many ways in which a citizen may work for his country. He may be active in political affairs, or work for the accomplishment of social goals. He may seek to improve the environment, or pursue better law enforcement methods, or render service through youth groups. Almost always he will serve in those capacities which give outlet for his best talents and abilities. By doing so, he gives the best of himself and accomplishes the greatest good.

I am no different. I am an author and publisher by profession. I seek to use my best skills as an expression of my patriotism and love of country. *Prophetic Warnings to Modern America* is my way of contributing something of worth towards the betterment of this great nation.

2. I seek to warn of difficult times and loss of freedoms which are rapidly approaching. As I study the scriptures and the teachings of those whom I regard as the authorized servants of God today, I find clear warning of an epoch in these last days when *"there shall be a time of trouble, such as never was since there was a nation."*[1] This series of cataclysmic events will be worldwide in scope and devastating in its effect. It will bring much death, suffering, and desolation.

The Savior warned that *"as a snare shall it come on all them that dwell on the face of the whole earth."*[2] I have learned of the terrible suffering mankind must endure if its wickedness causes the prophesied events of this era to transpire. With this insight, I seek to warn others: we must labor with our might to turn the world towards righteousness in the hope that this great wrath and punishment might be withheld.

I approach the events of the future with the understanding of a person trained primarily in one important area. My study and background have been focused in particular aspects of religion and theology. This background includes an advanced degree in Old and New Testament, a thesis study which focused on latter-day eschatology, the authorship of more than a dozen books on the last days and other theological themes, and extensive study for more than two decades on the messages of the scriptures concerning future events. Like Peter of old, "Such as I have give I thee."[3] Though this book will comment on many national and world events, trends, and conditions, my approach will be theological rather than political.

3. I seek to fulfill the God-given commandments that such a warning be given. In Biblical times God revealed to Ezekiel that if a watchman failed to warn his people of impending danger, responsibility for the destruction of that people would be required of that man.[4] In modern times the Lord has commanded that *"the voice of warning shall be unto all people, by the mouths of my disciples, whom I have chosen in these last days."*[5] While warning of this

---

1. Dan. 12:1.
2. Lk. 21:35.
3. Acts 3:6.
4. See Ezek. 33:2-6.
5. *The Doctrine and Covenants of The Church of Jesus Christ of Latter-day Saints* (Salt Lake City, Utah: The Church of Jesus Christ of Latter-day Saints), section 1, verse 4. Further references to this volume of scripture will be shown as *D & C*, with sections and verses cited as: 1:4.

terrible period (known scripturally as the "desolation of abomination"), the Savior revealed that *"it becometh every man who hath
been warned to warn his neighbor...and to prepare the saints for
the hour of judgment which is to come;* that their souls may escape
the wrath of God, *the desolation of abomination* which awaits the
wicked,..."[1]

This warning responsibility belongs to every Latter-day Saint,
not just to a few individuals. I am aware of the Lord's command to
the priesthood of the Church to

> *...go ye forth as your circumstances shall permit, in your several callings,*
> unto the great and notable cities and villages, reproving the world in
> righteousness of all their unrighteous and ungodly deeds, *setting forth
> clearly and understandingly the desolation of abomination in the last
> days.*[2]

His commandment to all who preach the gospel is that

> *...I send you out to reprove the world of all their unrighteous deeds,
> and to teach them of a judgment which is to come.*[3]

Those who labor within the Church sometimes find that the
Lord blesses them with talents, then prompts and uses them to fulfill particular responsibilities. If they fail to use the talents He gives
them, He is angered.[4] I feel that I have been given some understanding and talent on the subject treated in this book. I feel it appropriate, and I feel prompted, that I express such warnings as this
book contains. More important, I recognize that to fail to do so
God might see fit to retract the talent with which He has blessed
me.

4. **I seek to assess the degree of danger which confronts this
country and the members of the Church.** In any endeavor norms
must be set and evaluations conducted before trends and direction
of movement can be established. No business can know if it is profitable until it carefully counts its assets and liabilities. No educational system can determine if learning is taking place until valid
standards have been established and careful testing has been carried
out.

---

1. D & C 88:81, 84-85. See also verses 87-89.
2. D & C 84:117.
3. D & C 84:87.
4. D & C 60:2-3, 12-13. See also Mt. 25:24-30.

The Lord has revealed very definite standards with which the people of this country must comply if they are going to escape His judgments and gain blessings and prosperity in the land. One effort of this book is to closely report those standards—those prophetic warnings. Another objective is to gather facts and statistics which would indicate whether Americans are turning to God or abandoning His ways.

5. I seek to clearly portray what God has revealed will happen unless the nation returns to righteousness. The Lord has revealed to the latter-day prophets much of what will transpire in America in the future if wickedness prevails. Patterns are also found in the histories of other civilizations as they broke divine laws and underwent the same judgments.

Over the years I have found that people soon separate into two schools of thought when they begin to consider the prophetic warnings concerning the last days. Some want to know, understand, and prepare. Others, however, adopt the classic "head-in-sand" pose of the ostrich—they don't want to know of the warnings God has revealed. They rationalize His words of warning as "pessimism," and say they are "not uplifting," rather than giving heed to the revealed words of God. The same problem existed in the days of Heber C. Kimball, counselor to Brigham Young. He said:

> ...*if we do not take the right course, we are sure to see sorrow, and the greatest you have ever seen.* Those who were never without bread, and clothing, and good houses to dwell in, murmur the worst; and *those who never had any troubles and trials since they were in this Church, or since they have been on the earth, are the most ready to complain.*
>
> Go and read the prophets: They all say so. Don't be frightened; I tell you it will come; and *it would be better for you to believe it and go and make calculations accordingly.* Shall we ever be brought to want? I tell you, if we live our religion, we never shall.[1]

6. I seek to suggest possible solutions and appropriate actions. Over the years, many have proposed actions and policies which would help alleviate the nation's distress. I have assembled and sifted their proposals, and have attempted to suggest meaningful and realistic procedures which can serve to preserve and strengthen

---

1. Heber C. Kimball, as quoted by Weston N. Nordgren, "Shall We Go Hungry?—A Vital Question Answered Nearly a Century Ago by a Prophet of the Lord—Heber C. Kimball," Salt Lake City, Utah:*Improvement Era*, Vol. 43, No. 11, Nov. 1940, p. 662.

this country—policies which can be followed on an individual level for the betterment of this country.

7. I seek to make a contribution to patriotic literature and to the literature of the Church by assembling important materials and making them readily available to others.

In my profession as an author and publisher, I have learned that thoughts and materials must be available in useable form before they begin to have lasting impact upon large numbers of people.

In this book my role is that of reporter, compiler, and analyzer of teachings revealed in the scriptures and through modern prophets. I will assemble individual items together, point out relationships and trends, and draw such conclusions as would be appropriate for any editor or news analyst to make.

It should be understood that this book is a private endeavor; it is not an official publication of The Church of Jesus Christ of Latter-day Saints. From the beginning, the writing and compiling of Church-oriented books for commercial distribution has been left to individual authors who have functioned on their own initiative. Such books have been privately published and are the responsibility of the individual authors, not the Church itself. Church authorities have been wisely refrained from regulation and censorship of the writings of individual members. Members write, often seeking and receiving revealed guidance, but without any official status. The Lord has said,

> ...*It is not meet that I should command in all things;* for he that is compelled in all things, the same is a slothful and not a wise servant; wherefore he receiveth no reward.
>
> Verily I say, *men should be anxiously engaged in a good cause, and do many things of their own free will, and bring to pass much righteousness;*
>
> *For the power is in them, wherein they are agents unto themselves.*
> And inasmuch as men do good they shall in nowise lose their reward.[1]

A prominent LDS author once said to me, "You know, Duane, it's a blessing that there are members of the Church who write about Church history and doctrine on their own—*they are able to say a lot of important things that the Church can't say officially.*" His comment struck me with real force, and I am sure it is valid. There is definitely a place—an important place—for writ-

---

1. D & C 58:26-28.

ings other than the manuals and instructions issued by the Church
in its official capacity. The writings of individual Latter-day Saint
members throughout the history of the Church illustrate his premise
well. Such books soon find their own level. If their works furnish
information and insights of real value, they are widely read; if they
make little real contribution, they are soon discarded. The general
Church readership does a far better job than any official regulation
could do in determining true worth.

Pitfalls Avoided

There are several difficulties I have tried to avoid as I have
written *Prophetic Warnings to Modern America.*
First, I have sought to *avoid political bias* and party positions.
You can rest assured that you won't know whether I am a Republican, a Democrat, or an Independent when you have finished the
book. I have no political aspirations nor axe to grind.
Second, I have sought very carefully to *avoid extremism—*
I am not a "right-winger," nor do I lean to the opposite extreme.
I do not belong to any militant organization. I speak and write
only as a deeply-concerned citizen.
If I have any bias, it is religious rather than political or ideological. This book is a theological book, which accepts the validity
of Latter-day Saint scriptures and reveals my faith that the prophets who wrote them are inspired men who have expressed the Lord's
will concerning America in their teachings. You who are not LDS
may not accept the validity of this premise. I invite you, at least,
to consider their messages as the words of wise men and evaluate
them in the light of current world and national conditions. To do
less than that would be foolishness on your part.
Third, I believe that propaganda and loose interpretation of
documentation colors and falsifies truth. I have sought to *avoid
propaganda and also to avoid the assertion of improper doctrinal or
eschatological conclusions.* I have sought to quote the scriptures
accurately and to interpret them with care, remembering well the
words of the prophet Alma: "Behold, the scriptures are before you;
if ye will wrest them it shall be to your own destruction."[1]
When one deals with prophecy, the future always stands as
the final judge—erroneous data, improper conclusions, and incorrect interpretations are shown to be wrong with the passage of time.

---

1. Al. 13:20.

There is nothing to be accomplished by drawing an incorrect picture of the future.

It has been said that the two subjects one shouldn't discuss if he wishes to avoid controversy are religion and politics. *Prophetic Warnings to Modern America* focuses on both of these areas. After having written other books on doctrinal themes, I am not so naive as to expect that this work will completely escape the barbs of a few self-appointed critics. Certainly a book with the message which this one carries will receive scrutiny by those who might oppose its warning voice. I only ask that their evaluation be honest, and that it be made with care and with a desire for the ultimate well-being of this great land.

Be there criticism or not, this message must go forth. The Spirit has prompted and instructed, and has not allowed me to turn aside. I am like Martin Luther: "Here I stand. I can do no other."

Concern Because of Wickedness and Indifference

While I love this country and work for its preservation, I cannot help but feel deep concern for its future. That concern is evident throughout much of this book. I fear we are losing the liberties we presently enjoy because of the wickedness which is engulfing our nation and because of governmental actions and decisions which are robbing us of our freedoms.

I find my feelings reflected in the attitudes of Moroni, a Book of Mormon patriot who rallied his people under a "title of liberty," on which he had inscribed the words

> *In memory of our God,*
> *our religion, and freedom,*
> *and our peace,*
> *our wives, and our children.*[1]

He was a good man, possessed with the qualities I greatly admire:

> And Moroni was *a strong and a mighty man;* he was *a man of a perfect understanding;* yea, a man that *did not delight in bloodshed;* a man *whose soul did joy in the liberty and the freedom of his country,* and his brethren from bondage and slavery;
> Yea, a man *whose heart did swell with thanksgiving to his God,* for the many privileges and blessings which he bestowed upon his people; a man who *did labor exceedingly for the welfare and safety of his people.*

---

1. Al. 46:12-14.

> Yea, and he was a man who was *firm in the faith of Christ*, and he had
> sworn with an oath to defend his people, his rights, and his country, and
> his religion, even to the loss of his blood.[1]

Yet, as Moroni fought against the invading Lamanites he was concerned and angry because of the wickedness and indifference of his own Nephite people and government:

> And now, when Moroni saw that the city of Nephihah was lost he
> was exceeding sorrowful, and *began to doubt, because of the wicked-*
> *ness of the people, whether they should not fall into the hands of their*
> *brethren.*
> Now this was the case with all his chief captains. *They doubted and*
> *marveled also because of the wickedness of the people,* and this because
> of the success of the Lamanites over them.
> And it came to pass that *Moroni was angry with the government,*
> *because of their indifference concerning the freedom of their country.*[2]

It is that same concern which motivates the writing of this book.

Constructive Criticism is Chastening with Love

A parent does not act in the best interests of his children by allowing their misdeeds to go uncorrected. A teacher does not give his best to his students unless he shows them their weaknesses and challenges them to improve. A citizen does not act in the best interests of his community unless he speaks out for correction of dangerous conditions. In each case, such individuals are motivated by love and concern for the well-being of others as they point out their weaknesses. God also chastens those He loves. Concerning the Nephites, for instance, Samuel the Lamanite observed,

> ...they have been a chosen people of the Lord; yea, the people of Nephi
> hath he loved, and also hath he chastened them; yea, *in the days of their*
> *iniquities hath he chastened them because he loveth them.*[3]

When danger approaches, we call out with a warning voice to those we love. It is in that spirit that this book is written—it is an effort to warn and correct, so that we may be spared the terrible events which lie ahead if America continues on her present course. It is my sincere hope and prayer that its message will be heeded.

---

1. Al. 48:11-13.
2. Al. 59:11-13.
3. Hel. 15:3. See also D & C 95:1, 101:4-5.

Though there may be some who resent the warning message, we are commanded by God to deliver it, and

> ...notwithstanding their hardness, let us labor diligently; for *if we should cease to labor, we should be brought under condemnation; for we have a labor to perform whilst in this tabernacle of clay, that we may conquer the enemy of all righteousness, and rest our souls in the kingdom of God.*[1]

Duane S. Crowther

---

1. Moroni 9:6.

I

AMERICA— GOD'S CHOSEN LAND

America:
A Choice Land of Promise

I

An oft-cited principle in Latter-day Saint theology is that the Americas are a chosen land which God has designated and reserved for a righteous people. This belief has its origin in the Book of Mormon, which repeatedly refers to these continents as a land especially blessed by the Lord. That volume tells of several groups who were led to the Americas by the hand of God.

As early as the second chapter of the book, a revelation from the Lord to Nephi, the son of the prophet Lehi, is recorded:

> ...inasmuch as ye shall keep my commandments, ye shall prosper, and *shall be led to a land of promise;* yea, even *a land which I have prepared for you;* yea; a land which is *choice above all other lands.*[1]

While still in the Palestine area, Nephi was given instructions from the Holy Spirit, which caused him to comment on the expectations he held concerning the land of promise:

> *Behold the Lord slayeth the wicked to bring forth his righteous purposes.* It is better that one man should perish than that a nation should dwindle and perish in unbelief.
> And now, when I, Nephi, had heard these words, I remembered the words of the Lord which he spake unto me in the wilderness, saying that: *Inasmuch as thy seed shall keep my commandments, they shall prosper in the land of promise.*[2]

As Nephi was endeavoring to obtain a copy of the scriptures so that his people might have their sacred message, his father, Lehi, told his mother, Sariah, of the land of promise and rejoiced that they would be led there:

> ...I know that I am a visionary man; for if I had not seen the things of God in a vision I should not have known the goodness of God, but had tarried at Jerusalem, and had perished with my brethren.
> *But behold, I have obtained a land of promise, in the which things I do rejoice;*[3]

---

1. 1 Ne. 2:20. Nephi received this message in a wilderness area near the Red Sea, about 600 B.C., as he and his family were fleeing from Jerusalem.
2. 1 Ne. 4:13-14.
3. 1 Ne. 5:4-5.

13

Attaining the choice land was an ever-present goal for the Lehi colony as they traveled.[1]

Nephi's Vision of God's Guidance in America

Even before crossing the ocean to arrive in the Americas, Nephi was given a glorious vision in which he was shown many events which would transpire in the promised land. He saw that Lehi's descendants would multiply and become multitudes of people,[2] that there would be wars among them,[3] and that they would build many cities.[4] He saw that the Lamb of God would come among them, that Christ would choose and ordain twelve disciples here in the Americas,[5] and that the Savior's coming would be preceded by great destruction.[6] Nephi was shown that righteousness would prevail until the fourth generation after the Savior's advent, and then wars would again break out.[7] He saw that the descendants of his brother Laman (the Lamanites, forefathers of the American Indians) would conquer his descendants,[8] and that the Lamanites would then war among themselves for many generations,[9] as they dwindled in unbelief.[10]

Nephi's vision swept forward to the end of the dark ages when he saw many "nations and kingdoms of the Gentiles"[11] which were across the seas from the Lamanites here in the Americas.[12] In his vision he foresaw what many Latter-day Saints believe to be the coming of Columbus to the Americas, and observed that his coming would be inspired by the Spirit of God:

> And I looked and beheld a man among the Gentiles, who was sepa-
> rated from the seed of my brethren by the many waters; and *I beheld the*
> *Spirit of God, that it came down and wrought upon the man; and he*
> *went forth upon the many waters,* even unto the seed of my brethren,
> who were in the promised land.[13]

---

1. See 1 Nephi 5:4-5.
2. 1 Ne. 12:1.
3. 1 Ne. 12:2.
4. 1 Ne. 13:3.
5. 1 Ne. 12:6-10.
6. 1 Ne. 12:4-5.
7. 1 Ne. 12:11-15.
8. 1 Ne. 12:19-20.
9. 1 Ne. 12:21.
10. 1 Ne. 12:22-23.
11. 1 Ne. 13:1-9.
12. 1 Ne. 13:10.
13. 1 Ne. 13:12.

Nephi was then shown in his vision that the Spirit of God would inspire other Gentiles to leave the captivity and oppression of their homelands and to sail to the Americas.[1] He described the coming of these early American settlers and emphasized that they were led by God:

> And *I beheld the Spirit of the Lord, that it was upon the Gentiles, and they did prosper and obtain the land for their inheritance;* and I beheld that they were white, and exceedingly fair and beautiful, like unto my people before they were slain.
> And it came to pass that I, Nephi, beheld that the Gentiles who had gone forth out of captivity did humble themselves before the Lord; and *the power of the Lord was with them.*[2]

In his vision, Nephi foresaw the revolutionary struggles of these settlers as they won independence for the Americas. He was shown that *"the wrath of God was upon all those that were gathered together against them to battle"* and that they "were *delivered by the power of God* out of the hands of all other nations."[3]

Nephi was aware of the religious attitudes which would be manifested among the people of the Americas, and foretold the influence which the Bible would have among them.[4] He was also shown that the inhabitants of America would be *"lifted up by the power of God above all nations,* upon the face of the land which is choice above all other lands."[5]

Although he was aware that there would be contention between the American settlers and the Indian inhabitants,[6] Nephi saw that the Lamanites would be preserved by God and that they would not be destroyed.[7]

And then, in his vision, Nephi was told that God, in his mercy, would bring forth his "plain and precious" gospel here in the Americas,[8] and that the gospel would come first to the "Gentile" settlers and then would be carried to the Lamanites, the descendants of Lehi.[9] Those who would seek to establish the Lord's "Zion" in

1. 1 Ne. 13:13.
2. 1 Ne. 13:15-16.
3. 1 Ne. 13:17-19.
4. 1 Ne. 13:20-29.
5. 1 Ne. 13:30.
6. 1 Ne. 13:14.
7. 1 Ne. 13:30-31.
8. 1 Ne. 13:34-35.
9. 1 Ne. 13:34-35.

that day would be blessed with "the gift and power of the Holy Ghost."[1]

Nephi's powerful vision continued into the future and details significant events which must yet come to pass.[2] Every event in the prophetic timetable which he foresaw in this vision 600 years B.C. has come to pass so far. His inspired insight reveals repeatedly that God has guided and shaped the growth of America and that this is a choice land—a land of promise.

Statements by the Lehi Colony Concerning the Promised Land

When Lehi and his colony arrived in the Americas that great prophet bore witness of God's covenant concerning the land to which they had been led:

> ...we have obtained a land of promise, a land which is choice above all other lands; a land which the Lord God hath covenanted with me should be a land for the inheritance of my seed. Yea, the Lord hath covenanted this land unto me, and to my children forever, and also all those who should be led out of other countries by the hand of the Lord.
>
> Wherefore, I, Lehi, prophesy according to the workings of the Spirit which is in me, that there shall none come into this land save they shall be brought by the hand of the Lord.
>
> Wherefore, this land is consecrated unto him whom he shall bring.[3]

Lehi's son, the prophet Jacob, also spoke concerning the role of America as a promised land. He testified that

> ...this land, said God, shall be a land of thine inheritance, and the Gentiles shall be blessed upon the land.
>
> And this land shall be a land of liberty unto the Gentiles, and there shall be no kings upon the land, who shall raise up unto the Gentiles.[4]

Jacob reminded his followers that the Americas were consecrated by God as an inheritance for the descendants of Lehi.

---

1. 1 Ne. 13:37.
2. His prophecy concerning these future events will be considered later in this book. See the "Index to Scriptures Cited."
3. 2 Ne. 1:5-7. Lehi's statement is prophetic and continues into the future. It will be considered in detail later in this book.
4. 2 Ne. 10:10-11. The Savior, as He visited the Americas, spoke of the coming of the Gentiles in the last days, and observed that "it is wisdom in the Father that they should be established in this land, and *be set up as a free people by the power of the Father,...*" (3 Ne. 21:4.)

He repeated the Lord's word that

> ...I will *consecrate this land unto thy seed,* and them who shall be numbered among thy seed, *forever,* for the land of their inheritance; for *it is a choice land, saith God unto me, above all other lands,* wherefore I will have all men that dwell thereon that they shall worship me, saith God.[1]

A later admonition by Jacob to his people included his reference to "this land, *which is a land of promise unto you and to your seed.*"[2]

It is clear, then, that early Book of Mormon prophets recognized that God had shaped their lives for good by bringing them to a land which was to receive His special blessings and protection.

Jaredite Teachings Concerning the Land of Promise

The people of an earlier migration to the Americas also were shown by revelation that their destination was a land which was special in the eyes of God. This group, the Jaredites, left the Middle East at the time of the Tower of Babel. Like the Lehi colony, they also crossed the ocean under divine direction to settle in a land of promise. The Lord told the Brother of Jared:

> ...I will go before thee into *a land which is choice above all the lands of the earth.*
>
> And there will I bless thee and thy seed, and raise up unto me of thy seed, and of the seed of thy brother, and they who shall go with thee, a great nation. And there shall be none greater than the nation which I will raise up unto me of thy seed, upon all the face of the earth. And thus I will do unto thee because this long time ye have cried unto me.[3]

As he wrote the Jaredite history, the prophet Moroni told of the Jaredite migration to the Americas and commented that

> ...The Lord would not suffer that they should stop beyond the sea in the wilderness, but he would that they should come forth even *unto the land of promise, which was choice above all other lands, which the Lord God had preserved for a righteous people.*[4]

---

1. 2 Ne. 10:19.
2. Jac. 2:12.
3. Eth. 1:42-43.
4. Eth. 2:7. This passage also continues to become an inspired prophetic warning which will be discussed later in this book.

Moroni reported a revelation from the Lord to the brother of Jared which the Master concluded with the statement that "these are my thoughts upon the land which I shall give you for your inheritance; for *it shall be a land choice above all other lands.*"[1]

The promised-land concept remained with the Jaredites throughout their history. Moroni commented on a group of them many centuries later, observing that

> ...never could be a people more blessed than were they, and more prospered by the hand of the Lord. And they were *in a land that was choice above all lands, for the Lord had spoken it.*[2]

The last of the Jaredite prophets, Ether, told his people

> ...of all things, from the beginning of man; and that after the waters had receded from off the face of this land *it became a choice land above all other lands, a chosen land of the Lord; wherefore the Lord would have that all men should serve him who dwell upon the face thereof;*
> And that it was *the place of the New Jerusalem,* which should come down out of heaven, and the holy sanctuary of the Lord.[3]

Latter-day Revelations Concerning America as a Land of Promise

The theme of America being under the special providence of God continued into revelations given since the restoration of the gospel and the Lord's Church.

In the summer of 1828, the Lord spoke to Joseph Smith concerning the faith and prayers of the Book of Mormon prophets.

---

1. Eth. 2:15.
2. Eth. 10:28.
3. Eth. 13:2-3. His prophecy continued to tell of a New Jerusalem, a city which is to be built in America in the last days:

> And that *a New Jerusalem should be built upon this land, unto the remnant of the seed of Joseph,* for which things there has been a type.
> For as Joseph brought his father down into the land of Egypt, even so he died there; wherefore, the Lord brought a remnant of the seed of Joseph out of the land of Jerusalem, that he might be merciful unto the seed of Joseph that they should perish not, even as he was merciful unto the father of Joseph that he should perish not.
> Wherefore, *the remnant of the house of Joseph shall be built upon this land; and it shall be a land of their inheritance;* and they shall build up a holy city unto the Lord, like unto the Jerusalem of old; and they shall no more be confounded, until the end come when the earth shall pass away. (Eth. 13:6-8.)

He told Joseph that

> ...their faith in their prayers was that this gospel should be made known also, if it were possible that other nations should possess this land;
>
> And *thus they did leave a blessing upon this land in their prayers, that whosoever should believe in this gospel in this land might have eternal life;*
>
> Yea, that it might *be free unto all of whatsoever nation, kindred, tongue, or people they may be.* [1]

A revelation on January 2, 1831, at a Church conference at Fayette, New York, again conveyed the Lord's promise that America would be a land of inheritance for the saints:

> And I hold forth and deign to give unto you greater riches, even *a land of promise*, a land flowing with milk and honey, upon which there shall be no curse when the Lord cometh;
>
> And *I will give it unto you for the land of your inheritance*, if you seek it with all your hearts.
>
> And this shall be *my covenant with you, ye shall have it for the land of your inheritance, and for the inheritance of your children forever*, while the earth shall stand, and ye shall possess it again in eternity, no more to pass away.
>
> But, verily I say unto you that in time ye shall have no king nor ruler, for I will be your king and watch over you.
>
> Wherefore, hear my voice and follow me, and *you shall be a free people*, and ye shall have no laws but my laws when I come, for I am your lawgiver, and what can stay my hand? [2]

America Founded with Divine Assistance

A frequent message of LDS General Authorities has been that the founding fathers of America functioned under divine guidance

---

1. D & C 10:49-51.
2. D & C 38:18-22. His promise was followed a few verses later with a warning:

> *Ye hear of wars in far countries, and you say that there will soon be great wars in far countries, but ye know not the hearts of men in your own land.*
>
> *I tell you these things because of your prayers;* wherefore, treasure up wisdom in your bosoms, lest the wickedness of men reveal these things unto you by their wickedness, in a manner which shall speak in your ears with a voice louder than that which shall shake the earth; but *if ye are prepared ye shall not fear.*
>
> *And that ye might escape the power of the enemy, and be gathered unto me a righteous people, without spot and blameless—*
> (D & C 38:29-31.)

as they established this nation and led it through the perils of its first century. Over the years, they have cited numerous examples in world and American history to show how God has shaped the destiny of America. Their comments, when taken collectively, serve to illustrate that this view is widely held by Church leadership.

Columbus, for instance, bore witness of having received aid from God as he made his memorable voyage. The following statement made by the discoverer of America was cited in a recent general conference by Elder Mark E. Petersen of the Council of the Twelve:

> The Lord was well disposed to my desire and he bestowed upon me courage and understanding; knowledge of seafaring he gave me in abundance,...and of geometry and astronomy likewise.... *The Lord with provident hand unlocked my mind, sent me upon the sea, and gave me fire for the deed.* Those who heard of my enterprise called it foolish, mocked me and laughed. *But who can doubt that the Holy Ghost inspired me?*[1]

William Penn, the founder of the city in which the Declaration of Independence was later signed, recognized the need for divine guidance when he warned that *"those people who are not governed by God will be ruled by tyrants."*[2]

George Washington, on several occasions, acknowledged God's hand in the guiding of this country toward liberty. Following the battle of Yorktown, during the Revolutionary War, he gave instructions that

> *Divine service is to be performed tomorrow* in the several brigades and divisions. The Commander-in-Chief earnestly recommends that the troops not on duty should universally attend with that seriousness of deportment and gratitude of heart which *the recognition of such reiterated and astonishing interposition of Providence* demands of us.[3]

In his farewell address to the army made November 2, 1782, Washington told how "the singular interpositions of Providence in our feeble condition were such as could scarcely escape the observ-

---

1. Jacob Wasserman, *Columbus, the Don Quixote of the Seas* (New Brunswick: Rutgers University Press, 1959), pp. 19-20, as quoted in *CR*, April, 1967, pp. 111. A statement by Columbus to King Ferdinand is cited from the same source: *"I came to your majesty as the emissary of the Holy Ghost."* (Wasserman, pp. 46.)
2. William Penn, as cited by Elder Richard L. Evans of the Council of the Twelve, "Our Legacy of Liberty," *IE*, Vol. 54, No. 9, Sept., 1951, p. 656.
3. As cited by Elder Mark E. Petersen of the Council of the Twelve, *CR*, April, 1967, p. 111.

ance of the most unobserving."[1] While speaking to Congress on April 30, 1789, Washington spoke of the belief Americans held that God had aided them:

> *No people can be bound to acknowledge and adore the invisible hand which conducts the affairs of men more than the people of the United States.* Every step by which they have advanced to the character of an independent nation seems to have been *distinguished by some token of Providential agency.*[2]

He then commented on the place of religion and morality in the nation, observing that

> Of all the dispositions and habits which lead to political prosperity, *religion and morality are indispensable supports....* Reason and experience both forbid us to expect that national morality can prevail in exclusion of religious principle.[3]

---

1. *Ibid.*, p. 112.
2. *Ibid.*, also cited by Elder Ezra Taft Benson of the Council of the Twelve, *CR*, April, 1952, p. 59.
3. Benson, *Ibid.*, p. 59. Elder Wendell J. Ashton, the General Secretary of the Deseret Sunday School Union, cited other interesting items about George Washington:

To delve into the lives of these patriots reveals an abundance of strong religious conviction.... As a boy, George wrote his motto in his notebook: "Labor to keep alive in your breast that little spark of celestial fire, conscience." He was a regular attender at his church, taking an active part in his parishes at Alexandria and Pohick.

But Washington's deep-rooted faith branched out beyond chapel walls. Winthrop, the historian, tells us, "It is an interesting tradition that, during the prayers with which Dr. Duche opened that meeting [the First Continental Congress] at Carpenter's Hall on September 5, 1774, while most of the delegates were standing, Washington was kneeling." [Robert C. Winthrop, *Presidents of the United States*, edited by J. G. Wilson, p. 19.]

Washington's true humility shone out when Lewis Nicola, a colonel in his army, apprised him of a movement afoot, after the war, to make the general their king. "Banish these thoughts from your mind, and never communicate, from yourself or anyone else, a sentiment of a like nature," was the fiery reply. [*Ibid.*, p. 25.]

Two days after he had received a proclamation from Congress announcing the cessation of hostilities with Britain, Washington ordered the army chaplains to "render thanks to Almighty God." [*Ibid.*, p. 27].

Again, in his inaugural address, Washington's thought rose heavenward: "It would be peculiarly improper to omit in this first official act, my fervent supplication to that Almighty Being who rules over the universe, who presides in the councils of nations, and whose providential aids can supply every human defect." (The Signers of the Constitution," *IE*, Vol. 45, No. 9, Sept., 1942, pp. 563, 598.)

Patrick Henry's dramatic declaration at the Second Revolutionary Convention (Richmond, Virginia, March 23, 1775) was recalled by President David O. McKay:

> Is life so dear, or peace so sweet, as to be purchased at the price of chains and slavery? Forbid it, Almighty God! I know not what course others may take; but *as for me, give me liberty or give me death!* [1]

During the Constitutional Convention in 1787, a speech was made by **Benjamin Franklin** requesting that prayer be held. President J. Reuben Clark, Jr., cited it in a discourse illustrating the divinely-inspired nature of the U.S. Constitution:

> The small progress we have made after four or five weeks close attendance and continual reasonings with each other—our different sentiments on almost every question, several of the last producing as many noes as ays, is methinks a melancholy proof of the imperfection of the Human Understanding. We indeed seem to feel our own want of political wisdom, since we have been running about in search of it. We have gone back to ancient history for models of Government, and examined the different forms of those Republics which having been formed with the seeds of their own dissolution now no longer exist. And we have viewed Modern States all round Europe, but find none of their Constitutions suitable to our circumstances.
>
> In this situation of this Assembly, groping as it were in the dark to find political truth, and scarce able to distinguish it when presented to us, *how has it happened, Sir, that we have not hitherto once thought of humbly applying to the Father of lights to illuminate our understandings?* In the beginning of the Contest with G. Britain, *when we were sensible of danger we had daily prayer in this room for the divine protection.— Our prayers, Sir, were heard, and they were graciously answered. All of us who were engaged in the struggle must have observed frequent instances of a Superintending providence in our favor.* To that kind providence we owe this happy opportunity of consulting in peace on the means of establishing our future national felicity. *And have we now forgotten that powerful friend? or do we imagine that we no longer need his assistance?* I have lived, Sir, a long time, and the longer I live, the more convincing proofs I see of this truth—*that God governs in the affairs of men.* And if a sparrow cannot fall to the ground without his notice, is it probable that an empire can rise without his aid? We have been assured, Sir, in the sacred writings, that 'except the Lord build the House they labour in vain that build it.' I firmly believe this; and I also believe that without his concurring aid we shall succeed in this political building no better than the Builders of Babel: We shall be divided by our little partial local interest; our projects will be confounded, and we ourselves shall become a reproach and bye word down to future ages. And what is worse, mankind may hereafter from this

---

1. President David O. McKay, President of the Church, *CR*, October, 1961, p. 5.

unfortunate instance, despair of establishing Governments by Human Wisdom and leave it to chance, war and conquest.[1]

Elder Delbert L. Stapley quoted a statement made by **Daniel Webster** in 1852 in which he urged America to be true to God:

> *If we and our posterity shall be true to the Christian religion; if we and they shall live always in the fear of God and shall respect his commandments;...we may have the highest hopes of the future fortunes of our country,* and we may be sure of one thing: Our country will go on prospering. But if we and our posterity reject religious instruction and authority, violate the rules of eternal justice, trifle with the unjunctions of morality, and recklessly destroy the political constitution which holds us together, *no one can tell how sudden a catastrophe may overwhelm us, that shall bury all our glory in profound obscurity.*
>
> Should that catastrophe happen let it have no history. Let the horrible narrative never be written. Let its fate be that of the lost books of Livy which no human eye shall ever read, or the missing Pleiad of which no man can ever know more than that it is lost, and lost forever.[2]

Statements by **Abraham Lincoln** have frequently been cited by LDS General Authorities to show that divine guidance has shaped this nation. Mr. Lincoln said,

> Unborn ages and visions of glory crowd upon my soul, the realization of all which, however, is in the hands and good pleasure of Almighty God; but, *under His divine blessing, it will be dependent on the character and the virtues of ourselves, and of our posterity.*
>
> And let me say, gentlemen, that *if we and our posterity shall be true to the Christian religion—if we and they shall live always in the fear of God, and shall respect His commandments—if we and they shall maintain just, moral sentiments, and such conscientious convictions of duty as shall control the heart and life—we may have the highest hopes of the future fortunes of our country,* and if we maintain those institutions of government and that political union, exceeding all praise as much as it exceeds all former examples of political associations, we may be sure of one thing—that, while our country furnishes materials for a thousand masters of historic art, it will afford no topic for a Gibbon. It will have no decline and fall. It will go on prospering and to prosper.
>
> *But if we and our posterity reject religious instruction and authority, violate the rules of eternal justice, trifle with the injunctions of morality,*

---

1. President J. Reuben Clark, Jr., of the First Presidency, *CR*, April, 1957, pp. 51-52.
2. Elder Delbert L. Stapley, of the Council of the Twelve, *CR*, October, 1963, pp. 112-113. Mr. Webster was speaking to the New York Historical Society on Feb. 22, 1852. (Also cited by Elder Mark E. Petersen, (*CR*, Oct. 1967, p. 68), and Elder Sterling W. Sill (*CR*, Oct., 1970, p. 78).

and recklessly destroy the political constitution which holds us together, no man can tell how sudden the catastrophe may overwhelm us, that shall bury all our glory in profound obscurity.[1]

When leaving for Washington after being elected President, Lincoln commented to his neighbors that

Without the assistance of that Divine Being I cannot succeed. With that assistance I cannot fail. Trusting in him who can go with me and remain with you, and be everywhere for good, let us confidently hope that all may yet be well. To his care commending you, as I hope in your prayers you will commend me, I bid you an affectionate farewell.[2]

Another experience of Abraham Lincoln's, which followed the Battle of Gettysburg, was related by Elder Thorpe B. Isaacson:

General Sickles had noticed that before the battle of Gettysburg, upon the result of which, perhaps, the fate of this nation hung, President Lincoln was apparently free from the oppressive care which frequently weighed him down. After it was all past, the general asked President Lincoln how it was that he felt so free from the oppressive care previously noticeable. He answered:

'Well, I will tell you how it was. In the pinch of your campaign up there, when everybody seemed panic-stricken and nobody could tell what was going to happen, oppressed by the gravity of affairs, I went to my room one day and I locked the door and *I got down on my knees before Almighty God and prayed to him mightily for victory at Gettysburg.* I told him this war was his war and our cause was his cause, but we could not stand another Fredericksburg or Chancellorsville. *Then and there I made a solemn vow to Almighty God that if he would stand by our boys at Gettysburg, I would stand by him.* After that, I don't know how it was, and I cannot explain it, but soon *a sweet comfort crept into my soul. The feeling that God had taken this whole business into his own hands and that things would go right at Gettysburg,* and that is why I had no fears about you.'[3]

These statements, each of them cited by LDS Church leaders, all demonstrate the Latter-day Saint belief that this nation was brought into existence and preserved under the guidance and direction of God. They are typical of many other quotations cited in the frequently-delivered discourses and sermons on patriotic themes given by LDS Church leaders.

1. *Petersen, op. cit., CR,* April, 1967, p. 112.
2. *Ibid.*
3. Elder Thorpe B. Isaacson, Assistant to the Twelve, *CR,* October, 1962, p. 29.

The U.S. Constitution Inspired of God

A revelation given to Joseph Smith on December 16, 1833, contains the clear assertion that the Constitution of the United States of America is an inspired document. In this revelation, the Lord refers to the

> ...constitution of the people, which I have suffered to be established, and should be maintained for the rights and protection of all flesh, according to just and holy principles;
>
> That every man may act in doctrine and principle pertaining to futurity, according to the moral agency which I have given unto him, that every man may be accountable for his own sins in the day of judgment.
>
> Therefore, it is not right that any man should be in bondage one to another.
>
> And for this purpose have I established the Constitution of this land, by the hands of wise men whom I raised up unto this very purpose, and redeemed the land by the shedding of blood.[1]

Four months earlier, the Lord had revealed the principle that the

> ...law of the land which is constitutional, supporting that principle of freedom in maintaining rights and privileges, belongs to all mankind, and is justifiable before me.
>
> Therefore, I, the Lord, justify you, and your brethren of my church, in befriending that law which is the constitutional law of the land;[2]

Hundreds of discourses or statements on the Constitution and its divine origin have been delivered by the brethren over the years, primarily based on these two passages. Certainly one of the most outstanding was the penetrating summary of the Constitution's history and message given by President J. Reuben Clark, Jr., in general conference on Saturday, April 6, 1957. He said, in part:

Organization of Constitutional Convention

The Constitution of the United States was framed in Independence Hall, Philadelphia, May 14, 1787, to September 17, 1787. The Framers

---

1. D & C 101:77-80. The Prophet Joseph Smith, in the dedicatory prayer for the Kirtland, Ohio Temple, beseeched the Lord, saying, "May those principles, which were so honorably and nobly defended, namely, the Constitution of our land, by our fathers, be established forever." (D & C 109:54)
2. D & C 98:5-6.

were delegates sent thereto by the Thirteen Colonies. Seventy-four were
appointed; fifty-five reported at the Convention; nineteen did not attend; thirty-nine signed the Constitution. Representatives signed from
each of the Colonies except Rhode Island.

Bill of Rights

The Constitution as signed lacked a Bill of Rights, though these
rights were discussed in the Convention. As the Colonies voted to
ratify the Constitution, each proposed amendments to remedy the omis-
sion. Over one hundred amendments were proposed. Some forty to
fifty were eliminated as duplications. Seventeen were finally approved
by the House of the First Congress; the Senate reduced the number to
twelve, which were sent to the various legislatures for ratification. The
final returns showed that ten had been ratified.

Historical Experience of Framers

The Framers and their fathers had in the preceding seventy-five
years, fought through four purely European wars—in America between
the British and her colonists on one side, and the French and her
Indian allies on the other. The colonists had little, if any concern in
the European issues. They fought because the homelands fought. In
the first three of these wars the colonists lost much, suffered massacres.
Yet at the end of each war, each European government returned, each
to the other, the gains either had made in America. The colonists had
heavy losses, had no gains except the experience that builded up over
the decades, experience that aided them, first, in winning their independence, and, thereafter, in establishing this Government.

No wonder Washington in his Farewell Address counseled against
foreign entanglements. He stated the reasons drawn from colonial
experience.

The French and Indian War, the last of the four, broke the French
foothold on the Continent. Washington participated in that war as an
officer and suffered in Braddock's defeat at Fort Duquesne.

During a part of this whole period, the colonial legislatures had been
fighting against royal representatives; in the earlier decade the fathers of
the Framers carried on these contests; in the latter years, many of the
Framers were themselves involved.

Movement for Independence

The movement for independence began soon after the close of the
French and Indian War; for example, the Committees of Correspondence.
Some of the very best minds and ablest men in the Colonies participated. Framers served on these earlier revolutionary bodies. Many
Framers were members of the Continental Congress. When the Revolution came, they had the experiences, bitter as to both men and
money, that came to that Congress in raising troops and materials of
war. They had knowledge. Some were experienced in the actual
problems of conducting a war. One at least, Franklin, had seen distinguished service in the diplomatic field and continued so to serve.

Characters of Framers

The Framers were men of affairs in their own right. Some were distinquished financiers. More than half of them were university men, some educated in the leading American colleges—Harvard, Yale, Columbia, Princeton, William and Mary; others in the great colleges of Great Britain—Oxford, Glasgow, Edinburgh. Washington and Franklin were amoung those who had no college education. Altogether there were seventy-four delegates appointed; fifty-five who reported at the Convention, "all of them" it has been said, "respectable for family and for personal qualities." Of these fifty-five, only thirty-nine were present at the signing. Nineteen failed to attend.

They were men of varied political beliefs. Some were Federalists; some anti-Federalists. Some seemed favorable to a mere revamping of the Articles of Confederation.

No Political "Blueprint" Available

The amazing thing is that there was not in all the world's history a government organization even among confederacies, that could be taken by the Framers as a preliminary blueprint for building the political structure they were to build. Franklin declared:

"We have gone back to ancient history for models of Government, and examined the different forms of those Republics which, having been formed with the seeds of their own dissolution, now no longer exist. And we have viewed Modern States all round Europe, but find none of their Constitutions suitable to our circumstances."

They had been in session for about a month (June 26, 1787) when Madison declared:

"...as it was more than probable we were now digesting a plan which in its operation would decide forever the fate of Republican Gov't we ought not only to provide every guard to liberty that its preservation could require, but be equally careful to supply the defects which our own experience had particularly pointed out."

Who the Framers Were

A little further detail about the thirty-nine Framers who actually signed the document will be useful.

Of those thirty-nine signers, twenty-six had seen service in the Continental Congress. They knew legislative processes and problems. Thirteen had served both the Continental Congress and in the Army. What a wealth of experience they had obtained in both legislative and executive duties. Of the nineteen who served as officers—they knew the problems of armed forces in the field; and of these seventeen, four had served on Washington's staff.

Let us go down the roll: Washington, the "Father of his Country," and Madison, sometimes called the "Father of the Constitution," were later Presidents of the United States. Hamilton (a financial genius) was Secretary of the Treasury under Washington. McHenry (Maryland) was Secretary of War under Washington. Randolph (Virginia) acted as Attorney General for Washington and later as his Secretary of State. Rutledge (South Carolina), a distinguished jurist, was later Chief Justice

in the United States Supreme Court. Oliver Ellsworth (absent when the
Constitution was signed) was also later a Chief Justice of the Supreme
Court. Blair, Paterson, and Wilson were later Justices of the Supreme
Court. (Wilson had been on the Board of War and Ordnance in the
Second Continental Congress.)

Benjamin Franklin, a philosopher and scientist, had behind him years
of most distinguished and successful diplomatic service. King (Massachu-
setts) was later a Senator and thereafter Minister to Great Britain.
Charles Pinckney (South Carolina) was Minister to Spain. Dickinson
(Delaware) founded Dickinson College, and Johnson (Connecticut) was
President of Columbia College. Gerry (Massachusetts) was later Vice-
President of the United States, and Ingersoll (Pennsylvania) a candidate
for the Vice-Presidency.

Gorham (Massachusetts) and Mifflin (Pennsylvania) had been Presidents of the Continental Congress; Clymer (Pennsylvania), Continental
Treasurer; Robert Morris (Pennsylvania), Superintendent of Finances;
Sherman (Connecticut), a member of the Board of War and Ordnance,
all in the Continental Congress.

We might add, as among the most distinguished of this group, the
other Morris (Gouverneur) from Pennsylvania, and the other Pinckney
(Charles Cotesworth) from South Carolina.

There were many other distinguished men. They were distinguished
before the time of the Convention; they won great distinction after.
Men of affairs and influence, they were in their respective Colonies,
later States. They were all seasoned patriots of loftiest patriotism. They
were not backwoods men from the far-off frontiers, not one of them.

What a group of men of surpassing abilities, attainments, experience,
and achievements. *There has not been another group of men in all the
one hundred seventy years of our history, no group that even challenged
the supremacy of this group.* Gladstone solemnly declared:

"The American Constitution is the most wonderful work ever struck
off at a given time by the brain and purpose of man."

After departing from the theme of his explanation to comment
on the basic Doctrine and Covenants passages mentioned above,
he continued:

These Framers of the Constitution were the men who the Lord
"raised up unto this very purpose, and redeemed the land by the shedding of blood," making it ready for the blessings proclaimed for all.

Preparation of Framers

No more clearly does it appear that Moses was so trained in the
royal Egyptian courts that he could lead ancient Israel out of bondage,
or that Brother Brigham was so trained, in directing the exodus of the
Saints from Missouri to Nauvoo, that he could lead modern Israel from
the mobbings and persecutions of the East to the freedom of the mountain fastnesses of the West; neither one was more clearly trained for his
work than these Framers were trained for theirs—rich in intellectual
endowment and ripened in experience. They were equally as the others

in God's hands; he guided them in their epochmaking deliberations in Independence Hall.

The Framers were deeply read in the facts of history; they were learned in the forms and practices and systems of the governments of the world, past and present; they were, in matters political, equally at home in Rome, in Athens, in Paris, and in London; they had a long, varied, and intense experience in the work of governing their various Colonies; they were among the leaders of a weak and poor people that had successfully fought a revolution against one of the great Powers of the earth; they were among them some of the ablest, most experienced and seasoned military leaders of the world.

As to all matters under consideration by the Convention, the history of the world was combed for applicable experiences and precedents.

The whole training and experiences of the colonists had been in the Common Law, with its freedoms and liberties even under their kings. They knew the functions of legislative, executive, and judicial arms of government.

Then he explained the basic principles of the Constitution and their importance:

Some Constitutional Principles

Time is not available now to consider in detail the work of the Convention nor the Constitution that was framed. A very few principles only, and they among the basic ones, may be mentioned. You all know them; they are now merely recalled to your minds. Sometimes we miss the import of them.

Three Independent Branches

First—The Constitution provided for three departments of government—the legislative, the executive, and the judicial.

These departments are mutually independent the one from the other.

Each department was endowed with all the powers and authority that the people through the Constitution conferred upon that branch of government—the legislative, the executive, and the judicial, respectively.

No Encroachment by One Branch upon Another

No branch of the government might encroach upon the powers conferred upon another branch of government. In order to forestall foreseeable encroachments, the Convention provided in the Constitution itself for a very few invasions by one or the other, into one of the departments, to make sure that one department should not absorb the functions of the other or encroach thereon, or gain an overbalancing power and authority against the other. These have been termed "checks and balances."

Non-delegation of Powers

A third principle that was inherent in all the provisions of the Constitution was that none of the departments could delegate its powers to

others. The courts of the country have from the first insisted upon
the operation of this principle. There have been some fancy near-
approaches to such an attempted delegation, particularly in recent
years, and some unique justifying reasoning therefor, but the courts
have consistently insisted upon the basic principle, which is still operative.

An examination of the records of the Convention will show how
anxiously earnest the Framers were to set up these and other principles
of free government.

No Kings in America

The Convention seems to have experienced no really serious difficulty in setting up a judiciary department, nor in certain aspects, the
legislative department with its powers, until it came to those powers
which dealt with matters that in some governments had been regarded
as belonging to the executive. You will recollect that practically all of
these Framers had suffered under George III and his Minister, Lord
North. So they abandoned the British model, for, as Randolph said,
"...the fixt genius of the people of America required a different form of
Government." This ruled out royalty.

It might be noted that Washington, as the Revolution closed, had
definitively scotched at Newburgh, the kingship idea.

Kings and America

Of course, the Framers did not know (no living mortal then knew)
that centuries before a prophet of the Lord had declared as to America:

"Behold, this is a choice land, and whatsoever nation shall possess it
shall be free from bondage, and from captivity, and from all other
nations under heaven, if they will but serve the God of the land, who is
Jesus Christ, who hath been manifested by the things which we have
written." (Ether 2:12.)

Nor did the Framers know (again, no living mortal then knew) that
centuries after this prophecy, but still centuries before the Framers met,
another prophet had declared:

"And this land shall be a land of liberty unto the Gentiles."
(2 Nephi 10:11.)

The unhappy, short-lived experiences of the Dom Pedros in Brazil
and of Maximilian in Mexico seem the exceptions that prove the rule.
The Spirit of the Lord was leading.

The National Executive

In providing for the executive department, there was considerable
discussion as to whether the executive department should be one person or several. Commenting upon a proposal for three, Randolph said
their unity would be "as the foetus of monarchy."

Who should choose, elect, or appoint (the terms were used almost
interchangeably) the Chief Executive was exhaustively debated; so was
the problem of the length of his term, from one year, to Hamilton's
during "good behaviour," including the question whether he should be ineligible for re-election, and whether he should be subject to impeachment.

Power to Declare War

But one of their most searching examinations related to the war powers of government, including the power to declare war. It became clear very early in the debates that as Chief Executive, the President should execute the laws passed by Congress. But he was also made Commander in Chief of the Army and Navy of the United States and of the State Militia when called into the service of the United States. The delegates were fearfully anxious over this function of government. There was one suggestion that the Commander in Chief should not personally go into the field with the troops, so fearful were they of his power.

Where War Powers Rest

But in whom should rest the so-called war powers? This was the urgent problem. It soon became clear that the Convention was unalterably opposed to endowing the President with these war powers; it was conceded he should have the power to repel invasions, but not to commence war, which meant he could not declare war.

Chief Executives Conceived as Plain Human Beings

Some of the arguments made in this connection, involving the possibility of a military usurper, remind one of the potential calamities pictured by Lincoln in his prophetic Lyceum Address, where he sketched what an ambitious, fame-and-power-seeking executive might do.

Various other potential actions by the executive were explored. Future Presidents of the Republic were conceived as including men capable of doing the things that ambitious men in power had done over the ages. Men were still human, had the same urges and ambitions. The earnest effort was to make as nearly impossible as could be, the malfeasances of the past by men in high executive office in the future; and seemingly perhaps beyond everything else as a practical matter, *to prevent the President from taking us into war of his own volition.* The Framers therefore provided that the war powers, including the declaration of war, should rest exclusively in the Congress, both by express provisions, and, as the record shows, by the conscious intent of the Framers.

The Net Position of the National Executive

The net result may be stated thus: as Chief Executive the President was to enforce the laws passed by Congress, including those passed by Congress in the exercise of the war powers that were explicitly and exclusively possessed by Congress; as Commander in Chief of the Army and Navy of the United States and of the Militia of the States when called into the actual service of the United States, he was to direct the military operations thereof in the field, with the powers incident thereto.

These principles should never be forgotten by any free, liberty-loving American, the kind of American the Constitution and the Bill of Rights make of us, and in which they were designed to protect us.

The People Are Sovereign

Furthermore, under our form of government, we the people of the United States, as the Preamble to the Constitution declares, formed this government. We alone are sovereign. We are wholly free to exercise our sovereign will in the way we prescribe. The sovereignty is not personal, as under the Civil Law. The Constitution expressly provides the only way in which we may change our Constitution.

We may well repeat again: We the people have all the powers we have not delegated away to our government, and the institutions of government have such powers and those only as we have given to them. The total residuum of powers, including all rights and liberties not given up by us to Federal or State Governments, is still in us, to remain so till we constitutionally provide otherwise. Under the Civil Law that basically governs Continental Europe, the people have only such rights as a personal sovereign or his equivalent bestows, the residuum remaining in him or them. Wherever and whenever powers are exercised by any person or branch of our government that are not granted by the Constitution, such powers are to that extent usurpations.

He then related the Constitution to the religion of the Latter-day Saints:

The Constitution and Ourselves

Will not each of you ask yourself this question: What would probably have happened if Joseph Smith had been born and had attempted to carry on his work of the Restoration of the Gospel and the Holy Priesthood, if he had been born and had sought to go forward in any other country in the world?

Must we go far to seek why God set up this people and their government, the only government on the face of the earth, since the Master was here, that God has formally declared was set up at the hands of men whom he raised up for that very purpose, and the fundamental principles of which he has expressly approved?

Constitution Is Part of My Religion

Having in mind what the Lord has said about the Constitution and its Framers, that the Constitution should be "established, and should be maintained for the rights and protection of all flesh," that it was for the protection of the moral agency, free agency, God gave us, that its "principle of freedom in maintaining rights and privileges, belongs to all mankind," all of which point to the destiny of the free government our Constitution provides, unless thrown away by the nations—having in mind all this, with its implications, speaking for myself, I declare that the divine sanction thus repeatedly given by the Lord himself to the Constitution of the United States as it came from the hands of the Framers with its coterminous Bill of Rights, makes of the principles of that document an integral part of my religious faith. It is a revelation from the Lord. I believe and reverence its God-inspired provisions. My faith, my knowledge, my testimony of the Restored gospel, based on the divine principle of continuous revelation, compel me so to believe.

Thus has the Lord approved of our political system, an approval, so far as I know, such as he has given to no other political system of any other people in the world since the time of Jesus.

The Constitution, as approved by the Lord, is still the same great vanguard of liberty and freedom in human government that it was the day it was written. No other human system of government, affording equal protection for human life, liberty, and the pursuit of happiness, has yet been devised or vouchsafed to man. Its great principles are as applicable, efficient, and sufficient to bring today the greatest good to the greatest number, as they were the day the Constitution was signed. Our Constitution and our Government under it, were designed by God as an instrumentality for righteousness through peace, *not war*.

Our Constitutional Destiny

Speaking of the destiny that the Lord has offered to mankind in his declaration regarding the scope and efficacy of the Constitution and its principles, we may note that already the Lord has moved upon many nations of the earth so to go forward. The Latin American countries have followed our lead and adopted our constitutional form of government, adapted to their legal concepts, without compulsion or restraint from us. Likewise, the people of Canada in the British North America Act have embodied great principles that are basic to our Constitution. The people of Australia have likewise followed along our governmental footpath. In Canada and in Australia, the great constitutional decisions of John Marshall and his associates are quoted in their courts and followed in their adjudications. I repeat, none of this has come because of force of arms. The Constitution will never reach its destiny through force. God's principles are taken by men because they are eternal and true, and touch the divine spirit in men. This is the only true way to permanent world peace, the aspiration of men since the beginning. God never planted his Spirit, his truth, in the hearts of men from the point of a bayonet.

The Framers had their dark days in their work. There were discouragements, there were hours of near hopelessness for some. Yet, as they were engaged in God's work, and he was at the helm, we know it was as certain as the day dawn, that Satan would be there also, with this thwarting design.

But I see in their divers views, their different concepts, even the promotion of their different local interests, not the confusion which challenged Franklin, but a searching, almost meticulous study and examination of the fundamental principles involved, and the final adoption of the wisest and best of it all—I see the winnowing of the wheat, the blowing away of the chaff.

After telling of the request for prayer by Benjamin Franklin,[1] President Clark bore his personal witness concerning the Constitution and the role the Saints must play in its preservation:

---

1. See pp. 22-23.

My Witness

Out of more years, but of far, far less wisdom and experience, I echo Franklin's testimony "that God governs in the affairs of men," and that without his concurring aid we shall build in vain, and "our projects will be confounded, and we ourselves shall become a reproach and bye word down to future ages."

I bear my testimony that without God's aid, we shall not preserve our political heritage neither to our own blessing, nor to the blessing of the downtrodden peoples of the world.

In broad outline, the Lord has declared through our Constitution his form for human government. Our own prophets have declared in our day the responsibility of the Elders of Zion in the preservation of the Constitution. We cannot, guiltless, escape that responsibility. We cannot be laggards, nor can we be deserters.

On the back of the chair in which Washington sat as President during the Convention, was carved a half-hidden sun, showing just above a range of hills. As the signing of the Constitution was about over, Franklin observed to some fellow delegates:

"I have often and often, in the course of the session, and the vicissitudes of my hopes and fears as to its issue, looked at that (sun) behind the President, without being able to tell whether it was rising or setting; but now, at length, I have the happiness to know that it is a rising, and not a setting sun."

Such was the prophecy that marked the closing of the greatest political convention of all time, for the Lord was there working out his purposes in a system he could endorse.

God give us the power, each of us, to enshrine in our hearts the eternal truths of our Constitution; that come what may, we shall never desert these truths, but work always and unceasingly that, as Lincoln said, "government of the people, by the people, for the people, shall not perish from the earth."

Such is my prayer, and I ask it in the name of Jesus. Amen.[1]

An *Improvement Era* article by Wendell J. Ashton, entitled "The Signers of the Constitution," in September, 1942, presented an excellent introduction to the Constitution. Elder Ashton presented the accompanying chart which gives information on each of these men (see next page). He then commented on many of the men, as follows:

That the framers of the Constitution formed an assemblage of great men no student of History can doubt. Three-fourths of the delegates had served in Congress. But in the Mormon way of thinking, these pillars of government were more than intellectual giants; they, in the words of Brigham Young, "were inspired from on high to do that work." [*Journal of Discourses*, Vol. 7, pp. 9-15]   (Continued on page 36.)

---

1. President J. Reuben Clark, Jr., of the First Presidency, *CR*, April, 1957, pp. 44-52.

ORIGINAL SIGNERS OF THE CONSTITUTION OF THE UNITED STATES

Name	Birth Date	Birthplace	State Representing	Age at Convention	Death Date	Occupation
George Washington	Feb. 22, 1732	Popes Creek, Virginia	Virginia	55	Dec. 14, 1799	Farmer
John Langdon	June 26, 1741	Portsmouth, New Hampshire	New Hampshire	46	Sept. 18, 1819	Merchant
Nicholas Gilman	Aug. 3, 1755	Exeter, New Hampshire	New Hampshire	32	May 2, 1814	Statesman
Nathaniel Gorham	May, 1738	Charleston, Massachusetts	Massachusetts	49	June 11, 1796	Merchant
Rufus King	March 24, 1755	Scarboro, Maine (then part of Mass.)	Massachusetts	32	April 29, 1827	Lawyer
William Samuel Johnson	Oct. 7, 1727	Stratford, Connecticut	Connecticut	59	Nov. 14, 1819	Lawyer
Roger Sherman	April 19, 1721	Newton, Massachusetts	Connecticut	66	July 23, 1793	Merchant
Alexander Hamilton	Jan. 11, 1757	Island of Nevis, West Indies	New York	30	July 12, 1804	Lawyer
William Livingston	Nov., 1723	Albany, New York	New Jersey	63	July 25, 1790	Lawyer
David Brearly	June 11, 1745	Spring Grove, New Jersey	New Jersey	42	Aug. 16, 1790	Lawyer
William Paterson	Dec. 24, 1745	County Antrim, Ireland	New Jersey	41	Sept. 6, 1806	Lawyer
Jonathan Dayton	Oct. 16, 1760	Elizabethtown, New Jersey	New Jersey	26	Oct. 9, 1824	Lawyer
Benjamin Franklin	Jan. 6, 1706	Boston, Massachusetts	Pennsylvania	81	April 17, 1790	Publisher
Thomas Mifflin	Jan. 10, 1744	Philadelphia, Pennsylvania	Pennsylvania	43	Jan. 20, 1800	Merchant
Robert Morris	Jan. 31, 1734	Near Liverpool, England	Pennsylvania	53	May 8, 1806	Financier
George Clymer	March 16, 1739	Philadelphia, Pennsylvania	Pennsylvania	48	Jan. 24, 1813	Merchant
Thomas Fitzsimons	1741	Ireland	Pennsylvania	46	Aug. 26, 1811	Merchant
Jared Ingersoll	Oct. 27, 1749	New Haven, Connecticut	Pennsylvania	38	Oct. 31, 1822	Lawyer
Gouverneur Morris	Jan. 31, 1752	Morrisania, New York	Pennsylvania	35	Nov. 6, 1816	Lawyer
James Wilson	Sept. 14, 1742	Carskerdo, Scotland	Pennsylvania	45	Aug. 21, 1798	Lawyer
George Read	Sept. 18, 1733	North East, Maryland	Delaware	53	Sept. 21, 1798	Lawyer
Gunning Bedford, Jr.	1747	Philadelphia, Pennsylvania	Delaware	40	March 30, 1812	Lawyer
John Dickinson	Nov. 8, 1732	Talbot County, Maryland	Delaware	54	Feb. 14, 1808	Lawyer
Jacob Broom	1752	Wilmington, New Castle Co., Delaware	Delaware	35	April 25, 1810	Statesman
Richard Bassett	April 2, 1745	Cecil County, Maryland	Delaware	42	Sept. 15, 1815	Statesman
James McHenry	Nov. 16, 1753	Ballymena, Ireland	Maryland	33	May 3, 1816	Physician
Daniel of St. Tho. Jenifer	1723	Charles County, Maryland	Maryland	64	Nov. 16, 1790	Financier
Daniel Carroll	July 22, 1730	Upper Marlboro, Maryland	Maryland	57	May 7, 1796	Land Owner
John Blair	1732	Williamsburg, Virginia	Virginia	55	Aug. 31, 1800	Lawyer
James Madison, Jr.	March 16, 1751	Port Conway, Virginia	Virginia	36	June 28, 1836	Lawyer
William Blount	March 26, 1749	Bertie County, North Carolina	North Carolina	38	March 21, 1800	Realtor
Richard Dobbs Spaight	March 25, 1758	New Bern, North Carolina	North Carolina	29	Sept. 6, 1802	Statesman
Hugh Williamson	Oct. 5, 1735	West Nottingham, Pennsylvania	North Carolina	51	May 22, 1819	Physician
John Rutledge	Sept., 1739	Charleston, South Carolina	South Carolina	48	July 18, 1800	Lawyer
Charles Cotesworth Pinckney	Feb. 25, 1746	Charleston, South Carolina	South Carolina	41	Aug. 16, 1825	Lawyer
Charles Pinckney	1758	Charleston, South Carolina	South Carolina	29	Oct. 29, 1824	Lawyer
Pierce Butler	July 11, 1744	County Carlow, Ireland	South Carolina	43	Feb. 15, 1822	Planter
William Few	June 8, 1748	Baltimore, Maryland	Georgia	39	July 16, 1828	Banker
Abraham Baldwin	Nov. 6, 1754	Guilford, Connecticut	Georgia	32	1807	Lawyer

To frail, scholarly *James Madison* of Virginia has been accorded the distinquished title of "Father of the Constitution." Physically and mentally, he was quite different from Washington, being slight of build and never a general but always a brilliant student. Madison, like Washington, however, was favored with a rich religious background which on several occasions shaped his thinking—and that of whole legislative halls.

Madison studied for the ministry. The Hebrew language appealed to him. He "explored the whole history and evidences of Christianity on every side—a feature which bore fruit in his early years in the legislature, freedom of conscience being established by law in Virginia largely by Madison's own labors and influence." [Sarah K. Bolton, *Famous American Statesmen*, pp. 157-158].

He fathered the provisions in Virginia's Bill of Rights, copied by other states: "That religion, or duty we owe to our Creator, and the manner of discharging it, can be directed only by reason and conviction, not by force and violence; and, therefore, all men are equally entitled to the free exercise of religion according to the dictates of conscience."

Elected a member of the first Virginia legislature under its new constitution, Madison "failed of re-election because he refused to solicit votes or to furnish whiskey for thirsty voters." [John Fiske, *Presidents of the United States*, edited by J. G. Wilson, pp. 161-162].

Madison defended free agency in religion in his state on other occasions, and his "Religious Freedom Act," translated into French and Italian, was widely read and commented upon in Europe.

This same Madison, it was, who drew upon the groundwork for the Constitution, who was historiographer for its convention, and who successfully championed its ratification in Virginia in face of such formidable opposition as Patrick Henry and Richard Henry Lee.

No man did more for the Constitution of the United States than did a sandy-haired, handsome little figure with piercing gray-blue eyes, and pointed, classic nose who had come up as a youth to the States from the West Indies. He was *Alexander Hamilton*, who, more than any other, was responsible for the calling of the Constitutional Convention, and who was perhaps its most forceful exponent in bringing about its adoption by the several states.

But thirty of age at the Convention, Hamilton was indeed a prodigy. By the time he was fifteen years old he had worked his way up to the office of assistant manager in a trading business in the Indies. At that age he wrote an account of a hurricane on the islands which won him immediate recognition and the urge of friends to seek fortunes in the colonies.

One of Hamilton's earliest and warmest friends was a Presbyterian minister, the Reverend Hugh Knox, whose teachings no doubt made a lasting impression on the boy. Reverend Knox induced Hamilton to go to the States, and when Alexander departed he took with him a few belongings, including a box of books given him by the minister.

In many respects, Hamilton, as an American, was a modern David. He was fearless, brilliant in expression, full of honor and integrity, though his impetuousness sometimes led him to err. Through his life are incidents which reveal the importance he gave to spiritual affairs.

In 1793, he wrote concerning the French Revolution, which he abhorred: "...When I find the doctrines of atheism openly advanced in the convention with loud applause...when I behold the hand of rapacity outstretched to prostrate and ravish the monuments of religious worship erected by those citizens and their ancestors...I acknowledge that I am glad to believe there is no real semblance between what was the cause of America and what is the cause of France." [Henry Cabot Lodge, *Alexander Hamilton*, pp. 253-254].

Two years before his death, Hamilton, then "an elder statesman" at the age of forty-five, wrote to a friend, James A. Bayard, suggesting methods for building up the Federalist party. In part, he said: "Let an association be formed to be denominated 'The Christian Constitutional Society.' Its objects to be: 1st. The support of the Christian religion. 2nd The support of the Constitution of the United States." [*Ibid.*, p. 264].

When Hamilton's wife, Elizabeth Schuyler Hamilton, died fifty-two years after her husband, a little bag was found tied around her neck. In it was a faded paper containing love verses he had written her seventy-four years before.

Though he was advanced in years, *Benjamin Franklin* gave to the Convention added prestige, profound thought, and its clearest expression of the overruling providence of God at the gathering. Franklin once presented a picturesque explanation of immortality by writing his own epitaph: "The body of Benjamin Franklin, printer, (like the cover of an old book, its contents torn out, and stript of its lettering and gilding), lies here food for worms. Yet the work itself shall not be lost, for it will, as he believed, appear once more, in a new and more beautiful edition, corrected and amended by the Author." [Bernard Fay, Franklin, *The Apostle of Modern Times*, p. 116].

To go down the line of other illustrious personalities signing the Constitution, one finds many examples of characters strengthened by religious experiences. *Roger Sherman*, the only man to sign the four great documents of Revolutionary days (Articles of Association of 1774, Declaration of Independence, Articles of Confederation, and the Constitution), and author of the famous Compromise Plan at the Convention, was a profound student of theology. He published such papers as *A Short Sermon on the Duty of Self-Examination and Pre-paratory to Receiving the Lord's Supper*. A devout Congregationalist, he contributed heavily to the building of the chapel at Yale University. Dr. William Samuel Johnson, another outstanding delegate, studied for the ministry, and his appointment as first president of Columbia College was a departure from the traditional practice of choosing college presidents from the clergy. He was a leading layman in the Anglican Church. David Brearly, representative from New Jersey, was a delegate to the Episcopal General Convention of 1786 and helped compile the prayer book.

Thomas Fitzsimons of Pennsylvania, a strong supporter of Hamilton's views in government, was the largest single contributor to the erection of St. Augustine's Church in Philadelphia, and *Richard Bassett*, who was not only a Constitutional delegate but later served as Delaware's senator (1789-95) and Governor (1799-1801), was an enthusiastic Methodist. He paid approximately half of the cost of the first Methodist Church in Dover.

James McHenry, delegate from Maryland, who had served as major in Washington's army and who was Washington's choice for Secretary

of War in 1796, served as president of the first Bible Society founded
in Baltimore (1813). *Hugh Williamson,* representative from North Carolina at the Convention, studied theology prior to entering medicine,
and was once licensed to preach in Connecticut. He also served in the
Continental Congress (1784-6) and in the first United States Congress.
A Georgia delegate, *Abraham Baldwin,* was a chaplain in the war. He
later was a delegate to the Continental Congress, member of the House
of Representatives, and the Senate, and was founder and first president
of the University of Georgia.

"He was a staunch believer in revealed religion and a liberal giver of
his wealth to all good causes," [*Dictionary of American Biography,*
edited by Dumas Malone, Vol. VI, p. 352], is the way one biographer
characterizes *William Few,* the other Georgia delegate. He was one of
his state's first United States senators.[1]

References to the Latter-day Saint belief in the inspired nature of the Constitution have been made so often and by so many
LDS General Authorities that there is no need to compile them in
this context. Several examples, however, will serve to indicate the
messages which these references usually carry. President George
Albert Smith made this statement in the October, 1950 General
Conference:

> And that brings me to something that is frequently on my mind.
> *No nation in the world has a constitution that was given to it by our*
> *Heavenly Father except the United States of America.* I wonder if we
> appreciate that. The Lord gave us a rule of life for this great nation, and
> as far as we have lived up to it and taken advantage of it, the nation has
> grown, and the people have been blessed.... Why not hold on to what
> the Lord has given? The Constitution of the United States was written,
> it is true, by men, George Washington, Benjamin Franklin, and others
> who were their associates, but we have in this book that I have in my
> hand, the book of Doctrine and Covenants, *a revelation in which the*
> *Lord tells us that the Constitution of the Church was prepared by men*
> *raised up by him for this very purpose.*
>
> As Latter-day Saints we ought to know that there is nothing better
> anywhere else. And so *we should cleave to the Constitution of the*
> *United States and in doing so, earn the blessings of our Heavenly*
> *Father....* The Constitution guarantees us liberty that no other nation
> enjoys. Most of the nations are losing the liberties they have because
> they have not kept the commandments of the Lord.... I hold in my
> hand a copy of the Doctrine and Covenants, and in it the Lord tells us
> another thing, to pray for and sustain the Constitution of the land and
> those who represent us in its offices. So, *pray for the President of the*
> *United States, pray for those who have been elected to Congress, pray*

---

1. Wendell J. Ashton, General Secretary, Deseret Sunday School Union,
   "The Signers of the Constitution," *IE,* Vol. 45, No. 9, September, 1942,
   pp. 562-563, 598-600.

for your governor and the members of your legislature. If they have the spirit of the Lord, they cannot go wrong; but without it they can go a long way on the bypath. [1]

While telling of one man's love and allegiance to the United States, Elder Thorpe B. Isaacson again asserted the LDS doctrine that the Constitution is an inspired document:

I ask each of you now to consider with me for a few moments one of our most precious possessions—our citizenship in the United States of America, this nation under God.

A very fine man who came to the United States a few years ago from a foreign country and who now has his citizenship papers remarked to me that next to God and his loved ones, he considered his citizenship in the United States as his most precious and priceless possession. Yes, his most precious and priceless possession. *He said he loved the United States and was grateful for the freedom that it afforded him, because, you see, he had lived in a country where he did not know that freedom. When he said that he loved the United States and that he thanked God for his citizenship in this country, he said it with every fiber of his soul. He said he would fight for this country and this freedom, even if it meant his own life. He said that every citizen of the United States ought to feel that way; and if he did feel that way, talked that way, and loved that way, we would have no problem from within and no fear from without.* Yes, this nation under God means exactly what it says.

Let me quote from the Doctrine and Covenants:

"Let no man break the laws of the land, for he that keepeth the laws of God hath no need to break the laws of the land." [D & C 58:2.]

The Constitution of the United States is a document from inspired men. On August 6, 1833, the Church received a revelation that has gone far to establish a fixed attitude toward the Constitution and laws of the United States. Then came the word of the Lord:

"And now, verily I say unto you concerning the laws of the land, it is my will that my people should observe to do all things whatsoever I command them." [*Ibid.*, 101:79.]

Man could not so act save he live in a land of law, for only in a land of law can there be freedom as we know it.

"And for this purpose have I established the Constitution of this land, by the hands of wise men whom I raised up unto this very purpose, and redeemed the land by the shedding of blood." [*Ibid.*, 101:80.]

This revelation has a powerful influence in shaping the views of Latter-day Saints toward the Constitution of the United States, and it should also have a great influence on every citizen, for the *Lord suffered it to be by the hands of wise men.* [2]

---

1. President George Albert Smith, President of the Church, *CR*, September, 1950, pp. 7-8.
2. Elder Thorpe B. Isaacson, Assistant to the Council of the Twelve, *CR*, October, 1964, pp. 52-53.

Summary

1. Latter-day Saints hold as doctrine the belief that the American continents constitute a land which God has declared to be choice and consecrated above all other lands. This belief is often applied to the United States of America in particular.

2. The Americas were pledged by God as a land of inheritance to Lehi's descendants forever (2 Ne. 1:5-7). They are descendants of Joseph who was sold into Egypt (the son of the Old Testament patriarch, Jacob). The Americas will constitute a place of inheritance for a portion of the house of Joseph in the last days (Eth. 13:6-8). Because of this pledge, the Americas are considered a land of promise.

3. Because of a vision given to the prophet Nephi (1 Ne. 12 & 13) Latter-day Saint teachings include the beliefs that

   A. Columbus was inspired by God to sail to America,
   B. Early American settlers were inspired by God to leave their European homes and come to America,
   C. Early American settlers were caused by God to prosper here. His power was with them,
   D. God delivered America so it became independent, and that
   E. God lifted America above all other nations.

4. Latter-day Saint General Authorities frequently speak on themes of liberty and patriotism. Love and concern for country is a characteristic of the leadership of The Church of Jesus Christ of Latter-day Saints.

5. A frequent approach used by LDS General Authorities is to quote statements from non-LDS historical or modern sources which indicate that there was divine guidance in the founding of the United States of America.

6. Numerous founding fathers of America have given indication that they were aware of God's guiding hand in the formulative events of this nation's early history. Some of their statements are included in this book.

7. The Lord has revealed that He established the U.S. Constitution and raised up wise men for the very purpose of bringing

it forth. He has instructed the Saints to befriend the Constitutional law of the land.

8.   A discourse by J. Reuben Clark, Jr. emphasized important aspects of the Constitution. These include

A.   The Constitution provides for three independent departments of government—the legislative, the executive, and the judicial.

B.   Each of the three departments of government are to remain separate and are not to encroach upon the duties of another branch. This separation is to provide a system of "checks and balances."

C.   None of the three departments can delegate its powers to the others.

D.   As chief executive, the President is to execute the laws passed by Congress.

E.   The President was not given the power to declare war. That power was given to Congress.

F.   The President is the commander-in-chief of the army and the navy and is to direct their activities in time of war.

G.   The people of the nation are sovereign. They possess all the powers except those they have delegated to the government.

II

What's Right With America?

What's right with America? What freedoms do we enjoy? Americans would do well to consider these questions, and compare what they have to the conditions they would experience living in other parts of the world.

Imagine—what would your life be like if you lived under the political repression of the Soviet Union, or Red China, or East Germany? How would you fare if you lived under the jurisdiction of military dictators in South America, with their unbelievably sky-rocketing inflation? Or what would life be like in the poverty-stricken hands of rural Central America? Would you rather be in the midst of Africa's young nations, with tribal and racial wars an imminent prospect? What if the size of your family was limited by law, as in some of the Asian countries? Think back in time just one generation—would you have enjoyed the midnight abductions and reign of terror of Germany's Gestapo? or the Jewish pogroms? the Warsaw ghetto? Austwitz? life in occupied France, or Holland? Imagine! Compare!

The United States of America is truly a land of freedom. It is a nation with a great heritage, an inspiring history, and the potential for a glorious future. Settled by a unique mixture of freedom-loving peoples, it has been the symbol of hope and opportunity for the inhabitants of planet earth for more than two hundred years.

Its Constitution and government have served as models for emerging nations. The free enterprise economic system it fostered has made a vast panorama of goods and services available throughout the world, providing its citizens with a standard of living unparalleled until the past decade. Education has been fostered and creativity encouraged, resulting in an overwhelming array of unique inventions and technological advances. The land itself is a place of beauty—a fruitful land bringing forth rich harvests and yielding tremendous quantities of mineral wealth.

The nation's sovereignty has been protected, its continental borders have been shielded from invasion, its armies have been victorious in war. Truly America has been a God-protected land "blessed with victory and peace."[1]

---

1. Francis Scott Key, "The Star Spangled Banner," verse 4.

Though the liberties and privileges enjoyed in America are so abundant as to almost defy enumeration, it is appropriate that some basic freedoms and opportunities be recalled as a reminder to all that they form the basis for the happy and abundant life Americans enjoy. Indeed, these freedoms are what make life worth living.

Freedom of Worship

America has no state religion to which its citizens must belong, and the establishment of a prescribed religion is expressly prohibited by the Constitution.[1] The preaching of any and all religious philosophies, and the free exercise of religion, is a liberty guaranteed by law. Churches may proselyte freely and assemble when and where they desire without the necessity of government permission. They may build chapels, seminaries, and temples, subject only to the necessary regulation of local building codes, and the sanctity of these edifices is held inviolate by government officials. Church schools and universities may be established and operated on either a denominational or an open basis.

Religious and denominational literature can be freely written and disseminated without censorship, and is readily available in bookstores open to the public. The Bible is available in many editions and is even used as a measure of integrity in oaths taken in courts of law and in the swearing in of public officials. Religious sermons and related programming are heard on local and national radio and television. Churches can advertise in newspapers and other media.

The growth and well-being of religious institutions are encouraged by property and income tax exemptions which foster charitable donations. The uplifting influence of religion is accepted as an important element of community life, and religious officers hold positions of respect in communities throughout the nation.

Thus Americans have the privilege of worshipping according to the dictates of their own conscience, in full application of their God-given moral agency.

Freedom of Speech

Liberty to hold and publicly express one's personal views is a vital freedom enjoyed by American citizens. To be able to speak in support of one's beliefs on any subject without fear of governmental, social, or economic reprisal is a privilege not enjoyed in

---

1. Constitution of the United States, Amendments, Article I.

many other parts of the world. Americans enjoy the right to dissent from governmental policies if they so desire, and are free to work by a variety of lawful means to bring about change from laws and decisions which they may feel are improper or unjust. They are free to visit with or write to governmental leaders, to write and publish even materials which are critical of government policies, and to openly organize and influence others to accomplish their own ends. The privilege of free speech is a liberty which is soon lost under dictatorial and despotic governments. In a democracy, it serves as a check and balance to prevent governmental excesses or corruption.

Freedom of the Press and News Media

A free press and news media serve as powerful watchdogs, monitoring and reporting events of importance and concern to the community at large. Americans enjoy the right of having newspapers, television, radio, and other media owned and controlled by private rather than government sources. Thus the journalistic media are not instruments of official propaganda, but are independent institutions[1] that can examine issues from various viewpoints, expose improprieties, command accomplishments, and report bureaucratic weaknesses and failures when necessary. Their independent voices allow the citizenry to see and evaluate issues with perspective.

Columnists and editors present a host of viewpoints on major issues, exposing their readers to a broad spectrum of thought. Readers also enjoy the same intellectual freedom, being encouraged to respond with letters to the editor which are frequently published.

The media sometimes serve as catalysts, organizing community efforts to accomplish important objectives, or stimulating the masses to correct inequities at the polls.

A free press and news media serve as an effective check on governmental improprieties. They are essential to the maintenance of the nation's most fundamental liberties.

Freedom of Assembly

The right of the people peaceably to assemble is another liberty guaranteed in the Constitution.[2] Americans are free to

---

1. Constitution of the United States, Amendments, Article I.
2. Ibid.

meet together in groups for any purpose—religious, political, social, recreational, educational, or any other—without prior governmental consent. Such a privilege is quickly lost under a dictorial regime, where the right to assemble is almost always suppressed.

Freedom to Petition for Governmental Redress

The right to petition the government for a redress of grievances is another liberty expressly stipulated in the Constitution.[1] In many instances a private citizen or company may sue a local, state, or national government body for redress. Assistance can also be sought through communication with elected representatives who will work to sponsor and pass corrective legislation. In principle, government agencies and officials are responsible for their actions under the law just as are private citizens.

Freedom to Bear Arms

The U.S. Constitution also stipulates that "the right of the people to keep and bear Arms, shall not be infringed."[2] American citizens have the right to own guns both for sport and for purposes of personal protection.

Freedom from Unlawful Quartering of Soldiers in Private Homes

No soldier can be quartered in a private home during peacetime without the consent of the owner of the home, according to the Constitution.[3] The same prohibition exists in times of war, though soldiers can be stationed in private homes in wartime if it is done in a manner prescribed by law.

Freedom from Unreasonable Searches and Seizures

Citizens have the right to be secure from unauthorized searches and seizures in their persons, houses, papers, and effects.[4] Law enforcement officials must first obtain a warrant which particularly describes the place to be searched and the person or things to be seized. Such warrants are to be issued only when there is probable cause and when supported by an oath or affirmation.

---

1. *Ibid.*
2. *Ibid.*, Article II.
3. *Ibid.*, Article III.
4. *Ibid.*, Article IV.

Freedom from Imprisonment without Indictment

Citizens are protected from extended imprisonment unless a formal indictment is made charging them with a specific capital or infamous crime.[1] (Exceptions exist to this liberty in the military forces or militia during time of war or public danger.)

Freedom from Double Jeopardy

The Constitution guarantees that no person shall "be subject for the same offense to be twice put in jeopardy of life of limb."[2] If tried and acquitted for a crime, he cannot again be tried for the same offense.

Freedom from Forced Confession

Every citizen has the right to be silent and to refrain from any act or statement of self-incrimination in a criminal case. The Constitution expressly prohibits any situation in which an individual might be compelled to be a witness against himself.[3]

Freedom from Punishment without Due Process of Law

Another constitutional guarantee is that an individual shall "not be deprived of life, liberty, or property, without due process of law."[4] Thus a person cannot be fined, imprisoned, or executed unless found guilty in an authorized court of law.

Freedom from Public Confiscation without Renumeration

Yet another freedom enjoyed in America is the guarantee that an individual's private property shall not be taken for public use without just compensation being paid to him.[5] While a government body is considered to have sovereign power over all lands within its jurisdiction through the right of eminent domain, property owners are entitled to just payment for the property taken in such instances.

Freedom from Improper Trials

The U.S. Constitution guarantees a series of rights in connection with trial procedures in criminal prosecutions. An accused

---

1. *Ibid.*, Article V.
2. *Ibid.*
3. *Ibid.*

4. *Ibid.*
5. *Ibid.*

party is entitled to a "speedy and public trial,"[1] and to be judged
by an impartial jury from the state and district where the alleged
crime was committed. The accused person is entitled to be informed of the nature and cause of the accusation. The accused is
to be confronted with the witnesses against him.[2]

If a person is accused and brought to trial, he is entitled to
have compulsory process for obtaining witnesses in his favor. He
also has the right to have legal counsel to assist him in his defense.[3]

In common law suits where the value in controversy exceeds
twenty dollars, an accused person is entitled to a jury trial, and no
fact tried by a jury can be otherwise re-examined in any court of
the United States except according to the rules of common law.[4]

Freedom from Excessive Bail

The U.S. Constitution stipulates that "excessive bail shall not
be required."[5] Thus bail must be fixed in a manner proportional
to the seriousness of the crime for which an individual has been
charged.

Freedom from Excessive Fines

A further Constitutional guarantee is that excessive fines shall
not be imposed as payment for crimes for which individuals have
been found guilty.[6] A balance is to be maintained between the
seriousness of the crime and the degree of punishment meted out
to the offender.

Freedom from Cruel and Unusual Punishments

An important liberty enjoyed by Americans is the guarantee
that cruel or unusual punishments will not be inflicted upon
them.[7] Torture, beatings, and similar mistreatments are prohibited
and, if they do occur, are punishable by law.

Freedom from Slavery or Involuntary Servitude

Slavery or involuntary servitude, except as a punishment for
a crime whereof the party shall have been duly convicted, is

---

1. *Ibid.*, Article VI.   5. *Ibid.*, Article VIII.
2. *Ibid.*   6. *Ibid.*
3. *Ibid.*   7. *Ibid.*
4. *Ibid.*, Article VII.

prohibited in the United States or any place within U.S. jurisdiction.[1]

Freedom from State Laws Abridging Citizenship Rights

The Constitution prohibits the making or enforcing of any
state law which would abridge the privileges or immunities granted
under the Constitution to citizens of the United States.[2] No state
is allowed to deprive any person of life, liberty or property without
due process of law, nor deny to any person within its jurisdiction
the equal protection of the laws.

Freedom to Vote

The Constitution stipulates that neither the United States nor
any state can deny or abridge the right of any citizen to vote
because of his race, color, sex, or previous condition of servitude.[3]

American citizens enjoy the right to vote by secret ballot
for local, state, and national officials and to choose through the
ballot many of the laws which will be established.

The election system provides for a constant re-selection of
leaders and serves to prevent the establishment of dictatorial powers. All citizens registered to vote are entitled to a part in choosing
government officials. They are free to vote ineffective or incompe-
tent men out of office and to pursue necessary reforms by peaceful
and proper methods. This system of changeable leadership reduces
the possibility of government corruption and of unjust governmental intervention into the private affairs of the citizenry.

Freedom to Hold Public Office

American citizens are eligible to run for and be elected to
public office, subject only to minimum eligibility requirements
such as citizenship, residence, age, etc. They may also form new
political parties, campaign actively for themselves or others, and
establish any political ideological platform which they deem to be
appropriate.

Freedom to Own and Accumulate Property

The right to own and acquire property and tangible assets is a
fundamental liberty enjoyed by Americans. Indeed, it stands as the

---

1. *Ibid.*, Article XIII.   3. *Ibid.*, Article XV, Section I.
2. *Ibid.*, Article XIV, Section I.

key to the nation's vast economic system based on free enterprise. The privilege of ownership has been the stimulus and driving motivation for many who have immigrated to America's shores. It was the hope that moved homesteaders to settle virgin tracts and inspired pioneers to forge new lives in the west.

Freedom of Information

The right of Americans to have access to public records is another important liberty which adds stability to the nation and serves as a balancing influence. Government bodies are accountable for their actions, their policies, and their use of public monies. Citizen access to their records allows inspection and evaluation which will detect evidence of wrongdoing if such exists.

Historical records are also available, allowing a true transmittal of the American heritage without the intrusion of propaganda.

Americans are entitled to access to their own credit files, government dossiers, criminal records and other documents which comment upon their personal lives and habits. This gives them opportunity to correct misinformation which may have been erroneously added to the files.

Information of a general and educational nature is also readily available through libraries, bookstores, and the corner marketplace. Americans can read what they want, without having to participate in mandatory indoctrination programs established by government agencies.

Freedom of Communication

Americans enjoy the liberty to communicate with anyone they please throughout the world. Modern technology has extended the scope of this privilege, providing sophisticated telephone, telegraph, radio, satellite, and other equipment to speed the communication process.

Letters and packages can be sent through the mails with the expectation that the missives will arrive without being censored, tampered with, or stolen, a privilege not enjoyed in many countries today.

Freedom of Privacy

As modern living becomes more complex, increased protection is being given to insure individual privacy. Legislation has been enacted to guarantee American citizens protection against improper phone tapping, "bugging" and other electronic surveillance, and government scrutiny of foreign mail that might be politically sensitive. Controls have been set to protect citizens from unwarranted spying by the FBI and the CIA. Citizens have been given the right to inspect files kept about them by government agencies, local law enforcement officials, credit reporting firms, and others who may be maintaining records concerning their activities.

Freedom to Travel

Americans enjoy freedom to travel throughout the country without having to obtain governmental permission or having to pass through regulatory checkpoints. They can go where they want and do so when they please, without being bothered or influenced by stifling government regulations. Freedom to travel in America is enhanced by the high quality of the vast transportation network which stretches across the nation. Good highways, the easy availability of gasoline and service stations, and quality automobiles priced within the economic reach of the average citizen, increase the nation's mobility. Transportation networks have made air, bus, rail, and ship travel available to the masses. Municipal transit networks have also made local travel a reality in the nation's cities.

Travel abroad is easily undertaken also, with passports and visas readily obtainable.

Freedom to Choose Place of Residence

In this great land, people are free to choose their place of residence without the prohibiting influence of government controls. Caste, race, creed, or color do not provide bases for determining housing locations, nor do they affect zoning ordinances designed to protect the lifestyle and economic value of local subdivisions and neighborhoods. Citizens are free to move from state to state to obtain new employment or to meet other personal needs.

Americans can even move to foreign countries, taking up either temporary or permanent residence there, without jeopardizing the safety and well-being of family members who remain behind. These privileges are also extended to students and visitors from other countries who come to the United States.

Freedom of Education

Americans enjoy the right to gain a basic education in free public schools. This schooling, on both the primary and secondary levels, is available to all. Parents and youth have a voice in determining educational policies and curriculum, and local schoolboards are subject to community guidance, both through individual input and through the elective process. Schools can determine their curricula and texts without government censorship.

No government tests limit the amount or kind of schooling one may obtain, nor are students compelled to pursue careers deemed important by the state. Students are able to pursue advanced studies at a broad variety of universities and trade schools across the nation. Many scholarships, grants, and loans are available to assist needy and worthy students. College-level scholars are free to choose their major fields. They can change their courses, if they desire, and they can pursue their studies as long as they wish, subject only to their personal, scholastic, time, and economic limitations.

Freedom to Choose Medical Care

Under the American free enterprize system, citizens can exercise their personal choice in selecting doctors and dentists to administer to their physical needs—no government bureaucracy makes this choice for them. Both general practitioners and specialists are available within a reasonable travel distance of almost every community, as are hospitals and other advanced medical facilities. A wide spectrum of medicines and drugs is available. The American people are free from many of the diseases which wreck havoc in other parts of the world because of their progress in sanitation facilities, food processing technology, availability of adequate food supply, environmental care, etc.

Freedom from Want

Food, clothing, and other basic necessities are in plentiful supply in America. Citizens are able to obtain the goods needed to sustain life without having to wait in long lines or having them rationed. Fewer hours of work are required to earn the price of goods in the United States than in most other countries,[1] and

(Continued on p. 53.)

---

1. Dr. Joseph S. Peery, a professor of economics in the College of Business at the University of Utah, while speaking on the patriotic series presented in Utah's KSL radio and TV series, "What's Right With America?,"

added statistical insights to demonstrate the abundance enjoyed in this nation. He commented:

"American farms are unbelievably productive. Only 4% of our work force is in agriculture. In France it is 18%, in Japan 24%, in Russia 33%. We Americans spend a smaller part of our income on food than do any other people. We have the most varied diets, and the greatest surplus of food." (Program aired August 12, 1976.)

"A typical factory worker in the United States has to pay an equivalent of 4 years wages to buy a small house. In England the same worker would have to work 6 years, in France 8 years, and in West Germany 10 years. We Americans are the best housed in the world and it is only because our free market system is, by far, the most productive on earth." (Program aired July 24, 1976.)

"Food is a bargain for Americans. We spend only 17% of our income on food. In England and France, food consumes a quarter of total income; in Germany 32%; in Eastern Europe and Russia 40%. Food costs us less and we have the richest and most varied diet on earth." (Program aired May 24, 1976.)

"The 1976 standard of living of the average American family is twice as high as it was at the end of World War II; four times as high as it was in 1900; and over ten times as high as it was in 1776. The American system has produced affluence undreamed of by the founders of this country." (Program aired July 31, 1976.)

"The opportunity for college training really exists in this country. Over 20% of the young people who come from poverty homes with incomes below $5,000 a year are now enrolled in college. This is a higher percentage than the total rate for France, Germany, England, and Italy. Here, the children of all income groups have a greater chance to go to college than in any other country." (Program aired July 21, 1976.)

"Real family income has doubled in this country in the past 28 years, and that's with inflation removed. More than one-half of all American families now have incomes over $13,000 a year. We have a standard of living that is the envy of the whole world." (Program aired May 10, 1976.)

"Nine out of every 10 American families have radios, TV sets, automatic coffee makers, vacuum cleaners, and hot and cold running water. More than half of our homes are air conditioned and 40% of us have more than one car. All this in a world, where for most people, pure water alone is a luxury. Let's appreciate the good life we Americans have. It is the best in the world." (Program aired June 16, 1976.)

Others have added further insights. Booth Wallentine, executive vice president of the Utah Farm Bureau, observed that "America's two million farms and ranches produce enough food for nearly 23% of the world." (Program aired May 5, 1976.) Bob Halladay, executive vice president of the Utah Manufacturers Association, told of the nation's move towards affluence: "In 1959, one-fifth of all Americans were living below the poverty line. Now the total is half that and is still falling. The United States has the largest middle income class in the world." (Program aired July 16, 1976.)

many Americans have ample leisure time in addition to the time required to earn a living. Farming, food processing, transportation, and other related industries are so advanced that specialty foods grown only in limited areas are available to consumers throughout the nation.

Housing is available. Americans can build or buy a home, or remodel existing edifices if they choose to do so.

Automobiles, home appliances, and a wide variety of consumer goods are found in well-stocked stores across the land for all who wish to purchase them.

Electricity, natural gas, and telephone systems extend to homes across the country, making the use of home appliances practical.

The availability of consumer goods, plus economic conditions which allow ordinary citizens the discretionary income to purchase them in abundance, have combined to give Americans a high standard of living and an almost universal freedom from want of the basic commodities needed to sustain life.

Freedom of Vocational Choice

Unlike many other countries where vocational choices are limited because of government policy or severe economic conditions, America is still a "land of opportunity" where individuals may choose and pursue the vocational objectives which will best meet their personal needs. The free enterprize system is far-reaching in the vocational potential it offers. Individuals may choose whether to be self-employed or to work for others, and may select vocational goals from a broad spectrum. University, trade school, and on-the-job training programs make it possible for workers to learn the necessary skills. Laws prevent the exploitation of child laborers and require that acceptable working conditions be maintained. Freedom to move from one area to another also gives workers increased control over their vocational growth.

Freedom Through Economic Stability

Closely linked with the benefits of free vocational choice are privileges derived from America's economic system. Americans are able to invest their earnings, having confidence in the stability of their currency and banking system. They can save to meet future needs, investing with a reasonable hope and expectation of eventual profit. A consumer credit system makes the purchase of goods on a time-payment or credit card basis possible, thereby opening access to many purchases which would otherwise be impossible for many consumers to make. Capital is available for business investments, which eventually results in more goods being available in the well-stocked stores which are the envy of other nations around the world. The stability of the American economy makes it possible for the free enterprize system to flourish and for the people to enjoy the fruits of prosperity.

Freedom Through Social Acceptance

America takes pride in its role as the "melting pot" which has accepted immigrants from throughout the world. No rigid caste or social stratification system exists in this country. Opportunity for employment, schooling, housing, and personal growth exists for those of all ethnic and religious backgrounds. Though some integration problems may still exist, great strides have been made towards the elimination of discriminating practices based on race, religion, sex, or age. People can live in the neighborhood of their choice. A wide range of dress styles and standards is accepted. Varied art, folk, and traditional practices are maintained as people preserve the memories of their former cultures. Young people are free to marry whom they wish, even crossing over racial bounds. Individuals can choose their friends and associates, and are free to talk and openly discuss any matter they choose. Americans can trust and confide in one another, without fear that their neighbors are spies who will report their comments to critical police authorities. Social acceptance and equality of opportunity in America are choice liberties which add much to the value of life.

Freedom of Family Life

Americans are free to choose the family lifestyle they wish to pursue. Parents may determine the size of their families without having to submit to government population controls. Mothers can remain in the home and raise their own children, without being compelled to leave and work at government-assigned tasks. Children are not required to be raised in government-established nurseries. The family unit is still the basic building block of American society. Parents are free to teach their children moral and religious values and precepts. Schools are not government propaganda agents committed to a mission of political indoctrination. In the typical American home there are moments of leisure time and family recreation opportunities—the state makes no demand on one's time.

Freedom Through Police Protection

In America the police are regarded as the citizens' protectors and helpers rather than their enemies. Most communities have an efficient, high-quality police force comprised of competent officers who feel real concern for the well-being of residents in their jurisdictional area. Citizens expect their property and persons to be protected under the provisions of the law. In general, they are able to feel peace of mind and an attitude of security and safety. They see in the due process of law a system through which they can properly demand justice and receive redress for grievances they may receive. An effective police force, dedicated to the preservation of law and order, provides citizens with liberty and safety not found where government corruption or anarchy prevail.

Freedom of Artistic Expression

In America artists are free to draw what they choose. Performers can play music from any composer, or any style, without government restraint. Authors can write on the subjects of their choice. There are no forbidden subjects, or styles, or composers which they must avoid.

Freedom of Scientific Discovery

Research can be conducted in any field in private laboratories and in university facilities. No government prohibitions inhibit the continuing quest for knowledge or require inventors and scientists to avoid particular areas of exploration and investigation. Researchers can contribute to the best of their ability without government restraint.

Freedom to Limit Government

The framers of the Constitution recognized that government was to be the servant, not the master of the people. Though they used that inspired document to establish many of man's basic freedoms, they expressly stipulated that "the enumeration in the Constitution, of certain rights, shall not be construed to deny or disparage others retained by the people."[1] They also provided that

---

1. Constitution, *op. cit.*, Amendments, Article IX.

"The powers not delegated to the United States by the Constitution, nor prohibited by it to the States, are reserved to the States respectively, or to the people."[1]

The people, then, maintain the rights not specifically relegated to government. Theirs is the individual right through judicial suit, or collective right through the ballot box, to limit government if it begins to encroach upon their liberties. In the Constitutional plan, they are the masters. Power over government is theirs, if they will but use it.

Summary

America is a great nation, with stability and direction. Laws set forth at the highest level provide checks and balances which protect every man from a host of possible abuses. The pattern set forth in the Constitution has enabled the common man to maintain dignity, to work to achieve personal goals, and to resist the encroachment of tyranny.

1. To perceive the extent of the great freedoms enjoyed by American citizens, one has but to compare life in the United States with conditions in other countries throughout the world.

2. Many freedoms enjoyed by U.S. citizens were listed, including:

    A.   Freedom of worship.
    B.   Freedom of speech.
    C.   Freedom of press and news media.
    D.   Freedom of assembly.
    E.   Freedom of petition for governmental redress.
    F.   Freedom to bear arms.
    G.   Freedom from unlawful quartering of soldiers in private homes.
    H.   Freedom from unreasonable searches and seizures.
    I.   Freedom from imprisonment without indictment.
    J.   Freedom from double jeopardy.
    K.   Freedom from forced confession.
    L.   Freedom from punishment without due process of law.
    M.   Freedom from public confiscation without renumeration.

---

1. *Ibid.*, Article X.

N.   Freedom from improper trials.

O.   Freedom from excessive bail.

P.   Freedom from excessive fines.

Q.   Freedom from cruel and unusual punishments.

R.   Freedom from slavery or involuntary servitude.

S.   Freedom from state laws abridging citizenship rights.

T.   Freedom to vote.

U.   Freedom to hold public office.

V.   Freedom to own and accumulate property.

W.   Freedom of information.

X.   Freedom of communication.

Y.   Freedom of privacy.

Z.   Freedom to travel.

AA.   Freedom to choose place of residence.

BB.   Freedom of education.

CC.   Freedom to choose medical care.

DD.   Freedom from want.

EE.   Freedom of vocational choice.

FF.   Freedom through economic stability.

GG.   Freedom through social acceptance.

HH.   Freedom of family life.

II.   Freedom through police protection.

JJ.   Freedom of artistic expression.

KK.   Freedom of scientific discovery.

LL.   Freedom to limit government.

III

Will Unrighteousness Bring Judgments Upon America?

Why does a nation decline? What influences sap strength from a civilization and pave the way for its downfall? Which forces decrease the vitality of a people, weakening the national will and ability to repel internal degeneracy and external encroachments from tyrannical neighbors?

In his monumental work *The Decline and Fall of the Roman Empire*, Edward Gibbon made observations which give at least partial answers to these queries. He attributed the fall of that great civilization to

1. The rapid increase of divorce; the undermining of the dignity and sanctity of the home, which is the basis of human society.

2. Higher and higher taxes and the spending of public monies for free bread and circuses for the populace.

3. The mad craze for pleasure; sports becoming every year more exciting and more brutal.

4. The building of gigantic armaments when the real enemy was within, the decadence of the people.

5. The decay of religion—faith fading into mere form, losing touch with life and becoming impotent to warn and guide the people.[1]

The Cycle of Righteousness

The average age of the world's great civilizations has been approximately 200 years.[2] It has been observed that nations and civilizations pass through a cycle of righteousness, in which they rise from oppression to liberty and abundance, only to succumb through selfishness and corruption to governmental dependence and finally to oblivion. One author depicted this cycle in these words:

---

1. This summary is drawn from John D. Lawrence, *Down to Earth—The Laws of the Harvest* (Portland, Oregon: Multinomah Press, 1975), p. 26.
2. *Ibid.*

From Bondage to Spiritual Faith
From Spiritual Faith to Great Courage
From Courage to Liberty
From Liberty to Abundance
From Abundance to Selfishness
From Selfishness to Complacency
From Complacency to Apathy
From Apathy to Dependency
From Dependency back into Bondage.[1]

The Book of Mormon gives a vivid description of the cycle of righteousness, showing that God pours out rich blessings upon nations which trust and serve Him, but that God withholds His blessings when they forget Him, and finally pours out judgments upon them when they reject Him:

> ...We can see that the Lord in his great infinite goodness doth *bless and prosper those who put their trust in him.*
>
> Yea, and we may see at the very time when he doth prosper his people, yea, in the increase of their fields, their flocks and their herds, and in gold, and in silver, and in all manner of precious things of every kind and art; sparing their lives, and delivering them out of the hands of their enemies; softening the hearts of their enemies that they should not declare wars against them; yea, and in fine, doing all things for the welfare and happiness of his people; yea, *then is the time that they do harden their hearts, and do forget the Lord their God, and do trample under their feet the Holy One*—yea, and this because of their ease, and their exceedingly great prosperity.
>
> And thus we see that *except the Lord doth chasten his people with many afflictions, yea, except he doth visit them with death and with terror, and with famine and with all manner of pestilence, they will not remember him.* [2]

Where Does America Stand in the Righteousness Cycle?

Where does America stand in the cycle of righteousness? Is the nation still growing in liberty? Is this country still enjoying God's blessings and His influence in "doing all things for the welfare and happiness of His people"? Is the Master still "sparing their lives, and delivering them out of the hands of their enemies"? And

---

1. *Ibid.,* p. 27.
2. Hel. 12:1-3. The Book of Mormon gives an interesting chronicle of the decline-and-fall process of the Nephite nation, for instance. Trace it by reading the following passages in order: 4 Ne. 35-46; Morm. 1:13-19; 2:8-26; 4:5-12; 5:2; 6:1-15.

is the Lord still "softening the hearts of their enemies that they should not declare war against them"?

Or has the decline cycle begun? Have the people, "because of their ease, and their exceedingly great prosperity," now begun to "harden their hearts"? Have the people of America begun to "forget the Lord their God"? Are they approaching the stage where they will "trample under their feet the Holy One"? Will they soon bring upon themselves God's chastening "with death and with terror, and with famine and with all manner of pestilence"?

How does one assess the moral status of a nation, and evaluate its standing before God? In the previous chapter an attempt was made to recall "What's Right With America." Now the unpleasant task of taking the country's "spiritual pulse" must be undertaken, and drawing conclusions in areas where evidence is admittedly incomplete and sometimes partially inaccurate. Percentages may be in error by a point or two. Estimates may be the strongest source currently available. The figures only serve to reflect the nation's status at given points in time. Limited space prohibits extensive, in depth coverage. Yet with all these limitations, a grim picture of a nation being rapidly inundated by sin and the influences of Satan unavoidably emerges.

Violent Crime and Crimes Against Property

Rate of Crime Increase

Crime in the United States has increased at a frightening pace since World War II and is continuing to spiral upward at an alarming rate. The FBI's Uniform Crime Reports for 1975 indicate that crime has increased a frightening 179.9 percent since 1960 and summarize the trends as follows:

> The number of Crime Index offenses reported to law enforcement from throughout the United States increased 9 percent in 1975 when compared to 1974. Violent crimes as a group increased 5 percent. Robbery and aggravated assault rose 5 percent each and rape increased one percent. There was a one percent decrease in murder. As a group property crime increased 9 percent. Larceny-theft rose 12 percent, burglary increased 7 percent and motor vehicle theft was up 2 percent.
>
> Geographically the Southern States reported an 11 percent increase in the volume of Crime Index offenses. Reported crimes in the North Eastern States rose 10 percent, in the North Central States 8 percent and in the Western States 6 percent.[1]

---

1. "Uniform Crime Reports—1975 Preliminary Annual Release," Issued March 25, 1976 by Clarence M. Kelley, Director, Federal Bureau of Investigation, United States Department of Justice, Washington, D.C. 20535.

The 1975 preliminary report summarized the trend for the previous seven years, which had followed the continuous upward spiral from earlier years:

CRIME INDEX TRENDS[1]
(Percent change 1968-1975, each year over previous year)

Years	Total	Violent	Property	Murder	Forcible Rape	Robbery	Aggravated Assault	Burglary	Larceny-Theft	Motor Vehicle Theft
1969/1968	+10	+11	+10	+ 7	+17	+14	+ 9	+ 7	+12	+12
1970/1969	+ 9	+12	+ 9	+ 8	+ 2	+17	+ 8	+11	+ 9	+ 6
1971/1970	+ 6	+11	+ 6	+11	+11	+11	+10	+ 9	+ 5	+ 2
1972/1971	- 4	+ 2	- 5	+ 5	+11	- 3	+ 7	- 1	- 6	- 6
1973/1972	+ 6	+ 5	+ 6	+ 5	+10	+ 2	+ 7	+ 8	+ 5	+ 5
1974/1973	+18	+11	+18	+ 6	+ 8	+15	+ 8	+18	+21	+ 5
1975/1974	+ 9	+ 5	+ 9	- 1	+ 1	+ 5	+ 5	+ 7	+12	+ 2

The Uniform Crime Reports for 1975 reveal the following vital facts which are presented here in summary form:

1.   A total of 11,256,600 crimes were investigated in the seven major crime index areas. (The 1974 total was 10,192,000.)
2.   The "victim risk rate," or rate of serious crimes per 100,000 inhabitants, was 5,281.7, meaning that more than one citizen in twenty was the victim of a serious crime during the year. (The 1974 rate was 4,821.4.)
3.   There has been a 179.9 per cent increase in the rate of crime since 1960 (an annual average rate of increase of 11.99%). The rate of increase since 1960 for violent crime was 199.3%; for property crime it was 178.1%.

The following chart[2] furnished the basis for these statements:

NATIONAL CRIME, RATE, AND PERCENT CHANGE

Crime index offenses	Estimated crime 1975		Percent change over 1974		Percent change over 1970		Percent change over 1960	
	Number	Rate per 100,000 inhabitants	Number	Rate	Number	Rate	Number	Rate
Total	11,256,600	5,281.7	+9.8	+8.9	+39.0	+39.0	+232.6	+179.9
Violent	1,026,280	481.5	+5.3	+4.4	+38.9	+32.5	+255.8	+199.3
Property	10,230,300	4,800.2	+10.3	+9.4	+39.0	+32.6	+230.5	+178.1
Murder	20,510	9.6	- 1.0	-2.0	+28.2	+21.5	+125.1	+88.2
Forcible rape . . .	56,090	26.3	+1.3	+.4	+47.6	+40.6	+226.3	+174.0
Robbery	464,970	218.2	+5.1	+4.3	+32.9	+26.8	+331.2	+263.1
Aggravated assault . .	484,710	227.4	+6.2	+5.4	+44.7	+38.0	+214.1	+164.1
Burglary	3,252,100	1,525.9	+7.0	+6.1	+47.5	+40.6	+256.6	+200.0
Larceny-theft	5,977,700	2,804.8	+13.6	+12.7	+41.5	+34.9	+222.2	+171.1
Motor vehicle theft . .	1,000,500	469.4	+2.4	+1.6	+7.8	+2.8	+204.8	+156.5

1. *Ibid.* As is evident from the above chart, seven crimes are used as a statistical basis for recording changing trends in crime in the United States. These crimes are murder, forcible rape, robbery, aggravated assault,

The "crime clock" analysis in the 1974[1] and 1975[2] reports indicated the frequency of the major crimes on an hourly basis. A comparison of the two shows the increase in crime frequency in just one year:

	1974	*1975*
Serious crimes	19 each minute	21 each minute
Violent crimes (murder, forcible rape, robbery, or assault to kill)	one every 33 seconds	one every 31 seconds
Murder	one every 26 minutes	one every 26 minutes
Forcible rape	one every 10 minutes	one every 9 minutes
Aggravated assault	one every 70 seconds	one every 65 seconds
Robbery	one every 71 seconds	one every 68 seconds
Burglary	one every 10 seconds	one every 10 seconds

---

1. *Crime in the United States 1974*, issued November 17, 1975 by Clarence M. Kelley, Director—FBI (Washington, D.C.: U.S. Department of Justice), p. 9.
2. *Crime in the United States 1975, op. cit.*, p. 9.

---

burglary, larceny-theft, and motor vehicle theft. They are summarized as *violent* and *property* crimes.

2. *Crime in the United States 1975*, issued August 25, 1976 by Clarence M. Kelley, Director, U.S. Department of Justice, Washington, D.C., p. 11. Crime rates by region and area were summarized in charts on the same page as follows:

CRIME RATE BY REGION, 1975
[Rate per 100,000 inhabitants]

Crime index offenses	North-eastern States	North Central States	Southern States	Western States
Total	4,931.9	5,081.3	4,847.8	6,823.7
Violent	535.4	416.8	460.8	547.1
Property	4,396.4	4,664.6	4,387.0	6,276.6
Murder	7.6	8.1	12.7	9.0
Forcible rape	21.0	24.1	25.8	37.6
Robbery	300.4	207.3	168.6	216.5
Aggravated assault	206.4	177.2	253.8	284.0
Burglary	1,448.0	1,322.2	1,175.1	2,029.4
Larceny-theft	2,295.7	2,911.0	2,582.2	3,708.2
Motor vehicle theft	652.8	431.4	329.8	539.1

CRIME RATE BY AREA, 1975
[Rate per 100,000 inhabitants]

Crime index offenses	Total U.S.	Metropolitan areas	Rural	Other cities
Total	5,281.7	6,110.5	1,997.2	4,437.2
Violent	481.5	580.8	167.3	269.1
Property	4,800.2	5,529.7	1,829.9	4,168.1
Murder	9.6	10.6	8.1	5.5
Forcible rape	26.3	31.3	12.0	13.5
Robbery	218.2	284.0	23.5	57.8
Aggravated assault	227.4	254.9	123.7	192.2
Burglary	1,525.9	1,747.9	785.9	1,103.3
Larceny-theft	2,804.8	3,195.6	941.6	2,849.2
Motor vehicle theft	469.4	586.2	102.4	215.5

	1974	*1975*
Larceny-theft	one every 6 seconds	one every 5 seconds
Motor vehicle theft	one every 32 seconds	one every 32 seconds

Significant facts about increasing crime rates in the United States as of 1975:

1. Crime has increased 179.9% since 1960.
2. Crime is increasing at an average annual rate of 12 percent.
3. The chance of being a victim of one of the seven major crimes was one in twenty.
4. Twenty-one serious crimes occurred each minute.

Number of Arrests

Arrests were made for many crimes besides the seven index crimes summarized in the FBI Uniform Crime Reports. According to the FBI figures,

> In 1975, law enforcement agencies made an estimated 9.3 million arrests nationally for all criminal acts except traffic offenses. *The arrest rate was 45 arrests for each 1,000 persons.* The arrest rate for big cities as a group was 53 per 1,000 inhabitants, for suburban areas 37, and in the rural areas the arrest rate was 32.[1]

High Percentage of Juvenile Offenders

The majority of crimes in America today are committed by youthful offenders. More than half of all who are arrested are under 25 years of age, according to the 1975 Uniform Crime Reports:

> Nationally, persons under 15 years of age made up 9 percent of the total police arrests [all offenses except traffic violations]; under 18, 26 percent; under 21, 42 percent; *and under 25, 57 percent....* When only the Index crimes are considered, 17 percent of all persons arrested in 1975 were under the age of 15 and 43 percent were under 18 years of age.[2]

---

1. *Ibid.*, 1975 report, p. 37.
2. *Ibid.*, 1975 report, p. 41.

The very young—juveniles seventeen or younger—are the objects of more than one in four arrests:

The latest statistics compiled by the U.S. Department of Justice show that over *1,683,000, or 27 percent of all arrests (excluding traffic violations) were of persons seventeen years of age and under.* Of these, over 71,000 were under the age of eleven.[1]

Figures released by Sen. Birch Bayh, chairman of the Subcommittee to Investigate Juvenile Delinquency in the U.S., reveal the involvement of teen-agers in the nation's "serious" crime categories:

(1)   Although youngsters from 10 to 17 account for only 16% of our population, they account for nearly 50% of all persons arrested for serious crimes.

(2)   31% of all crimes solved [for FBI Crime Index offenses] involved persons under 18.

(3)   The peak age for arrests for violent crime is 18, followed by 17, 16, and 19.

(4)   The peak age for arrests for major property crime is 16, followed by 15 and 17.[2]

---

1. Emily Rhoads Johnson, "Your Child Is Under Arrest," *Parents Magazine*, May, 1976, p. 44. The author points out that

Children may be arrested not only for criminal acts but also for so-called, status offenses—acts for which an adult would not be arrested. These are called status offenses because it is the state of being a child which makes the act an offense. Behavior such as running away, truancy, consensual sexual activity, suspected or actual sexual promiscuity, refusal to obey parents, using vile, obscene, or vulgar language in public, associating with immoral persons, sleeping in the streets, wandering about a railroad yard or track, jumping a train, frequenting places where drinks are sold, refusing to obey authorities—all may be judged status offenses. (*Ibid.*, p. 58.)

2. Pamela Swift, "Juvenile Crime," *Parade*, July 11, 1976. Senator Bayh attributed much of the problem to teen-age unemployment.

We can trace at least part of this unequal distribution of crime," says Bayh, "to the idleness of so many of our children."

The rate of unemployment among teen-agers is at a record high, and among minority teen-agers it is an incredible 50%. Teen-agers are at the bottom rung of the employment ladder. In hard times they are the most expendable.

We are living in a period in which street crime has become a surrogate for employment and vandalism a release from boredom.... (*Ibid.*)

Juvenile violence in the schools has become a major problem. During the 1972-1975 period *there was an 85% increase in assaults on students and a 77% increase in attacks on teachers*[1] committed by students. In 1975 American students committed 100 murders, 12,000 armed robberies, 9,000 rapes, and 204,000 aggravated assaults against teachers and other students.

The annual cost of vandalism to schools runs to almost $600 million a year—an amount equal to the cost of textbooks.[2]

Juvenile court cases have increased dramatically, as has the rate of cases per 1,000 population of 10-17 year-old youths. 510,000 juvenile court cases were handled in 1960, while the case load had spiraled to 1,143,000 in 1974. The rate per thousand in the 10-17 age group was 20.1 in 1960, *but the rate had increased dramatically to 34.2 per 1,000 in 1974.*[3]

Significant facts about juvenile crime and arrests, as of 1975:

1.   The arrest rate for criminal offenses was 45 arrests for each 1,000 persons (one arrest for every 22 inhabitants).
2.   57% of all who were arrested (for offenses except traffic violations) were under age 25.

Percentage of Crimes Solved and Punished

It is alarming to note that most crimes go unsolved. The 1975 Uniform Crime Report notes that

...Law enforcement agencies do not clear or solve most crimes. Only one-fifth of the serious crimes committed during 1975 were solved by arrest.[4]

Even a criminal's being arrested for a crime is no guarantee that he will be convicted and punished for his crime. A study prepared by U.S. News & World Report indicates that less than 33% of criminals arrested are convicted or plead guilty to the crime, and

---

1. "Violence—A Growing Blot That Hurts U.S. Schools," *Deseret News,* August 30, 1976.
2. *Ibid.* The article commented on Utah's school vandalism rate, observing that "In Utah, the figure comes to around $500,000, which is below the national average but still anything but a reason for feeling complacent."
3. U.S. Bureau of the Census, *Statistical Abstract of the United States: 1975* (96th edition), Washington, D.C., 1975, p. 166.
4. *Uniform Crime Reports,* 1975, *op. cit.,* p. 43.

that of those convicted, less than half are sent to prison. The report shows, for example, the rates in six major cities, indicating that of all persons arrested on felony charges—[1]

City	Convicted	Sent to Jail or to Prison
Washington, D.C.	33%	18%
Chicago	26%	15%
Baltimore	44%	28%
Detroit	58%	20%
Los Angeles County	46%	28%
San Diego County	34%	14%

After presenting the above figures, the record of Washington D.C. is presented as an example of how the criminal justice system works—"or doesn't work:"

> To begin with, you find that most criminals are never caught. For example, *arrests are made in only 1 out of 4 reported robberies.* So, only a small fraction of all crimes committed ever reach the criminal-justice system at all.
>
> Starting with those who are arrested, you find *only 33 out of 100 will eventually be convicted of any crime.* The attrition among the ranks of the arrestees begins early. Typically, for a variety of reasons, *the prosecutor declines to prosecute 24 out of 100 cases that the police bring in. An additional 40 cases out of the original 100 will be dropped later by the prosecutor or dismissed by a judge. Only 10 cases will go to trial. About 26 defendants will plead guilty to some charge*—sometimes a lesser charge than that on which they were originally arrested. *Out of the original 100 arrested, only 3 will go free because of an acquittal at trial. The other 7 who stand trial will be convicted.*
>
> Of those who are convicted, about 4 in 10 will not be sentenced to jail or prison. Instead, they will be fined or placed on probation. Of the 6 in 10 who are incarcerated, 2 out of 3 will be paroled when they first become eligible—usually after serving the minimum time set in the sentence imposed by the judge. Even before parole or final release from prison, many inmates will be released temporarily into the community on "furlough" to work, study or visit.
>
> In addition, most of the persons who are prosecuted will be released while awaiting disposition of their cases.[2]

---

1. " 'Revolving Door' Justice—Why Criminals Go Free," *U.S. News & World Report*, May 10, 1976, p. 37. The source given for the above chart was: Institute for Law and Social Research: "Felony Justice," (to be published in the fall of 1976 by Little, Brown & Company), and the California Bureau of Criminal Statistics.
2. *Ibid.*

Majority Arrested Are Repeat Offenders

The FBI statistics indicate that 65% of all the persons arrested in the 1970-1974 period for "serious" crimes were repeat offenders. A chart in the Uniform Crime Reports listing "Percent Repeaters by Type of Crime"[1] showed these figures:

Auto Theft	79%	Assault	65%
Robbery	79%	Burglary	64%
Stolen Property	78%	Narcotics	59%
Forgery	73%	Fraud	58%
Weapons	72%	Larceny	55%
Murder	68%	Embezzlement	23%
Gambling	65%	All others	68%
Rape	65%	Total	65%

Significant facts about crimes solved and repeat offenders, as of 1975:

1. Most crimes go unsolved. Only 20% of serious crimes are solved by arrest.
2. Less than 33% of arrested criminals are eventually convicted of their crime.
3. 60% of criminals, after being convicted, are not sentenced to jail or prison—they are only fined or placed on probation.
4. 65% of criminals arrested are repeat offenders. Repeaters on an average, were arrested four times in a five-year period.

Dollar Cost of Crime

The dollar cost of crime is enormous, and has increased 50% within the past five years, as reported in a UPI release:

CRIME COSTS UP 50 PCT.

Crime cost United States business more than $23.6 billion last year, about 50 percent more than five years ago, according to an expert on industrial security.

1. Uniform Crime Reports, 1974, *op. cit.*, p. 49. Supporting charts indicated that the above figures were based on a total number of subjects of 207,748. The average age of the "repeater" criminals arrested during the four year period was 31, and that the average "repeater" had already been charged 4 times during his average criminal career of 5 years. (*Ibid.*, p. 48.)

About $6 billion of that total was paid by businesses for private security systems and guards, Arthur J. Bilek told the American Society of Industrial Security.

Bilek, vice president of Pinkerton's Inc., is chairman of the National Private Security Council of the U.S. Law Enforcement Assistance Administration.

"Today there are over one million persons employed in private security and less than one-half million public law enforcement officers," Bilek said, yet increased private security has not been able to stem the crime rate.

"It is now painful and unalterably clear that *police alone cannot make a business, a home, a citizen safe from criminal attack,"* he said.[1]

Another report indicates that "U.S. merchants lose $2 billion annually to shoplifters, far more than is lost from burglaries and robberies combined."[2]

Significant facts about the cost of crime, as of 1975:

1.   Crime cost $23.6 billion, or $111 for every American inhabitant. Shoplifting alone cost $9.39 per individual.
2.   The dollar cost of crime has increased 50% in the last 5 years.
3.   As much is spent to repair school vandalism as to buy school textbooks.

Soaring Crime a Character Sickness

The tremendous seriousness of the continually-spiraling crime rate cannot be minimized. Attorney General Edward Levi, with his overview of the national problem, has warned that *"crime remains an enormous national problem and current levels are—and must be— seen as unacceptable."*[3]

What are the conditions which have caused crime to increase? There are no simple answers to the question, though many offer helpful insights. Dr. Victor B. Cline, nationally-known researcher, observed that *"crimes of violence in the U.S. are currently increasing at nine times the population growth,"* and suggested that "rising crime is caused by a combination of factors, but mainly

---

1. *Deseret News,* September 2, 1976.
2. $2 Billion Lost to Shoplifting," *Deseret News,* October 8, 1976. This was the report of Richard Mellard, coordinator for the National Crime Prevention Institute, Louisville, Ky.
3. "No Let-up in Crime Epidemic," *Deseret News,* October 1, 1975.

the breakdown of the family and the vast amount of violence to which people are exposed on TV and in plays, movies, magazines and books."[1]

Many of the diverse factors which have contributed to increased crime were touched on by a report issued by the Educational Testing Service. (The report was dealing with why student scores on national tests have dropped, rather than the rise in crime, yet it effectively summarizes some of the sociological factors which are shaping the nation's morality.) The report is summarized by Lavor Chaffin:

>—The *family* has become too permissive, parents have abdicated their authoritative role, are too indulgent, too coddling; the women's liberation movement has had an effect on women who are full-time mothers.
>
>—*Religion* is partly responsible. There has been a growing rejection of traditional western religions.
>
>—*Civil rights:* We are seeing increased encroachment by the courts, increased legislative involvement in education, having the effect of tying the hands of school personnel in such matters as discipline, access to higher education.
>
>—*A crisis of values:* There is a revolution in values, including a decline in the Protestant ethic, specifically the outmoding of the idea of success through hard work and the impact of the counter culture with its hostility to reason, science, technology and industry.
>
>—The decline is a result of the *rapid enrollment increases* following World War II when schools were overcrowded and *many inadequate teachers* were employed. Critics point out that the pupils receiving the poor scores beginning in about 1964 were the ones born in 1946.
>
>—A possible explanation is that *teachers have lost perspective* and allowed academic demands to be reduced. This may have been accompanied by an erosion of traditional values and a decline in both social and academic discipline....
>
>—Utah's Dr. Terrel H. Bell, while still U.S. Commissioner of Education, said today's learning environment is "suffering from pollution." He said the increased use of alcohol and drugs is contributing to the decline in the learning environment. Another source of pollution, he said, "is television." He said TV is "pandering to the lowest common denominator of public taste."[2]

James J. Kilpatrick, a nationally-syndicated columnist, attempted to analyze the increase in crime and mentioned many possible causes, but finally concluded that *"this is a sickness of character, and God, alone, knows how we treat that":*

---

1. Douglas Palmer, "3 Ways to Reverse Crime Rise," *Deseret News,* October 30, 1975.
2. Lavor Chaffin, "What's Dropping Test Scores?" *Deseret News,* September 16, 1976.

What accounts for this cancerous growth within our society? How do you explain the figures?

If we were dealing with crimes of violence, perhaps *some blame might rationally be laid on TV.* It seems reasonable to surmise that a generation of young people, reared to seeing blood shed in living color on the screen, might incline toward violence on the streets. You could turn around on the *easy availability of handguns.* You might find a farfetched explanation in the *experience of violence in Vietnam.* In the matter of rape, which now occurs on an average of once every nine minutes, you might talk of *changing sexual mores.*

But one searches in vain for an explanation of the soaring increase in crimes against property. Doubtless, *drugs* are a factor; addicts steal to support their habits. *Poverty* may account for some thefts; people steal to eat—but our people have been poor before, much poorer than they are now, and the country experienced no such fearful invasion of property rights.

The worst of the situation, perhaps, is that the FBI's Report depicts only a part—the most obvious part—of the appalling picture. *Across the country, merchants suffer from a plague of shoplifting that hurts every consumer. At the highest levels tales of bribery abound. Within the medical profession, the number of fraudulent Medicare Medicaid claims increases. We have cheating scandals in our greatest universities and in the service academies.*

Has the machinery of law enforcement failed? Evidently it has. Barely one out of every five crimes against property is cleared by arrest. Of those arrested, only two-thirds are found guilty as charged. Of those two-thirds, perhaps one-third actually serve time in jail.

But it is an inadequate answer to lay the blame upon the business community, police, prosecutors and judges. *Somewhere is a deeper, more troublesome explanation.* Only a short time ago, our people generally respected the simple commandment: Thou shalt not steal. *This was a discipline imposed in the home, in the schools, in the churches, in business and human relationships.*

A few years ago, writing these end-of-August essays, I was urging more police, more courts, larger prisons, longer sentences. It still strikes me as important to crack down on the repeaters—the "career criminals"—and to impose punishments that may not rehabilitate but surely will incarcerate. But massive injections of law enforcement may treat only the symptoms without touching the underlying illness. *This is a sickness of character, and God alone knows how we treat that.*[1]

---

1. James J. Kilpatrick, "Soaring Crime: A Character Sickness," *Deseret News*, September 2, 1976. The figures he was describing were the FBI Uniform Crime Report update concerning crimes against property released in August, 1976, which he summarized as follows:

> Most Americans of middle age can remember a time when houses were seldom locked, and bicycles were not casually stolen, and the rare bank robbery was a national news event. There once was a time when property was generally, if not perfectly, respected. Even in the

When will we see relief from soaring crime? Who knows? There are many theories,[1] but they fail to take into account the effects of "the cycle of righteousness" and the fury of the last days struggle between the forces of good and evil. Time will prove or disprove their validity, as it does the truthfulness of any prophecy.

Significant facts about the increase in crime, as of 1975:

1. Crimes of violence are increasing nine times as fast as the population.
2. Crimes against property are increasing twelve times as fast as the population.

---

1. Some sociologists, for instance, believe that crime will abate as the population age of the nation shifts:

    The current crime wave sweeping the United States can be expected to end by 1980, law enforcement officers attending a crime prevention seminar at the University of Utah were told Monday.
    In all other major crime waves in the country—1870 to 1875, 1930-1935, and from 1962 to the present—the country's population 25 or under outnumbered the remainder of the population.
    By 1980 the U.S. population 25 or older will outnumber the population under 25.
    Joe Mele, instructor from the National Crime Prevention Institute, Louisville, Ky., said that leading sociologists believe in that theory because 80 percent of all crimes are committed by those 25 or under.
    He said the earlier crime waves abated when the older residents began to outnumber the younger ones and sociologists expect it to happen again in 1980.
    However, *he emphasized that crime prevention efforts must continue and that crime will still be a serious problem in 1980,* when it is expected to abate. (Robert D. Mullins, "Crime Wave May Ebb by '80, Lawmen Told," *Deseret News,* October 5, 1976.)

---

depths of the Depression, when millions of our people were desperately poor, stealing was not pervasive.

What has gone wrong? *Over the 15 years between 1960 and 1975, our population increased by roughly 15 percent. In this same period, crimes against property increased by 178 percent.*

In 1960, the FBI reported 1,034 larcenies per 100,000 population. Last year the rate was 2,805. In 1960, the rate on motor vehicle thefts was 183; last year it was 469.

Perhaps whole numbers carry greater impact. In 1960, the FBI reported 912,000 burglaries. Last year the figure was 3,252,000 burglaries, an increase of 256 percent. The increase in robberies was even greater, from 108,000 in 1960 to 465,000 last year.

Sexual Immorality

Of major concern is the continually-rising tide of sexual sin, in direct defiance of the commandment on Mt. Sinai that "Thou shalt not commit adultery."[1] Accurately measuring the extent of sexual immorality in America today is an impossible task, but the available indicators clearly show that it is widespread and on the increase.

Adultery

In their study of *Sexual Behavior in the Human Male* published in 1948, Dr. Alfred C. Kinsey and his associates startled the nation with their revelation of the widespread sexual activities. In their research, based on large samples, they found over a third of their male subjects admitting to extra-marital intercourse, and felt that "*it is probably safe to suggest that about half of all the married males have intercourse with women other than their wives, at some time while they are married*":

> It has so far been impossible to secure hundred percent samples from men of the type that belongs to business organizations, business executive groups, and service clubs; and we have every reason for believing that extra-marital intercourse is the source of the hesitance of many of the individuals in such groups to cooperate. Consequently, *the incidence and frequency figures which are given here must represent the absolute minimum, and it is not at all improbable that the actuality may lie 10 to 20 per cent above the figures now given.*
>
> *Hamilton (1929) found 28 per cent of his hundred men with records of extra-marital intercourse.* His figure would have been higher if he had dealt with older men. *In the present study, something over a third (27% to 37%) of the married males in each of the five-year age periods have admitted some experience in extra-marital intercourse.... Since these are active incidence data, the accumulative figure must amount to something more than that.* Because of the inadequacy of the record it has been impossible to construct accumulative incidence curves by the usual techniques..., and we can only estimate from these active incidence figures.
>
> On the basis of these active data, and *allowing for the cover-up that has been involved, it is probably safe to suggest that about half of all the married males have intercourse with women other than their wives, at some time while they are married.*[2]

---

1. Ex. 20:14. See also Ro. 2:22; 1 Cor. 6:9-13; Eph. 5:3-5; etc.
2. Alfred C. Kinsey, Wardell B. Pomeroy, Clyde E. Martin, *Sexual Behavior in the Human Male*, (Philadelphia & London: W. B. Saunders Company, 1948), p. 585.

Five years later, the Kinsey group released their *Sexual Behavior in the Human Female.* In this study they reported their findings that

> In their late teens, 7 per cent of the married females in the sample were having coitus with males other than their husbands. The accumulative incidences did not materially increase in the next five years, *but after age twenty-six they gradually and steadily rose until they reached their maximum of 26 per cent by forty years of age....* After that age only a few females began for the first time to have extra-marital coitus. [1]

Their report of 26% of the women having been participants in adulterous relations was presented with the comment that "Since the cover-up on any socially disapproved sexual activity may be greater than the cover-up on more accepted activities, it is possible that the incidences and frequencies of extra-marital coitus in the sample has been higher than our interviewing disclosed."

In 1974 Dr. Robert R. Bell, of Temple University, studied the questionnaire replies of 2,372 American wives in an effort to learn whether the sexual-response patterns of married women have changed since the Kinsey report. In his summary he reported:

> On the average, *one out of every four women surveyed said she had had extra-marital coitus, and there is every indication this rate is on the increase.* One out of six women under the age of 25 reported extra-marital liasons; between the ages of 26 and 30 the rate doubled. *I predict that as the wives in both these groups get older, the number who have experienced extramarital affairs will grow, eventually including nearly half of all wives under 30.* [2]

Dr. Bell also reported that *"One out of twenty women in this survey—most of them under 30—said they had mate-swapped at*

---

1. Alfred C. Kinsey, Wardell B. Pomeroy, Clyde E. Martin, Paul H. Gebhard, *Sexual Behavior in the Human Female* (Philadelphia & London: W. B. Saunders Co., 1953), p. 416. The sample was based on interviews with 8,000 women.
2. Robert R. Bell, with Norman M. Lobsenz, "How Uninhibited Can a Woman Dare to Be?", *Redbook,* September, 1974, Vol. 143, No. 5, p. 179. He reported that "Most of the women do not seem to think of adultery in terms of a single, impulsive affair. *Half of them felt that they 'certainly' or 'probably' would have an extramarital involvement in the future.*" He observed that *"Forty per cent of the adulterous wives had had sex with two to four men; 17 per cent, with five or more. Most wives had had several encounters with each extramarital partner."* (Ibid.)

least once, and most of them plan to keep on doing it.... About one out of four women who had never swapped mates said they might like to try it."[1]

In October, 1974, Redbook published a similar questionnaire and received responses from more than 100,000 women which were tabulated and published in the October, 1975 issue. In the survey, 38% of the participants admitted to adultery by the time they had reached the 35-39 age group:

> *Thirty out of 100 wives who participated in the survey have engaged in sex outside of marriage....* About one third of all married women who took part in the survey report having sexual relations with men other than their husbands. The longer they have been married, the more likely it is to happen. Twelve out of 100 women married less than a year have had extramarital intercourse; and so have 21 out of 100 women married 1 to 4 years; 30 out of 100 women married 5 to 10 years; and *38 out of 100 women married more than 10 years.*[2]

The conclusion that there is a high percentage of married individuals who have committed adultery—certainly at least one

---

1. *Ibid.*, p. 181.
2. Robert J. Levin, "The Redbook Report on Premarital and Extramarital Sex—The End of the Double Standard?", *Redbook*, October, 1975, Vol. 145, No. 6, p. 40. That author, by comparing the Redbook findings with the earlier Kinsey report, demonstrated the significant increase in adulterous relationships which has occurred within the past quarter-century:

    Some sociologists and sex researchers predict that eventually half of all American wives will engage in extramarital sex. As questionable as that may seem at first, some of our findings put the issue into focus.

    A rough comparison with Kinsey reveals a sharp change in just 21 years. Among 25-year-old women, Kinsey found, 9 per cent had had extramarital intercourse; in the Redbook survey, among 20- to 24-year-old wives, extramarital sex was reported by 25 per cent. *Among 40-year-old women Kinsey found that 26 per cent had had extramarital sex; among Redbook's 35- to 39-year-old wives—the group with the highest percentage of extramarital activity—it is 38 per cent.*

    In that age group, however, we discovered that for certain women the likelihood of extramarital sex is even higher. We separated the replies of the 35- to 39-year-old wives into three categories: those women who work part or full time, those who work as volunteers and those who remain at home. Twenty-seven out of 100 women who remain at home and 32 out of 100 volunteers report extramarital sex; *but among wage-earning wives, almost half (47 out of 100) say they have had intercourse with men other than their husbands. (Ibid.,* p. 42.)

third or more of all married individuals in the United States—is inescapable. Equally evident is that the per cent is rising rapidly.

Significant facts about adultery in the United States:

1. Various surveys indicate that at least 38 per cent of married men and women, by age 39, admit having had sexual intercourse with someone other than their spouse at some time during their marriage.
2. Researchers estimate that 50% of husbands and wives commit adultery, having intercourse with individuals other than their spouses, sometime during their marriage.
3. Working wives are almost twice as likely to be involved in adultery as wives who remain in the home.

Fornication and Premarital Intercourse

Kinsey, after his study of the American male almost three decades ago, reported that

> *The highest incidence of pre-marital intercourse comes in the late teens, where nearly three quarters (70.5%) of the total U.S. population is involved....* From that point the incidence drops, but still stays high. In every age group between 16 and 50, more than half (from 70.5% down to 51.3%) of the single males engage in heterosexual intercourse.[1]

The Kinsey report showed an even higher fornication rate for American males with lower educational levels:

> The accumulative incidence figures for pre-marital intercourse vary considerably for different social levels.... Among the males who go to college, about *67 per cent* has coital experience before marriage; among those who go into high school but not beyond, about *84 per cent* has such intercourse; and among the boys who never go beyond grade school the accumulative incidence figure is *98 per cent.*[2]

Concerning male relationships with prostitutes, Kinsey wrote that "we find that *about 69 percent of the total white male population ultimately has some experience with prostitutes.*"[3] And the Kinsey report concerning male homosexuality recorded that

---

1. Kinsey, Male, *op. cit.*, p. 249.   3. *Ibid.*, p. 597.
2. *Ibid.*, pp. 551-552.

In these terms (of physical contact to the point of orgasm), the data in the present study indicate that *at least 37 per cent of the male population has some homosexual experience between the beginning of adolescence and old age....* This is more than one male in three of the persons that one may meet as he passes along a city street.[1]

The 1953 Kinsey report on the American female reported that *"nearly 50 per cent of the females in our sample had had coitus before they were married....* A considerable portion of the pre-marital coitus had been had in the year or two immediately preceding marriage, with a portion of it confined to the fiancé in a period just before marriage."[2]

The Kinsey report also made reference to lesbianism, indicating that "By age forty, *19 per cent of the females in the total sample had had some physical contact with other females* which was deliberately and consciously, at least on the part of one of the partners, intended to be sexual."[3]

The 1974 Redbook survey revealed how dramatically the moral standard has been abandoned, for 90 per cent of the women under 25 admitted that they had had premarital intercourse:

> *Ninety per cent of women under 25 who participated in Redbook's survey say that they have had premarital intercourse. In 1953, however, Kinsey found that only 33 per cent of 25-year-old women had had premarital intercourse (and, incidentally, as his 1948 study showed, only 80 per cent of 25-year-old men).*
>
> The likelihood that young women will have intercourse before marriage has been steadily increasing over the last 10 years. *Sixty-nine per cent of the women in Redbook's survey who were married before 1964 have experienced premarital intercourse. Among women married between 1964 and 1969, it is 81 per cent; among those married between 1970 and 1973, 89 per cent; and among those married after the end of 1973, 93 per cent.*
>
> In all age groups the strongly religious woman is more likely than other women to remain a virgin until marriage, but *the influence of religion is certainly less inhibiting in this respect than might be expected.* Thus, for example, *among strongly religious women under 25 years of age, 75 out of 100 have had premarital intercourse.* At the same time the contrast with nonreligious women under 25 is striking—96 out of 100 have had intercourse before marriage.[4]

Earlier studies also demonstrated the rapid increase in pre-marital sex. A Pennsylvania sociologist, Dr. Carlfred B. Broderick,

---

1. *Ibid.*, p. 623.
2. Kinsey, female, *op. cit.*, p. 286.
3. *Ibid.*, p. 453.
4. "The Redbook Report...," *op. cit.*, p. 38.

professor of family relationships at Pennsylvania State University, reported in 1971 a series of studies which were already indicating the dramatic increase of premarital sex which would lead to the Redbook figures:

> Sexual attitudes and behavior of American women are becoming vastly more liberal. Premarital sexual intercourse is increasing dramatically across the nation....
>
> In one survey of newly-weds in Pennsylvania,... *75 per cent admitted to premarital intercourse. Thirty percent of the wives in the survey admitted, too, that they were pregnant prior to marriage.*

Broderick also contends that the rise in premarital sex is not limited to college students, but "it applies equally to non-students and older couples as well.

"Not only are more women engaging in premarital sex nowadays statistically," he contends, "but fewer who do so have regrets about it. It's more accepted."[1]

The rapid increase in fornication is leading to an increase in children born out of wedlock. A March 4, 1976 UPI release from Washington entitled "Illegitimate Births Are On the Rise," reported that

> *Illegitimate births are steadily increasing, especially among white teen-agers,* the National Center for Health Statistics reports.
>
> The Center estimates there were 418,000 illegitimate births nationwide in 1974, the latest year for which figures were available, for an increase of nearly 3 percent over the previous year.... *More than one-third of all 1974 births to girls aged 15-19 were classified as illegitimate....*[2]

---

1. "Sex and Guilt," *Parade*, March 7, 1971. Coupled with increased premarital sex is the tendency to postpone marriage. "The census bureau reports that young Americans are getting married later in life than they used to. In the last two decades the median age for a man getting married has risen 6 months to age 23.1. Young women now get married at age 21, up a year from the 1950's." (Waiting for Weddings, *Parade*, December 22, 1974.)
2. "Illegitimate Births Are on the Rise," *Deseret News*, March 4, 1976. Earlier figures add insights to the extent of illegitimacy. A *Parade* article published August 31, 1969, entitled "Education and Sex," reported that

    > *For every 1,000 unmarried girls in this country, ages 15 to 19, approximately 18 bear an illegitimate child.* At this moment there are 145,000 known, unwed American mothers in that particular age group, with their illegitimacy rate steadily rising....

    (Cont. bottom p. 78.)

The number of illegitimate births is not nearly as great a concern as is the knowledge that *almost seventy-five percent of the babies born to teen-age mothers are conceived out of wedlock.* These were the findings of sociologists from Johns Hopkins University in an extensive study on 1971 statistics:

> *Three-fourths or about 75 percent of American teen-age girls pregnant for the first time are unwed when they conceive.* So report two professors from Johns Hopkins University in Baltimore, Melvin Zelnik and John Kantner.
>
> *The two sociologists researched 4,600 girls in the 15-to-19 age bracket.*
>
> *"To marry and then to conceive is the exception among teen-agers, characterizing about one-fourth of all first conceptions in this age group,"* the two professors point out, revealing that *30 percent of the girls they surveyed said they engaged in sexual relations without marriage. About a third of these girls eventually become pregnant.*
>
> The Zelnik-Kantner report, published by the Planned Parenthood Federation of America, is described as "the first extensive study of pregnancy rates among teen-agers in the United States." The research was based on 1971 statistics, two years before the 1973 Supreme Court ruling made abortions easier to obtain....
>
> Among other facts, the survey shows that *58 percent of girls who married in their teens engaged in sex relations prior to marriage. The pregnancy rate for black girls was higher than for whites. About 25 percent of the blacks conceived before marriage, and 6 percent of the whites.* Promiscuity studies show that black girls are not appreciably different from white girls. Both have just about the same number of male partners. Because of their lower economic status, however, blacks probably have less access to contraceptive devices and sex education than do whites, which may account for their higher pregnancy rate.[1]

A Utah study, which closely parallels the national average and reflected similar results, was reported as follows:

> *Seven out of 10 Utah teen-agers having their first baby conceived the child out of wedlock,* according to a study of 1972 births by the State Division of Health.

---

1. "Teen-agers and Sex," *Parade,* August 18, 1974.

> It is no secret that, proportionately, the illegitimacy rate of non-white girls is higher than that of white girls—80.2 per thousand is the non-white rate in the 15 to 19 age-group as opposed to 9.0 for whites.

> A UPI release from Washington published in the *Deseret News* on August 16, 1976, entitled "Unwed Mom Riskier as Wife," contained Census Bureau findings as follows:

> The report also said that *10.1 percent of first births among whites and 52.6 percent among blacks were reported illegitimate in 1969.*

That is close to the national average for teen-age mothers, according to Dr. Peter C. Van Dyck, deputy director of health for Family Health Services, who released the study with John E. Brockert, director of the Bureau of Health Statistics....

The study involved 2,963 babies born to Utah teen-aged mothers during 1972. Of these, 578 were listed as illegitimate, 1,147 were born within eight and a half months after marriage, and 597 were not listed as illegitimate, but no marriage certificates for parents were found.[1]

Ann Landers was apparently using similar national figures as her guide when she asked,

Did you know that six out of 10 teen-age mothers are unmarried or get married just before their babies are born? Over 10 percent of the pregnant teen-age girls interviewed did not use any contraceptives and didn't realize they could become pregnant. More than 55 percent of the girls said they thought they were too young to become pregnant.

Most teen-age mothers and their babies face greater health risks than older mothers. Teen-agers who marry as a result of pregnancy are more likely to be economically disadvantaged and to be divorced.

These conclusions were based on statistics from the Department of Health, Education and Welfare and a survey by the Census Bureau.[2]

Many participants in premarital intercourse remain unwed and bring offspring into the world without the advantages of a proper home. A UPI release concerning the report issued at the end of 1966 indicated that *"Illegitimate births last year represented 14.2 percent of all births, the highest ever."*[3] Teen-age pregnancies without the stabilizing effect of marriage are a major problem of society today:

The extent of *extra-marital pregnancies* among women, white and black, indicate a tremendous breakdown in religious values and practice. *Among teen-agers alone, more than a million became pregnant.*[4]

---

1. "Problems of Unwed Teen Moms," *Deseret News,* February 3, 1976.
2. Ann Landers, "Ignorance Gets Teen-Agers in Trouble," *Salt Lake Tribune,* December 28, 1975.
3. "Birth Rate Falls to Record Low," *Deseret News,* December 31, 1976.
4. Michael Novak, "Abortion and the Blacks," *Deseret News,* November 13, 1976. Figures cited are for 1974. A comparison with census figures places this figure in shocking perspective—that *one teen-age girl out of twenty in the United States became pregnant as the result of fornication during the year, 1974.*

   The Statistical Abstract gives a population breakdown based on the 1970 Census as follows:

10,231,994	girls ages 10-14
9,476,628	girls ages 15-19
19,708,622	Total

Figures released at a conference on teen-age sexuality in early February, 1976, indicate a high degree of teen participation in sex:

> Statistics released at the conference indicated there were one million teen-age pregnancies last year—some 400,000 ending in abortions. Of the pregnancies, 50,000 involved girls 15 or under.
>
> Alfred Moran, executive vice-president of Planned Parenthood in New York City, made a "conservative estimate" that between three and four million, or about 25 percent of all teen-agers, engage in sexual activity.[1]

Parental disapproval of premarital sex has greatly diminished. Less than one-fourth of parents surveyed indicate that they would even object to children participating in fornication. In the Redbook survey parents "were asked whether they would object if their sons engaged in premarital sex. *Twelve percent said they would object.* Asked the same question about their daughter, *24 percent objected.*[2]

According to Dr. Elliott Landau, "In 1974 (the most recent year for which we have statistics), more than 200,000 teen-agers (85,000 whites and 121,000 blacks) gave birth to out-of-wedlock children."[3]

In another study related to teen-age pregnancies,

> *Twenty percent of 3,000 teen-agers having their first baby were not married during pregnancy or after the child was born. Another 50 percent married sometime during the pregnancy. Only 30 percent became pregnant after marriage.*[4]

---

1. "Psychologist Urging Teen Girls to Say 'No,' " *Deseret News*, February 5, 1976. In the light of figures cited above concerning illegitimacy, Moran's estimate was extremely conservative.
2. "The Redbook Report...," *op. cit.*, p. 192.
3. Dr. Elliott Landau, "Today's Teen-Age Mother," *Deseret News*, March 31, 1976.
4. Douglas Palmer, "Teen Pregnancies, Many Expenses—Not All Monetary," *Deseret News*, May 6, 1976. The study was conducted in Utah under the direction of Dr. Peter Van Dyck, deputy state director of health and head of the state's Family Health Services Branch. The study showed that there is greater than normal danger in births to teen-age mothers:

   > Studies made during the past nine months show that about one out of every 10 babies born to teen-agers will be premature. The studies also show that teen-agers have two to five times more injuries occurring to their child at birth than mothers in their 20's and 30's. *At least a third of all teen-age mothers will have some kind of medical complication during pregnancy which can harm the child. (Ibid.)*

Premarital intercourse is often more than a brief encounter. Unmarrieds living together has become accepted practice on many college campuses. A 1972 survey on cohabitation at Cornell University by Dr. Eleanor Macklin, a psychologist, revealed that

> ...*31 percent of the unmarried students at Cornell lived with a person of the opposite sex for at least three months.*
>
> Dr. Macklin defined "living together" as sharing a bed or bedroom with a single person of the opposite sex for four or more nights per week for at least three consecutive months.
>
> Almost 80 percent of the students who lived together, the psychologist learned, tried to hide the relationship from their parents.[1]

According to recent studies, "An emerging social trend of the 1970's is the escalating number of men and women living together out of wedlock, the Census Bureau says."[2] A report issued in February, 1977 indicated that

> The number of unmarried couples in the United States who have decided to share living quarters has more than doubled....
>
> Arthur Norton, who directed preparation of the study, said the phenomenon is not a passing fad. "This is a true, accepted social trend," he said, adding that he expected the number of unmarried roommates to increase even more.
>
> The report said that in March 1976, when the statistics were compiled, *1,320,000 unmarried Americans lived with a member of the opposite sex in a two-person household, compared with 654,000 in 1970.*
>
> *Forty-eight percent of the men and 43 percent of the women involved had never been married, the report said.*[3]

It appears that the compilers of the Redbook survey understood well the extent of the fornication problem in America when they felt compelled to observe that

> It seems almost self-evident that *having intercourse before marriage is, in 1975, a virtually universal experience—an irreversible pattern....*[4]

---

1. "Campus Cohabitation," *Parade*, December 22, 1974.
2. "Unwed Roommates Now Social Trend," *Deseret News*, February 9, 1977.
3. *Ibid.*
4. "The Redbook Report...," *op. cit.*, p. 40.

Significant facts about fornication and illegitimate births in the United States

1. The number of participants in pre-marital intercourse has skyrocketed during the last decade as the moral standard has been abandoned. A recent survey shows that of wives married after 1973, 93% had committed fornication prior to their marriage.
2. One teen-age girl out of every twenty became pregnant as the result of fornication in 1974.
3. Of births classified as legitimate, in more than 50% the parents were married after the baby was conceived.
4. Almost seventy-five percent of the babies born to teen-age mothers are conceived out of wedlock.
5. Illegitimate births are on the rise. In 1975, illegitimate births constituted 14.2% of all births, the highest illegitimacy rate ever.
6. In 1974 more than one-third of all births to girls aged 15-19 were classified as illegitimate.

Venereal Disease

Closely associated with the rapid increase in adultery and fornication is the alarming epidemic of venereal disease which is sweeping the country. The extent of this epidemic was reported in 1972 in an outspoken article reprinted in the Reader's Digest:

From July 1970 through 1971 alone, there were 624,371 new cases of gonorrhea reported by U.S. public-health officials, plus 23,336 new cases of syphilis. These frightful figures represent only the tip of a fast-growing iceberg. For although all states require physicians to report venereal-disease cases to public-health authorities, only a fraction— perhaps fewer than one out of five—are actually reported which could mean that *our VD epidemic is now reaching more than 2.5 million Americans annually.* [1]

1. Grace Naismith, "The Plain Truth About VD," *Reader's Digest,* September, 1972, p. 65. The rapid growth of VD was reported later in the article as follows:

   VD rates in "inner cities" are 10 to 12 times as high as in other parts of the country. The rate of increase in gonorrhea alone during the year was 15 percent. U.S. taxpayers laid out $42.5 million in 1969 to support the thousands of syphilitics in our mental hospitals.

A serious new strain of venereal disease, Herpes Simplex Virus Type 2, has recently emerged as a new and fearful threat.

> Herpes Simplex is now recognized as the second-most-common venereal disease in America. Currently *it attacks twice as many victims as syphilis, and is beginning to challenge gonorrhea for first place.... Conservative guesses put the number of cases at about 300,000 per year and increasing.*[1]

As venereal diseases sweep through the country on a rapidly increasing scale, warnings of their ravages become more frequent. A December 7, 1975 UPI dispatch from St. Louis, for instance, stated:

> It's no secret that there is a VD epidemic in this country. Information from the American Social Health Assn. shows *a new case is caught every 11 seconds* and *more than 5,000 girls are absent from school each day because of gonorrhea....* Gonorrhea in the United States is primarily a disease of youth,... In Sweden, they say every hour a teen-ager catches gonorrhea. In the United States, a teen-ager catches gonorrhea every 40 seconds.[2]

Under the headline "Venereal Diseases—At Epidemic Proportions," a September, 1976 newspaper article from Salt Lake City indicated the seriousness of both national and Utah trends:

> *If venereal disease continues at its present rate, within the next ten years one out of five students will become infected before graduating from high school.*

---

1. David R. Reuben, M.D., "The Grim New Venereal Disease in Our Midst," *Reader's Digest*, November, 1974, pp. 114-115.
2. "Whatever the Name, VD War Necessary," *Salt Lake Tribune*, December 7, 1975.

> We spent $4.7 million in 1969 just for the syphilitic blind. (*Ibid.*, p. 67.)
> The *Reader's Digest* follow-up article the following month told how the nation almost defeated VD before the advent of "the pill" and "the new morality:"
> We thought we had VD licked once—in the early '50's. With the advent of penicillin treatment for VD in 1943, reported new cases of syphilis rapidly decreased—from 106,539 in 1947 to a low of 6,251 in 1957. Gonorrhea, too, had decreased. But with the incidence, and therefore the risk, of infection subsiding, government funds for control and educational programs were curtailed and the public lost interest. (Grace Naismith, "How to Stop the VD Epidemic," *Reader's Digest*, October, 1972, p. 166.)

This startling news is predicted both locally and nationally, according to Bonnie Bullock, director of the free VD clinic at the Salt Lake City-County Health Department.

Based on sheer numbers, Mrs. Bullock (a registered nurse) reports *the incidence of venereal disease is at epidemic proportions....*

Utah statistics indicate the highest rate of venereal disease increase is in the 15- to 24-year-old age group. But *the age of those coming into clinics, who think they have the disease, is lowering.*[1]

Unreported cases of VD complicate the problems of treatment and statistical analysis, but medical authorities usually assume a much larger incidence of venereal disease than has been reported. Typical is the release reporting that *"On a national level, gonorrhea has been classed as an epidemic in the past four years, with one million cases reported and another two million suspected unreported cases."* [2]

Significant facts about venereal disease in the United States:

1. A venereal disease epidemic is sweeping the country, and is believed by health authorities to be reaching more than 2.5 million Americans annually. A new case is contracted by someone in the country every 11 seconds. Gonorrhea has actually been classed as an epidemic in health statistics for the past five years.
2. More than 5,000 girls are absent from school each day because of gonorrhea.
3. If venereal disease continues to spread at the present rate, by 1986 one out of five students will become infected before graduating from high school.
4. The highest rate of venereal disease increase is in the 15-24 year-old age group, with the average age lowering.

---

1. Sue Thurman, "Venereal Disease—At Epidemic Proportions," *Deseret News,* September 9, 1976. The article told of the detection of primary cases of syphilis and observed that "Health authorities have found these *primary cases usually multiply to six that number within a year,* since people with syphilis are more sexually active." The article also explained that *"there are some 40 venereal diseases.... VD is any communicable disease sexually transmitted."*
2. "Area Clinics Begin New Methods to Check for New Strain of VD," *Deseret News,* September 17, 1976. This article, which dealt with local VD treatment problems, carried the observation that "Salt Lake health officials don't think the problem is that bad locally." Yet it describes

Abortion

Abortion has become commonplace in American society since it was legalized by the courts in 1974. By 1975, four out of ten teen-age pregnancies were ending in abortion. "Statistics released at the conference [on teen-age sexuality held in February, 1976] indicated that there were one million teen-age pregnancies last year—some 400,000 ending in abortions. Of the pregnancies, 50,000 involved girls 15 or under."[1]

Though current figures are yet unavailable, statistics for 1974 show that in that first year of legalized abortion, one out of five pregnancies was already being aborted and that 73 percent of those receiving abortions were unwed. This information was released in an AP news service article issued from Atlanta under the title "Abortion Rate Rises 24 Pct.":

> The first nationwide survey of abortions shows *there was one legal abortion for every four live births in the United States in 1974*, according to the National Center for Disease Control (CDC).
> *There were 763,476 legal abortions performed, an increase of 24 percent over 1973. Most women who had abortions were young, white, unmarried and in the early stages of pregnancy*, the Atlanta-based federal health agency reported Friday.
> The CDC said the report included the most recent statistics available and represented the first time that each of the 50 states and the District of Columbia had reported on abortions within its borders.
> Prior to 1974, the year in which the U.S. Supreme Court legalized abortions, the CDC surveys did not include states where abortions were illegal. The percentage figures were derived from using previous year reports from states that had legalized abortion and comparing them with the same state figures reported for 1974.
> The report said 87 percent of the abortions occurred within the women's home states in 1974, compared with 75 percent in 1973 and 56 percent in 1972.

---

1. "Psychologist Urging Teen Girls to Say 'No,' " *Deseret News*, February 5, 1976.

> what is happening in a typical medium-size urban VD center, Salt Lake City's City-County Clinic, as the VD epidemic rages:
> The City-County Clinic has gone from a one-day-a-week operation at the time of the 1970 merger to a five-day-a-week situation now.
> The clinic costs about $83,000 a year to operate and *sees about 10,000 persons a year. Some 20 percent of these turn out to be positive cases of VD and are given treatment. (Ibid.)*

It showed that 64 percent of the women obtaining abortions were under age 25, 75 percent were white and 73 percent were not married.
The report said 48 percent of the women had no living children, 20 percent had one living child and 5 percent had five or more children.[1]

The vast acceptance of abortion in some areas is reflected by the early 1976 report that

Almost one in five women of child-bearing age in New York City has had a legal abortion since New York State liberalized its abortion law in 1970.
A study in the current issue of the magazine published by the Planned Parenthood Federation reveals that *about 850,000 legal abortions were performed in New York City between 1970-75, half of them on city residents.*[2]

Abortion is used primarily by the young and unmarried and is seen as "a device for coping with the unwanted consequences of not following ancient codes of morality." Michael Novak summarized the impact which abortion has had on America with these observations:

According to a fact sheet on abortion prepared by Zero Population Growth in 1976, black women had 29% of all abortions in 1974 (the latest figures available). *Almost 33% of all abortions occurred among young women 19 years old or younger. (A total of 66% includes all women under 25.) Finally, 73% of all abortions occurred among the unmarried.*
Far more than I had realized, abortion is disproportionately a problem of the young, the black, and (overwhelmingly) the unmarried.
Two things surprised me in these figures. First, the shock of contemplating the estimated one million abortions in 1975 still affects me. For those who do not believe that abortion is a form of killing, of course, there is no moral shock....
Secondly, it surprises me that black leaders so easily go along with the abortion rate among black women. When 15% of the population has 29% of the abortions (I allow for the larger percentage of black women in the age cohort 25 and under), the black population suffers, it seems, disproportionate population loss. In addition, it suffers a disproportionate share of the psychological effects of abortion upon mothers and upon other children. The power to abort is power over life and death of a special kind.
Approximately 300,000 blacks were aborted last year: 1.3 percent of the population of blacks. A staggering figure.

---

1. "Abortion Rate Rises 24 Pct.," *Deseret News*, June 12, 1976.
2. "Abortion in N.Y.," *Parade*, March 7, 1976.

The extent of extra-marital pregnancies among women, white and black, indicates a tremendous breakdown in religious values and practice. *Among teen-agers alone, more than a million became pregnant. Of these, more than 300,000 had abortions. Over 730,000 abortions among unmarried women occurred last year.*

These figures show that *abortion is pre-eminently a way of preventing childbirth for pregnancies out-of-wedlock.* Abortion is primarily a device for coping with the unwanted consequences of not following ancient codes of morality. It is a massive means of *overcoming the consequences of a massive change in ethics.*

It remains that *27% of abortions—almost 270,000—occurred among married women. About 33% occurred among women over 25. About 67% occurred among white women* (including Spanish surname).[1]

The legalization of abortion, while allowing the reported number of abortions to increase, did not have a strong demographic influence on the nation's birthrate because most of the abortions would have been performed illegally anyway, according to a survey released in early February, 1975, by the Alan Guttmacher Institute of the Planned Parenthood Federation of America:

"The results show that the number of legal abortions in the nation rose from nearly 600,000 in 1972 to 750,000 during the year after the Supreme Court ruling. *By the end of last year, the figure had reached nearly 900,000.* According to Dr. Christopher Tietze, a senior consultant with the Population Council, *the demographic impact of the increase has been small. He estimates that two-thirds or more of the abortions would have been performed under illegal auspices* had not the decision been handed down—so only a third have actually affected the birth rate."[2]

A majority of the nation apparently favors the abortion principle in the mid '70's:

"After last fall's elections, an NBC News poll found that 58 per cent of the voters questioned (and 46 per cent of the Roman Catholics) approved of laws permitting abortion during the first three months of pregnancy—or wanted them liberalized."[3]

Government funds have been used to finance the performance of abortions:

1. Michael Novak, "Abortion and the Blacks," *Deseret News*, November 13, 1976.
2. "Report on Abortion," *Newsweek*, February 17, 1975, p. 97.
3. "Abortion and the Law," *Newsweek*, March 3, 1975, p. 19.

HEW spends an estimated $40 million to $45 million annually for 250,000 to 300,000 abortions, primarily through Medicaid for the needy.[1]

The seriousness of the effect of abortion is emphasized in the warning issued by LDS President Spencer W. Kimball when he said, *"If nations begin to destroy families by abortion or other means, they will destroy the nation."*[2]

Significant facts about abortion in the United States:

1. Abortion is primarily used by the young and unmarried.
2. Of more than one million teen-age pregnancies in 1975, 400,000 of them ended in abortions.
3. 66% of all abortions performed were on women under 25 (in 1974).
4. 73% of all abortions occurred among the unmarried. Over 730,000 abortions were performed on unmarried women in 1975.
5. Abortions are highest among black women. Blacks, who comprise 15% of the population, had 29% of the abortions.

Divorce

The rapid disintegration of home and family life in America is recognized across the nation as a cause for serious concern. *In 1975, "For the first time, American divorces passed the one million mark.* According to the National Center for Health Statistics, the U.S. divorce rate has been rising steadily since 1962. It has now reached the point of about 4.7 per 1,000 population, possibly higher."[3]

---

1. "Alternative to Abortions," *Deseret News,* February 2, 1977.
2. "LDS Growth Foreseen," a UPI release from Helsinki, Finland, *Deseret News,* August 2, 1976. President Kimball was addressing an audience of 1,800 Finnish members in an area conference of the Church.
3. "New Divorce Record," *Parade,* February 29, 1976. When divorce statistics were first recorded in 1867, the rate was .3 per 1,000 population.

The national "average divorce rate" increased 92 percent during the decade between 1965 and 1975.[1] On a national level, *53*

---

1. Douglas D. Palmer, "Divorce Rate Comparisons Misleading, Utah Aide Says," *Deseret News*, March 8, 1976. During this period, Utah experienced a 76 percent increase in its divorce rate.

    The 1975 divorce rate in Utah was 5.1 per 1,000 population, while the average rate for the United States was 4.8 per 1,000, he said, adding that 1975 data for individual states are not presently available.

    In 1974 the Utah divorce rate was 4.8 divorces per 1,000 population, with the U.S. average being 4.6 per 1,000, he said.

    In 1974, 20 states had a higher rate of divorce than Utah, with the highest rate being 17.2 per 1,000 for Nevada. Twenty-seven states had a lower divorce rate than Utah, with the lowest being 2.3 per 1,000 population in Wisconsin. Not all states have centralized reporting of divorces.

    The health statistician said it is "erroneous" to compare divorce rates between states, since divorce is a "legal status determined by the laws of each state." *(Ibid.)*

The ratio of LDS to non-LDS divorces in Utah is informative, and indicates that non-Latter-day Saint divorces have exceeded the divorce rate among Mormons. In 1972, according to LDS Church Social Services:

    The LDS total divorce rate per 1,000 population in Utah was 4.22.
    The non-LDS divorce rate per 1,000 population was 4.67.
    The overall divorce rate in Utah per 1,000 population was 4.28.
    The U.S. national average divorce rate per 1,000 population was 4.00.

An analysis of Utah divorces within the Church for 1972 indicates that

    The LDS temple-marriage divorce rate per 1,000 population was 1.46.
    The LDS non-temple-marriage divorce rate per 1,000 population was 6.68.

When calculated on the basis of actual divorces occurring instead of the percentage per 1,000 population, the statistics for 1972 in Utah are quite different:

    The LDS temple-marriage divorce rate was 8.2% of total divorces.
    The LDS church-marriage divorce rate was 7.97% of total divorces.
    The LDS civil marriage divorce rate was 36.91% of total divorces.
    The non-LDS in-church-marriage divorce rate was 8.09% of total divorces.
    The non-LDS civil-marriage divorce rate was 38.83% of total divorces.

Figures released by the LDS Church Information Services in early 1976 gave church-wide figures on divorce, as follows:

    Six out of 205 temple marriages end in divorce (2.93%).
    Twenty-one out of 150 non-temple marriages end in divorce (14%).
    Six out of 25 marriages of an LDS member to a non-member end in divorce (24%).

(Source for the above information: Joyce Worthen Walker, *Divorce—How to Prevent or Survive It* (Bountiful, Utah: Horizon Publishers, 1976), pp. 24-25.

out of 1,000, or one out of twenty adults are either divorced or separated from their spouses.[1]

With the rapid increase in the divorce rate, there is now one divorce for every 2.3 marriages in the nation each year. During 1974, for instance, "...there were approximately 970,000 divorces in the United States. That was 57,000 more than in 1973. On the other hand, the number of marriages that took place in the year, 2,235,000, was unexpectedly small.... Because of the decrease in marriages and the increase in divorces, *there was one divorce in the year for every 2.3 marriages.*"[2]

Divorce is taking a terrible toll on the family as American couples are divorcing more frequently. Now

> *More than one-half of all black school children and more than one-fourth of all white school children live in one-parent homes, in homes with one or more stepparents, or apart from either parent.*[3]

Six out of ten divorcing couples have young children who must endure the difficulties which are inherent in the divorce process. ("In 1973, 40% of divorcing couples had no children under 18 years of age, 25% had 1 child, 19% had 2 children, and 15% had 3 children or more."[4]) In 1973, 1,079,000 children were involved in divorces and annulments.[5] The effect of divorce on children is cumulative, with more and more youth each year becoming the unwilling members of broken families. "Even just considering the 22 years beginning with January 1954 and ending with December 1975, *over 15 million children under 18 years of age have been subjected to all the suffering divorce brings.*"[6]

Children from broken homes are responsible for a high percentage of the nation's juvenile delinquency and serious crime:

> According to figures based on 1968 census records, 83% of the youth ages 10-17 in our nation lived in families with both a father and a mother; 11.7% lived in mother only families; 1.6% lived in father only families; and the remaining 3.7% lived in a situation without either parent.

---

1. "Fewer Divorces Among Davisites," Bountiful, Utah: *Davis County Clipper*, June 27, 1975. "In the Mountain States the rate is 52, and in the State of Utah, 40." *(Ibid.)*
2. *Ibid.*
3. "Marriage and Divorce," *Parade*, September 19, 1976.
4. Joyce Worthen Walker, *Divorce—How to Prevent or Survive It* (Bountiful, Utah: Horizon Publishers, 1976), p. 156.
5. *Ibid.*, p. 157.
6. *Ibid.*, p. 85

A further examination of the data reveals that *the 17% of the youth not living in normal two-parent homes are responsible for almost 40% of the total juvenile delinquency,* with the greatest percentage coming from children with neither parent.[1]

The cost of divorce to the taxpayer is enormous. *"About 77 percent of the money spent in welfare is for children under 14 and their mothers.* Marriages seem to be breaking up right and left. Hundreds of fathers are abandoning their responsibility."[2]

Certainly one reason for the rapid increase in divorce is the tremendous increase in teen-age promiscuity. The unexpected pregnancies which result force many youth into marriages for which they are ill-prepared and which are unable to endure:

> Studies indicate that the actual percentage of premarital pregnancies among teen-agers having a first birth may be as high as 70 percent.
> It seems relatively obvious that the high rate of teen-age marriages and of teen-age premarital conceptions must influence the increasing rate of divorce.[3]

---

1. *Ibid.,* p. 92.
2. "Family Breakups Called Top Concern," *Deseret News,* October 10, 1976. Figures cited are for Utah, but are typical of welfare conditions across the nation. The heavy load which new divorces will place on welfare loads during the next decade is a cause for alarm. If the present divorce rate of one divorce per 2.3 marriages (43.48 divorces per hundred marriages) continues (and the proportion of divorces is actually expected to increase markedly), there will be approximately 11,437,848 divorces in the nation during the next decade. This projection is based on current marriage projections:

   > "The fact that there will be 26,306,000 marriages in the next 10 years (of which 75 per cent will be first marriages) is reason enough to examine carefully these couples who are about to launch new lifestyles, form new households and begin their dynamic union as married people.

   > ### FIRST-MARRIAGE BRIDES

   > "Two per cent of the U.S. population, comprised of all socioeconomic, ethnic and regional groups, marries each year.
   > "And because of increased education, as well as greater emphasis on working and travel before marriage, the average age for first-marriage brides has risen in the last several years from just 18 to 20.7 years. (Add a couple of years for the bridegroom.)..."

   ("Young People Still Getting Married, Says Editor," *Salt Lake Tribune,* April 10, 1977.
3. Douglas D. Palmer, "Divorce Rate Comparisons Misleading...," *op. cit.*

Violence in Homes and Schools

With the accelerated divorce rate has come a disintegration of home and family values. This has resulted in a marked increase in violent attacks on family members. A nationwide survey reported by Richard J. Gelles of the University of Rhode Island indicates that

> For more than 5 million American children, punishment at home has meant being shot, stabbed, kicked, beaten and bitten by their parents,... three of every 100 parents, an estimated 1.2 million parents nationwide, have used knives and guns on their youngsters.
> Another 1.2 million have threatened to harm their children with the weapons,...
> And more than 80 percent of the 1,146 parents surveyed said they sometimes spank or slap their children,...
>
> WHAT LEADS TO VIOLENCE
> The survey was designed to find out what leads to violence in the family and how it can be stopped, Gelles said. It included families of differing social and economic background and was among the first on a national level on violence toward children in the home.
> The survey indicated that from 3.2 million to 3.9 million children between 3 and 17 have been kicked, bitten or punched by their parents, Gelles said. An additional 1.6 million to 2.2 million have been "beaten up" during childhood, he said.
> While parents often express concern about violence on television, Gelles said many of them might better be worried about how violence in the home affects their youngsters.
> "While television may reinforce some of this behavior, what the child experiences in the home is much more important," he said.[1]

The same level of violence is moving into the schools, where *"70,000 serious physical assaults on teachers and literally hundreds of thousands of assaults on students"*[2] take place each year. The rate of school crime is increasing dramatically. A study by the National Education Association showed that

> *...between 1970 and 1974, assaults in schools increased 58 percent; sex offenses by 62 percent; drug-related crimes by 81 percent; and robberies by 117 percent.*[3]

---

1. "Report Marks Violence in U.S. Homes," *Salt Lake Tribune*, February 27, 1977.
2. "School Violence Called Shocking," *Deseret News*, February 25, 1977. This article is a summary of statistics released by Sen. Birch Bayh, chairman of the Senate juvenile delinquency subcommittee.
3. *Ibid.*

The cost of this school crime on a national scale is a heavy burden:

> This staggering waste of scarce educational resources is more money than we spent for textbooks in 1972 and is enough to hire 50,000 additional teachers without increasing taxes by one cent,...
>
> Problems involving home environment, severe unemployment among young people, and a lack of adequate recreational facilities have a tremendous influence on youth, yet remain largely outside of the school's ability to directly control.[1]

Significant facts about divorce and family violence in the United States:

1. In 1975 divorces passed the one million mark for the first time. The national divorce rate increased 92 percent between 1965 and 1975.

2. In America, one out of twenty adults are either divorced or separated from their spouses.

3. There is now one divorce for every 2.3 marriages (1974).

4. More than one-half of all black school children and more than one-fourth of all white school children now live in one-parent homes, in homes with one or more step-parents, or apart from either parent.

5. Six out of ten divorcing couples have young children who are affected. Seventeen percent of America's youth not living in normal homes are responsible for almost 40% of the total juvenile delinquency.

6. Divorce swells welfare rolls. About 77% of welfare funds are spent for children under 14 and their mothers.

7. If present divorce rates continue, there will be about 11½-million divorces in the next decade.

8. Violence is increasing in the homes. Three out of every 100 parents have used knives and guns on their youngsters. About 3½-million children between ages 3 and 17 have been kicked, bitten, or punched by their parents.

9. Between 1970 and 1974, crime in schools increased dramatically: assaults 58%, sex offenses 62%, drug-crimes 81%, and robberies 117%.

---

1. *Ibid.*

Narcotics and Alcohol Abuse

Drug Usage

During the fifteen-year period between 1960 and 1975, the use of narcotics increased at an alarming rate in the United States. Drug abuse was associated with a youth counter-culture whose life styles defied the established social order. Drug usage became a symbol of rejection of traditional social principles and values. Sexual promiscuity, lack of work-related incentive, and social protest were all linked to its use.

The number of reported active narcotics abusers leaped astronomically, with the percent of change between 1960 and 1975 up 112% in New York City, 1543.2% in Norfolk, Virginia, 1065.5% in Paterson, N.J., 243.9% in Philadelphia, 587.7% in Phoenix, 110.9% in San Francisco, and 227.2% in Washington, D.C.[1]

"By 1970...the amount of marijuana and heroin being used in the U.S., particularly by young people, increased so rapidly in four or five years that *sociologists began talking about the drug abuse 'epidemic.' After that, the use of illicit drugs continued to grow rapidly.*"[2]

The number of heroin addicts in the nation soared to over half a million. A government campaign against heroin temporarily reduced the supply, but the drug traffic soon managed to draw from other sources and heroin addiction has skyrocketed to an all-time high:

> The estimated number of heroin addicts dropped from 600,000 in 1970 to 300,000, or less, in early 1974, after a successful blockade of Turkish heroin. *But now the total has risen again to 600,000, according to the White House Strategy Council on Drug Abuse.*
>
> Drug Enforcement Administration officials say unofficially that *the number of heroin users may actually be much higher—up to 725,000....*
>
> In all, White House experts say, *drug abuse is now linked to more than 15,000 American deaths each year and costs the nation 10 to 17 billion dollars annually.*[3]

---

1. "Reported Active Narcotics Abusers in Selected Cities," *1977 Information Please Almanac Atlas & Yearbook* (Simon & Schuster), p. 730.
2. "The Losing Battle Against Heroin," *The New Republic*, February 7, 1976, p. 7.
3. "Return of the Hard-Drug Menace," *U.S. News & World Report*, June 30, 1975, p. 29. Unfortunately, "Fewer than 100,000 of our 600,000 addicts are being treated." (Steve Slade, "The Holy War Against Heroin," *The Progressive*, January, 1974, p. 28.)

The use of other hard drugs such as LSD, cocaine, and methedrine hit alarming peaks, but has substantially diminished in the mid 1970's. The use of marijuana, however, has increased, and *"...No one is optimistic that the growth in use of marijuana can be cut back.... It is estimated that some 33 million Americans have tried the drug and perhaps 12 million, many of them young, use it with some regularity."*[1]

The use of marijuana has penetrated deeply into the national way of life. Results of three nationwide surveys taken by the National Institute on Drug Abuse indicate that

> After cigarettes and alcohol, Americans use more marijuana than any other psychoactive substance. Among many young people, marijuana use has become a way of life:
>
> *53 percent of those aged 18-25 have used marijuana,* and 25 percent are current users;
>
> *22 percent of those aged 12-17 have used marijuana,* and 15 percent consider themselves regular or occasional users;
>
> *53 percent of the high school seniors surveyed have tried marijuana,* and 32 percent are current users.[2]

The use of marijuana doubled between 1973 and 1976 with adults as well as juveniles involved in its usage. According to a Gallup Poll:

> *The percentage of Americans who have tried marijuana has doubled during the last four years, with one adult in four having now tried "grass" at least once.*
>
> In the latest Gallup survey of marijuana use in America, *24 per cent of the nation's adults, 18 and older, report they've sampled the substance at least once.* Half, 12 per cent, can be considered recent users, having last tried it during the past year.
>
> The overall usage figure is double what it was in 1973 and six times what it was in 1969 when the Gallup Poll's first survey of marijuana use found only 4 per cent had tried it.
>
> As has consistently been the case, young adults in the latest survey are more likely to be users than those in any other population group.

---

1. "Drugs: A \$17-Billion-A-Year Habit That U.S. Can't Break," *U.S. News & World Report,* May 10, 1976, p. 26.
2. Pamela Swift, "Drug Stabilization," *Parade,* February 20, 1977, p. 6. Concerning the use of cocaine the reports indicated that

     Cocaine, better known as "coke," continues to circulate widely among the young:

     3 percent of those aged 12-17 have experimented with it;

     13 percent of those 18-25 have used it at least once, 2 percent using it in the past month. *(Ibid.)*

Fully 56 per cent of those under 30 years of age (and 59 per cent of those between 18 and 24) say they have tried marijuana. Among people between 30 and 49 years old the percentage who have tried it (16 per cent) is less than one-third that of young people. And with those over 50 years old only 5 per cent have indulged.[1]

"The feds confiscate about 1,000 tons of grass [marijuana] a year—only about 10% of the estimated traffic."[2] Arrests of marijuana trafficers and users have climbed so high that the states have struggled to find appropriate means and facilities for handling the offenders. The heavy court and police loads have caused some states to alter their laws:

According to FBI statistics, more than 700,000 persons in the U.S. were arrested for marijuana offenses during the years 1970-72. Arrest figures show a steady increase: from 188,682 in 1970 to 292,179 in 1972. A 1971 analysis revealed that 93 per cent of all marijuana arrests were for possession, with two-thirds of those involving quantities of one ounce or less.

Interestingly, as arrest statistics rose, more and more states reduced penalties for possession.[3]

Yet it is clear that continual usage of marijuana leads to addiction to hard drugs: *"Nine of every ten teen-agers who smoke marijuana eventually end up on heroin, "mainliners," full-fledged dope addicts."*[4]

---

1. Dr. George Gallup, "Marijuana Use Doubles Since '73 to 1 Out of 4," *The Salt Lake Tribune*, May 15, 1977. His findings indicates highest usage among males, the college trained, and non-whites:
    Sex and educational background present interesting contrasts. *Men (31 per cent) continue to be more likely to have tried marijuana than women (17 per cent). And those with college training include more who have used it (36 per cent)* than people whose education stopped at the high school level (23 per cent) or grade school level (5 per cent).
    One of the largest and most interesting differences is that between whites and non-whites. In 1973 the percentage of whites and non-whites who had tried marijuana was about the same. Today, *the level among non-whites (36 per cent) is significantly higher than that of whites (22 per cent).*
2. "Pity Those Who Take Pot Luck," *Time*, December 27, 1976, p. 17.
3. "Decriminalization of Marijuana: Dealing with the Reality, Not the Symbol," *The Christian Century*, Sept. 4, 1974, p. 822.
4. *Help Detect and Prevent Narcotic Addiction* (Bountiful, Utah: Bountiful Police Department), p. 2. Reprinted from information by Detective Sergeant Louis W. Rustolo of the East Brunswick Police Department.

Cost of Drug Abuse

The cost of drug abuse is a major burden to society, and a cause of national alarm:

Despite billions of dollars in spending and years of effort—
Drug abuse in the U.S. is still spreading dramatically, running virtually out of control in many parts of the nation.
In Los Angeles County, officials report at least 60,000 heroin addicts.
In South Carolina, *36.8 per cent of the students in 13 high schools reported using marijuana.* That's up from 14.7 per cent in just four years.
New York City police officials expect *at least 1,000 deaths from drug overdoses this year.* And the heroin death rate in Detroit is up 20 per cent....
Such reports are only the visible tip of *a drug culture that is vast and growing....* It is against this background that President Ford sent a message to Congress on April 27 in which he said:
"The cost of drug abuse to this nation is staggering. *More than 5,000 Americans die each year from the improper use of drugs. Law enforcement officials estimate that as much as one half of all 'street crime'— robberies, muggings and burglaries—are committed by drug addicts to support their expensive and debilitating habits.*
"*In simple dollar terms, drug abuse costs us up to 17 billion dollars a year.*"[1]

Another report indicates that

"*As much as half of major city crime is attributable to addicts. Estimates of the cost of addict crime range between $10 billion and $30 billion a year....* Addicts are forced by the high priced black market to support $20-$50-a-day habits. Most addicts need to steal goods worth between $60-$100 a day to raise that kind of money."[2]

An analysis of how drug addicts obtain the money required to sustain their drug habit is indicative of the manner in which drugs lead to crime:

Sources of funds for heroin have been estimated by Moore as follows:

Shoplifting	22.5%
Burglary	19.0

1. "Drugs: A $17-Billion-A-Year Habit that U.S. Can't Break," *U.S. News & World Report*, May 10, 1976, p. 25.
2. Steve Slade, "The Holy War Against Heroin," *The Progressive*, January, 1974, p. 26.

Pickpocketing	5.4%
Larceny	7.4
Robbery	3.4
Confidence Games	4.7
Prostitution	30.7
Welfare	3.0
Other, Legal Sources	3.9
	100.0%[1]

Alcohol Usage

The use of alcohol in the United States, as throughout the world, has increased dramatically during the past two decades. The record in recent years shows the proportion of Americans over 18 who drink alcoholic beverages:

Year	Drinkers
1958	55%
1960	62%
1964	63%
1966	65%
1969	64%
1974	68%
1977	71%[2]

As reported by a Gallup Poll taken January 14-17, 1977, only 29% of the nation's adults are now total abstainers:

> The percentage of drinkers in the United States has reached a 38-year high point while the proportion of families where liquor is cited as a cause of trouble has increased dramatically in just three years.
> The latest nationwide audit of drinking *shows 71 percent of adults, 18 and older, saying they use alcoholic beverages such as liquor, wine or beer. Only 29 percent are total abstainers. The percentage of drinkers in 1974 was 68 percent.*

---

1. Selma Mushkin, "Politics and Economics of Government Response to Drug Abuse," *The Annals of the American Academy of Political and Social Science* (Philadelphia: The American Academy of Political and Social Science, 1975), p. 30. "Moore" is Mark Moore, writing in Vol. 2, *Economics of Heroin Distribution* (Crotonon-Hudson: Hudson Institute, 1970), p. 64.
2. "How Business Grapples With Problem of the Drinking Worker," *U.S. News & World Report*, July 15, 1974, p. 75. Figures are based on Gallup polls, with the final figure added by the author based on the Gallup Poll taken January 14-17, 1977, reported above.

The rise in the percentage of drinkers over the last three years has come about *almost entirely among women.* While the proportion of male drinkers has remained at about the same level, the proportion of female imbibers is up 5 points. Men, however, continue to be more likely to drink than women.

One American in five (18 percent) says alcohol has been a cause of trouble in their families. In 1974 the comparable figure was 12 percent— the same as recorded in a survey in 1966.

Social observers have expressed alarm at excessive drinking and alcoholism in American society, pointing to findings that *show alcohol to be involved in about half of highway fatalities and in about half of all homicides.*[1]

From 1960 to 1970, per capita consumption of alcohol increased a startling 26%, to an all-time high level:

In the past few years alcoholism—among youths and adults alike— has at last been recognized as a plague. *From 1960 to 1970, per capita consumption of alcohol in the U.S. increased 26%*—to the equivalent of 2.6 gal. of straight alcohol per adult per year. *It is now at an alltime high,* probably surpassing the levels during such notoriously wet eras as the pre-Civil War and pre-Prohibition years. Moreover, according to the NIAAA, *about one in ten of the 95 million Americans who drink is now either a full-fledged alcoholic or at least a problem drinker* (defined by NIAAA as one who drinks enough to cause trouble for himself and society). Uncounted thousands of the problem drinkers are under 21 and, in fact, *the approximately 9 million excessive drinkers* are representatives of—and affect—the whole spectrum of American society.

The facts gathered by NIAAA about alcohol abuse are as depressing as they are impressive:

After heart disease and cancer, alcoholism is the country's biggest health problem. Most deaths attributed to alcoholism are caused by cirrhosis of the liver (13,000 per year). *An alcoholic's life span is shortened by ten to twelve years.*[2]

---

1. Dr. George Gallup, "Drinking Percentage Hits 38-Year High Mark," *The Salt Lake Tribune,* February 13, 1977. In his summary of the Gallup Poll, Lloyd Shearer observed that "Among those who drink, the largest percentage are Catholic men with college backgrounds in the 18-29 age group who reside in the East." "Drinking Problem," *Parade,* May 8, 1977.
2. "Alcoholism: New Victims, New Treatment," *Time,* April 22, 1974, p. 75. Figures on the state of Utah bear out the national trend, but show it moving higher among the states in terms of its alcoholism:

   Utah, historically an antidrinking state, has taken a significant step upward (if that is the right word) from 46th to 35th of the states in terms of its alcoholism.

   Actually, that statistic measures the time from 1960 to 1973, as researched by the American Business Men's Research Foundation. But Mr. Dinsmore says the story is still true.

(Cont. bottom p. 100.)

The use of alcohol is greatest among the youth, as is the use of narcotics. A combination of more than 200 different student surveys analyzed by the National Commission on Marijuana and Drug Abuse in 1972 presented the following usage data for students on America's college campuses:

Drug Type	Student Survey Data (Mean %)
Alcohol	83%
Marijuana	50
Hallucinogens	14
Stimulants	24
Depressants	15
Opiates	6[1]

---

1. Gerald L. Robinson and Stephen T. Miller, "Drug Abuse and the College Campus," *The Annals of the American Academy of Political and Social Science, op. cit.,* p. 104.

In fact, he calls any statistic such as this conservative, like the one which reads there were 29,316 alcoholics in Utah in 1973. Consider the closet drinkers, and the ones closeted by their families, he says.

Also, estimates of the cost to the state resulting from alcoholism range from $20 million to more than $50 million a year. Important, says Mr. Dinsmore, but consider the price of suffering which doesn't carry a dollar tag....

Researchers say 11 percent of the heavy drinkers in the state are still in high school or of high school age. They number 5,698. "Heavy" here means one who drinks daily a minimum of four drinks, and sometimes up to six or more.

There are reportedly 198,110 regular drinkers in Utah. Of these, 98,820 are light drinkers; 47,500 are moderate drinkers, and 51,800 are heavy drinkers.

Researchers say "it may safely be presumed that *50 percent of heavy drinkers are alcoholic.*"

And, according to the state statistics, *60 percent of the regular drinkers are male; 40 percent are female, and 64 percent of them are members of The Church of Jesus Christ of Latter-day Saints.* Additionally, 8 percent of all regular drinkers are still in adolescence. They number 15,848.

(George Raine, "Agency's Statistics Show Dramatic Increase in Utah Drinking, Alcoholism," *The Salt Lake Tribune,* January 11, 1976. Statistics are from a report issued in early January by the Utah Alcoholism Foundation.)

A national survey taken in December, 1976, demonstrated that the high percentage of drinkers extends down to high school and junior high levels:

> Statistics show how serious the problem is becoming. *A national study in December, 1976 indicated that 74 percent of the young people in grades seven to 12 and living in the contiguous 48 states had had a drink more than two or three times. Half of those surveyed were under 16, and 54.8 percent drank once a month or more.*
>
> *Almost one of four of the kids said they had been drunk four or more times during the previous year.* "This frequency is three or four times greater than for all drinkers," said Christiansen....
>
> —A million young Americans a year run away from home. *Over half of all teen-age runaways and their families appear to be heavy alcohol users.* By age 14, half of the runaways said they used alcohol, and use by females in this category was three times that of males.
>
> —*Suicide is the second leading cause of death for young people between 15 and 24. Juvenile delinquency has increased, while the number of youth nationally arrested for serious crimes of murder, rape, robbery and assault has gone up 254 percent since 1960.*[1]

There is a high correlation between teen-age drinking and smoking, sexual promiscuity, and drug usage, as is demonstrated in a report issued by the American Cancer Society and released through UPI:

> *One of four teen-age girls who smoke cigarettes also uses marijuana regularly,* an American Cancer Society report shows.
>
> A new profile of *the 2.7 million* girls smoking regularly also shows:
>
> —*81 percent drink* compared to 42 percent of nonsmokers.

---

1. Robert L. Christiansen, Director, Utah State Division of Alcoholism and Drugs, "Teen-age Alcoholism," *Deseret News*, May 24, 1977. Director Christiansen commented on teen-age drinking in Utah, observing that "11 percent of all drinkers in the state are adolescents," and noting that "In 1975, 30 percent of the alcohol-related fatal accidents in Utah involved people under the age of 21."

   He warned that breaking the Church's Word of Wisdom code is likely to cause severe drinking problems to the offenders:

   The issue of teen-age alcohol abuse is complicated in Utah by another factor—*a little over 70 percent of the population is affiliated with a religion which teaches abstinance.* The goal is to keep young people from ever drinking, but those who do drink have a much higher probability of experiencing problems. Christiansen said that one of every 10 adults who drinks will become a problem drinker, but studies show that *one of every two individuals who drink and whose religious training has been in an abstinance background will have problems.*

—Smokers are more likely to have a current boyfriend than non-smokers—64 to 38 percent.
—Smokers are more likely to have had sexual intercourse—31 to 8 percent.
—Only 3 percent of nonsmokers use marijuana....
The profile was based on interviews with 10 million girls between the ages of 13 and 17.[1]

The increased use of alcohol by women is also taking its toll. "Nationally, there are about 5 million alcoholic women."[2] According to the National Institute of Mental Health, the ratio of female to male alcoholics is now *"one woman for every four men."*[3]

Cost of Alcohol Usage

Like drug abuse, alcohol usage results in tremendous losses to society, both in lives, in time, and in dollars. An article in *Time* reports that

> In half of all murders in the U.S., either the killer or the victim—or both—have been drinking. A fourth of all suicides are found to have

---

1. "Teen Girl Smoking, a Health Crisis," *Deseret News*, February 12, 1976. Cancer Society President Benjamin Byrd called smoking among teen-age girls "an urgent public health crisis."

    He said the society is disturbed because half a million more teen-age girls smoke today than in 1969, even though they are more aware of warnings that smoking may harm their health.

    The survey showed girl smokers are more likely to be found in the Northeast and urban areas, to be from blue collar families with family incomes under $10,000 a year and to have fathers who were high school dropouts.

    Forty-nine percent of the teen-age girl smokers go to schools having smoker rooms. Two of three said doctors warned them against smoking. But nearly a third said they smoke with parental approval.

    The report traced the increase in smoking to the growth and acceptance of the "new values" generated by college youth in the sixties.

    "The new values," the report said, "represent the breakdown of previous moral norms and are characterized by the rejection of authority, emphasis on the emotional rather than rational, freer sexual morality, strong accent on self and self-fulfillment, the acceptability of illegal drugs and a more informal lifestyle."

    A 1976 report from the National Institute on Drug Abuse showed that "about a fourth of all those aged 12-17 and four out of 10 adults remain smokers. Roughly a third of the youths and six out of 10 adults remain drinkers." (Pamela Swift, "Drug Stabilization," *Parade*, February 20, 1977, p. 6.)
2. "Women Trying to Beat Alcohol," *Deseret News*, May 27, 1977.
3. "Alcoholism: New Victims, New Treatment, *Time*, April 22, 1974, p. 76.

significant amounts of alcohol in their bloodstreams. People who abuse alcohol are seven times more likely to be separated or divorced than the general population.

The dollar cost of alcoholism may be as much as $15 billion a year, much of it from lost work time in business, industry and the Government.

At least half of each year's 55,500 automobile deaths and half of the 1 million major injuries suffered in auto accidents can be traced directly to a driver or pedestrian "under the influence."

Many of the deaths and injuries are caused by the under-21 age group, and arrests of young people for drunken driving have skyrocketed since states began lowering the drinking age from 21. In the year following its lowering of the drinking age, for example, Michigan reported a 141% increase in such arrests.[1]

Criminologist Dr. Walter C. Reckless observed that *"one out of every five murders is committed while the subject is under the influence of alcohol. And an overwhelming proportion of parole violations, job failures, and family breakups are caused by alcohol."*[2]

---

1. "Alcoholism: New Victims...," *Ibid.*, p. 75. The article notes that "In virtually all states, that influence is legally set at a blood concentration of .1% or more alcohol. A 150-lb. man can reach this level if he takes three one-jigger (1½ oz. per jigger) drinks within an hour.

   A Utah study showed the relationship between alcohol and youthful drivers involved in accidents to be highly significant:

   Mix alcohol with inexperienced drivers and you have the makings of another traffic fatality.

   That fact was borne out again this week with release of a study dealing with the ages of drivers involved in alcohol-related fatal traffic accidents in Utah.

   In 1975, *29.7% of all such accidents occurred among drivers under the age of 21. An additional 28.1% involved those 21 to 25 years of age—or a total of 57.8% for all drivers 25 years of age or younger.*

   Those statistics should be a strong argument against any move to get Utah to join several other states which have lowered the drinking age to 18,...

   As experience in Iowa showed, lowering the drinking age made liquor more available to those even younger. After the legal drinking age was lowered to 18 in 1973, the number of 19-and-under drivers involved in fatal accidents jumped from just over 10% of the total to nearly 26%. ("Alcohol and Teen-Age Drivers," *Deseret News*, February 28, 1976.)

2. "Attitudes Toward Addicts," *Intellect*, January, 1974, p. 214.

Significant facts about narcotics and drug abuse in the United States:

1. Drug abuse is linked to more than 15,000 American deaths annually and costs the nation about 17 billion dollars each year. Approximately half of major city crime is attributed to addicts.
2. The use of marijuana doubled between 1973 and 1976. 56% of the population under 30 years of age have tried it. 32% of high school seniors are classified as current users.
3. 71% of the nation's adults now drink alcoholic beverages—only 29% are total abstainers. 83% of America's college-age youth drink alcohol. 55% of the children in grades 7 through 12 drink once a month or more.
4. Alcohol is involved in about half of the nation's highway fatalities and homicides. Alcoholism costs the nation about $15 billion a year.

Decline in Religious Participation and Values

The past 15 years have been an era of major religious unrest, both in the United States and throughout international Christianity. A wave of religious disenchantment has brought about significant changes, some of which are here summarized:

Protestants accuse their religion of "being run like a business." Catholics say birth control is a private matter and reject the Pope's infallibility. Nuns abandon convents to live in downtown apartments. Priests leave the church in unprecedented numbers to marry. One of the nation's best known Episcopal Bishops is accused of heresy. Teachers of religion announce that "God is dead."

What is happening to religion...?

For a decade after World War II, religious books such as "The Greatest Story Ever Told" and "The Power of Positive Thinking" dominated the best-seller lists and religious spokesmen such as Fulton Sheen enjoyed unprecedented popularity on television. Church membership soared, religion seemed influential and secure.

Today, chaos, acrimony and confusion are apparently the order of the day. Church attendance has declined for several years,...

ARE TODAY'S CHURCHES OUT-OF-DATE?

The question is legitimate. But it is a little like asking a volcano why it erupted. The fact is that *today's religious unrest, in both the Protes-*

*tant and Catholic churches, is focused on the church as an institution.
Like buildings that grow old and need renovation, every institution has
a tendency to cling to habits of life that no longer mean very much to a
new generation. To protect these habits, the institution insists on discipline and loyalty from its members.*

In December, 1966, Catholics in England gasped in disbelief when
Charles Davis, considered one of the ranking theologians of the decade,
announced he was leaving the priesthood and the church—to get married. "I do not think the claim the church makes as an institution rests
upon any adequate Biblical and historical basis," he said. *"I don't believe
the Church is absolute and I don't believe any more in Papal infallibility."* Davis went on to castigate the church hierarchy. *"There is concern for authority at the expense of truth,"* he declared, "as I am con-
stantly saddened by instances of the damage done to persons by the
workings of an impersonal and unfree system."

The late Pope John XXIII tried to head off a confrontation between
freedom and authority within the Catholic Church. Unfortunately, the
Vatican Council was half-hearted about following his lead, and John
died before the council ended. The new Pope, Paul VI, has followed a
one-step-forward, two-steps-back approach to change, and the result has
been vast dissatisfaction within the church.

*Vatican authorities report more and more priests are asking to be re-
leased from their vow of celibacy* which, of course, means, at present,
resignation from the priesthood....

Nuns are equally restless with their traditional isolation behind con-
vent walls. *An estimated more than 2,000 young women are leaving the
various sisterhoods each year to resume secular lives,...*

Nowhere is the reaction against the institutional church more visible
than among young people....

*"We are tired of bored priests who have built walls of procedure and
respect and propriety around themselves,"* wrote one youngster. Said
another, "Teens avoid the Mass because *it just stands for Father Fire-
and-Brimstone and his collection box.* They would rather have a personal
relationship with God instead, *without the grumpy middle man."*

Older Catholics are equally restive, particularly about the issue of
birth control. Pope Paul VI has refused to acknowledge repeated calls
to clarify the church's position. Meanwhile, recent polls show as many
as 75 per cent of all Catholics using some form of artificial contracep-
tion. And in Holland, the church hierarchy came dangerously close to
repudiating the Vatican's stand-pat position against anything except
so-called natural rhythm and abstinence.

*Within the Protestant churches, there is the same dissatisfaction with
the institutional approach to religion,* as well as some more radical suggestions for correction. Arthur J. Moore, Jr., the editor of "World Out-
look," a leading Methodist publication, recently suggested that *it was
time to stop running the church "like a business." It was dangerously
frustrating, he said, to feel "that the church is a machine, not a community, and that the machine is running us, not we the machine."*

In Protestant seminaries, another kind of problem has been manifest-
ing itself. *Young clergymen are being attracted to other fields* such as

the poverty program, pastoral counseling in hospitals and industry. Result: *an estimated 70,000 congregations are without full-time pastors.*

Another remarkable religious phenomenon of the '60s is the way *clergymen have been participating in what has heretofore been considered secular problems.* In one single year, for instance, the Friends Committee on National Legislation, a Quaker group, held 780 interviews with Congressmen. Nuns, priests and ministers have marched in support of civil rights, protested slum housing and Vietnam, and backed striking farm workers.

This so-called "involvement" has worried many people. Clergymen's statements on the Vietnam war and other aspects of U.S. foreign policy have been particularly naive and dubious. Another problem, aptly stated by Dr. Carl F. H. Henry, editor of "Christianity Today," is that *"a clergyman can profess to speak for himself (on social issues) but he is heard as the voice of his church."* This may explain why a national poll found that 56 per cent of all white Americans disapproved of clerical participation in racial demonstrations....

But all this may well be the voice of an older generation. *In the future, the churches and the churchmen may speak out on all kinds of issues, but their voices will no longer be clothed in accents of infallibility.* [1]

Religious organizations became deeply involved in political ideology and social controversies, which was a cause for dismay to many of their adherents. One such organization was the National Council of Churches, which drew the scathing fire of political columnist Tom Anderson, as well as others in the conservative camps of American politics:

Know your enemy! If you are a Christian-American, freedom-loving patriot, one of your most dangerous enemies is the National Council of Churches.

The following objectives of the National Council of Churches also happen to be objectives of the American Communist party: (1) Peaceful coexistence, (2) Disarmament, (3) Kill the proposed ABM system, (4) Ban nuclear testing, (5) Abolish loyalty-security laws and loyalty oaths, (6) Abolish all investigating committees on Communism, (7) Force racial integration, (8) Change the social order, using violence if necessary, (9) More foreign aid to Communist countries, (10) Recognition of Red China, Cuba and East Germany, (11) Advance Marxist and one-world propaganda efforts through the church, (12) Recruit for one-world socialist conspiracy in political and labor movements, (13) End capital punishment, (14) Discredit J. Edgar Hoover and the F.B.I., (15) Kill immigration and passport laws, (16) Clemency for convicted spies,

1. Thomas J. Fleming, "What's Happening to Religion?" *This Week Magazine,* February 25, 1968. See also Jenkin Lloyd Jones, "A Storm Signal for Churches in America," *Deseret News,* June 27, 1970, and James J. Kilpatrick, "Changing Role of the Churches," *Deseret News,* July 16, 1970.

(17) Reconstruct religion on the basis of scientific materialism, (18) Remove restrictions on imports from Communist countries and on cultural exchanges between the U.S. and the Soviet Union, (19) Promote sex education in churches, synagogues and schools, press and networks.

(20) Adopt the "open society sociologically" (world socialism) and the "open society ideologically" (end all supernatural religion, especially Christianity), (21) Enforce "open-housing" and the "closed shop" (compulsory labor union membership), (22) Oppose and discriminate against "super-patriots," "radical rightists" and anti-Communists, (23) "New internationalism" to replace national sovereignty, (24) Take from the "haves" and give to the "have-nots." (Land reform, guaranteed annual income, etc.) (25) Put political and economic pressure on South Africa and Rhodesia, (26) Surrender American sovereignty to the Communist-dominated World Court, (27) Greatly strengthen the power of the United Nations, (28) Vastly increase the foreign aid program with no thought of whether any aid is to the best interest of the U.S.A., (29) Liberalize "welfare laws," (30) Firearms control, (31) Promote intermarriage of blacks and whites, (32) Remove all prayer and Bible reading from the public schools, (33) Advocate "situation ethics" and free love, (34) Sponsor and train agitators for the invasion of some of our southern states, (35) Censorship of radio and TV with respect to "conservative" broadcasters like Carl McIntyre, Dean Manion, "Lifeline," Tom Anderson, Dan Smoot, Dr. Billy James Hargis.[1]

The participation of Americans in church religious activities underwent a steady decline from 1958 to 1971, as the crime rate of the nation increased. Measurement of national church attendance has been monitored since 1955 through annual surveys conducted under the direction of Dr. George Gallup. The survey takers would ask the question, "Did you, yourself, happen to attend church or synagogue in the last seven days?" Their findings show a 9% drop in church attendance during the fifteen-year period beginning in 1958:[2]

Year	% Attendance	Year	% Attendance
1958	49	1960	47
1959	47	1961	47

---

1. Tom Anderson, "Straight Talk—The National Council of Churches—Part I," Southern Utah Free Press, October 23, 1969.
2. Figures were drawn from two Gallup Poll reports: "Public Opinion Poll: Churchgoing Levels Off Across Nation," Salt Lake Tribune, January 13, 1974; and "Disenchantment with Church Subsiding," Salt Lake Tribune, January 4, 1976. The surveys show that fewer Americans participate in religious activities other than church services such as prayer group meetings, Bible reading classes, with a national average of only 20% indicating participation during the preceding week. ("Disenchantment..., Ibid.)

Year	% Attendance		Year	% Attendance
1962	46		1969	42
1963	46		1970	42
1964	45		1971	40
1966	44		1972	40
1967	43		1973	40
1968	43		1974	40
			1975	40

The decline in religious attendance during the above period was primarily among Catholics,[1] as was recorded by the Gallup surveys. It should be noted that in spite of its continuing decline, Catholic attendance still is, considerably higher than Protestant attendance:[2]

Year	Catholics	Protestants
1964	71%	38%
1965	67	38
1966	68	38
1967	66	39
1968	65	38
1969	63	37
1970	60	38
1971	57	37
1972	56	37
1973	55	37
1974	55	37
1975	54	38

---

1. Catholics have experienced a remarkable increase in membership in the United States since World War II. From 1947 through 1967, Roman Catholicism increased from 17.7238% of the American population to 23.8392%—a shift of over 6% of the U.S. population to that church in twenty years. With the exception of the Baptists (who increased 2.5265%), no other major American church increased in percent of population more than 1½ percent. The Latter-day Saints increased in percent of population 0.3323% during this period.) From 1947 to 1967 Roman Catholic population in the United States increased from 25,268,173 to 47,468,333. Today one American in four is a Catholic. (Figures compiled by the author in 1969, based on data supplied by the National Council of the Churches of Christ in the U.S.A., which he compared with national population statistics.)
2. "Disenchantment...", op. cit. The poll analysis pointed out that church-going among Protestants has been remarkably stable since 1964, fluctuating only by a point or two from year to year over this entire period of time. (Cont. bottom p. 109.)

WILL UNRIGHTEOUSNESS BRING JUDGMENTS? 109

By way of comparison, average Latter-day Saint attendance at Sacrament Meeting was 37% in 1974 and up to 41% in 1976, rising from 17% in 1943. Sunday School attendance was slightly higher with 1974 attendance reaching a peak of 42.2%.[1]

Of real concern is the fact that "age is a key factor related to church attendance, with persons under 30 considerably less likely to attend church than those 30 and older."[2] Attendance comparisons by age show that only 30% of those in the "under 30" group attend church, while 57% attendance by the "over 50" group is raising the overall percentage:[3]

	National	Protestant	Catholic
Under 30	30	30	41
30 - 49 yrs.	40	36	57
50 yrs. & older	47	42	66

The figures for the first half of the 70's indicate a stabilization of church activity at a significantly lower plateau than the level of the previous decade. But the religious problems of the 60's had already taken their toll before the stabilization took place:

> After showing signs of decline for several years, the post-World War II religious boom has gone into a full-scale recession.
> Almost every new statistical report from a religious body shows further evidence of the downward trend....
> Whether or not religion is losing its influence, most people think it is—75 per cent, according to a recent Gallup poll, compared to 14 per cent who thought so in 1957.[4]

---

1. Data furnished to the author by Jerry Cahill of the LDS Church Public Communications Department, August 25, 1977.
2. Dr. George Gallup, "U.S. Churchgoing Remaining Stable," *Salt Lake Tribune*, December 22, 1974.
3. *Ibid.* The findings of the survey also indicate that
   — 9% more women than men attend church,
   — churchgoing is less frequent in the far west than in other major regions,
   — married persons have better attendance records than single persons.
4. Tracy Early, "Religious Poll: Declining Activity," *Deseret News*, July 16, 1970. This article reported significant downward trends throughout the nation.

Catholic attendance, on the other hand, is down 17 percentage points from 1964. Most of this decline, however, occurred in the 1960s.
...Attendance among Jews at synagogue has remained fairly stable over the last 12 years, with 17 percent having attended in a typical week in 1964 compared to 21 percent in 1975. (*Ibid.*)

Significant facts about the decline in religious activity and influence in America:

1. Institutionalized religion in America received strong criticism during the 1960s. Questions of authority, infallibility, birth control, celibacy, social relevancy and the role of the churches in secular and political conflicts caused serious declines in church membership and finances.
2. U.S. church attendance dropped nine percent between 1958 and 1971, to an average weekly attendance of 40%.

The Mafia

Organized crime has spread across America, and is believed to control as many as 50,000 criminals in the United States. At the heart of this criminal structure is the Mafia—an organization of approximately 5,000 mobsters of Italian ancestry:

> For all of its impact on American life, the Mafia is a remarkably small organization. *As reckoned by the FBI, the Mafia numbers about 5,000 "made men," or members. All are of Italian ancestry, most with roots in Sicily. Of course, the nationwide number of mobsters involved in organized crime is far higher and knows no ethnic limits.* Rednecks dominate the Georgia underworld. Blacks and Hispanics run most of the rackets in their neighborhoods. Jews, Greeks, Chinese and Irish Americans all help swell the totals.
> Then why does the Mafia attract so much attention? Many Italian Americans complain that the notoriety is excessive, and damaging to millions of lawabiding citizens; to assuage their sensibilities, *the Justice Department has stopped referring to the Mafia by name. No matter what the organization is called, it dominates much of American crime. Many nonmember gangsters are allied to it, usually kicking back a share of their take to the dons; some criminologists estimate that at least 50,000 hoods can be considered confederates of the Mafia. The Mafia is by far the best organized criminal group in the U.S. and the only one with a national structure:* 26 families—five of them in New York City—of from 20 to 1,000 "button men," or soldiers.[1]

During the past 15 years, the federal government has sought to combat the Mafia influence through "strike forces" which utilize the resources of numerous government agencies:

---

1. "The Mafia—Big, Bad and Booming," *Time*, May 16, 1977, p. 35.

The Strike Forces, *with a budget of 8.3 million dollars a year, pool the resources of 10 federal law enforcement agencies.* They are scattered in 16 cities, but their 151 lawyers report directly to William S. Lynch, chief of the organized-crime section of the Justice Department in Washington, D.C.[1]

Yet "despite a 15-year offensive that has made heavy inroads into the leadership ranks of the Mafia syndicates, *there is still as much mob-run gambling, narcotics traffic and loan sharking as ever—maybe more.*"[2]

The Mafia has moved into legitimate businesses to provide outlets through which it can "launder" illegal funds, and to provide "respectability" to its operations. Yet the result of Mafia-caused crime costs the average citizen an extra two cents for every dollar he spends:

For the Mafia, and indeed for all organized crime...business has seldom been better. As during Prohibition, big-time criminals profit by providing goods and services that are either downright illicit or, where legal, are handled by people who are highly vulnerable to underworld pressures. *The Mafia now dominates the manufacture and distribution of pornographic books, magazines and movies, a business that has doubled in a decade to $2.2 billion a year.* It has become heavily involved in *bootleg cigarettes and coffee.* Most of the Mob's mainstay businesses are doing better than ever: *gambling, loansharking, narcotics, hijacking, extortion and labor racketeering.* No one outside the tight-knit Mafia organization knows the full extent of its operations, but estimates culled from a variety of law enforcement agencies suggest that *the Mafia takes in at least $48 billion in annual gross revenues and nets an incredible $25 billion or so in untaxed profits.* By contrast, Exxon, the largest industrial corporation in the U.S., reported sales of $51.6 billion and net profits of $2.6 billion in 1976.

The criminals plow lots of their profits back into their rackets or, even more ominously, into a wide range of legitimate businesses that affect Americans' lives from cradle (diaper services) to grave (funeral parlors). Increasing amounts of Mob money are pouring into real estate, construction companies, liquor stores, meat-packing companies, truck-

1. "War on Organized Crime Takes a New Turn," *U.S. News and World Report,* May 31, 1976, p. 64. The cities in which major efforts to combat Mafia activities have been centered are Boston, Brooklyn, Buffalo, Chicago, Cleveland, Detroit, Kansas City, Los Angeles, Miami, Newark, New Orleans, New York, Philadelphia, Pittsburgh, San Francisco, and St. Louis. Changes are anticipated in the location of these strike forces, and "manpower may be shifted from the Northeast to cities of the South and Southwest where gangsters are developing newer, more sophisticated kinds of organized crime." (*Ibid.,* p. 66)
2. *Ibid.,* p. 64.

ing firms, hotels, bars, restaurants, laundries and vending machines. Indeed, *no facet of U.S. commercial life is safe from Mafia infiltration* in the form of investment offers—often handled through lawyers or front men, of course. Justice Department officials believe that *the Mafia may own as many as 10,000 legitimate firms, which generate annual profits estimated at $12 billion.*

In addition to the sums that Americans pay directly for the mobsters' wares, there are substantial hidden charges. Chicago authorities estimate that because of Mob operations, *the average citizen pays an additional 2 cents on the dollar for almost everything he purchases on the legal market—the passed-along business costs of extra theft insurance, additional security forces and outright extortion.*[1]

The Mafia reaps huge profits from its illegal activities. Authorities estimate their profits to be as follows:

REVENUES FROM THE RACKETS

Estimates in
billions of dollars

	Gross	Net	
Gambling	$38.0	$ 7.6	*$2.5 to $3.5 billion loaned out
Loan-Sharking	*	10.0	at any given time calculations
Narcotics	5.0	4.0	based on data from the National
Hijacking	1.5	1.2	Gambling Commission, the Drug
Pornography and			Enforcement Administration, the
Prostitution	2.0	1.7	Tobacco Tax Council, the Senate
Cigarette Boot-			Small Business Committee, the
legging	1.5	.8	New York State Commission of
			Investigation and various law-en-
Total	$48.0	$25.3	forcement agencies.[2]

John E. Mettale, second in command of the Criminal-Intelligence and Organized Crime section of the FBI, has stated that *"the Mafia is the biggest single crime group,...it has to be our prime target."*[3] He observed that "now the gangs are more sophisticated. They are into stock exchanges, financial markets, labor unions and interstate shipping."[4] These relationships with national organizations have given the Mafia additional power and finances. For instance, they have established close ties with the Teamsters, the

---

1. "The Mafia—Big, Bad and Booming," *op. cit.*, p. 33.
2. *Ibid.*, p. 36.
3. "War on Organized Crime Takes a New Turn," *op. cit.*, p. 64.
4. *Ibid.*

largest and richest union in the nation. "Millions upon millions of Teamster pension fund dollars have been funneled into Florida, and one of the chief beneficiaries has been the mob."[1]

Significant facts about organized crime in the United States:

1. The 5,000 members of the Mafia control approximately 50,000 criminals in the United States today. The Mafia is the best organized criminal group and the only one with a national structure.
2. The Federal government is spending 8.3 million dollars annually to combat the Mafia, with "strike forces" functioning across the nation.
3. The Mafia dominates national crime in the areas of pornography, gambling, loan sharking, narcotics, hijacking, extortion, labor racketeering, prostitution, and cigarette bootlegging. It may now own as many as 10,000 legitimate businesses which serve as fronts for its activities.
4. Mafia criminals gross over 48 billion dollars annually. As a result of their actions, the average citizen pays an additional 2 cents on the dollar for everything he purchases.

Corruption and Mismanagement in Government

The affairs of the nation took an abrupt turn for the worse with the June, 1972 attempted burglary of the Democratic Party headquarters in the Watergate office building. President Richard Nixon publicly denied having any knowledge of the crime, but surreptitiously instructed the Central Intelligence Agency to obstruct and halt the FBI investigation of the break-in. For more than two years he lied to the public, the Congress, and to his own staff, maintaining that he had no prior knowledge of the break-in affair. Yet continued investigation continued to link him to the crime. American prestige and authority began a rapid decline, both at home and abroad, as the truth of the matter unfolded. Finally, the President's personal tape recording of his conversation on June 23, 1972, provided conclusive evidence of his misdeeds. The House Judiciary Committee, in July, 1974, voted to recommend impeachment of the President on three counts: obstruction of justice,

---

1. "Teamsters and the Mob," *Newsweek*, August 18, 1975, p. 17.

abuse of power, and defiance of committee supoenas. As the pressure of the investigation increased, the personal work of the President stopped, his personality and actions became increasingly erratic and unstable, and the nation stood at the brink of national crisis. Faced with the choice of being either the first U.S. president to resign or the first to be impeached, President Nixon went before the nation and tendered his resignation, which became effective August 9, 1974.[1]

In accompanying legal action, many of Nixon's aides received criminal sentences, including John Mitchell, the former attorney general, and H. R. Haldeman, the President's chief of staff.

In 1973, while the Watergate investigation was underway, the nation discovered that Vice President Spiro T. Agnew was also guilty of serious crimes. In Baltimore County, Maryland, it was found that for a decade, up to 1972, Agnew had accepted and perhaps even solicited cash payments from contractors in return for official favors. The U.S. Justice Department presented evidence against him to a Baltimore grand jury. As the probe continued, the nation was in danger of having a U.S. administration too tarnished to function, especially as the spectre of a constitutional snarl over the question of vice presidential and presidential immunity from court procedures loomed. "On October 10, 1973, Vice President Spiro T. Agenw resigned from office, pleaded *nolo contendre* to a single count of income tax evasion and agreed to the government's publishing a statement that he had extorted bribes for a decade. He was sentenced to three years of unsupervised probation and received a $10,000 fine, which he has now paid."[2]

Revelations of immoral actions by other recent presidents of the United States have served to weaken the confidence of the public in the nation's highest offices. Americans have become aware of John F. Kennedy's illicit involvement with Judith Campbell Exner, traveling companion of a Mafia don. His administration, like Nixon's, has been found to have been involved in political malpractices such as illegal wiretapping and the use of federal agencies for personal political gain. The hero-worshipping public was dismayed to learn that his alleged heroism on PT-109 in a World War II encounter with Japanese destroyers was far from

1. For an account of the events leading to the President's resignation, see Theodore H. White, "Breach of Faith," *Reader's Digest*, May, 1975, pp. 204-258.

2. "The Decline and Fall of a Vice President," *Reader's Digest*, January, 1974, p. 98. See also "Spiro Strikes Back," *Newsweek*, October 8, 1973, pp. 30-33.

heroic and his war hero image was in reality well-orchestrated public relations hoopla.[1]

Lyndon B. Johnson's administration was also marred by political malpractice, including illegal spying on U.S. citizens. President Johnson had access to secret FBI files containing information on the indiscretions of public figures, and "Johnson had a voracious appetite for gossip."[2]

With his difficulties in connection with the Vietnamese War, President Johnson lost the confidence of the nation to the extent that he finally chose not to run for re-election in 1968.

Even the reputation of President Eisenhower was stained with the release, four years after his death, of *Past Forgetting—My Love Affair with Dwight D. Eisenhower.*[3] The author, Kay Summersby Morgan, was an English fashion model who became Ike's wartime driver, aide, secretary, and more. This liason took place while the married Eisenhower was Supreme Commander of Allied Forces in Europe, prior to becoming President of the nation.

Congress has also suffered a tremendous loss in prestige in the eyes of the American populace during the past decade, due to the improper conduct of some of its members. In October, 1974, Representative Wilbur Mills, chairman of the House Ways and Means Committee, was arrested near the Washington, D.C. Tidal Basin while he was entertaining "Fanne Fox—the Argentine Firecracker," a stripper at a Washington strip joint.[4] Several months later, she called him up on stage when she finished her strip act at Boston's Pilgrim burlesque theatre. A local newspaper photographed him there and the scandal spread. Overnight it completed the ruin of one of Washington's most powerful men. He was stripped of his political power and was compelled to seek clinical aid for alcoholism.[5]

Playgirl Elizabeth Ray leaped into public scrutiny with her revelation that she had been kept on the staff of Congressman

1. See "Closets of Camelot," *Newsweek*, January 19, 1976, p. 31.
2. "L.B.J., Hoover and Domestic Spying," *Time*, February 10, 1975, p. 16. Moyers wrote, for instance, that "Shortly after Johnson took office, the transcript and tapes of Martin Luther King's bedroom activities were spirited to him. He read the accounts, which an aide described as being 'like an erotic book.' He listened to the tapes that even had the noises of the bedsprings." *(Ibid.)*
3. Released in *Ladies Home Journal,* December, 1976.
4. "Scandals: A Firecracker Explodes," *Newsweek*, October 21, 1974, p. 42.
5. "Wilbur in Nighttown," *Newsweek*, December 16, 1974, pp. 21-23.

Wayne Hayes to serve as his mistress, at a cost to the public of $14,000 per year. Ms. Ray also made it known that her services were provided to numerous other high government officials, and made thinly-disguised reference to these liasons in her book "The Washington Fringe Benefit." Congressman Hayes lost the chairmanship of his party's Congressional Campaign Committee and was forced to give up his chairmanship of the House Administration Committee when the matter became public.[1] He later attempted suicide to escape the scandal.

Government secretary Colleen Gardner, secretary to Congressman John Young, revealed that her annual salary jumped from $8,500 to almost $26,000 because she met the employment requirement that she sleep with her boss. Congressman Charles Vanik admitted keeping a prostitute on his payroll at the expense of the citizenry, even continuing her pay after she became ill and was unable to work. Congressman Allan T. Howe lost his bid for reelection after being arrested for allegedly soliciting sexual services from two policewomen posing as prostitutes. Joe D. Waggoner was involved in an encounter with Washington D.C. police for soliciting sex from a policewoman.[2]

The courts have taken their toll on members of the nation's highest legislative bodies. "Since 1970, payoff convictions have touched three senator's offices. In the House, four congressmen have been pronounced guilty, and influence-peddling charges have gone as high as the office of the Speaker."[3] Sixteen members of Congress were indicted between 1955-1975, according to a Library of Congress survey, on charges ranging from tax evasion to taking kickbacks on defense contracts.[4] Others have fled to escape local prosecution. The public still remembers, for instance, Adam Clayton Powell's retreat on the island of Bimini to avoid legal action in New York.[5]

Congressional abuses of taxpayers funds have become a cause of growing concern. There are patronage jobs that pay well but require little work or professional preparation. The size of congressional staffs, and the expense of maintaining them, has increased at an alarming rate:

---

1. See "What Liz Ray Has Wrought," *Time*, June 21, 1976, p. 22, and "The Sex Saga," *Time*, June 28, 1976, p. 20.
2. *Ibid.*
3. James R. Polk, "The Secret Fringe Benefits Enjoyed by Congress," *The New Republic*, September 13, 1975, p. 14.
4. "Questions of Ethics," *Newsweek*, June 14, 1976, pp *21-27.
5. *Ibid.*

With the winds of reform blowing over Capitol Hill, the Senate really ought to deal with one of Washington's biggest open secrets—*the scandalous and hypocritical way in which it spends taxpayers' money on its own staff aides and committee operations.*

In the past five years, as the prestige and power of the Congress were on the decline, the cost and the size of Senate staffs nearly doubled. The bill was $10 million in fiscal 1971 and it will be above $20 million in fiscal '76."[1]

Abuses relating to congressional committees and subcommittees have become prevalent. Senators and Congressmen appropriate the services of members of standing committees to work on their personal staffs, and use committee funds to further personal political goals. They also make use of committee projects and budgets to enhance their personal re-election potential. For instance, "The *Post* found that 85.1 percent of all field hearings held in 1973 and 1974 were in the home states of members of those committees."[2]

Many members of the American public were dismayed at the manner in which the 94th Congress gave itself a pay raise on July 30, 1975. The Congress attached it to a minor postal bill, and allowed news of the bill to surface publicly only five days before the bill was finally passed. Congress granted itself another pay raise, of 25%, in February, 1977.[3]

Overseas travel privileges by legislators have been seriously abused, and the nation has learned of excursions that are little more than vacation trips taken at taxpayers' expense, often by "lame duck" legislators who have been defeated in their bids for re-election. The Congressional report of the cost of such trips was incorrect, and "government records kept secret until recently show that the overseas travel and entertainment of lawmakers has been *costing two-thirds more than the Congress's reports to the public have disclosed.*"[4]

---

1. Walter Pincus, "Committee Chicanery—The Scandalous Senate," *The New Republic*, February 22, 1975, p. 16.
2. *Ibid.*, p. 18.
3. "How Congress Rammed Through Its Pay Hike," *U.S. News & World Report*, September 1, 1975, p. 29. See also "Up and Up—The Money Congress Spends on Itself," *U.S. News & World Report*, March 10, 1975, pp. 16-17.
4. "Our Junket-Happy Congress," *U.S. News & World Report*, June 27, 1977, p. 19. The actual costs were summarized as follows:
   What was the cost to the public of these overseas treks? Congress gave its answer this spring when it published in the Congressional Record what was purported to be a full accounting of overseas travel

Serious problems have arisen in the Congress in many situations where the possibility of unethical or illegal conduct becomes
suspect: lawmakers receiving free rides on corporation jets bound
for convenient locations, legislators using private hunting lodges
maintained by business firms, auto makers providing leased sports
cars to families of lawmakers without cost, free vacation trips being
furnished to members of Congress, etc. The nation's highest legislative body has been receiving increased public pressure to establish tighter rules on financial disclosure, open lawmakers' books
on their outside income, crack down on secret private expense
funds, shed more light on lobbying, eliminate the taking of free
favors, correct nepotism situations, and eliminate hidden profi-
teering made possible through the holding of high public office.[1]

Government investigative agencies have also been guilty of
criminal activities. Following the death of F.B.I. Director J. Edgar
Hoover, it was found that he kept improper dossiers on many public officials, recording details concerning their sex lives, drinking
problems, and other indiscretions. Much of the material contained
in the files was rumor, unsubstantiated, as sensational as it was
spurious. Yet it served Hoover's power-hungry purpose as he drib-
bled the information out to men in high places.[2] The Federal
Bureau of Investigation also made illegal "surreptitious entries"
into various places including foreign embassies and missions and

---

1. See "Questions of Ethics, *Newsweek*, June 14, 1976, pp. 21-27; "Uses
   of Corruption," *Newsweek*, March 22, 1976, p. 73; "Businessman and
   the Government: Corruption Yesterday and Today," *American Heritage*,
   June, 1977, pp. 66-73; "Public Officials For Sale: Bribery, Graft, Kick-
   back," *Newsweek*, February 28, 1977, pp. 36-38; "Wrongdoing at High
   Levels," *Nation*, September 18, 1976, pp. 227-28; "Sexless Orgies of
   Morality," *N.Y. Times Magazine*, January 23, 1977, p. 33.
2. "The Pandora's Box at the FBI," *Time*, February 3, 1975, pp. 11-12.

---

expenditures for the previous year. This annual report has been the
basis for articles in many home-town newspapers on how much jun-
keting the local Congressman has been doing. The report for 1976
showed a total of $1,431,828 spent on overseas travel.

State Department and Pentagon records, however, tell a different
story. These records, plus interviews with Pentagon officials, indicate
that spending on congressional overseas trips totaled $2,513,169 last
year, more than one million dollars in excess of what legislators
owned up to in their reports to the public. This suggests the possibility that the House and Senate have been understating the true costs
of globe-trotting by their members since the publication of reports
on such spending began in 1959. (*Ibid.*)

headquarters of extremist groups—making at least 1,500 such break-ins between World War II and 1966.[1] "Attorney General Edward H. Levi told congress that abuses of the FBI had spanned three different generations."[2]

Though the Central Intelligence Agency has no jurisdiction to monitor the affairs of Americans, it too kept illegal files on American political figures and regularly opened the confidential mail of U.S. citizens. Of even greater concern, the CIA has been shown to have been involved in assassination plots against foreign political figures: South Viet Nam's President Ngo Dinh Diem, who was killed in a military uprising in 1963; the Communist-leaning dictator of the Dominican Republic, Rafael Trujillo; 1961 attempts on the life of Cuba's Fidel Castro using Mafia killers; and the attempted bombing of Francois "Papa Doc" Duvallier's palace in Haiti during a 1963 rebel uprising. CIA meddling extended to the internal political affairs of other nations, with involvement in the overthrow of the Arbenz regime in Guatemala and Allende in Chile. As recently as early 1976 the CIA funneled $6 million to non-Communist parties in Italy in an effort to keep the coalition of Christian Democratic Premier Aldo Moro from collapsing.[3] Many Americans have shown deep concern about the "invisible government" of these investigative agencies because they have exerted unbridled power and illegal influence in both foreign entanglements and domestic snooping.

Excessive government spending and serious financial mismanagement has created an astronomical national debt which has continually fed inflationary fires. A Taxpayer's Liability Index, prepared by the National Taxpayers Union, showed the U.S. national indebtedness at more than $131,000 per citizen:[4]

---

1. "The FBI's 'Black-Bag Boys,' " *Newsweek*, July 28, 1975, pp. 18-21.
2. Bill Moyers, "LBJ and the FBI," *Newsweek*, March 10, 1975, p. 84.
3. "The CIA—Prying Into Mail, Plotting Murder," *Time*, March 17, 1975, p. 10; "Cape-and-Dagger Stories," *Time*, August 11, 1975, pp. 61-62; "Red Star Over Rome," *Newsweek*, January 19, 1976, p. 40.
4. "Statement of Account," a brochure published by the National Taxpayers Union, 325 Pennsylvania Avenue, S.E., Washington, D.C. 20003. The brochure asserted that the liability per citizen had increased $17,000 in just one year and stated that, "As it is, you spend some five months a year working to pay all taxes, direct and hidden. The serfs of old were required to spend only three months toiling for their masters. The remainder of the year they were free to work for themselves. We want you to be at least as free as a serf." Examples of federal projects with limited value were listed: $375,000 for a Pentagon study of the frisbee; $159,000 to teach mothers how to play with their babies; $80,000 to

TRANSACTION DESCRIPTION	GROSS COST	YOUR SHARE
National Debt	$ 544,000,000,000.00	$ 10,880.00
Other Fiscal Liabilities	$ 69,000,000,000.00	$ 1,380.00
Undelivered Orders	$ 130,000,000,000.00	$ 2,600.00
Long-term Contracts	$ 12,000,000,000.00	$ 240.00
Financial Commitments	$ 175,000,000,000.00	$ 3,500.00
Insurance Commitments	$1,481,000,000,000.00	$ 29,620.00
Annuity Programs	$3,499,000,000,000.00	$ 69,980.00
Unadjudicated Claims	$ 10,000,000,000.00	$ 200.00
International Commitments	$ 10,000,000,000.00	$ 200.00
Miscellaneous Commitments	$ 31,000,000,000.00	$ 620.00
Subtotal as of June 30, 1975	$5,961,000,000,000.00	$119,220.00
Liability Growth in Fiscal 1976	$ 600,000,000,000.00	$ 12,000.00
Total	$6,561,000,000,000.00	$131,220.00

Government agencies are extending their power and prying deeper into the personal lives of Americans, as well as into almost every conceivable aspect of American business. In recent years, public cries of outrage have been raised concerning abuses by OSHA, the Internal Revenue Service, the Food and Drug Administration, and other federal agencies. The government is rapidly de-

---

develop a zero-gravity toilet; $121,000 to find out why some people say 'ain't; and $29,324 for a study of the mating calls of the Central American toad." Other examples of "staggering amounts...spent in ways which bring little benefit" were listed:

Item: $3 billions stolen annually from health programs—yet the federal government has fewer people investigating than it has manicuring the White House lawn.

Item: $600,000 in subsidy payments to a single beekeeper in Washington.

Item: $6.5 billions each year for the Pentagon to buy five times as many routine supplies (not weapons) as are actually used. 80% of its purchases are later scrapped in unused condition or sold for pennies on the dollar.

Item: Billions wasted annually on 900,000 "totally ineligible" welfare recipients.

Item: $200 millions annually to perform useless research and shower favored professors with grants. There are 23 biographies of Isaac Newton in the Library of Congress, yet the federal government wants to spend $10,000 for another one.

Item: $85,000 *per minute* to pay interest on the "national debt."

Item: $250 billions for foreign aid, including money for the U.S. to finance both sides in 14 wars during the last 20 years.

parting from the role of servant and has become the master of the people. As one commentator has observed,

> *What is the proper function of government?* One would suppose, where the police power is concerned, that *a proper function of government is to protect the citizen against fraud, mislabeling, and serious danger. But this function ought to be severely limited.* Government was not meant to be the One Great Nannie of Us All to hold our hands, blow our noses, and tie down our little mittens. *At some point responsibility has to be personal.* At some point parents, children, ice skaters and skiers have to learn for themselves that life is filled with sharp edges, thin ice, and bumps in the snow.[1]

Significant facts about corruption and mismanagement in national government in the United States:

1. For the last decade-and-a-half, America has endured the pains of a severe loss of confidence in its government. This was manifested in the internal strife during the Viet Nam War, and reached its zenith with the resignations of Richard Nixon and Spiro Agnew following the Watergate scandal of 1972-1974.
2. Several of the nation's recent presidents have engaged in immoral acts which have resulted in a lowering of the esteem in which the nation's highest office is held.
3. Sex scandals influenced the affairs of the nation's congress, and evidence of serious congressional ethical abuses raised extensive public criticism.
4. The CIA and FBI were found to have participated in numerous illegal acts which infringed upon the civil rights of many Americans.
5. Government spending has created a national debt of $6.5 trillion—an obligation of more than $131,000 for every citizen. Americans spend five months of the year working to pay taxes—two months more than the serfs of medieval times.

Will Unrighteousness Bring Judgments?

Will the decline in righteousness bring God's judgments upon America? The above statistics clearly establish the trend of rapidly-

---

1. James J. Kilpatrick, "How Much Government Is Too Much?" *Deseret News*, January 8, 1974.

declining morality which is evident in the nation. Of perhaps greatest concern is that the problems exist to the highest degree among
the youth. Their involvement in crime, sexual immorality, drug
and alcohol abuse, abortion, divorce, and lack of religious participation bodes ill for the future. What will happen in another twenty
years when they have sired another generation? If the nation continues its degenerating plunge at the same rate as it did from 1960
to 1975, only one conclusion can be drawn—that God's chastening
hand will soon come upon us, and unless we repent as a nation, He
will pour out His judgments until the wicked are destroyed!

Summary

1. History has shown that certain influences, attitudes, and
events weaken nations and lead to their downfall. Rome fell because
    A.   the sanctity of the home was undermined,
    B.   high taxes and unwise government spending ruined
         the economy,
    C.   people sought for pleasure rather than striving to ful-
         fill the basic needs of life,
    D.   the nation built armaments to repel external enemies
         but did not counteract the increasing decadence of
         its citizens, and
    E.   the people abandoned their religious and moral values.

2. The average age of the world's great civilizations has been
approximately 200 years.

3. There is a cycle of righteousness through which nations
pass:
    A.   God blesses and prospers people when they trust him,
    B.   the people are industrious and work to support and
         improve themselves,
    C.   the people become wealthy and live lives of ease and
         luxury,
    D.   the people harden their hearts and forget God's bless-
         ings,
    E.   God chastens the people with many afflictions,
    F.   God pours out judgments upon the people, destroy-
         ing them and their prosperity until a remnant hum-
         bled again remembers and trusts Him.

4. America is experiencing the events of the cycle of righteousness. The events of the past 15 years indicate that many Americans have hardened their hearts, forgotten God's blessings, and ceased to trust in Him. A grim picture of a nation being rapidly inundated by sin has unavoidably emerged. If that trend continues, it must be expected that God will first chasten the nation with many afflictions and eventually pour out His judgments upon the people, destroying them until a remnant humbles itself and remembers Him.

5. Crime has increased 179.9% since 1960, at an average annual rate of 12%. Crimes of violence are increasing nine times as fast as the population; crimes against property twelve times as fast. The majority of crimes are committed today by youthful offenders. 65% of criminals arrested are repeat offenders.

6. Based on their surveys, researchers estimate that 50% of America's husbands and wives commit adultery. Fornication is almost universal, and studys show that 93% of the wives married after 1973 have committed fornication. Almost 75% of the babies born to teen-age mothers are conceived out of wedlock.

7. Venereal disease is sweeping the country in epidemic proportions, particularly among the youth. If it continues to spread at its present rate, by 1986 one out of five students will be infected before graduating from high school.

8. One out of five pregnancies end in abortion. 73% of abortions are performed on unwed mothers. Almost a million abortions were performed in the United States in 1974 and the number is increasing annually.

9. American divorces passed the million mark in 1975, an increase of 92% in a decade. There is now one divorce for every 2.3 marriages each year. Divorce causes heavy increase in welfare expense—about 77% of the money spent in welfare is for children under 14 and their mothers.

10. Violence has increased in schools. Between 1970 and 1974, assaults in schools increased 58%, sex offenses 62%, drug-related crimes 81%, and in-school robberies 117%. More is spent on school vandalism than was spent in 1972 for textbooks. The cost of vandalism is enough to hire 50,000 teachers.

11. Drug abuse increased at an alarming rate between 1960 and 1975. Drugs are linked to more than 15,000 American deaths each year. 56% of those under 30 years of age have tried marijuana. Half of major city crime is attributed to drug addicts, and drug abuse costs the nation 17 billion dollars a year.

12. Seventy-one percent of the nation's adults drink alcoholic beverages, 83% of college students, and 74% of youth in grades seven through twelve had had a drink two or more times, with 54.8 percent of them drinking once a month or more. Alcohol is involved in a fifth of the nation's murders and half of its automobile deaths and injuries. Drinking costs the nation about 15 billion dollars a year.

13. Church attendance dropped nine percent from 1958 to 1971, with the national average attendance then stabilizing for several years at 40%. Disenchantment with organized religion has increased, with Catholics challenging papal authority and Protestants discontent with churches run like big business and lacking social relevancy. Age is a factor in church attendance—people under 30 average only 30% attendance, while the activity level of those more than 50 years old is 47%.

14. The Mafia has spread organized crime across America, and controls 50,000 criminals in crime operations such as gambling, loansharking, narcotics, pornography, hijacking, labor racketeering, bootlegging, and prostitution. Americans pay 2 cents more on the dollar as passed-along business costs businesses experience for theft protection, and outright extortion.

15. Corruption in the U.S. government has caused a serious lack of confidence in the integrity of government officials. Watergate, the resignation of the president and vice president, congressional sex scandals, serious breaches of ethical conduct by the nation's lawmakers, illegal acts by the CIA and FBI, and abuses by federal agencies have added to the nation's discontent.

16. Government spending has created a national debt of $6.5 trillion—an obligation of more than $131,000 for every citizen. Americans spend five months of the year working to pay taxes—two months more than the serfs of medieval times.

II

THE
PROPHETIC
WARNINGS

First Warning: IV
Those Who Do Not Believe In God Will Be Destroyed

The Conditional Nature of Book of Mormon Warnings

Many important warnings to last days inhabitants of America are recorded in the Book of Mormon. These warnings are usually given in conditional prophecies concerning future events. The Lord's promises made concerning this choice land are often based on alternatives—they contain an all-important *IF*. Implicit in each warning is a specific principle. The prophetic warnings describe what will happen *if* the people of America obey the principle in righteousness, they also warn what will transpire *if* the people choose to disobey that principle and work iniquity.

Each chapter in this section carefully considers one or more of these conditional warnings. The combined message is a matter of grave concern for all America, for it is a presentation of principles which *must* be obeyed if this nation is to survive.

While the chapters allude to many events which are prophesied to take place in the future, the chapters in this section are devoted to gaining an understanding of the principles upon which survival depends. Later chapters will consider the prophesied events to which the prophetic warnings allude.

Jacob's Warning: Unbelievers Will Be Destroyed by Fire, Tempest, Earthquakes, Bloodsheds, Pestilence, and Famine (2 Ne. 6:14-18)

The prophet Jacob, while preaching to the Nephites more than five centuries before the birth of Christ, made a sweeping prophecy concerning a period of conflict which is to occur in a time still future. Taking as his theme a passage from the prophet Isaiah,[1] Jacob tells how the people of Israel are to be gathered to the lands of their inheritance in the last days. He describes how God will pour out His judgments during the time of their gathering. He then

---

1. Is. 49:22-23 (quoted by Jacob in 2 Ne. 6:6-7), and Is. 49:24-52:2 (quoted by Jacob in 2 Ne. 6:16-8:25). For interpretive comment on these chapters see the author's book, *Prophets and Prophecies of the Old Testament* (Bountiful, Utah: Horizon Publishers, 1973, 644 pp.) pp.351-352, 356-357, 342.

sets forth the principle which will determine who escapes the judgments which will be sent from God in that day. That principle, he says, is belief in the Messiah, the Holy One of Israel:

> And behold, according to the words of the prophet, the Messiah will set himself again the second time to recover them [Zion and the covenant people of the Lord]; wherefore, he will manifest himself unto them in power and great glory, unto *the destruction of their enemies*, when that day cometh when they shall believe in him; and *none will he destroy that believe in him.*
>
> *And they that believe not in him shall be destroyed,* both by *fire*, and by *tempest*, and by *earthquakes*, and by *bloodsheds*, and by *pestilence*, and by *famine*. And they shall know that the Lord is God, the Holy One of Israel.
>
> For shall the prey be taken from the mighty, or the lawful captive delivered?
>
> But thus saith the Lord: Even the captives of the mighty shall be taken away, and the prey of the terrible shall be delivered; for *the Mighty God shall deliver his covenant people.* For thus saith the Lord: *I will contend with them that contendeth with thee—*
>
> *And I will feed them that oppress thee, with their own flesh; and they shall be drunken with their own blood* as with sweet wine; and all flesh shall know that I the Lord am thy Savior and thy Redeemer, the Mighty One of Jacob.[1]

Note that his prophecy is conditional: men will be able to escape destruction *if* they believe in God, but they will be destroyed by a series of judgments *if* they fail to meet the condition of belief in God.

Note also that the prophecy has a specific time of fulfillment: the unbelievers will be destroyed in the period when God moves to fulfill His covenants with Israel[2] by gathering and recovering her.[3] This event is clearly placed in the future in a chronological order of last days events set forth by the Savior Himself, as will be seen later in this book.[4]

Observe, too, that all people will not suffer the same fate: some will believe and escape while others who are unbelievers will be struck down. Thus the prophecy divides the people of that era into two distinct groups, believers and non-believers—a pattern established by many Book of Mormon prophecies.

---

1. 2 Ne. 6:14-18.
2. 2 Ne. 6:12.
3. 2 Ne. 6:11.
4. See p. 325

The Savior's Warning: Unbelieving Gentiles Will Be
   Trodden Down by the House of Israel When They
   Sin Against the Gospel (3 Ne. 16:4-15)

Another conditional prophecy, which specifically concerns
America in the last days, also places belief in God as the criterion
for escape from future disaster. This prophecy is found in the
words of Jesus Christ recorded in Third Nephi, chapter 16. The
time of prophetic fulfillment is the same: the future era when the
Savior will fulfill his covenant with Israel by gathering them from
the four quarters of the earth. [1] This prophecy is directed specifically to the Gentiles—the Caucasian people of America. [2]

The preparatory verses (3 Ne. 16:4-13) paint the scenario.
As in Jacob's prophecy, the criterion of belief in God divides the
last days' people of America into two groups. One portion of
the Gentiles believes, and receives the gospel:

> And *blessed are the Gentiles, because of their belief in me,* in and
> of the Holy Ghost, which witnesses unto them of me and of the Father.
> Behold, *because of their belief in me,* saith the Father, and because
> of the unbelief of you, O house of Israel, in the latter day shall the
> truth come unto the Gentiles, that the fulness of these things shall be
> made known unto them. [3]

The other portion of America's Gentiles does not believe, and
"wo," says God, *"unto the unbelieving of the Gentiles."* [4] This
group will sin against the gospel and turn to gross wickedness.

With the background clearly established by these preliminary
verses, the Savior delivers His prophetic message. Like Jacob's,
His warning is conditional—*if* the Gentiles of the last days reject
the fulness of the gospel, they will lose their opportunity to hear it:

> ...*At that day when the Gentiles shall sin against my gospel, and shall
> be lifted up in the pride of their hearts above all nations, and above all
> the people of the whole earth, and shall be filled with all manner of
> lyings, and of deceits, and of mischiefs, and all manner of hypocrisy,*

---

1. 3 Ne. 16:5.
2. Note that these Gentiles are the descendants (the fulness) of the American
   Gentiles who received the Book of Mormon (3 Ne. 16:4; compare with
   1 Ne. 13:14-39, which clearly identifies the Gentiles of America as
   those who receive the Book of Mormon in the last days).
3. 3 Ne. 16:6-7.
4. 3 Ne. 16:8.

and murders, and priestcrafts, and whoredoms, and of secret abomina-
tions; and *if* they shall do all those things, and shall reject the fulness of
my gospel, behold, saith the Father, *I will bring the fulness of my gospel*
from among them.[1]

The conditional nature of the prediction continues to be seen
throughout the warning portion of prophecy: *if* these wicked
American Gentiles will repent they will be numbered among Israel
and won't be trodden down,[2] but the Lord warns what will happen
if they don't repent:

> But if they will not turn unto me, and hearken unto my voice, *I*
> *will suffer them, yea, I will suffer my people, O house of Israel, that*
> *they shall go through among them, and shall tread them down,* and
> they shall be as salt that hath lost its savor, which is thenceforth good
> for nothing but *to be cast out, and to be trodden under foot of my*
> *people,* O house of Israel.
> Verily, verily, I say unto you, thus hath the Father commanded me—
> that I should give unto this people this land for their inheritance.[3]

Belief in God is again stated as the principle which will determine the difference between safety and destruction in this future event.

The Savior's Warning: Unbelieving Gentiles Will Be
Cut Off By a Remnant of Jacob (3 Ne. 21:1-14)

The Lord presents a similar prophecy in a different context,
but again sets belief in God as the criterion which will allow some
to escape destruction in America in the last days. Christ is speaking
of the same time and place as in His former prophetic warning:
He speaks of an event in connection with the future gathering
of Israel[4] which takes place *"in this land"* where the Gentiles are
"set up as a free people by the power of the Father."[5] He describes, once again, two groups who are differentiated by the belief in God. He tells of the righteous portion of the Gentiles, who
are willing to believe in God, that the Father

---

1. 3 Ne. 16:10. Note that this verse intimates a separating of the righteous
   from the wicked as the fulness of the gospel is taken from the unbelieving
   Gentiles. Whether this is a gathering out of the righteous, or a cessation
   of missionary work among the wicked, or both, is not indicated.
2. 3 Ne. 16:13-14.
3. 3 Ne. 16:15-16. Note that verse 16 clearly places this prophecy in the
   Americas. See also D & C 103:5-11.
4. 3 Ne. 21:1.
5. 3 Ne. 21:4.

...may show forth his power unto the Gentiles, for this cause that *the Gentiles, if they will not harden their hearts, that they may repent and come unto me* and be baptized in my name and know of the true points of my doctrine, that they may be numbered among my people, O house of Israel;...[1]

These believing Gentiles are contrasted with the unbelieving who will reap destruction as the Savior gives His prophetic warning. According to the Master, the unbelieving Gentiles will be destroyed by a remnant of Jacob which will cut them off:

> Therefore it shall come to pass that *whosoever will not believe in my words, who am Jesus Christ,* which the Father shall cause him to bring forth unto the Gentiles, and shall give unto him power that he shall bring them forth unto the Gentiles, (it shall be done even as Moses said) *they shall be cut off from among my people who are of the covenant.*
>
> *And my people who are a remnant of Jacob shall be among the Gentiles, yea, in the midst of them as a lion among the beasts of the forest, as a young lion among the flocks of sheep, who, if he go through both treadeth down and teareth in pieces, and none can deliver.*
>
> Their hand shall be lifted up upon their adversaries, and all *their enemies shall be cut off.*
>
> Yea, wo be unto the Gentiles except they repent;...[2]

Mormon's Warning: The Sword of Vengeance for the Blood of the Saints Hangs Over the Unbelieving (Morm. 8:27-9:6)

The prophet Mormon also presents belief in God as the principle which will separate those who will suffer God's vengeance in the last days from those who will be spared. He describes the day when *"the blood of the saints shall cry unto the Lord, because of secret combinations,"*[3] when *"the power of God shall be denied,"*[4] and there will be *wars* and *earthquakes,*[5] and *"persecutions, and all manner of iniquities,"*[6] and *"secret abominations to get gain."*[7]

---

1. 3 Ne. 21:6.
2. 3 Ne. 21:11-14. His prophecy continues in detail, describing the great destruction which will be brought upon the Gentiles. The remainder of this prophecy is considered later in the book.
3. Morm. 8:27.
4. Morm. 8:28.
5. Morm. 8:30.
6. Morm. 8:36.
7. Morm. 8:40.

Then he warns:

> Behold, *the sword of vengeance hangeth over you;* and the time soon
> cometh that *he avengeth the blood of the saints* upon you, for he will
> not suffer their cries any longer.[1]

Speaking "concerning those who do not believe in Christ,"[2] he
warns,

> Behold, *will ye believe* in the day of your visitation—behold, when
> the Lord shall come, yea, even that great day when the *earth shall be
> rolled together as a scroll,* and *the elements shall melt with fervent heat,*
> yea, in that great day when *ye shall be brought to stand before the
> Lamb of God*—then will ye say that there is no God?[3]

Then he shows that his prophecy is conditional—he contrasts
the scene he has depicted with the state of those who will repent
and believe in God:

> *O then ye unbelieving, turn ye unto the Lord;* cry mightily unto the
> Father in the name of Jesus, that *perhaps ye may be found spotless,
> pure, fair, and white,* having been cleansed by the blood of the Lamb,
> at that great and last day.[4]

Nephi's Warning: God Will Cause a Great Division Among the People and Will Destroy the Wicked (2 Ne. 30:1-10)

Yet other Book of Mormon passages present belief in God
as the criterion which will distinguish between those who are to be
spared and those who are to be destroyed in a last days period of
destruction connected with the gathering of Israel. Nephi spoke
of the Gentiles in the last days, telling how some of them through
belief in God might be among the covenant people:

> For behold, I say unto you that *as many of the Gentiles as will
> repent are the covenant people of the Lord;* and as many of the Jews
> as will not repent shall be cast off; for *the Lord covenanteth with none
> save it be with them that repent and believe in his Son,* who is the
> Holy One of Israel.[5]

---

1. Morm. 8:41.
2. Morm. 9:1.
3. Morm. 9:2.
4. Morm. 9:6.
5. 2 Ne. 30:2.

Then, after talking of the gathering of Israel[1] when *God* will cause a great division among the people and will destroy those who are not His people, he said:

> For the time speedily cometh that *the Lord God shall cause a great division among the people, and the wicked will he destroy;* and he will spare his people, yea, even if it so be that he must destroy the wicked by fire.[2]

Moroni's Warning: Those Who Deny the Word of the Lord Shall Be Accursed and Destroyed By Fire (Eth. 4:6-18)

Moroni, writing to the Gentiles in the last days, cited the Lord's warning to unbelievers among both the Gentiles and among Israel in the last days. As he did so, he told of the portion of the revelation given to the brother of Jared which has not yet been given to the Church in the last days. He explained that it, and other revelation, is to be restored to the Saints. Some of the Gentiles will believe it, while others will deny the Lord's word and will be destroyed:

> ...I have written upon these plates the very things which the brother of Jared saw; and there never were greater things made manifest than those which were made manifest unto the brother of Jared....
>
> ...*They shall not go forth unto the Gentiles until the day that they shall repent of their iniquity, and become clean before the Lord.*
>
> And in that day that they shall exercise faith in me, saith the Lord, even as the brother of Jared did, that they may become sanctified in me, *then will I manifest unto them the things which the brother of Jared saw, even to the unfolding unto them all my revelations,* saith Jesus Christ, the Son of God, the Father of the heavens and of the earth, and all things that in them are.
>
> *And he that will contend against the word of the Lord, let him be accursed; and he that shall deny these things, let him be accursed; for unto them will I show no greater things,* saith Jesus Christ; for I am he who speaketh.
>
> *And at my command the heavens are opened and are shut; and at my word the earth shall shake; and at my command the inhabitants thereof shall pass away, even so as by fire.*[3]

---

1. 2 Ne. 30:3-8.
2. 2 Ne. 30:10.
3. Eth. 4:4, 6-9. Then there followed this beautiful explanation of belief:
   And he that believeth not my words believeth not my disciples; and if it so be that I do not speak, judge ye; for ye shall know that it is I that speaketh, at the last day.
   But he that believeth these things which I have spoken, him will I visit with the manifestations of my Spirit, and he shall know and bear

After promising rich blessings to those who would believe during the future period (when the gathering process will be the sign God has remembered His covenant with Israel and has commenced His work), Moroni repeated the Lord's prophetic warning that believers would be saved while unbelievers would be damned:

> *Behold, when ye shall rend that veil of unbelief which doth cause you to remain in your awful state of wickedness, and hardness of heart, and blindness of mind,* then shall the great and marvelous things which have been hid up from the foundation of the world from you—yea, when ye shall call upon the Father in my name, with a broken heart and a contrite spirit, *then shall ye know that the Father hath remembered the covenant which he made unto your fathers, O house of Israel.*
>
> *And then shall my revelations which I have caused to be written by my servant John be unfolded in the eyes of all the people. Remember, when ye see these things, ye shall know that the time is at hand that they shall be made manifest in very deed.*
>
> Therefore, when ye shall receive this record ye may know that the work of the Father has commenced upon all the face of the land.
>
> Therefore, repent all ye ends of the earth, and *come unto me, and believe in my gospel, and be baptized in my name; for he that believeth and is baptized shall be saved; but he that believeth not shall be damned;* and signs shall follow them that believe in my name.[1]

Summary

1. The Book of Mormon contains important warnings to the last days' inhabitants of the Americas. These warnings are usually found in conditional prophecies concerning last days events.

---

1. Eth. 4:15-18. Note that the revelation written by John is the final book of the New Testament, "The Revelation of St. John the Divine." This verse is telling when the last days events it prophecies will find fulfillment.

---

record. For because of my Spirit he shall know that these things are true; for it persuadeth men to do good.

And whatsoever thing persuadeth men to do good is of me; for good cometh of none save it be of me. I am the same that leadeth men to all good; *he that will not believe my words will not believe me—that I am;* and he that will not believe me will not believe the Father who sent me. For behold, I am the Father, I am the light, and the life, and the truth of the world.

Come unto me, O ye Gentiles, and I will show unto you the greater things, the knowledge which is hid up because of unbelief. (Eth. 4:10-13)

2. Many of the conditional warnings state a specific gospel principle. They say what blessings will be reaped by those who obey the principle, then warn of destruction which will come upon those who are disobedient to that law.

3. The chapters in section II are devoted to gaining an understanding of the principles upon which survival depends. Later chapters will consider the prophesied events to which the prophetic warnings allude.

4. The people of America must believe in God or they will be destroyed in a future period of God-sent judgments. This is the first of the principles for survival cited and the central theme of this chapter.

5. Six key prophetic warnings are cited to demonstrate this principle. They are prophecies made by:

A.   Jacob (2 Ne. 6:14-18)
B.   the Savior (3 Ne. 16:4-15)
C.   the Savior (3 Ne. 21:1-14)
D.   Mormon (Morm. 8:27-9:6)
E.   Nephi (2 Ne. 30:1-10)
F.   Moroni (Eth. 4:6-18)

6. A major theme of the prophecies is that the people of the Americas will be divided into two factions, one righteous and the other wicked. They will be separated; the righteous will be spared while the wicked are destroyed.

7. The prophecies generally refer to a specific time of fulfillment: a time of future conflict during which God will fulfill His covenant with Israel by gathering that people to the lands of their inheritance. Some of the prophecies, however, may have reference to the destruction of the wicked to take place at the time of Christ's coming in glory to begin His millennial reign.

8. The prophecies are usually directed to the "Gentiles," or Caucasian inhabitants who settled in the Americas following the coming of Columbus. According to the Book of Mormon, the gospel is restored to and through the Gentiles. It appears that Church members may be found among both the "believing" and "unbelieving"categories of the Gentiles in the last days.

9. The prophecies allude to unrighteous conditions which will exist in America as the time of conflict and destruction draws near:

A. The Gentiles will sin against the gospel (3 Ne. 16:10)

B. The Gentiles will be lifted up in pride above all people of the whole earth (3 Ne. 16:10)

C. The Gentiles will be filled with lyings, deceits, mischiefs, hypocrisy, murder, priestcrafts, whoredoms, and secret abominations (3 Ne. 16:10)

D. The blood of the Saints will cry unto the Lord because of secret combinations (Morm. 8:27)

E. The power of God shall be denied (Morm. 8:28)

F. There will be persecutions (Morm. 8:36)

G. There will be secret abominations to get gain (Morm. 8:40)

H. The people will be unbelieving (Morm. 9:6)

I. Some will contend against the word of the Lord (Eth. 4:8)

J. Some will deny the validity of newly-revealed revelations (Eth. 4:7-8)

K. People will be in an awful state of wickedness (Eth. 4:15)

The degree in which these conditions exist at present may be some indication as to how close this future period of conflict and destruction is in time.

10. The warnings allude to specific events which will transpire as the prophecies are fulfilled:

A. God will begin to recover and gather Israel (2 Ne. 6:12-14; 3 Ne. 16:5; 21:1)

B. Those who don't believe in God will be destroyed by fire, tempest earthquakes, bloodsheds, pestilence, and famine (2 Ne. 6:15)

C. People will contend with Israel and oppress her (2 Ne. 6:17-18)

D. Israel (or some of Israel) will be captive to a mighty enemy but will be delivered from it (2 Ne. 6:16-18)

E. God will deliver His covenant people (2 Ne. 6:17)

F. Believers will be spared from destruction (2 Ne. 6:14-15)

G. Enemies of Israel will fight among themselves (2 Ne. 6:18)

H.   Some Gentiles will receive the gospel (3 Ne. 16:6-7; 21:6)
I.   The gospel will be taken away from the wicked Gentiles (3 Ne. 16:10, 21:11)
J.   Members of the House of Israel (the remnant of Jacob) will tear and tread down the Gentiles (3 Ne. 16:15; 21:12-13)
K.   There will be wars and earthquakes (Morm. 8:30)
L.   God will avenge the blood of the Saints upon the Gentiles (Morm. 8:41)
M.   God shall cause a great division among the people (2 Ne. 30:10)
N.   God will destroy the wicked by fire (2 Ne. 30:10; Eth. 4:9)
O.   Things shown to the Brother of Jared, plus other revelations, will be manifested to righteous Gentiles (Eth. 4:7)
P.   Men will contend against these new revelations and deny them (Eth. 4:8)
Q.   The revelations given to John [the Revelator] will be unfolded (Eth. 4:16)
R.   The Lord will come. The elements will melt with fervent heat (Morm. 9:2)

Second Warning: $\qquad$ V
Those Who Will Not Serve
God Will Be Destroyed

Failure to serve God is also cited as a cause for past and future destruction of the inhabitants of the promised land in Book of Mormon warnings. It stands as the second of the principles which must be obeyed if the peoples of the Americas are to escape God's judgments.

Moroni's Warning: Nations Not Serving God Will Be Swept Off When the Fulness of God's Wrath Comes Upon Them (Eth. 2:7-12)

Moroni, while referring to "the land of promise, which was choice above all other lands, which the Lord God had preserved for a righteous people,"[1] told of God's everlasting decree and promise to the brother of Jared:

> And *he had sworn* in his wrath unto the brother of Jared, that *whoso should possess this land of promise, from that time henceforth and forever, should serve him, the true and only God, or they should be swept off when the fulness of his wrath should come upon them.*
> And now, we can behold the decrees of God concerning this land, that it is a land of promise; and *whatsoever nation shall possess it shall serve God, or they shall be swept off when the fulness of his wrath shall come upon them.* And the fulness of his wrath cometh upon them when they are ripened in iniquity.
> For behold, this is a land which is choice above all other lands; wherefore *he that doth possess it shall serve God or shall be swept off; for it is the everlasting decree of God.* And it is not until the fulness of iniquity among the children of the land, that they are swept off.[2]

He then directed his writing to the American Gentiles of the last days, whom he knew would eventually read his words in the Book of Mormon. He knew that iniquity would come among them, and warned that they must repent and not allow their wickedness to reach a "fulness:"

---

1. Eth. 2:7.
2. Eth. 2:8-10.

And this cometh unto you, O ye Gentiles, *that ye may know the decrees of God—that ye may repent, and not continue in your iniquities until the fulness come,* that ye may not bring down the fulness of the wrath of God upon you as the inhabitants of the land have hitherto done.

Behold, *this is a choice land, and whatsoever nation shall possess it shall be free from bondage, and from captivity, and from all other nations under heaven, if they will but serve the God of the land, who is Jesus Christ,* who hath been manifested by the things which we have written.[1]

Lehi's Warning: If Iniquity Abounds, the Land Will Be Cursed (2 Ne. 1:5-7)

Lehi, in his prophecy concerning "the land of promise, a land which is choice above all other lands,"[2] saw that *if* the people brought here by God would serve Him, then this would be a land of liberty unto them. But *if* they turned to wickedness they might be brought into captivity and the land would be cursed for their sakes:

Wherefore, I, Lehi, prophesy according to the workings of the Spirit which is in me, that *there shall none come into this land save they shall be brought by the hand of the Lord.*

Wherefore, this land is consecrated unto him whom he shall bring. And *if it so be that they shall serve him* according to the commandments which he hath given, it shall be a land of liberty unto them; wherefore, they shall never be brought down into captivity; *if so, it shall be because of iniquity; for if iniquity shall abound cursed shall be the land for their sakes,* but unto the righteous it shall be blessed forever.[3]

Thus Lehi, like Moroni, foresaw that serving God would be a criterion which would determine whether the people of this land would enjoy liberty and divine blessings or would be cursed and destroyed.

King Limhi's Warning: If the People Sow Filthiness They Shall Reap Immediate Destruction (Mos. 7:29-33)

Past situations in the Book of Mormon indicate the importance of serving God as being the key to retaining liberty and escaping from divine judgments. King Limhi (leader of the people

1. Ether 2:11-12.
2. 2 Ne. 1:5.
3. 2 Ne. 1:6-7. Note that Lehi, in his prophecy, also follows the procedure of dividing the people into two groups: those iniquitous ones for whom the land will remain blessed forever. This is the pattern of prophecies in the preceding section.

of Lehi-Nephi who were in bondage to the Lamanites) assembled his people and taught them that serving God would be the only way they could escape from captivity. After telling how their wickedness led to their being conquered, he warned that[1]

> ...the Lord hath said: *I will not succor my people in the day of their transgression, but I will hedge up their ways that they prosper not;* and their doings shall be as a stumbling block before them.
> And again, he saith: *If my people shall sow filthiness they shall reap the chaff thereof in the whirlwind; and the effect thereof is poison.*
> And again he saith: *If my people shall sow filthiness they shall reap the east wind, which bringeth immediate destruction.*
> And now, behold, the promise of the Lord is fulfilled, and ye are smitten and afflicted.
> But if ye will *turn to the Lord* with full purpose of heart, and *put your trust in him,* and *serve him with all diligence of mind,* if ye do this, he will, according to his own will and pleasure, deliver you out of bondage.[2]

Serving God the Key to Escaping Divine Retribution: Examples from Book of Mormon History

A Famine Sent to Stir Up Warring People in Remembrance of Their God

An important example of how serving God is the key to enjoying blessings from God and escaping divine retribution occurred in the period shortly before the birth of Christ. During the days of the Prophet Nephi,[3] the people had become so wicked that God sent His prophet to them with the message that *"Except ye repent ye shall be smitten, even unto destruction."*[4]

---

1. Concerning the cause of their downfall, he said:

> ...Great are the reasons which we have to mourn; for behold how many of our brethren have been slain, and their blood has been spilt in vain, and *all because of iniquity.*
> *For if this people had not fallen into transgression the Lord would not have suffered that this great evil should come upon them.* But behold, *they would not hearken* unto his words; but *there arose contentions among them,* even so much that *they did shed blood* among themselves.
> And *a prophet of the Lord have they slain;* yea, a chosen man of God, who told them of their wickedness and abominations, and prophesied of many things which are to come, yea, even the coming of Christ. (Mos. 7:24-26)

2. Mos. 7:29-33.
3. The Son of Helaman II. See Hel. 3:37.
4. Hel. 10:11.

Wars were raging throughout the land because of the inroads made by the Gadianton robbers. Rather than allow all his people to be destroyed, Nephi pled with the Lord to send a famine to stir them up in remembrance of their God. Drought and famine came, and *"they did perish by thousands in the more wicked parts of the land."*[1] Then Nephi beseeched the Lord that the famine might end and that the people might again be tested whether they would serve God:

> And now, O Lord, wilt thou turn away thine anger, and *try again if they will serve thee?* And if so, O Lord, thou canst bless them according to thy words which thou hast said.[2]

After three years of drought-caused famine, the rains fell once again. The people now were sufficiently ready to serve God. Because of their repentant attitude, the Church spread throughout the land and they lived in peace.[3]

War and Seige Humble Wicked Nephites Until They Serve God

Another prophet named Nephi[4] saw his people endure terrible war and bloodshed until they were willing to serve God with diligence. The people saw the new star which was the sign of Christ's birth,[5] yet so many of them were corrupted and led astray by the "secret society of Gadianton"[6] that they engaged in the war which brought the greatest slaughter among the people of Lehi since that prophet came to the promised land.[7] It was not until the Nephites had endured a harsh seige that God delivered them out of the hands of their enemies "and *they knew it was because of their repentance and their humility that they had been delivered from an everlasting destruction."*[8] What did they then do?

> ...They did forsake all their sins, and their abominations, and their whoredoms, and *did serve God with all diligence day and night.*[9]

Again, service to God was linked with escape from destruction.

---

1. Hel. 11:6.
2. Hel. 11:16.
3. Hel. 11:17-21.
4. The son of the above Nephi and grandson of Helaman (II). See 3 Ne. 1:10.
5. 3 Ne. 1:19-21. This was the sign prophesied by Samuel the Lamanite. See Hel. 14:1-6.
6. 3 Ne. 3:9. See all of 3 Ne. 3 and 4.
7. 3 Ne. 4:11.
8. 3 Ne. 4:33.
9. 3 Ne. 5:3.

Moroni's Warning to Last Days' Unbelievers: Despisers of God's Works Shall Wonder and Perish (Morm. 9:26-28)

Moroni, in his address to the unbelievers who would read his words in the last days, warned that those who will rise up against the power of the Lord will perish. His admonition was that the Gentiles follow the course of wisdom by serving God:

> ...Who can stand against the works of the Lord? Who can deny his sayings? Who will rise up against the almighty power of the Lord? Who will despise the works of the Lord? Who will despise the children of Christ? Behold, all ye who are despisers of the works of the Lord, for ye shall wonder and perish.
>
> O then despise not, and wonder not, but hearken unto the words of the Lord, and ask the Father in the name of Jesus for what things soever ye shall stand in need. Doubt not, but be believing, and begin as in times of old, and come unto the Lord with all your heart, and work out your own salvation with fear and trembling before him.
>
> Be wise in the days of your probation; strip yourselves of all uncleanness; ask not, that ye may consume it on your lusts, but ask with a firmness unshaken, that ye will yield to no temptation, but that ye will serve the true and living God. [1]

Service to God thus stands as a second important criterion for America's survival in the perilous last days' scene. In warning after warning, inspired prophets have held this principle as a vital key to the receiving of divine blessings and the avoiding of God-sent judgments.

There can be no compromise nor mixed allegiance. As the Savior taught:

> No man can serve two masters; for either he will hate the one and love the other, or else he will hold to the one and despise the other. Ye cannot serve God and Mammon. [2]

Summary

1. Prophetic warnings concerning the Americas as a land of promise show service to God as a necessary criterion for escaping

---

1. Morm. 9:26-28.
2. 3 Ne. 13:24. Nor is there room for discouragement among God's people. The Savior, while among the Nephites, quoted them His former revelation to Malachi in which he observed their diminished faithfulness: "Ye have said: It is vain to serve God, and what doth it profit that we have kept his ordinances and that we have walked mournfully before the Lord of Hosts?" (3 Ne. 24:14).

God's judgments. If the people serve God, they will be blessed and protected. If they do not serve God, His judgments will come upon them.

2. Four prophetic warnings on this theme are cited in this chapter:

A. Moroni (Eth. 2:8-12)
B. Lehi (2 Ne. 1:5-7)
C. King Limhi (Mos. 7:29-33)
D. Moroni (Morm. 9:26-28)

3. With the warnings are promises of blessings if the people of the land will truly serve God:

A. Whatever nation possesses the "choice land" of America shall be free from bondage and captivity, and from all other nations if they will serve Jesus Christ (Eth. 2:12).
B. The people brought to this "consecrated" land will enjoy liberty and shall never be brought into captivity if they will serve the Lord by keeping His commandments (2 Ne. 1:7).
C. If people will turn to the Lord, trust Him, and serve Him with all diligence, He will deliver them out of bondage (Mos. 7:33).

4. God's actions when wickedness prevails are also described in the prophetic warnings:

A. The fulness of the wrath of God comes upon those who continue in iniquities until the fulness comes (Eth. 2:11).
B. If iniquity abounds, the people may go into captivity and the land will be cursed because of the wicked people (2 Ne. 1:7).
C. The Lord won't succor His people if they transgress. He will hedge up their ways so they won't prosper and their doings will be their stumbling blocks (Mos. 7:29).
D. Those who rise up against the Lord's power and despise His works will wonder and perish (Morm. 9:26).

5. According to the prophet Lehi, "there shall none come into this land save they be brought by the hand of the Lord"

(2 Ne. 1:6). This does not necessarily mean that no enemies can ever come here, but rather that if they were to come, they would be brought by God (as often happened in both Biblical and Book of Mormon accounts when the people became wicked).

6. People have been humbled so that they would serve God through bondage, famines, and wars. The examples of the Lehi-Nephi colony captivity to the Lamanites (Mos. 7), the famine sought by the prophet Nephi (Hel. 11), and the Nephite war against the Gadianton robbers (3 Ne. 3-5) were cited.

7. Moroni's address to unbelievers in the last days indicates another aspect of last days conditions: men will stand against the work of God, deny His sayings, and despise both His works and His children [followers] (Morm. 9:26).

Third Warning: VI
If The People Turn To Wickedness, They And The Land Will Be Cursed

Alma's Warning: The Land is Cursed Unto Destruction Unto Every People Which Do Wickedly (Al. 45:16)

The Lord has set high standards for the inhabitants of America—the land "choice above all other lands." He expects them to believe in Him, He expects them to serve Him, and He expects them to refrain from wicked deeds. Though many are aware of the promises of blessings He has made if the people are righteous, relatively few seem to know of the curses He has pronounced on the land if the inhabitants choose wickedness.

Alma, while giving a father's blessing to his sons, taught them of this conditional curse:

> ...Thus saith the Lord God—*Cursed shall be the land, yea, this land, unto every nation, kindred, tongue, and people, unto destruction, which do wickedly, when they are fully ripe;* and as I have said so shall it be; for this is the cursing and the blessing of God upon the land, for the Lord cannot look upon sin with the least degree of allowance. [1]

He taught his son that

> ...*There is a curse upon all this land, that destruction shall come upon all those workers of darkness,* according to the power of God, *when they are fully ripe;* therefore I desire that this people might not be destroyed. [2]

Lehi's Warning: If Iniquity Abounds,
Cursed Shall be the Land (2 Ne. 1:7)

Lehi, it will be remembered, taught the same principle, saying that "*if iniquity shall abound, cursed shall be the land* for their sakes...." [3] He taught his sons that God had said that

> ...Inasmuch as ye shall keep my commandments ye shall prosper in the land; but *inasmuch as ye will not keep my commandments ye shall*

---

1. Al. 45:16. See also D & C 1:31.
2. Al. 37:28. See also verse 31.
3. 2 Ne. 1:7.

be cut off from my presence.

And now that my soul might have joy in you, and that my heart might leave this world with gladness because of you, that I might not be brought down with grief and sorrow to the grave, *arise from the dust, my sons, and be men, and be determined in one mind and in one heart, united in all things, that ye may not come down into captivity;*

That ye may not be cursed with a sore cursing; and also, that ye may not incur the displeasure of a just God upon you, unto the destruction, yea, the eternal destruction of both soul and body.[1]

He also described the nature and extent of such a curse:

My heart hath been weighed down with sorrow from time to time, for I have feared, lest for the hardness of your hearts the Lord your God should come out in the fulness of his wrath upon you, that ye be cut off and destroyed forever;

Or, that a cursing should come upon you for the space of many generations; and ye are visited by sword, and by famine, and are hated, and are led according to the will and captivity of the devil.[2]

Instances of God's Curse Upon the Land: Book of Mormon Examples

The Book of Mormon gives striking examples of what takes place when the Lord's curse becomes operative. Five-and-a-half centuries after Lehi's warning, the people of Nephi witnessed the effects of the Lord's curse:

And they did prosper exceedingly, and they became exceedingly rich; yea, and they did multiply and were strong in the land.

And thus we see how merciful and just are all the dealings of the Lord, to the fulfilling of all his words unto the children of men; yea, we can behold that his words are verified, even at this time, which he spake unto Lehi, saying:

Blessed art thou and thy children; and they shall be blessed, inasmuch as they shall keep my commandments they shall prosper in the land. *But remember, inasmuch as they will not keep the commandments they shall be cut off from the presence of the Lord.*

And we see that *these promises have been verified to the people of Nephi;* for it has been their quarrelings and their *contentions,* yea, their *murderings,* and their *plunderings,* their *idolatry,* their *whoredoms,* and their *abominations,* which were among themselves, *which brought upon them their wars and their destructions.*

And *those who were faithful in keeping the commandments of the Lord were delivered* at all times, whilst *thousands of their wicked brethren have been consigned to bondage, or to perish by the sword, or to dwindle in unbelief, and mingle with the Lamanites.*[3]

---

1. 2 Ne. 1:20-22.
2. 2 Ne. 1:17-18.
3. Al. 50:18-22.

A thousand years after Lehi's day, Mormon saw that God no longer would send His word to the wicked Nephites and, because of the hardness of their hearts, the land again was cursed:

> And I did endeavor to preach unto this people, but my mouth was shut, and I was forbidden that I should preach unto them; for behold *they had wilfully rebelled against their God;* and the beloved *disciples were taken away out of the land,* because of their iniquity.
>
> But I did remain among them, but I was forbidden to preach unto them, because of the hardness of their hearts; and *because of the hardness of their hearts the land was cursed for their sake.*
>
> And these Gadianton robbers, who were among the Lamanites, did infest the land, insomuch that the inhabitants thereof began to hide up their treasures in the earth; and *they became slippery, because the Lord had cursed the land, that they could not hold them, nor retain them again.*[1]

The curse continued until a quarter-of-a-million Nephite warriors, plus their women and children, were slain in a single day. The entire nation was destroyed.[2]

Jacob's Warning: The People Must Keep the Lord's Commandments, or Cursed Be the Land (Jac. 1:29; 3:3)

The prophet Jacob, on several occasions, warned of the Lord's curse. When his people became unchaste, he proclaimed that "*this people shall keep my commandments, saith the Lord of Hosts, or cursed be the land for their sakes.*"[3] His warning cry was "Wo, wo unto you that are not pure in heart, that are filthy this day before God; for *except ye repent the land is cursed for your sakes....*"[4]

Nephi's Warning: The Lord Destroys the Wicked, and Curses the Land for Their Sakes (1 Ne. 17:36-38)

The words of Nephi summarize this principle or warning:

> Behold, the Lord hath created the earth that it should be inhabited; and he hath created his children that they should possess it.
>
> And he raiseth up a righteous nation, and *destroyeth the nations of the wicked.*
>
> And he leadeth away the righteous into precious lands, and *the wicked he destroyeth, and curseth the land unto them for their sakes.*[5]

---

1. Morm. 1:16-18.
2. See Morm. 6:10-15.
3. Jac. 2:29.
4. Jac. 3:3. He alluded to the Lord's cursing of the wicked in the last days. See Jac. 6:2-3.
5. 1 Ne. 17:36-38.

What more need be added? Just three brief observations from the scriptures. First, Alma the Younger's comment:

> Now I would that ye should see that *they brought upon themselves the curse; and even so doth every man that is cursed bring upon himself his own condemnation.* [1]

Second, the same prophet's observation concerning who might receive the greatest cursing:

> And now, how much *more cursed is he that knoweth the will of God and doeth it not,* than he that only believeth, or only hath cause to believe, and falleth into transgression? [2]

And finally, an observation by Mormon:

> But, behold, the judgments of God will overtake the wicked; and *it is by the wicked that the wicked are punished;* for it is the wicked that stir up the hearts of the children of men unto bloodshed. [3]

Summary

1.   The third principle which must be obeyed, if America is to escape future destruction, is that wickedness must not become commonplace. The prophets have repeatedly warned that the promised land will be cursed if wickedness abounds and prevails.

2.   Prophetic warnings on this theme are cited in this chapter from four prophets:

A.   Alma (Al. 45:16, 37:28)
B.   Lehi (2 Ne. 1:7, 17-18, 20-22)
C.   Jacob (Jac. 2:29, 3:3)
D.   Nephi (1 Ne. 17:36-38)

3.   Book of Mormon examples indicate that the threatened cursing of the land comes in varying degrees. As people move toward national wickedness their economy is affected, and they can't retain their riches (Morm. 1:18; Hel. 13:30-36). If iniquity

---

1. Al. 3:19.
2. Al. 32:19.
3. Morm. 4:5.

progresses until it is fully "ripe," the people are visited with God's judgments by famine, sword, and pestilence.

4. Every man that is cursed by God brings upon himself his own condemnation.

5. Those who know but do not obey the will of God are more cursed than those with lesser belief and knowledge.

Fourth Warning: VII
If The People Do Not Repent, They Will Be Destroyed

Book of Mormon prophecies repeatedly warn of a last days' period when there will be great wickedness among the people of America. At that day, according to the prophecies, the people must repent or they will be destroyed. If they do repent, however, they will be spared and blessed.

Alma's Warning: Unless Nations That Possess the Promised Land Repent, They Will Be Destroyed (Al. 37:22-25)

Repentance from wickedness has been required by the Lord from every nation that has possessed this land throughout its history, and that principle stands as a fundamental requirement to national survival. Alma explained this great truth to his son, Helaman, as he spoke of the previous destruction of the Jaredite nation and of the records of their downfall:

> ...the Lord saw that his people began to work in darkness, yea, work secret murders and abominations; therefore the Lord said, *if they did not repent they should be destroyed* from off the face of the earth.
>
> And the Lord said: I will prepare unto my servant Gazelem, a stone, which shall shine forth in darkness unto light, that *I may discover unto my people who serve me, that I may discover unto them the works of their brethren, yea, their secret works, their works of darkness, and their wickedness and abominations.*
>
> And now, my son, these interpreters were prepared that the word of God might be fulfilled, which he spake, saying:
>
> I will bring forth out of darkness unto light all their secret works and their abominations; and *except they repent I will destroy them from off the face of the earth;* and I will bring to light all their secrets and abominations, *unto every nation that shall hereafter possess the land.*[1]

---

1. Al. 37:22-25. Alma made this observation concerning the Jaredites: "And now, my son, *we see that they did not repent; therefore they have been destroyed,* and thus far the word of God has been fulfilled;"... (Al. 37:26).

Thus repentance, or the lack of it, becomes another criterion for the survival of America as the Book of Mormon prophecies foretell the future of this nation. As with the previous prophetic warnings, the prophecies are conditional.

Nephi's Warning: In the Day the Earth's Inhabitants are Fully Ripe in Iniquity, They Shall Perish (2 Ne. 28:16-17)

For instance, Nephi prophesied concerning the people of the last days, observing that they will all have *"gone astray save it be a few, who are the humble followers of Christ,"*[1] and that there will come a time when they will *"turn aside the just for a thing of naught"* and that the devil will *"stir them up to anger against that which is good."*[2] In close chronological proximity to the fall of the great and abominable church[3] and a period of great wickedness and apathy in Zion,[4] he gives this warning concerning the necessity of repentance:

> Wo unto them that turn aside the just for a thing of naught and revile against that which is good, and say that is of no worth! For the day shall come that *the Lord God will speedily visit the inhabitants of the earth; and in that day that they are fully ripe in iniquity they shall perish.*
>
> But behold, *if the inhabitants of the earth shall repent of their wickedness and abominations they shall not be destroyed,* saith the Lord of Hosts.[5]

His prophetic utterance contains the Lord's warning that the Gentiles of the last days will deny Him, but also holds the promise of God's love if the people will repent:

> Wo be unto the Gentiles, saith the Lord God of Hosts! For notwithstanding I shall lengthen out mine arm unto them from day to day, *they will deny me;* nevertheless, *I will be merciful unto them, saith the Lord God, if they will repent and come unto me;* for mine arm is lengthened out all the day long, saith the Lord God of Hosts.[6]

---

1. 2 Ne. 28:14.
2. 2 Ne. 28:16, 20. See 1 Ne. 14:7 and 2 Ne. 30:10.
3. 2 Ne. 28:18. See pp. 171-197.
4. 2 Ne. 28:21-31. See pp. 227-258.
5. 2 Ne. 28:16-17.
6. 2 Ne. 28:32.

Nephi's Warning: Whoso Repenteth Not Must Perish (1 Ne. 14:5-6)

In earlier prophecy, Nephi had warned of the future dominion, power and wickedness of the great and abominable church.[1] He spoke of the Gentiles as two factions, the repentant and the wicked:

> And it came to pass that the angel spake unto me, Nephi, saying: Thou hast beheld that *if the Gentiles repent it shall be well with them;* and thou also knowest concerning the covenants of the Lord unto the house of Israel; and thou also hast heard that *whoso repenteth not must perish.*
>
> Therefore, *wo be unto the Gentiles if it so be that they harden their hearts against the Lamb of God.*[2]

The Savior's Warning: The Gentiles Shall Not Have Power Over The House of Israel (3 Ne. 16:12-14)

In the vivid prophecies concerning events yet future made by the resurrected Christ, repentance plays the determining role concerning the escape or fall of the Gentiles. In the approaching era of great wickedness,[3] as the Gentiles are about to suffer the wrath of the remnant of Jacob,[4] the great need for repentance among the Gentiles is described:

> ...*I will show unto thee, O house of Israel, that the Gentiles shall not have power over you;* but I will remember my covenant unto you, O house of Israel, and ye shall come unto the knowledge of the fulness of my gospel.
>
> But *if the Gentiles will repent and return unto me,* saith the Father, *behold they shall be numbered among my people,* O house of Israel.
>
> *And I will not suffer my people, who are of the house of Israel, to go through among them, and tread them down,* saith the Father.[5]

The Savior's Warning: A Remnant of Jacob Will Tread Down and Tear the Unrepentant Gentiles (3 Ne. 20:14-16)

In the second of His three great prophecies describing this future event, the Lord portrays the necessity of repentance even

---

1. 1 Ne. 14:9-17. Note the chronological relationship of verse 17: it is in the era that judgments are to be poured out upon this great church that the major period of the gathering of Israel begins (see 3 Ne. 20:22, 27-46; 21:1-29).
2. 1 Ne. 14:5-6. Note that the next verse alludes to some important but undefined future event which will clearly separate the people into these two groups, the repentant and unrepentant.
3. See 3 Ne. 16:10.
4. See 3 Ne. 16:15, 20:16-17, 21:12-19.
5. 3 Ne. 16:12-14.

more vividly. While speaking unto the Book of Mormon descendants of the House of Israel He warned that

> ...The Father hath commanded me that I should give unto you this
> land, for your inheritance.
>
> And I say unto you, that *if the Gentiles do not repent after the
> blessing which they shall receive,* after they have scattered my people—
> *Then shall ye, who are a remnant of the house of Jacob, go forth
> among them; and ye shall be in the midst of them who shall be many;*
> and ye shall be among them as a lion among the beasts of the forest,
> and *as a young lion among the flocks of sheep, who, if he goeth through
> both treadeth down and teareth in pieces, and none can deliver....*
>
> And it shall come to pass, saith the Father, that *the sword of my
> justice shall hang over them at that day; and except they repent it shall
> fall upon them,* saith the Father, yea, even upon all the nations of the
> Gentiles.[1]

The Savior then foretold that blessings to the Gentiles would
make them "mighty above all," but warned that "when they shall
have received the fulness of my gospel, then *if they shall harden their
hearts against me I will return their iniquities upon their own
heads,* saith the Father."[2]

The Savior's Warning: He Will Cut Off the Unrepentant
and Execute Vengeance and Fury Upon Them (3 Ne. 21:20-22)

Again, in His third prophecy depicting this great series of
future events, the Master emphasized the need for repentance
among the Gentiles in the era when the remnant of Jacob will
move against them. He warned that "*...wo be unto the Gentiles
except they repent;* for it shall come to pass in that day, saith the
Father, that *I will cut off thy horses out of the midst of thee, and
I will destroy thy chariots;...*"[3] Yet repentance will provide the
means of bringing some of the Gentiles to dwell among the Saints:

> For it shall come to pass, saith the Father, that at that day *whosoever
> will not repent and come unto my Beloved Son, them will I cut off from
> among my people, O house of Israel;*

---

1. 3 Ne. 20:14-16, 20. Note that in this passage, as in 1 Ne. 14:5-17, the
   need for repentance and the impending judgments pertain to "all the
   nations of the Gentiles." Though much of this chapter pertains specifically to the inhabitants of the Americas, the international scope of this
   warning should not be overlooked.
2. 3 Ne. 20:27-28.
3. 3 Ne. 21:14. See also verse 6.

> *And I will execute vengeance and fury upon them,* even as upon
> the heathen, such as they have not heard.
>
> But *if they will repent and hearken unto my words, and harden not
> their hearts, I will establish my church among them,* and they shall
> come in unto the covenant and be numbered among this the remnant of
> Jacob, unto whom I have given this land for their inheritance;... [1]

Mormon's Admonition to Last Days' Gentiles: Repent of Your Evil Doings (3 Ne. 30:2)

After receiving revealed insights concerning the Gentiles in
the last days, the prophet Mormon responded in this manner to
God's command that he admonish them to repent in his writings:

> *Turn, all ye Gentiles, from your wicked ways; and repent of your
> evil doings,* of your *lyings* and *deceivings,* and of your *whoredoms,* and
> of your *secret abominations,* and your *idolatries,* and of your *murders,*
> and your *priestcrafts,* and your *envyings,* and your *strifes,* and from
> *all your wickedness and abominations,* and come unto me, and be
> baptized in my name, that ye may receive a remission of your sins,
> and be filled with the Holy Ghost, that ye may be numbered with my
> people who are of the house of Israel. [2]

Repentance Necessary to Escape Destruction: Book of Mormon Examples

Examples of repentance being necessary to escape destruction
constitute a major message of the Book of Mormon. The inhabitants
of Jerusalem were warned that they must repent or suffer the
destruction of their city. [3] Nephi's wicked brothers found that

---

1. 3 Ne. 21:20-22. Note Nephi's prediction that "as many of the Gentiles
   as will repent are the covenant people of the Lord." (See 2 Ne. 30:1-2.)
   In Alma's day only the repentant were numbered among the people
   (Mos. 26:30-32. See Al. 6:3.).
2. 3 Ne. 30:2. The prophet Alma had previously warned of the danger of
   procrastinating repentance. He wrote:

   ...I beseech of you that ye do not procrastinate the day of your repentance until the end;...

   Ye cannot say, when ye are brought to that awful crisis, that I will
   repent, that I will return to my God....

   For behold, if ye have procrastinated the day of your repentance
   even until death, behold, ye have become subjected to the spirit of the
   devil, and he doth seal you his;... (Al. 34:33-35).
3. 1 Ne. 1:4.

"the judgments of God were upon them, and that they must perish save they should repent of their iniquities" [1] when they bound Nephi during their ocean crossing. Jacob warned the Nephites that "except ye repent the land is cursed for your sakes," and prophesied that the Lamanites would scourge them "even unto destruction." [2] Abinadi warned the priests of the wicked King Noah that "except they repent in sackcloth and ashes, and cry mightily to the Lord their God" the Lord would deliver them into the hands of their enemies and would not hear their prayers nor deliver them from their afflictions. [3] Alma was sent by an angel to warn the people of the city of Ammonihah that "except they repent the Lord God will destroy them."[4]

Near the time of the birth of Christ, the missionaries, Nephi and Lehi, preached and prophesied to the people "what should come unto them if they did not repent of their sins."[5] Later Nephi returned to the land of Zarahemla and observed the great wickedness of the people even there at the center of the church. With the cry, "O repent ye, repent ye! Why will ye die?" [6] he warned that they would be utterly destroyed unless they repent:

> ...Wo shall come unto you except ye shall repent. For if ye will not repent, behold, this great city, and also all those great cities which are round about, which are in the land of our possession, shall be taken away that ye shall have no place in them; for behold, the Lord will not grant unto you strength, as he has hitherto done, to withstand against your enemies.
>
> For behold, thus saith the Lord: I will not show unto the wicked of my strength, to one more than the other, save it be unto those who repent of their sins, and hearken unto my words. Now therefore, I would that ye should behold, my brethren, that it shall be better for the Lamanites than for you except ye shall repent.
>
> For behold, they are more righteous than you, for they have not sinned against that great knowledge which ye have received; therefore the Lord will be merciful unto them; yea, he will lengthen out their days and increase their seed, even when thou shalt be utterly destroyed except thou shalt repent. [7]

---

1. 1 Ne. 18:15.
2. Jac. 3:3-4.
3. Mos. 11:20-21, 25. He warned them, in even harsher terms, of famine, pestilence, hail, insects, and complete destruction. See Mos. 12:1-8.
4. Al. 8:15-16. The reason for the warning is significant: "They do study at this time that they may destroy the liberty of thy people." (verse 17.) See also Al. 8:29.
5. Hel. 4:14. Because of his warning, the people repented and began to prosper.
6. Hel. 7:17. See verses 19-21.
7. Hel. 7:22-24. See verses 25-29; 9:22, 10:11-12, 14; 15:17.

Samuel the Lamanite looked four hundred years into the future and warned that only repentance would save the Nephites from utter destruction:

> ...the sword of justice hangeth over this people; and four hundred years pass not away save the sword of justice falleth upon this people.
>
> Yea, heavy destruction awaiteth this people, and it surely cometh unto this people, and *nothing can save this people save it be repentance and faith on the Lord Jesus Christ,...* [1]

When the time for the fulfillment of Samuel's prophecy drew near, Mormon recorded that *"notwithstanding the great destruction which hung over my people, they did not repent of their evil doings; therefore there was blood and carnage spread throughout* all the face of the land." [2]

These examples should suffice to indicate that God has required repentance of the inhabitants of the Americas throughout Book of Mormon history. When the people have abandoned their wickedness, they have been preserved and blessed. When they have not repented, God has visited them in His wrath with bondage, suffering, and even with total destruction. When these prophetic warnings speak so clearly of the need for repentance in the last days, recognition of the need for repentance as a criterion for the preservation of this nation is an absolute necessity.

Summary

1. Book of Mormon prophecies repeatedly warn of a last days period when there will be great wickedness among the people of America. At that day, according to the prophecies, the people

---

1. Hel. 13:5-6. See also verses 8-10. He made a similar warning to those of his day. See verses 11-13 and 3 Ne. 9:1-2.
2. Morm. 2:8. He wrote to his son concerning the effects of his preaching upon the unrepentant Nephites:

   ...I fear lest the Lamanites shall destroy this people; for *they do not repent, and Satan stirreth them up continually to anger one with another.*

   Behold, I am laboring with them continually; and *when I speak the word of God with sharpness they tremble and anger against me;* and *when I use no sharpness they harden their hearts against it;* wherefore, I fear lest *the Spirit of the Lord hath ceased striving with them.*

   For so exceedingly do they anger that it seemeth me that *they have no fear of death;* and *they have lost their love,* one towards another; and they *thirst after blood and revenge continually.* (Moro. 9:3-5).

must repent or they will be destroyed. If they do repent, however, they will be spared and blessed.

2. Prophetic warnings concerning a need for repentance to avert judgments from God in the last days were cited from:

    A.   Alma (Al. 37:22-25).
    B.   Nephi (2 Ne. 28:16-17).
    C.   Nephi (1 Ne. 14:5-6).
    D.   The Savior (3 Ne. 16:12-14).
    E.   The Savior (3 Ne. 20:14-16).
    F.   The Savior (3 Ne. 21:20-22).

3. The scriptures frequently indicate that there will be great wickedness among the Gentiles in the last days, and give details concerning the nature and extent of their wickedness:

    A.   Secret works of darkness, wickedness and abominations (Al. 37:22).
    B.   All have gone astray save a few humble followers of Christ (2 Ne. 28:14).
    C.   They turn aside the just for a thing of naught (2 Ne. 28:16).
    D.   They revile against good, saying it has no worth (2 Ne. 28:16).
    E.   In the day they are fully ripe in iniquity they shall perish (2 Ne. 28:16).
    F.   The Gentiles will deny Christ (2 Ne. 28:32).
    G.   Gentiles may harden their hearts (3 Ne. 20:28; 21:22).
    H.   The Gentiles wicked ways: lyings, deceivings, whoredoms, secret abominations, idolatries, murders, priestcrafts, envyings, strifes (3 Ne. 30:2).

4. The Savior, in three separate passages, warns that a remnant of Jacob [the Lamanite] will tread down and tear the unrepentant Gentiles in the last days, and none can deliver them (3 Ne. 16:12-14; 20:14-16, 20; 21:12-21).

5. The Gentiles will not have power over the House of Israel in the day that God remembers His covenant with Israel (3 Ne. 16:12-14).

6. The impending last days' judgments pertain to all the nations of the Gentiles, not just to the Gentiles in the Americas (3 Ne. 20:20; 1 Ne. 14:5-17).

7. Mormon admonished the Gentiles of the last days to turn from their wicked ways by coming unto Christ, being baptized, receiving a remission of sins and the Holy Ghost, and being numbered among the house of Israel (3 Ne. 30:2).

8. There is a danger in procrastinating repentance, for Satan may seal you his as death approaches (Al. 34:33-35).

9. Examples of repentance being necessary to escape destruction were cited from the Book of Mormon:

A.   The inhabitants of Jerusalem (1 Ne. 1:4).
B.   Laman and Lemuel (1 Ne. 18:15).
C.   The wicked Nephites (Jac. 3:3-4).
D.   The city of Ammonihah (Al. 8:15-16).
E.   Nephites shortly before the birth of Christ (Hel. 4:14).
F.   The city of Zarahemla (Hel. 7:17-24).
G.   The final generation of Nephites (Hel. 13:5-6; Morm. 2:8).

10. One reason the unrepentant reap God's judgments is that they seek to destroy the liberty of His people (Al. 8:17).

11. The nearness of destruction does not necessarily cause people to repent. The wicked tend to be angry, hard of heart, lack fear of death, have no love, and seek for blood and revenge (Moro. 9:3-5).

12. When people become wicked, God withholds His strength from them (Hel. 7:22-23), withdraws His Spirit (Moro. 9:4), and prevents His prophets from preaching to them (Morm. 1:16-17).

Fifth Warning: VIII
If The People Fight Against Zion, They Will Be Destroyed

Jacob's Warning: Gentiles Who Fight Against Zion Shall be Destroyed (2 Ne. 6:12-15)

The prophet Jacob added another important item to the list of prophetic warnings found in the Book of Mormon concerning the future. He warned that in the last days, in the era of the return of the House of Israel to the lands of their inheritance, [1] there would be those who would fight against the Lord's people. He foresaw the destruction that would come upon those who would fight against Zion, and described it in this manner. Again, his words are in the nature of conditional prophecy: *if* the people don't fight against Zion, they'll be saved; *if* they do, they will be destroyed:

> And *blessed are the Gentiles*, they of whom the prophet has written; for behold, *if it so be that they shall repent and fight not against Zion*, and do not unite themselves to that great and abominable church, they shall be saved; for the Lord God will fulfill his covenants which he has made unto his children; and for this cause the prophet has written these things.
>
> Wherefore, *they that fight against Zion and the covenant people of the Lord shall lick up the dust of their feet; and the people of the Lord shall not be ashamed.* For the people of the Lord are they who wait for him; for they still wait for the coming of the Messiah.
>
> And behold, according to the words of the prophet, the Messiah will set himself again the second time to recover them; wherefore, he will manifest himself unto them in power and great glory, *unto the destruction of their enemies*, when that day cometh when they shall believe in him; and none will he destroy that believe in him.
>
> And *they that believe not in him shall be destroyed, both by fire, and by tempest, and by earthquakes, and by bloodsheds, and by pestilence, and by famine.* And they shall know that the Lord is God, the Holy One of Israel. [2]

---

1. 2 Ne. 6:11.
2. 2 Ne. 6:12-15.

Nephi's Warning: All That Fight Against Zion Shall be Destroyed (1 Ne. 22:14, 19)

Nephi also taught this principle concerning the last days, saying that *"all that fight against Zion shall be destroyed,"*[1] and teaching that "the righteous shall not perish; for the time surely must come that *all they who fight against Zion shall be cut off.*"[2]

And who, or what, or where, is Zion? The scriptures speak of three Zions which are to exist in the last days:

1. The city of Jerusalem, in Israel,
2. The city of the New Jerusalem, to be built in Jackson County, Missouri,
3. The Lord's people who are pure in heart.

Zion—the City of Jerusalem

When Bible and Book of Mormon passages speak of Zion, they almost always have reference to the city of Jerusalem in Israel and the area which surrounds it. Zion was the name of the Jebusite fortress which David conquered and made his capital in Old Testament times, as is described in Second Samuel, chapter 5:

> David was thirty years old when he began to reign and he reigned forty years.
>
> In Hebron he reigned over Judah seven years and six months: and in Jerusalem he reigned thirty and three years over all Israel and Judah.
>
> And *the king and his men went to Jerusalem unto the Jebusites, the inhabitants of the land:* which spake unto David, saying, Except thou take away the blind and the lame, thou shalt not come in hither; thinking, David cannot come in hither.
>
> Nevertheless *David took the stronghold of Zion: the same is the city of David.*[3]

---

1. 1 Ne. 22:14. Note that this destruction is related to the fall of the great and abominable church. This relationship is considered further in the chapter.
2. 1 Ne. 22:19.
3. 2 Sam. 5:4-7. There is no question among Bible scholars that Zion is a synonym for Jerusalem. For instance, the listing for *Zion* in the *Dictionary of the Bible* (ed. by James Hastings, revised ed. by Frederick C. Grant and H. H. Rowley; New York: Charles Scribner's Sons, 1963, p. 1058), says: "ZION (AV Sion in NT).—*The name of the fortress of the pre-Israelite city of Jerusalem* (2 S 57), which was conquered by David and made his capital. *The name is frequently used in the Psalms and the Prophets as a synonym for Jerusalem.*"
   Merrill Unger, in *Unger's Bible Handbook* (Chicago: Moody Press, 1966, p. 202) explains further: "The towns of Jerusalem had been taken in the time of the judges (Jud. 1:8), but not the stronghold of

the Jebusites. *This was the southeast hill, later called the city of David or Zion.* Zion is closely connected with David's being made king over all Israel."

The Bible Dictionary of the Cambridge Bible (specially bound for The Church of Jesus Christ of Latter-day Saints, 1950) in its article says:

Zion, or 'the city of David' (2 S. 5. 7-9), one of the hills of Jerusalem on which the Temple stood. The sanctity of Z. may be accounted for by the fact that it was for many years the resting place of the Ark; *Z. thus became the sacred name for the whole city,* and on the return from Exile may have been specially applied to the Temple Mount, though this was not the original Zion.

The Westminster Historical Atlas to the Bible, by George Ernest Wright and Floyd Vivian Filson (Philadelphia: The Westminster Press, 1946, p. 97), describes the topography of early Jerusalem in this manner:

The location of the water supply determined that the earliest settlements should be located on the Eastern Hill, south of the Temple area and above the Gihon spring. In ancient times this hill was called, in its northern part at least, Ophel (XVII:A D-E 5; Micah 4:8, R.V. marg.; II Chron. 27:3, 33:14; Neh. 3:26f; 11:21). *This was also the site of the City of David, or Zion, and of the Jebusite city before it.* This part of the Eastern Hill is not formidable in appearance, and since the fourth century A.D. tradition has associated Zion with the southern part of the Western Hill, where guides still show tourists the traditional Tomb of David (XVII:D, C-6). Archaeological investigation, however, has proved that Zion was south of the Temple area, as indeed it had to be in order to be near its water supply. In Old Testament times it was higher than at present; the Hasmonaeans in the second century B.C. removed the top of the Eastern Hill in order that it might not rival the Temple in height.

A recent work by an LDS author, LaMar C. Berrett, *Discovering the World of the Bible* (Provo, Utah: Brigham Young University Press, 1973, p. 281), adds other insights:

Mount Zion ("fortress"). Zion was the name of the citadel of the Jebusite city of Jerusalem, captured by David. Today, tradition (probably in error) says this was on the southwest hill of the city. Zion was also a title applied to the temple area. The present traditional site of Mount Zion is on a hill close to the southwest corner of the old walled city. In A.D. 340, a large basilica, called Hagia Zion, was built on the mount and it was probably from this building that the mount received its name. The basilica was destroyed by the Persians in 614. This area was once within the city wall, and is very sacred to the Jews because they believe David is buried here. On the slope of Mount Zion is a Protestant cemetery in which Sir Flinders Petrie, the noted archaelogist, is buried.

He then cites Biblical references pertaining to Zion:

The ark was carried from here to the temple (1 Kings 8:1; 2 Chron. 5:2).

"Out of Zion shall go forth the law" (Isa. 2:3).

Mount Zion was spoken of as Temple Hill (Isa. 8:18; Jer. 31:6; Mic. 4:7).

Zion was the name of the whole city (Ps. 102:21; Mic. 3:10-12).

Here Jesus was taken before Annas and Caiaphas (Matt. 26:3-5, 57-75; John 18:12-24).

Here Peter denied Jesus at the palace of Caiaphas (Matt. 26:59-75; Luke 22:54-62).

Solomon expanded Jerusalem to the north and encompassed Mt. Moriah, the area where Solomon's temple was built. He moved the ark of the covenant from Zion to the new temple location in the city (1 Ki: 8:1, 2 Chron. 5:2) but the term Zion remained a synonym for Jerusalem and was frequently used in that manner (see Ps. 51:18; 147:12; Is. 2:3; 33:20; 40:9; 41:27; 51:16-17; 52:1, 7-9; 62:1; 64:10; Jer. 4:6, 14; 26:18; 51:35; Lam. 1:17; Amos 1:2; Mi. 3:10, 12; 4:2; Zech. 1:14, 17; 8:3).[1] In many other passages, the term Zion is used in a historical or a prophetic sense which clearly applies to Jerusalem.[2]

Zion—the New Jerusalem

Passages referring to Zion in the Doctrine and Covenants usually have reference to the city to be known as the New Jerusalem, which is to be built in Jackson County, Missouri in the last days.

3 Ne. 21:14-29 clearly establishes the building of this city in close chronological proximity to the destruction of many of the Gentiles by the remnant of Jacob and just prior to the major period of the gathering of Israel worldwide.

As He described the New Jerusalem in the last days, the Lord said that

---

1. In almost all of these references, the passages have been examples of *Synonymous Parallelism*, a characteristic form of Hebrew poetry. In this poetic style,

    The second line restates the first, not merely by repetition, however, as in many of the Near Eastern liturgies, but by enriching, deepening, and even transforming it with new words, by adding fresh nuances, and by giving it a symmetry and balance, as in

    > O Lord, who shall sojourn in thy tent?
    >   Who shall dwell on thy holy hill?—(Ps 15[1])

    or

    > The heavens are telling the glory of God;
    >   and the firmament proclaims his handiwork.—(Ps 19[1])

    (Hastings, *Dictionary of the Bible, op. cit.*, p. 779.)

2. Many biblical references cited or repeated in the Book of Mormon fall into these categories: 1 Ne. 21:14-21, for instance, refers to Jerusalem in its desolate state prior to the gathering of Israel, as does 2 Ne. 8:3, 11, 16-17. Zion (Jerusalem) putting on her strength (2 Ne. 8:24; 3 Ne. 20:36) is interpreted in a last days setting in D & C 113:7-10 in relation to the redemption of Israel, etc.

...it shall be called the New Jerusalem, a land of peace, *a city of refuge, a place of safety for the saints of the Most High God;*

And the glory of the Lord shall be there, and the terror of the Lord also shall be there, insomuch that *the wicked will not come unto it, and it shall be called Zion.* [1]

In 1831 the Lord revealed that Independence, Missouri was the exact place for the city to be built, and designated that location as an "everlasting inheritance." [2]

Some of the early saints moved to this area but were subsequently driven out by mobs. The Lord rebuked the saints for disobedience [3] and said that

...in consequence of the transgressions of my people, it is expedient in me that *mine elders should wait for a little season for the redemption of Zion—*

That they themselves may *be prepared*, and that my people may *be taught more perfectly*, and *have experience*, and *know more perfectly concerning their duty*, and the things which I require at their hands. [4]

Further instruction from the Lord has led the Saints to believe that the New Jerusalem will be regained in a time of conflict and unrest. The Savior has said:

For behold, I do not require at their hands to fight the battles of Zion; for, as I said in a former commandment, even so will I fulfil—*I will fight your battles.*

Behold, *the destroyer I have sent forth to destroy and lay waste mine enemies; and not many years hence they shall not be left to pollute mine heritage*, and to blaspheme my name upon the lands which I have consecrated for the gathering together of my saints. [5]

And also:

Behold, I say unto you, *the redemption of Zion must needs come by power;*

Therefore, I will raise up unto my people a man, who shall lead them like as Moses led the children of Israel.

For ye are the children of Israel, and of the seed of Abraham, and *ye must needs be led out of bondage by power, and with a stretched-out arm.*

And as your fathers were led at the first, *even so shall the redemption of Zion be.* [6]

---

1. D & C 45:66-67.
2. D & C 57:1-5. See D & C 84:2-5.
3. D & C 105:1-8.
4. D & C 105:9-10.
5. D & C 105:14-15.
6. D & C 103:15-18.

And concerning the New Jerusalem when it is finally established:

> And *it shall come to pass among the wicked, that every man that will not take his sword against his neighbor must needs flee unto Zion for safety.*
> And there shall be gathered unto it out of every nation under heaven; and it shall be the only people that shall not be at war one with another.
> And it shall be said among the wicked: Let us not go up to battle against Zion, for the inhabitants of Zion are terrible; wherefore we cannot stand,
> And it shall come to pass that *the righteous shall be gathered out from among all nations, and shall come to Zion,* singing with songs of everlasting joy....
> For when the Lord shall appear he shall be terrible unto them, that fear may seize upon them, and they shall stand afar off and tremble.
> And *all nations shall be afraid because of the terror of the Lord,* and the power of his might. [1]

Zion—the Pure in Heart

A revelation in 1833 indicated that Zion was not only a name for geographical places, but also a name for people. This revelation also indicated that the Zion people would exist in the last days' era of terrible calamities:

> Therefore, verily, thus saith the Lord, let Zion rejoice, for *this is Zion—THE PURE IN HEART;* therefore, let Zion rejoice, while *all the wicked shall mourn.*
> For behold, and lo, *vengeance cometh speedily upon the ungodly* as the whirlwind; and who shall escape it?
> *The Lord's scourge shall pass over by night and by day,* and the report thereof shall vex all people; yea, it shall not be stayed until the Lord come;
> *For the indignation of the Lord is kindled against their abominations and all their wicked works.* [2]

Fight Against Zion, a Worldwide Conflict
Against the House of Israel and the Church

To which of these Zions do the Book of Mormon warnings refer? It appears that all three, God's people and both places of

---

1. D & C 45:68-71, 74-75. See also D & C 97:18-20.
2. D & C 97:21-24. Biblical passages occasionally use the term "Zion" in reference to the Lord's people, as in Zech. 2:6-8.

gathering, are involved in the period of this great conflict. Jacob, in 2 Ne. 6:13-14, seems to refer to Zion as the covenant people of the Lord who are being recovered for the second time and "gathered again to the lands of their inheritance." [1] Nephi, in connection with his warning that all that fight against Zion will be destroyed, observes that *"every nation which shall war against thee, O house of Israel,* shall be turned one against another, and they shall fall into the pit which they digged to ensnare the people of the Lord." [2] He links the fall of these nations with the collapse of the great and abominable church in the same verse. His description of this event is of the wrath of God being poured out upon the earth by blood, smoke, and fire:

> For behold, saith the prophet, the time cometh speedily that Satan shall have no more power over the hearts of the children of men; for the day soon cometh that all the proud and they who do wickedly shall be as stubble; and the day cometh that they must be burned.
>
> For the time soon cometh that *the fulness of the wrath of God shall be poured out upon all the children of men; for he will not suffer that the wicked shall destroy the righteous.*
>
> Wherefore, *he will preserve the righteous by his power,* even if it so be that the fulness of his wrath must come, and the righteous be preserved, *even unto the destruction of their enemies by fire.* Wherefore, the righteous need not fear; for thus saith the prophet, they shall be saved, even if it so be as by fire.
>
> Behold, my brethren, I say unto you, that these things must shortly come; *yea, even blood, and fire, and vapor of smoke must come;* and it must needs be upon the face of this earth; and it cometh unto men according to the flesh if it so be that they will harden their hearts against the Holy One of Israel.
>
> For behold, *the righteous shall not perish; for the time surely must come that all they who fight against Zion shall be cut off.* [3]

This account bears similarities to Nephi's earlier description of the "wars and rumors of wars among all the nations which belonged to the mother of abominations." [4] These wars, it appears, will result from the actions of the "great mother of abominations" who will *"gather together multitudes upon the face of all the earth, among all the nations of the Gentiles, to fight against the Lamb of God."*[5] At that time, according to Nephi's vision, there will be two groups who will be granted protective power from God: "the saints of

---

1. 2 Ne. 6:13-14, and also verse 11.
2. 1 Ne. 22:14.
3. 1 Ne. 22:15-19.

4. 1 Ne. 14:16. See 14:10-17.
5. 1 Ne. 14:13.

the church of the Lamb," and "the covenant people who were scattered upon all the face of the earth." [1] It appears that both the Lord's Church and the entire house of Israel, both scattered throughout the world, will bear the onslaught of Satan's forces fighting against Zion.

Jacob's Warning: The Whore of the Earth that Fights Against Zion Shall Perish (2 Ne. 10:11-16)

Jacob locates some of this conflict in the Americas, and associates it with the influence of "the whore of all the earth:"

> ...This land shall be a land of liberty unto the Gentiles, and there shall be no kings upon the land, who shall raise up unto the Gentiles.
> *And I will fortify this land against all other nations.*
> *And he that fighteth against Zion shall perish*, saith God.
> For he that raiseth up a king against me shall perish, for I, the Lord, the king of heaven, will be their king, and I will be a light unto them forever, that hear my words.
> Wherefore, for this cause, that my covenants may be fulfilled which I have made unto the children of men, that I will do unto them while they are in the flesh, *I must needs destroy the secret works of darkness, and of murders, and of abominations.*
> *Wherefore, he that fighteth against Zion, both Jew and Gentile, both bond and free, both male and female, shall perish; for they are they who are the whore of all the earth; for they who are not for me are against me, saith our God.* [2]

Nephi's Warning: The Nations that Fight Against Zion will be Visited with Earthquake, Storm, and Devouring Fire (2 Ne. 27:1-5)

Nephi saw that the wickedness and judgments of this era will involve "those who shall come upon this land and those who shall be upon other lands, yea, even upon all the lands of the earth," and that the judgments will involve "all the nations that fight against Zion:"

> But behold, *in the last days, or in the days of the Gentiles*—yea, behold all the nations of the Gentiles and also the Jews, *both those who shall come upon this land and those who shall be upon other lands, yea, even upon all the lands of the earth, behold, they will be drunken with iniquity and all manner of abominations*—

---

1. 1 Ne. 14:14.
2. 2 Ne. 10:11-16.

And when that day shall come they shall be visited of the Lord of Hosts, with *thunder* and with *earthquake*, and with a *great noise*, and with *storm*, and with *tempest*, and with *the flame of devouring fire*.
   And all the nations that fight against Zion, and that distress her, shall be as a dream of a night vision; yea, it shall be unto them, even as unto a hungry man which dreameth, and behold he eateth but he awaketh and his soul is empty; or like unto a thirsty man which dreameth, and behold he drinketh but he awaketh and behold he is faint, and his soul hath appetite; *yea, even so shall the multitude of all the nations be that fight against Mount Zion*.
   For behold, all ye that doeth iniquity, stay yourselves and wonder, for ye shall cry out, and cry; yea, ye shall be drunken but not with wine, ye shall stagger but not with strong drink.
   For behold, the Lord hath poured out upon you the spirit of deep sleep. For behold, ye have closed your eyes, and *ye have rejected the prophets; and your rulers, and the seers hath he covered because of your iniquity*. [1]

Nephi's Warning: Those Who Fight Against His People Israel will be Shown the Lord is God (2 Ne. 29:12-14)

Nephi's predictions show that the future conflict will involve a fight against God's word and God's people, and will come in a period when other sacred records will have come to light:

For behold, I shall speak unto the *Jews* and they shall write it; and I shall also speak unto the *Nephites* and they shall write it; and I shall also speak unto the *other tribes of the house of Israel, which I have led away*, and they shall write it; and I shall also speak unto *all nations of the earth* and they shall write it.
   And it shall come to pass that the Jews shall have the words of the Nephites, and the Nephites shall have the words of the Jews; and the Nephites and the Jews shall have the words of the lost tribes of Israel; and the lost tribes of Israel shall have the words of the Nephites and the Jews.
   And it shall come to pass that *my people, which are of the house of Israel, shall be gathered home unto the lands of their possessions; and my word also shall be gathered in one. And I will show unto them that fight against my word and against my people, who are of the house of Israel, that I am God*, and that I covenanted with Abraham that I would remember his seed forever. [2]

Thus it appears that the future conflict in which many will fight against Zion will be international in scope. It will involve the tribes of Israel as they gather home to the lands of their inheritance.

---

1. 2 Ne. 27:1-5.
2. 2 Ne. 29:12-14.

It will involve the Church. It will involve the saints who participate in the return to the New Jerusalem. It will be Satan-inspired with a vast evil church leading much of the onslaught against the Lord's people. The conflict will culminate with the collapse of this great and abominable church, which is the subject of the next chapter.

Summary

1. A fifth principle which must be obeyed if America and the other Gentile nations are to escape future destruction is that they must not fight against Zion. Again, the principle is conditional: if the people don't fight against Zion, they will be saved; if they do, they will be destroyed.

2. Prophetic warnings on this theme are cited in this chapter:

A.   Jacob (2 Ne. 6:12-15)
B.   Nephi (1 Ne. 22:14, 19)
C.   Jacob (2 Ne. 10:11-16)
D.   Nephi (2 Ne. 27:1-5)
E.   Nephi (2 Ne. 29:12-14)

3. The destruction of those who fight against Zion will come by a variety of judgments: fire, tempest, earthquakes, bloodsheds, pestilence, famine, and nations warring among themselves (2 Ne. 6:12-15; 1 Ne. 22:14-19; D & C 45:68-69).

4. As the judgments are poured out, God will preserve the righteous while He destroys the wicked (2 Ne. 6:14; 1 Ne. 22:16, 19) and will fight the battles for the righteous (D & C 105:14-15; 45:74-75).

5. The fight against Zion will be instigated by the great and abominable church which is called the whore of all the earth (2 Ne. 6:12; 1 Ne. 22:14; 1 Ne. 14:13).

6. The conflict will be worldwide in scope, involving a multitude of nations including America (D & C 45:69; 1 Ne. 22:14; 1 Ne. 14:13, 16; 2 Ne. 27:1-4; 2 Ne. 10:11-16).

7. The scriptures speak of three Zions which will be in existence at the time of the great conflict:

A.   The city of Jerusalem, in Israel.

    B.   The city of the New Jerusalem, in Jackson County, Missouri.

    C.   The Lord's people who are pure in heart.

The great conflict will involve all three of them.

    8.   Zion is the name of the fortress of the pre-Israelite city of Jerusalem which David conquered from the Jebusites and made his capital, the "city of David." The term Zion has remained a synonym for Jerusalem and is frequently used in that manner in the Bible (particularly in instances of synonymous parallelism, a common Hebrew poetic form).

    9.   The city of the New Jerusalem, to be built in Jackson County, Missouri, will be

    A.   A land of peace (D & C 45:66).

    B.   A city of refuge (D & C 45:66).

    C.   A place of safety for the saints (D & C 45:66).

    D.   Protected from the wicked by the glory and terror of God which will be there (D & C 45:67).

    E.   Consecrated for the gathering of the saints (D & C 105:15).

    F.   Redeemed by power through a man God will raise up to lead the saints out of bondage (D & C 103:15-18).

    G.   A gathering place for those who won't fight against their neighbors (D & C 45:68).

    H.   A gathering place for righteous people of every nation (D & C 45:69, 71).

    I.   The only people not at war with one another (D & C 45:69).

    J.   A source of fear to the wicked (D & C 45:70, 74-75).

    10.   Zion also refers to people who are pure in heart as well as to the two geographical places mentioned above (D & C 97:21). This, apparently, embraces both righteous Church members and righteous members of the scattered House of Israel.

    11.   The Lord has revealed that a terrible scourge will come upon the wicked in the last days which will vex all people and which will continue until He comes (D & C 97:21-24).

    12.   As is seen in this chapter and later in this book, the fight against Zion will be so far-reaching that it will involve all three of

the Zions mentioned. The New Jerusalem Zion, apparently, will rise to power and will be strong enough to resist enemy onslaught. Both the Church and the House of Israel will be subjected to distress and Jerusalem will see much strife which will culminate in the Battle of Armageddon.

Sixth Warning: IX
The Great And Abominable Church Will Persecute The Saints

Jacob's Warning: To Be Saved, the Gentiles Must Not Unite with the Great and Abominable Church (2 Ne. 6:12)

In the same passage in which he warned of the fate of those who would fight against Zion in the last days, the prophet Jacob cautioned the Gentiles of the danger of affiliating with a great and abominable church. Avoiding unity with or participation in that body was one of the criteria he specified as being necessary for the Gentiles to be saved from God's judgments:

> And blessed are the Gentiles, they of whom the prophet has written; for behold, *if it so be that they shall repent and fight not against Zion, and do not unite themselves to that great and abominable church,* they shall be saved; for the Lord God will fulfill his covenants which he has made unto his children; and for this cause the prophet has written these things.[1]

Numerous scriptural passages foretell the existence in the last days of this great and abominable church which is depicted as being opposed to the true work of Christ. The identity of this organization is subject to many different interpretations—indeed, it has been the source of much controversy throughout the entire Christian world since the time of the Reformation. Its identity is especially of vital concern to Latter-day Saints, however, because of the numerous prophetic warnings concerning it found in the Book of Mormon.

Important to Be Forewarned of Future Danger to the Saints

In recent years some Latter-day Saints have been content to ignore the numerous scriptural warnings of the persecutions which this great world-wide organization will bring upon them. Yet signs of the times indicate that the prophesied conflict involving this

---

1. 2 Ne. 6:12.

great church is approaching. The time must soon come when the passive attitudes of yesterday must give way to the alertness necessary to preserve God's people. God, through His prophets, has revealed His warning of the oppressive role this abominable church will play in a broad scriptural pattern based on dozens of passages.[1] To refuse to ponder those revealed warnings, as to refuse to consider any pattern of revealed scripture, is a serious matter before the Lord.

This author does not seek to bring criticism nor create animosity towards any existing church or sect. Indeed, this chapter will contain no statement by the author which labels any existing church as being the fulfillment of the prophecies reported, nor will it advocate any action or procedure against any existing religious organization. If any sects impute offense against themselves from what is written herein, let them recall the proverb that "the wicked flee when no man pursueth."[2]

Past Activities of the Great and Abominable Church Recorded in Scriptures

The scriptures describe both the past and future activities of the great and abominable church in considerable detail. Nephi told of being visited by an angel who showed him its origin. The vision was part of a chronological overview which indicated that the time of the foundation of the church was to be following the ministry of Christ,[3] yet preceding the discovery and settling of America by Columbus and European Gentiles:[4]

---

1. In such a case, the Lord's warning through Ezekiel must be heeded:

   Son of man, speak to the children of thy people, and say unto them, When I bring the sword upon a land, if the people of the land take a man of their coasts, and set him for their watchman:

   If when he seeth the sword come upon the land, he blow the trumpet, and warn the people;

   Then whosoever heareth the sound of the trumpet, and taketh not warning; if the sword come, and take him away, his blood shall be upon his own head.

   He heard the sound of the trumpet, and took not warning; his blood shall be upon him. But he that taketh warning shall deliver his soul. (Ezek. 33:2-5)

2. Prov. 28:1. See also Lev. 26:17, 36-37.

3. See 1 Ne. 11:15-33; 12:6-10.

4. See 1 Ne. 13:10-14.

And it came to pass that I saw *among the nations of the Gentiles the foundation of a great church.*

And the angel said unto me: Behold the foundation of a church which is *most abominable above all other churches,* which *slayeth the saints of God,* yea, and *tortureth them* and *bindeth them down,* and yoketh them with a yoke of iron, and *bringeth them down into captivity.*

And it came to pass that I beheld this great and abominable church; and I saw the devil that he was the foundation of it.

And I also saw gold, and silver, and silks, and scarlets, and fine-twined linen, and all manner of precious clothing; and I saw many harlots.

And the angel spake unto me, saying: Behold the gold, and the silver, and the silks, and the scarlets, and the fine-twined linen, and the precious clothing, and the harlots, are the desires of this great and abominable church.

And also for the praise of the world do *they destroy the saints of God, and bring them down into captivity.*[1]

The above passage is meaningful in its rich detail. It locates the foundation of the church as being centered in the nations of the Gentiles,[2] or European nations. It clearly identifies the organization as actually being a church and not just general wickedness, and specifies that in the era prior to the settling of America it is "most abominable above all other churches."[3] The passage characterizes the church as using fine and precious clothing,[4] being

---

1. 1 Ne. 13:4-9.

2. It is from these Gentile nations that America is settled (1 Ne. 13:10-19). Hence the conclusion that the Gentile nations are the nations of Europe. Orson Pratt equated the Gentile nations with "the nations of Christendom." (See JD, 7:186.) In prophetic terminology the Gentile nations are contrasted with the heathen, or non-Christian nations.

3. Note the approximate dates of the formation of some of the earliest "other churches" in Christianity:

Mennonites (1525)	(Swiss brethren)
Evangelical Lutherans (1526)	(Luther, Melanchthon)
Church of England (1533)	(Henry VIII)
Anabaptist (1534)	(Phillips, Simons)
Reformed Churches (1536)	(Calvin, Zwingle, Knox)
Presbyterians (1559)	(Calvin, Zwingle, Bucer)
Congregationalists (1560)	(English brethren)
Quakers (1666)	(Fox)
Methodists (1739)	(Wesley, Whitefield)

4. How expensive is clerical garb? A 1967 AP News dispatch gives some indication of the expense involved for one denomination:

ROME (AP)—The ecclesiastical tailors of Rome were busy Saturday making final adjustments on the new scarlet garments for 27 new cardinals being elevated by Pope Paul VI in consistory Monday.

involved with harlotry,[1] and begins the warning theme that this church would eventually slay the saints, torture them, bind them, bring them into captivity, and destroy many of them.[2] These evil deeds will be done in a world climate of antagonism against the the Lord's people, when persecuting the saints will bring "the praise of the world."[3] Nephi leaves no doubt about the origin of this church: the devil is its founder.[4]

Nephi's vision contained other insights concerning the identity of the great and abominable church. He saw the writings which were to be the Bible come forth from the Jews[5] and that they were carried forth in purity by the Savior's twelve apostles.[6] The vision then indicated that that period immediately following the labors of the twelve in the meridian of time would be the time of the great church's beginning,[7] and that the church would take away many portions of both Christ's gospel[8] and the book that was to become the Bible.[9] According to the vision, the great and abominable church would take away these truths before the Bible would go forth to the Gentile nations and before the Bible would be brought to the Americas:[10]

Wherefore, *these things go forth from the Jews in purity unto the Gentiles*, according to the truth which is in God.

And *after they go forth by the hand of the twelve apostles* of the Lamb, from the Jews unto the Gentiles, *thou seest the foundation of a great and abominable church, which is most abominable above all other*

1. 1 Ne. 13:7.
2. 1 Ne. 13:5, 9.
3. 1 Ne. 13:9.
4. 1 Ne. 13:6
5. 1 Ne. 13:20-24.
6. 1 Ne. 13:25-26.
7. 1 Ne. 13:26.
8. 1 Ne. 13:26.
9. 1 Ne. 13:28.
10. 1 Ne. 13:29.

What does it cost to dress a cardinal in the rich red cassock and cape and buckled shoes that go with his princely rank in the Roman Catholic Church?

At least $1,400 is the figure given by one of Rome's best ecclesiastical outfitters—and that's only for a minimum wardrobe of 23 items, exclusive of ring and pectoral cross.

Most expensive item on the typical price list is the three-yard long scarlet silk "Capa Magna" or Great Cape. It goes for $176. Least costly is a Roman collar of red silk with square white cutout in front. They cost 80 cents.

The new cardinals are saving at least $448 thanks to papal-ordered changes just put into effect for simplifying the dress and protocol for all cardinals. ("Beau Cardinal Costs Less," Salt Lake Tribune, June 25, 1967.)

churches; for behold, *they have taken away from the gospel of the Lamb many parts which are plain and most precious; and also many covenants of the Lord have they taken away.*

And all this have they done that they might pervert the right ways of the Lord, that they might blind the eyes and harden the hearts of the children of men.

Wherefore, thou seest that after the book hath gone forth through the hands of the great and abominable church, that *there are many plain and precious things taken away from the book,* which is the book of the Lamb of God.

And *after these plain and precious things were taken away it goeth forth unto all the nations of the Gentiles;* and after it goeth forth unto all the nations of the Gentiles, yea, even across the many waters which thou hast seen with the Gentiles which have gone forth out of captivity, thou seest—because of the many plain and precious things which have been taken out of the book, which were plain unto the understanding of the children of men, according to the plainness which is in the Lamb of God—*because of these things which are taken away out of the gospel of the Lamb, an exceeding great many do stumble, yea, insomuch that Satan hath great power over them.* [1]

Nephi observes repeatedly that the withholding of gospel and scriptural truths by this great church would cause many to "stumble exceedingly[2] and be in an "awful state of blindness"[3] and be subject to Satan's power,[4] and that this effect would be manifest even before the Lord would bring forth His gospel and the Book of Mormon in the Americas.[5]

A "Great and a Marvelous Work" and the Lord's "Strange Act"— A Future Event Causing Men to Join Either the Church of God or the Church of the Devil

As the chronological prophetic picture left by Nephi sweeps from the past into the future,[6] a highly-significant change is to be noted concerning the identity of the great and abominable church. Nephi prophesies that some undefined event will cause men to move into two distinct factions which cause them to align themselves with either the church of the Lamb of God or with the church

---

1. 1 Ne. 13:25-29.
2. 1 Ne. 13:29, 34.
3. 1 Ne. 13:32.
4. 1 Ne. 13:29.
5. 1 Ne. 13:34-35.
6. Note that the chronological account moves past Gentile persecution of the American Indians (1 Ne. 13:30-31), the restoration of the gospel (1 Ne. 13:34), the coming forth of the Book of Mormon (1 Ne. 13:35-36, 39-41), and the preaching of the gospel to the Lamanites (1 Ne. 13:38).

of the devil. This devisive event, when *the Lord God shall cause a great division among the people, and the wicked shall he destroy,*[1] is called by an angel "a great and a marvelous work."[2] As a result of this event, men will no longer be lukewarm "fence-sitters," but will be moved to take a definite position either for or against the Lord's people. When this situation aligns men into opposing camps of good and evil, then *"whoso belongeth not to the church of the Lamb of God belongeth to that great church, which is the mother of abominations."*[3] This is the angel's prophecy recorded by Nephi:

> For *the time cometh,* saith the Lamb of God, that *I will work a great and a marvelous work among the children of men; a work which shall be everlasting, either on the one hand or on the other—either to the convincing of them unto peace and life eternal, or unto the deliverance of them to the hardness of their hearts* and the blindness of their minds unto their being *brought down into captivity, and also into destruction, both temporally and spiritually,* according to the captivity of the devil, of which I have spoken.
>
> And it came to pass that when the angel had spoken these words, he said unto me: Rememberest thou the covenants of the Father unto the house of Israel? I said unto him, Yea.
>
> And it came to pass that he said unto me: *Look, and behold that great and abominable church, which is the mother of abominations, whose foundation is the devil.*
>
> And he said unto me: *Behold there are save two churches only; the one is the church of the Lamb of God, and the other is the church of the devil; wherefore, whoso belongeth not to the church of the Lamb of God belongeth to that great church, which is the mother of abominations; and she is the whore of all the earth.*[4]

The term "marvelous work and a wonder" has sometimes been assumed to mean the restoration of the gospel,[5] but careful study of passages which use the term indicates the full meaning involves a future latter-day event related to the cataclysmic era surrounding the restoration of Israel.

---

1. 2 Ne. 30:10.
2. 1 Ne. 14:7.
3. 1 Ne. 14:10.
4. 1 Ne. 14:7-10.
5. For instance, Elder LeGrand Richards, in his useful and widely read missionary volume entitled "A Marvelous Work and A Wonder," assumes that the term refers to the "conundrum of Joseph Smith and the work he established," but offers no interpretational substantiation to justify his assumption, only a question after citing Isaiah 29:13-14: "How could this prediction possibly be more literally fulfilled than in the case of Joseph Smith and the work the Lord established through him?" (LeGrand Richards, *A Marvelous Work and A Wonder* (Salt Lake City, Utah: Deseret Book Company, 1953), pp. 364-365.)

The term "a marvelous work and a wonder" is rarely used in scripture. Its most frequently cited source is the 29th chapter of Isaiah, a chapter with clear allusions to at least three different periods of time.

Verses 1-6 seem to be a comparison of destruction in Jerusalem ("Ariel, the city where David dwelt," Is. 29:1) to the fall of the Nephites about 385 A.D. This comparison becomes clear when Is. 29:1-6 is considered in the light of 2 Ne. 26:14-18 and the fulfillment of the prophecy recorded in Mormon 6.[1]

Isaiah 29:11-13 apparently refers to the coming forth of the Book of Mormon to Joseph Smith, and the delivery of words from that manuscript to a scholar by the name of Charles Anthon. A comparison of Is. 29:11-13 with 2 Ne. 27:15-22 and J.S. 2:64-65 (in The Pearl of Great Price) will give understanding of these verses.[2]

A third event is also prophesied in Isaiah 29: a future campaign against Mount Zion by many nations. It is to this event that the term "marvelous work and a wonder" appears to be related. This event is to take place in an era when the love of God will be diminished upon the earth and the righteous will be persecuted by the wicked. Note the message of these verses selected from Isaiah 29:

> And *the multitude of all the nations that fight against Ariel [Jerusalem]*, even all that fight against her and her munition, and that distress her, shall be as a dream of a night vision.
>
> It shall even be as when an hungry man dreameth, and, behold, he eateth; but he awaketh, and his soul is empty: or as when a thirsty man dreameth, and, behold, he drinketh; but he awaketh, and, behold, he is faint, and his soul hath appetite: *so shall the multitude of all the nations be, that fight against mount Zion.*
>
> Stay yourselves, and wonder; cry ye out, and cry: they are drunken, but not with wine; they stagger, but not with strong drink.
>
> For the Lord hath poured out upon you the spirit of deep sleep, and hath closed your eyes: *the prophets and your rulers, the seers hath he covered....*
>
> Wherefore the Lord said, Forasmuch as this people draw near me with their mouth, and with their lips do honour me, but have removed their heart far from me, and their fear toward me is taught by the precept of men:
>
> Therefore, behold, *I will proceed to do a marvellous work among this people, even a marvellous work and a wonder: for the wisdom of their wise men shall perish, and the understanding of their prudent men shall be hid.*

1. For a discussion of these passages see the author's book, *The Prophecies of Joseph Smith* (Salt Lake City, Utah: Bookcraft, 1963), pp. 174-179.
2. See *The Prophecies of Joseph Smith*, pp. 76-86.

Woe unto them that seek deep to hide their counsel from the Lord, and their works are in the dark, and they say, Who seeth us? and who knoweth us?

Surely your *turning of things upside down* shall be esteemed as the potter's clay: for shall the work say of him that made it, He made me not? or shall the thing framed say of him that framed it, He had no understanding?...

For the terrible one is brought to nought, and the scorner is consumed, and all that watch for iniquity are cut off:

That make a man an offender for a word, and lay a snare for him that reproveth in the gate, and turn aside the just for a thing of nought.[1]

In this context, the marvelous work and a wonder does not appear to be the restoration of the gospel, but rather a later last days event which leads to the fall of those who have persecuted the Lord's people.

Passages related to "a marvelous work and a wonder" or to a "marvelous work" in the Book of Mormon consistently link those phrases to the cataclysmic events of the last days which will involve the restoration of Israel. In addition to 1 Nephi 14:6-17, which is under consideration in this section, other passages carry the same intent.

In 1 Nephi 22:8-19, Nephi prophesies that the Lord will do a "marvelous work" among the Gentiles, which he links with the message that the Lord will bring "the house of Israel...out of captivity, and they shall be gathered together to the lands of their inheritance."[2] In the passage he prophesies that members of the great and abominable church "*shall war among themselves,*"[3] and that "*every nation which shall war against thee, O house of Israel, shall be turned one against another,*"[4] and that "*all that fight against Zion shall be destroyed.*"[5] In the series of events which he describes, people are clearly divided into two opposing factions, and Nephi prophesies that "*the wicked shall not destroy the righteous,*"[6] and that the righteous will "*be preserved, even unto the destruction of their enemies by fire.*"[7] Surely the "marvelous work" of this passage refers to a last days era far later than the 1820-1830 restoration of the gospel—it focuses on the results of that future devisive event when men will "harden their hearts against the holy one of Israel."[8]

---

1. Is. 29:7-10, 13-16, 20-21.
2. 1 Ne. 22:11-12.
3. 1 Ne. 22:13.
4. 1 Ne. 22:14.

5. *Ibid.*
6. 1 Ne. 22:16.
7. 1 Ne. 22:17.
8. 1 Ne. 22:18.

2 Nephi 25:15-18 also links "a marvelous work and a won-der"[1] to the gathering of Israel when "the Lord will set his hand again the second time to restore his people from their last and fallen state."[2] This passage may give a clue to the nature of the devisive event under discussion, for it alludes to "a false Messiah which should deceive the people."[3]

2 Nephi 27 is a commentary and paraphrase of Isaiah 29 and subject to the same analysis as that suggested for Isaiah 29 above. But the context stated in the beginning of 2 Nephi 27 places the fulfillment "in the last days, or in the days of the Gentiles," when the people of America ("this land") and other lands *will be drunken with iniquity and all manner of abominations.*"[4] This will be the era when the *"multitude of all the nations" will "fight against Mount Zion."*[5] The devisive event will have taken place, for the people will have *"rejected the prophets."*[6] That day when the Lord will "do a marvelous work among this people, yea, a mar-velous work and a wonder,"[7] will be the time when scorners and those who "watch for iniquity"[8] will *"make a man an offender for a word, and lay a snare for him that reproveth in the gate, and turn aside the just for a thing of naught."*[9] Certainly the "mar-velous work" of this passage refers to an era later than the time of the restoration of the gospel through Joseph Smith.

2 Nephi 28:32 through 2 Ne. 29:14 bears the same message. In the last days era when the Gentiles will deny Christ,[10] the Lord will "do a marvelous work among them,"[11] and set his hand again "to recover my people, which are of the house of Israel."[12] As he gathers Israel, the Savior will deal with *"them that fight against my word and against my people."*[13] Again evidence that a devisive event will have occurred is presented in a marvelous work prophecy.

---

1. 2 Ne. 25:17.
2. *Ibid.*
3. 2 Ne. 25:18.
4. 2 Ne. 27:1. Compare 2 Ne. 27:1-5, 25-32 with Is. 29:7-10, 13-16, 20-21.
5. 2 Ne. 27:3.
6. 2 Ne. 27:5.
7. 2 Ne. 27:26.
8. 2 Ne. 27:31.
9. 2 Ne. 27:32.
10. 2 Ne. 28:32.
11. 2 Ne. 29:1.
12. *Ibid.*
13. 2 Ne. 29:14.

In 3 Nephi 21:7-29, in the era when the Lamanites have already begun to hear the gospel and "know these things"[1] and when the Lord has already commenced fulfilling his covenant to the house of Israel,[2] the Lord prophesies that his "servant" or representative will declare God's word to "those who will not believe it,"[3] and that servant will be "marred because of them,"[4] and then healed. Perhaps the ministry of this last days servant is closely connected with the devisive event, for after he brings forth the words of Christ "unto the Gentiles,"[5] the Savior says that the unbelieving Gentiles "shall be cut off from among my people who are of the covenant"[6] and great destruction will be worked by the remnant of Jacob upon the cities of the Gentiles and God will *"execute vengeance and fury upon them, even as upon the heathen."*[7] This is the era described when the Lord says that the Father shall "work a work, which shall be a great and a marvelous work among them."[8]

In 3 Ne. 28:25-32, Mormon prophesies of the role of the three Nephite apostles in the last days. The lives of these three Nephites were extended so they could minister unto the earth until the second coming of the Lord. Mormon prophesies that they shall be "among the Gentiles" and "among the Jews," in the last days, and that the Lord will eventually send them to "minister unto all the scattered tribes of Israel, and unto all nations, kindreds, tongues and people."[9] In that era "before the great and coming day when all people must surely stand before the judgment-seat of Christ"[10] they will "bring out of them unto Jesus many souls."[11] Mormon says that "great and marvelous works shall be wrought by them"[12] in that era when they will be separating the righteous from the nations (and doesn't the "bring out" process indicate that the dividing and separating process will be underway at that time?)

---

1. 3 Ne. 21:7.
2. *Ibid.*
3. 3 Ne. 21:9.
4. 3 Ne. 21:10.
5. 3 Ne. 21:11.
6. *Ibid.*
7. 3 Ne. 21:12-21. Note that the context indicates that this will occur before the building of the New Jerusalem. (See 3 Ne. 21:22-24, which follow in chronological order.)
8. 3 Ne. 21:9.
9. 3 Ne. 28:27-29.
10. 3 Ne. 28:31.
11. 3 Ne. 28:29.
12. 3 Ne. 28:31.

Thus all the major scriptural passages dealing with a "marvelous work" or "a marvelous work and a wonder" relate to a future era—the time of the major gathering of Israel, persecution of the Lord's people, and the pouring out of God's judgments. Those who might still hold to the theory that the "marvelous work" of 1 Ne. 14:7 refers only to the 1820-1830 restoration and the missionary labor which has followed it, should recall that the restored gospel has been preached for a century-and-a-half, and many have either accepted or rejected it. Those who have rejected it may even have reaped captivity by the devil in hell when they died—but it was an eventual thing, and a spiritual rather than an immediate temporal result. More preaching of the gospel, in the way it has been done previously, does not appear to fulfill the criteria of Nephi's prophecy of delivering men into captivity and destruction, *both temporally and spiritually.*

This future event of which Nephi speaks is different! On the basis of Nephi's prophecy in 1 Ne. 14:7, it appears that when this future "marvelous work" transpires, all men will be obliged to take a stand for or against the Lord's work, and those who unite themselves with the great and abominable church will reap actual, temporal destruction! No, this is more than missionary work, in a sense the saints have known it in the past.

The nature of this event that will divide men into opposing factions is not clearly defined in the scriptures, but some clues may shed light on it. While prophesying of the fall of the great and abominable church, Nephi warned that there will be those at that day who will *"turn aside the just for a thing of naught* and *revile against that which is good, and say that is of no worth!"*[1] He also taught that at that day Satan will "rage in the hearts of the children of men, and *stir them up to anger against that which is good."*[2] Can this be a cryptic explanation of what will happen as men divide themselves into two opposing camps—one following the Lord and one following Lucifer?

In a revelation given in 1833, the Lord said that a time would come when he would proceed to *"bring to pass my act, my strange act, and perform my work, my strange work."*[3] This strange act will have the same result as the "great and a marvelous work" prophesied by Nephi: it will cause that *"men may discern between the righteous and the wicked."*[4] In the revelation, the Master

1. 2 Ne. 28:16.
2. 2 Ne. 28:20.
3. D & C 101:95.
4. *Ibid.*

related the parable of a "woman and the unjust judge,"[1] in which
he likened the future Zion to a woman who sought and finally received vengeance on her adversary. He then revealed that a time
will come when, because of the unwillingness of governmental officials to heed the requests of the saints (for release from the offenses
of their adversaries), the Lord will "arise and come forth out of
his hiding place, and *in his fury vex the nation,*"[2] and *"cut off
those wicked, unfaithful, and unjust stewards.*"[3] This is his prophetic utterance:

> Thus will I liken the children of Zion.
> Let them importune at the feet of the judge;
> And if he heed them not, let them importune at the feet of the
> governor;
> And if the governor heed them not, let them importune at the feet
> of the president;
> *And if the president heed them not, then will the Lord arise and
> come forth out of his hiding place, and in his fury vex the nation;*
> *And in his hot displeasure, and in his fierce anger, in his time, will
> cut off those wicked, unfaithful, and unjust stewards, and appoint them
> their portion among hypocrites, and unbelievers;*
> Even in outer darkness, where there is weeping, and wailing, and
> gnashing of teeth.
> Pray ye, therefore, that their ears may be opened unto your cries,
> that I may be merciful unto them, that these things may not come
> upon them.
> What I have said unto you must needs be, that all men may be left
> without excuse;
> That wise men and rulers may hear and know that which they have
> never considered;
> *That I may proceed to bring to pass my act, my strange act, and
> perform my work, my strange work, that men may discern between the
> righteous and the wicked, saith your God.*[4]

Again, the passage does not say what the specific situation is
that will cause the oppression against the saints and bring God's
wrath upon the nation. Yet there appears to be obvious relationships between the "great and a marvelous work" prophesied by

---

1. D & C 101:81-85.
2. D & C 101:89.
3. Note that they are to be consigned to hell ["outer darkness"—see Al.
   40:13-14], just as are the evil ones who choose to follow Satan at the
   time of the "marvelous work" of 1 Ne. 14:7.
4. D & C 101:85-95. This revelation was given in a time when the saints
   were undergoing persecution, yet the prophetic warning was not fulfilled in that era. Presumably fulfillment is yet future.

Nephi, the time when men will "turn aside the just for a thing of naught," the Lord's "strange act" and "strange work," and the time when "the Lord God shall cause a great division among the people."

What issue will serve to focus adverse attention upon the church and bring intense pressure and persecution upon the saints? Is it the Negro and the priesthood? the ERA and women's rights? abortion? taxation of church properties? released time religious education? Or is it some other issue which is not yet visible? Certainly when Satan stirs men to anger, he will be able to provide them with some excuse to "revile against that which is good."

The important thing to understand in this context is that until this change takes place, the great and abominable church is neither fully functioning in its antagonistic role, nor truly discernible as the great church which is to be the "whore of all the earth."

Paul's Warning: Some Will Heed Doctrines of Devils and Speak Lies in Hypocrisy (1 Tim. 4:1-3)

Others besides Nephi have warned of the great and abominable church in the last days. Paul identified it as one which would teach Satan-inspired doctrines, speak lies, function without conscience, forbid marriage and which would command abstention from meats:

> Now the Spirit speaketh expressly, that in the latter times some shall depart from the faith, *giving heed to seducing spirits, and doctrines of devils;*
> *Speaking lies in hypocrisy;* having their conscience seared with a hot iron;
> *Forbidding to marry, and commanding to abstain from meats,* which God hath created to be received with thanksgiving of them which believe and know the truth.[1]

John's Warning: The Dragon Will Make War With the Remnant (Rev. 12:17-13:18)

John the Revelator also saw the role that Satan and his followers would play in this last days sequence.[2] He pictured Satan as

---

1. 1 Tim. 4:1-3.
2. Note the guidance to understanding the chronology of the Book of Revelation found in D & C section 77. The sequence of events from

a dragon,[1] the Lord's church as a woman, and Jesus Christ as a man child, and saw that "the dragon...persecuted the woman which brought forth the man child."[2] From his vision John reported that "the dragon was wroth with the woman, and *went to make war with the remnant of her seed*, which keep the commandments of God, and have the testimony of Jesus Christ.[3]

In symbolic form John described Satan's followers (functioning in political as well as religious roles) as beasts. He spoke of one of them, saying that "the dragon (Satan) gave him his power, and his seat, and great authority."[4] John warned of the power this "beast" will wield when the time comes for the conflict with the saints to take place:

> And it was given unto him to *make war with the saints, and to overcome them:* and *power was given him over all kindreds, and tongues, and nations.*
>
> And all that dwell upon the earth *shall worship him,* whose names are not written in the book of life of the Lamb slain from the foundation of the world.[5]

John spoke of another "beast" which would arise in this period, and foretold the great power he would exert:

> ...*he exerciseth all the power of the first beast before him,* and *causeth the earth and them which dwell therein to worship the first beast,* whose deadly wound was healed.
>
> And he *doeth great wonders,* so that he maketh fire come down from heaven on the earth in the sight of men,
>
> And *deceiveth them* that dwell on the earth *by the means of those miracles* which he had power to do in the sight of the beast; saying to them that dwell on the earth, that they should make an image to the beast, which had the wound by a sword, and did live.

---

1. Rev. 12:9.
2. Rev. 12:13.
3. Rev. 12:17.
4. Rev. 13:2.
5. Rev. 13:7-8. Verse 8 does not appear to indicate a universal alignment with Satan when this period transpires, but rather warns that those who follow him at that day will not have their names recorded in the Lamb's book of life. (See D & C 88:2; 76:68; Heb. 12:23; Rev. 21:24-27; Phil. 4:3; Rev. 3:5; Dan. 12:1-2; D & C 128:8; 132:19; Ex. 32:33.)

Revelation, chapters 8-19, lead up to the coming of the Savior in glory and the beginning of the millennium. D & C 77:12 indicates that these events take place after the beginning of the seventh thousand years (a time yet future, but drawing near).

And he had power to give life unto the image of the beast, that the image of the beast should both speak, and *cause that as many as would not worship the image of the beast should be killed.*

And he causeth all, both small and great, rich and poor, free and bond, to receive a mark in their right hands, or in their foreheads:

And that no man might buy or sell, save he that had the mark, or the name of the beast, or the number of his name.

Here is wisdom. Let him that hath understanding count the number of the beast: for it is the number of a man; and his number is *Six hundred threescore and six.* [1]

---

1. Rev. 13:12-18. Note that the Savior also warned of deception in the last days through miracles that "shall deceive the very elect." (Mt. 24:24, Mk. 13:22, J.S. 1:22. Compare with 2 Ne. 25:18, D & C 64:37-39; Mos. 15:13; Rev. 2:2).

   The number 666 has provided an interpretational field day for Bible commentators, who since the reformation have devised a continually growing list of numerical explanations. Protestants asserted that the number referred to the Roman Catholic Pope, drawing the Roman numeral equivalents from the title on the papal crown: VICARIVS/FILII/ DEI.

   A second protestant interpretation is based on the word *Lateinos,* which also contains numerical letters totaling 666—the assertion being that the church of Rome is the Latin church because of its origin and language. A corollary to this interpretation is that the Hebrew word for Lateinos is *Romiith,* which also produces numerical letters totaling 666 in the Hebrew language.

   A third interpretation is that the prophecy was filled in Roman times by Nero redivivus. The name Neron Caesar is translated into Hebrew letters, which give the numerical equivalent of 666.

   An interpretation based on the Preterist interpretational viewpoint of the book of Revelation is similar to the above. It goes into Pythagorean numerology, seeing 666 as a triangular number being the sum of numbers 1-36 inclusive; 36 is the sum of numbers 1-8, so 666 is resolved into the number 8, connected with Rev. 17:11, and comes out with the conclusion that the Antichrist is Nero redivivus.

   A fifth interpretation is aimed against the founder of the Seventh-day Adventists, Helen Harmon White. Her name, in Greek numerology, also yields 666.

   Hitler becomes 666 in a numbering system that assumes A is 100, B is 101, C is 102, etc.

   Stalin is 666 when his Russian name Dzugashvili is used in a system that assumes that A is 49, B is 50, C is 51, etc.

   The author has even seen in print a numbering system in which "Church of Jesus Christ of Latter-day Saints" is asserted to total 666.

   Latest in the interpretational assertions to come to the author's attention is reference to a giant computer at the headquarters of the Common Market Confederacy. It is asserted that computer experts are working on a plan to computerize all world trade, assigning a number to every human on earth which would be invisably laser-tatooed on the forehead or back of the hand. The number would show up under

Daniel's Warning: The Horn Will Wear Out the Saints and They Shall Be Given Into His Hand (Dan. 7:21-27)

The prophet Daniel also saw key events of the last days in vision. He described a great power as a "beast" and a "horn," warning that the horn would make war against the saints. Like John, he saw that the saints would fare poorly in this conflict:

> I beheld, and the *same horn made war with the saints, and prevailed against them;*
> *Until the Ancient of Days came,* and judgment was given to the Saints of the most High; and the time came that the saints possessed the kingdom.
> Thus he said, The fourth beast shall be the fourth kingdom upon earth, which shall be diverse from all kingdoms, and shall devour the whole earth, and shall tread it down, and break it in pieces.
> And the ten horns out of this kingdom are ten kings that shall arise: and another shall rise after them; and *he shall be diverse from the first,* and he shall subdue three kings.
> And *he shall speak great words against the most High, and shall wear out the saints of the most High, and think to change times and laws: and they shall be given into his hand* until a time and times and the dividing of time.
> But the judgment shall sit, and they shall take away his dominion, to consume and to destroy it unto the end.
> And the kingdom and dominion, and the greatness of the kingdom under the whole heaven, shall be given to the people of the saints of the most High, whose kingdom is an everlasting kingdom, and all dominions shall serve and obey him.[1]

---

1. Dan. 7:21-27. These passages from John and Daniel have proved controversial throughout Christianity and, indeed, within Mormondom. Early LDS leaders expressed varying opinions concerning how they should be used and interpreted. Joseph Smith, for instance, expounded at length on the images and beasts of both the book of Daniel and the Revelation of St. John, (Apr. 8, 1843: TPJS pp. 287-294; HC 5:339-345), and in doing so expressed his opinion that "It is not very essential for the elders to have knowledge in relation to the meaning of beasts, and heads and horns, and other figures made use of in the revelations; *still, it may be necessary, to prevent contention and division and do away with suspense.*" (TPJS p. 287) He regarded the persecution of the saints prophesied by Daniel as an actual event which will occur in the last days scenario, for he commented that "*The 'Horn' made war with the Saints and overcame them, until the Ancient of Days came;* judgment was given to the Saints of the Most High from the Ancient of Days;..." (HC 3:389. This prophecy is linked with an extensive prophetic statement warning the church of future suffering the saints must endure. See HC 3:389-391.)

---

infra-red scanners at all checkout counters and places of business. Without his assigned number, no one would be able to buy or sell. The program is being devised as a restoration plan to be implemented in the aftermath of world chaos.

While these passages are difficult to interpret with exactness, their major messages are clear, and in harmony with Nephi's visions, and interpretative wrangling must not be allowed to obscure them:[1]

1. There will be conflict between the church of the devil and the saints of the Lamb of God in the last days.
2. The conflict, for a time, will go badly for the saints. Satan will prevail over them and overcome them to a degree. This will be a period of great distress.
3. The turning point will be the arrival of the Ancient of Days, when judgment is given to the Saints.

Nephi's Warning: Multitudes Will Gather Among Gentile Nations to Fight Against the Lord's Church (1 Ne. 14:11-13)

Nephi's continuing prophecy describes what will happen after the future "marvelous work"—a divisive event which will cause people to muster into two distinct factions. He describes the buildup of the antagonism and locates it primarily among the Gentile (Caucasian) nations. He also emphasizes that the wickedness of the abominable church will have restricted the size and growth of the Lord's church:

> And it came to pass that I looked and beheld the whore of all the earth, and *she sat upon many waters; and she had dominion over all the earth, among all nations, kindreds, tongues, and people.*
>
> And it came to pass that I beheld the *church of the Lamb of God, and its numbers were few,* because of the wickedness and abominations of the whore who sat upon many waters; nevertheless, I beheld that *the church of the Lamb, who were the saints of God, were also upon all the face of the earth;* and their dominions upon the face of the earth were small, because of the wickedness of the great whore whom I saw.
>
> And it came to pass that I beheld that *the great mother of abominations did gather together multitudes upon the face of all the earth, among all the nations of the Gentiles, to fight against the Lamb of God.*[2]

Nephi's prophecy continues by describing the fall of the great and abominable church, as do several other prophetic passages. A significant aspect of these passages, however, is that they contain

---

1. For comment on portions of this chapter pertaining to the Council at Adam-ondi-Ahman see the author's book, *Prophecy—Key to the Future* (Salt Lake City, Utah: Bookcraft, 1962), pp. 167-176. See also Duane S. Crowther, "Daniel," *Prophets and Prophecies of the Old Testament*, (Bountiful, Utah: Horizon Publishers, 1973), pp. 496-527.
2. 1 Ne. 14:11-13.

clues to what the saints must endure during this period of tribulation. These clues will be considered in this chapter in the form of prophetic warnings before the prophesied fall of the great and abominable church is described.

Nephi's Warning: Nations Shall Dig a Pit to Ensnare the People of the Lord and Pervert the Lord's Ways (1 Ne. 22:14)

As he tells how the great and abominable church will be destroyed by nations warring among themselves in a far-reaching world war, Nephi indites the wicked with three prophetic accusations. According to his prophecy, they will:

1. fight as nations against the house of Israel,
2. dig a pit to ensnare the people of the Lord, and
3. pervert the right ways of the Lord.

This is his prophetic utterance:

> *Every nation which shall war against thee*, O house of Israel, shall be turned one against another, and they shall fall into *the pit which they digged to ensnare the people of the Lord.* And all that *fight against Zion* shall be destroyed, and that great whore, who hath *perverted the right ways of the Lord*, yea, that great and abominable church, shall tumble to the dust and great shall be the fall of it.[1]

The nature of the pit, or entrapment, which the unrighteous will attempt to use against the people of the Lord is not described in the passage. However, the possibility that it is related to the "marvelous work" which will divide people into "save two churches only"[2] is great.

Nephi's Warning: The Wicked Will Turn Aside the Just and Revile Against Good (2 Ne. 28:16)

As he prophesies of the wickedness of organized religion in the last days[3] and foretells the fall of the great and abominable church,[4] Nephi again indites the wicked for their persecution of the saints. He warns:

---

1. 1 Ne. 22:14.
2. Review 1 Ne. 14:7-10.
3. 2 Ne. 28:1-17.
4. 2 Ne. 28:18.

> Wo unto them that *turn aside the just for a thing of naught and revile against that which is good, and say it is of no worth!* For the day shall come that the Lord God will speedily visit the inhabitants of the earth; and in that day they that are fully ripe in iniquity they shall perish.[1]

He adds that at that day Satan will "rage in the hearts of the children of men, and *stir them up to anger against that which is good.*"[2]

Again the picture is portrayed: anger against the saints for doing good while others are committed to evil.

Jacob's Warning: The Lord's People Shall Be Oppressed, Prey, and Captives of the Mighty (2 Ne. 6:17-18)

Yet another passage which will be considered as the fall of the great and abominable church is described and yields clues as to what the Lord's people must first endure. Jacob describes the saints as being:

1. captives of the mighty,
2. prey of the terrible,
3. contended with, and
4. oppressed by their enemies.

His prophecy, which details the fall of the great and abominable church,[3] ends with this warning to the wicked:

> But thus saith the Lord: Even the *captives of the mighty* shall be taken away, and the *prey of the terrible* shall be delivered; for the Mighty God shall deliver his covenant people. For thus saith the Lord: I will contend with *them that contendeth with thee—*
>
> And I will feed *them that oppress thee,* with their own flesh; and they shall be drunken with their own blood as with sweet wine; and all flesh shall know that I the Lord am thy Savior and thy Redeemer, the Mighty One of Jacob.[4]

John's Warning: The Woman Will Be Drunken with Blood of the Saints and Martyrs (Rev. 17:6)

John the Revelator characterizes the capital city of the great and abominable church as a "great city, which reigneth over the

---

1. 2 Ne. 28:16.
2. 2 Ne. 28:20.
3. 2 Ne. 6:12-18.
4. 2 Ne. 6:17-18.

kings of the earth."[1] As he begins to describe the fall of the great and abominable church, he gives grim reminder of the death and slaughter she will have brought upon the Lord's people:

> And I saw the woman *drunken with the blood of the saints, and with the blood of the martyrs of Jesus:* and when I saw her, I wondered with great admiration.[2]

John's Warning: Ten Kings Will Make War with the Lamb (Rev. 17:12-14)

As John the Revelator described the woman, or capital city of the great and abominable church, he indicated that the city had "ten horns," or control over ten kings or nations which would function for a short interval in the last days scenario. He indicated that these nations would give their strength to the beast and wage war against the Lord's people:

> And the *ten horns which thou sawest are ten kings,* which have received no kingdom as yet; but *receive power as kings one hour with the beast.*
> These have one mind, and shall *give their power and strength unto the beast.*
> *These shall make war with the Lamb,* and the Lamb shall overcome them....[3]

Thou we do not yet know who these nations will be, John's warning is similar to those of the other prophets previously cited, that the Lord's people will have to endure war with the forces of Antichrist—war on a large, multi-nation scale—world war!

Prophecies of World War as the Great and Abominable Church is Destroyed

Nephi, in his great chronological prophecy of 1 Nephi 11-14, describes the disunity and chaos which will come upon the great and abominable church as it prepares to wage war against the saints. After foretelling how the mother of abominations will gather among all the Gentile nations to fight against the Lamb of God, he describes the power of God which will be with the saints and also

---

1. Rev. 17:18.
2. Rev. 17:6.
3. Rev. 17:12-14.

the divine wrath which will cause the nations dominated by the mother of abominations to fight among themselves:

> And it came to pass that I, Nephi, beheld *the power of the Lamb of God, that it descended upon the saints of the church of the Lamb, and upon the covenant people of the Lord,* who were scattered upon all the face of the earth; and they were armed with righteousness and with the power of God in great glory.
>
> And it came to pass that I beheld that *the wrath of God was poured out upon the great and abominable church, insomuch that there were wars and rumors of wars among all the nations and kindreds of the earth.*
>
> And as there began to be wars and rumors of wars among all the nations which belonged to the mother of abominations, the angel spake unto me, saying: Behold, the wrath of God is upon the mother of harlots; and behold, thou seest all these things—
>
> *And when the day cometh that the wrath of God is poured out upon the mother of harlots, which is the great and abominable church of all the earth, whose foundation is the devil, then, at that day, the work of the Father shall commence, in preparing the way for the fulfilling of his covenants, which he hath made to his people who are of the house of Israel.*[1]

In another prophecy made by Nephi, the fall of the great and abominable church is also described. Again the event is linked to the time of the gathering of Israel.[2] Again the description is one of international war, with nations who had been warring against the Lord's people suddenly turning on one another and wreaking great destruction:

> *And the blood of that great and abominable church, which is the whore of all the earth, shall turn upon their own heads; for they shall war among themselves, and the sword of their own hands shall fall upon their own heads, and they shall be drunken with their own blood.*
>
> *And every nation which shall war against thee, O house of Israel, shall be turned one against another,* and they shall fall into the pit which they digged to ensnare the people of the Lord.
>
> *And all that fight against Zion shall be destroyed, and that great whore, who hath perverted the right ways of the Lord, yea, that great*

---

1. 1 Ne. 14:14-17. Verse 17 provides an important chronological clue, when linked with verses 27-29 of the Lord's prophetic panorama of 3 Nephi, chapter 21. This relationship indicates that the fall of the great and abominable church will not occur until after internal warfare in the Americas (3 Ne. 21:12-22), the building of the New Jerusalem (3 Ne. 21:23), the gathering to the New Jerusalem of the Lamanites (3 Ne. 21:24), an appearance of Christ there (3 Ne. 21:25), and the preaching of the gospel among the dispersed of Israel, including the lost tribes (3 Ne. 21:26).
2. 1 Ne. 22:9-11.

and abominable church, shall tumble to the dust and great shall be the fall of it.

For behold, saith the prophet, the time cometh speedily that Satan shall have no more power over the hearts of the children of men; for the day soon cometh that all the proud and they who do wickedly shall be as stubble; and the day cometh that they must be burned.

For the time soon cometh that the fulness of the wrath of God shall be poured out upon all the children of men; for *he will not suffer that the wicked shall destroy the righteous.*

Wherefore, he will preserve the righteous by his power, even if it so be that the fulness of his wrath must come, and *the righteous be preserved, even unto the destruction of their enemies by fire.* Wherefore, the righteous need not fear; for thus saith the prophet, they shall be saved, even if it so be as by fire.

Behold, my brethren, I say unto you, that these things must shortly come; yea, even *blood, and fire, and vapor of smoke must come;* and it must needs be upon the face of this earth; and it cometh unto men according to the flesh if it so be that they will harden their hearts against the Holy One of Israel.

For behold, *the righteous shall not perish; for the time surely must come that all they who fight against Zion shall be cut off.*[1]

That the fall of the evil church is an event of major significance was emphasized by Nephi, who in yet another prophetic context taught that the "great and abominable church, the whore of *all the earth*, must tumble to the earth, and *great must be the fall thereof.*[2]

As John the Revelator described "the judgment of the great whore that sitteth upon many waters,"[3] he told of the destruction which would come upon the "woman," or capital city of the great and abominable church. He identified this city as being "arrayed in purple and scarlet colour, and decked with gold and precious stones and pearls,"[4] and being full of abominations, filthiness and fornication.[5] The city will be situated on seven mountains,[6] and be a large or "great" city which reigns over kings[7] and which is noted for its trade.[8] It will be sufficiently near to the ocean that men on ships will be able to see "the smoke of her burning."[9]

John sees that the great city is suddenly destroyed, "in one hour,"[10] by the ten kings or nations who had previously supported it and made war[11] against the Lamb of God:

---

1. 1 Ne. 22:13-19.
2. 2 Ne. 28:18.
3. Rev. 17:1.
4. Rev. 17:4.
5. *Ibid.*
6. Rev. 17:9.
7. Rev. 17:18.

8. Rev. 18:3, 11-16.
9. Rev. 18:17-18.
10. Rev. 18:17. And what instrument of war has modern man devised that can instantly destroy a huge, sprawling city, leaving smoke billowing high into the sky above the mountains?
11. See again Rev. 17:12-14.

And the ten horns which thou sawest upon the beast, these shall hate the whore, and shall make her desolate and naked, and shall eat her flesh, and burn her with fire.[1]

John saw and described her downfall:

And I heard another voice from heaven, saying, *Come out of her, my people, that ye be not partakers of her sins, and that ye receive not of her plagues.*

For her sins have reached unto heaven, and God hath remembered her iniquities.

Reward her even as she rewarded you, and double unto her double according to her works: in the cup which she hath filled fill to her double.

How much she hath glorified herself, and lived deliciously, so much torment and sorrow give her: for she saith in her heart, I sit a queen, and am no widow, and shall see no sorrow.

Therefore shall her plagues come in one day, death, and mourning, and famine; and she shall be utterly burned with fire: for strong is the Lord God who judgeth her.

And the kings of the earth, who have committed fornication and lived deliciously with her, shall bewail her, and lament for her, when they shall see the smoke of her burning,

Standing afar off for the fear of her torment, saying, Alas, alas, that great city Babylon, that mighty city! for *in one hour is thy judgment come.*[2]

Its downfall will serve to avenge the saints for the many losses they will have suffered at her hands:

Rejoice over her, thou heaven, and *ye holy apostles and prophets;* for God hath avenged you on her....

And in her was found the blood of prophets, and of saints, and of all that were slain upon the earth.[3]

Summary

1. Both Book of Mormon and Biblical passages warn of the existence of a great and abominable church. The message of these passages is that this church will persecute and make war upon the saints, but will collapse and fall when nations previously under its control war among themselves and then destroy the church's capital city.

---

1. Rev. 17:16.
2. Rev. 18:4-10.
3. Rev. 18:20, 24.

2. Numerous clues from the scriptures help to identify the great and abominable church:

A.   The church was founded shortly after the ministry of Christ in the meridian of time (1 Ne. 13:26; compare the chronological relationship of 1 Ne. 13:5-9 with 1 Ne. 11:15-23, 12:6-10).

B.   The church was founded prior to the voyage of Columbus and the settling of America by the European Gentiles (compare the chronological relationship of 1 Ne. 13:5-9 with 1 Ne. 13:12-13).

C.   The church is founded across the waters from America among the nations and kingdoms of the Gentiles (1 Ne. 13:3-4, 10).

D.   The church is abominable above all other churches (1 Ne. 13:5), so it is a church, and not "general wickedness" or a combination of churches.

E.   The church slays, tortures, binds, and imprisons the saints of God (1 Ne. 13:5).

F.   The devil is its foundation (1 Ne. 13:6).

G.   The church has gold, silver, silks, scarlets, fine linen and precious clothing (1 Ne. 13:7).

H.   The church has many harlots (1 Ne. 13:7).

I.   The church desires riches (1 Ne. 13:8).

J.   The church destroys and imprisons the saints for the praise of the world (1 Ne. 13:9).

K.   The church receives the gospel from Christ's apostles and the Jews, but takes away many plain and precious parts and many covenants (1 Ne. 13:26-27).

L.   The church takes away many plain and precious things from the book of the Lamb of God—the Bible (1 Ne. 13:28).

M.   The church removes portions of the Bible before that book goes to the nations of the Gentiles or is brought to America (1 Ne. 13:29).

N.   The church removes portions of the Bible, which causes many to stumble, prior to the restoration of the gospel (1 Ne. 13:34).

O.   The capital city of the church sits on seven mountains (Rev. 17:9).

P.   The capital city of the church is a great city which reigns over the kings of the earth (Rev. 17:18).

Q.   The capital city of the church is a great center of
     commerce which has made many merchants rich
     (Rev. 18:3, 11-15).

R.   The capital city is located close enough to the sea that
     people on ships will be able to see smoke rising from
     it as it burns (Rev. 18:17-18).

3. Book of Mormon prophecies indicate that in the future
God will do a "marvelous work," by bringing to pass some event
which will divide people into two distinct groups, the righteous
and the wicked. After this event there will be "two churches only."
(1 Ne. 14:7-10.)

4. The "marvelous work" which is also mentioned in 1 Ne.
22:8-19; 2 Ne. 25:17-18; 2 Ne. 27:1-5, 25-32; 2 Ne. 28:32-29:14;
3 Ne. 21:9-29; and 3 Ne. 28:25-32, is continually linked in the
scriptures with future last days events and is therefore regarded as
being an event other than the restoration of the gospel through
Joseph Smith. It may be the same as the Lord's "strange act"
mentioned in D & C 101:85-95, in which the saints are depicted as
importuning before judges, governors, and the president just before
the Lord in his fury vexes the nation.

5. Prophetic warnings concerning the tribulations which will
come to the saints and the house of Israel because of the great and
abominable church in the last days were cited from:

A.   Jacob (2 Ne. 6:12).
B.   Paul (1 Tim. 4:1-3).
C.   John (Rev. 12:17-13:18).
D.   Daniel (Dan. 7:21-27).
E.   Nephi (1 Ne. 14:11-13).
F.   Nephi (1 Ne. 22:14).
G.   Nephi (2 Ne. 28:16).
H.   Jacob (2 Ne. 6:17-18).
I.   John (Rev. 17:6).
J.   John (Rev. 17:12-14).

6. Several of the prophetic warnings indicate that the Lord's
people will be the recipients of false charges and evil allegations
brought by the great and abominable church as the last days conflict takes shape:

A. Nephi: Satan will stir them to anger against that which is good (2 Ne. 28:20).

B. Paul: They will speak lies in hypocrisy, without conscience (1 Tim. 4:2).

C. Daniel: The horn shall speak great words against the most High (Dan. 7:25).

D. Nephi: The nations will dig a pit to ensnare the people of the Lord (1 Ne. 22:14).

E. Nephi: The whore shall pervert the right ways of the Lord (1 Ne. 22:14).

F. Nephi: They will turn aside the just for a thing of naught (2 Ne. 28:16).

G. Nephi: They will revile against that which is good, and say it is of no worth (2 Ne. 28:16).

H. Jacob: They will contend with the covenant people (2 Ne. 6:17).

7. The prophecies warn that the great and abominable church will exercise great control over the saints during the period of persecution and tribulation:

A. John: The beast will make war with the saints and overcome them. Power is given him over all kindreds, tongues, and nations (Rev. 13:7-8).

B. John: Another beast has power to cause that as many as would not worship the image of the beast should be killed (Rev. 13:15).

C. John: The beast causes all to receive a number in their right hands or foreheads; they cannot buy or sell without it (Rev. 13:16-17).

D. Daniel: The horn made war with the saints, and prevailed against them (Dan. 7:21).

E. Daniel: The horn shall wear out the saints, and they shall be given into his hand (Dan. 7:25).

F. Jacob: The captives of the mighty shall be taken away, for God shall deliver his covenant people (2 Ne. 6:17).

8. The great and abominable church will wield international political power.

A. Nephi: She had dominion over all nations, kindreds, tongues, and people (1 Ne. 14:11).

B. Nephi: The mother of abominations did gather multitudes upon the face of all the earth, among all the nations of the Gentiles (1 Ne. 14:13).

C. John: Ten kings receive power one hour, and shall
give their power and strength unto the beast (Rev.
17:12-13).

D. John: The "woman," or capital city, reigns over kings
(Rev. 17:18).

9. The effort to fight against the saints will disintegrate into
world war—international war in which the Gentile nations do battle with one another and finally destroy the capital city of the
great and abominable church:

A. Nephi: Every nation which shall war against the house
of Israel shall be turned one against another (1 Ne.
22:14).

B. Jacob: I will feed them that oppress thee with their
own flesh (2 Ne. 6:18).

C. Nephi: There were wars and rumors of wars among all
the nations and kindreds of the earth (1 Ne. 14:15).

D. Nephi: The great and abominable church shall war
among themselves (1 Ne. 22:13).

E. John: The ten horns shall hate the whore and shall
burn her with fire (Rev. 17:16).

F. John: Her plagues shall come in one day: death, famine, and fire (Rev. 18:8).

10. Though many of the saints will be slain by the great and
abominable church (Rev. 13:15; 17:6), the righteous will ultimately be preserved while they who fight against Zion will be cut
off and destroyed (1 Ne. 22:16-19).

Seventh Warning: X
If Secret Combinations Are Allowed To Spread, The Nation Will Be Destroyed

Moroni's Warning: If a Nation Allows Secret Combinations to Spread Over It, the Nation Will Be Destroyed (Eth. 8:21)

The Book of Mormon bears strong and compelling testimony concerning one of man's most corrupt practices: the organizing of secret combinations to obtain power and wealth through evil deeds. The message of the scriptures is that such a *"combination is most abominable and wicked above all, in the sight of God; For the Lord worketh not in secret combinations,* neither doth he will that man should shed blood, but in all things hath forbidden it."[1]

A powerful warning was given by Moroni to the last days inhabitants of the Americas as he wrote concerning the danger of secret combinations. After warning that secret combinations had caused the destruction of two great cultures, the Jaredites and the Nephites,[2] the last Book of Mormon prophet wrote a warning which may have far-reaching significance during the great panorama of last days events:

> *...whatsoever nation shall uphold such secret combinations, to get power and gain, until they shall spread over the nation, behold, they shall be destroyed;* for the Lord will not suffer that the blood of his saints, which shall be shed by them, shall always cry unto him from the ground for vengeance upon them and yet he avenge them not.[3]

His admonition was specifically addressed to the latter-day Gentiles, or inhabitants of America, as a preliminary to a second, and more specific warning concerning a last days secret combination which he saw would be international in scope and objectives:

Moroni's Warning: A Secret Combination Will Seek to Overthrow the Freedom of All Nations (Eth. 8:23-26)

As he prophesied to the "Gentiles" who would read his words in the last days, he not only warned of a specific secret combination

---

1. Eth. 8:18-19.
2. Eth. 8:21.
3. Eth. 8:22.

of international proportions which would come, but *commanded* the inhabitants of America that they must awake to the sense of their awful situation because of the presence of the combination among them:

> Wherefore, O ye Gentiles, it is wisdom in God that these things should be shown unto you, that thereby ye may repent of your sins, *and suffer not that these murderous combinations shall get above you, which are built up to get power and gain—and the work, yea, even the work of destruction come upon you, yea, even the sword of the justice of the Eternal God shall fall upon you, to your overthrow and destruction if ye shall suffer these things to be.*
>
> Wherefore, the Lord *commandeth* you, *when ye shall see these things come among you that ye shall awake to a sense of your awful situation, because of this secret combination which shall be among you;* or wo be unto it, because of the blood of them who have been slain; for they cry from the dust for vengeance upon it, and also upon those who built it up.
>
> For it cometh to pass that *whoso buildeth it up seeketh to overthrow the freedom of all lands, nations, and countries; and it bringeth to pass the destruction of all people,* for it is built up by the devil, who is the father of all lies; even that same liar who beguiled our first parents, yea, even that same liar who hath caused man to commit murder from the beginning; who hath hardened the hearts of men that they have murdered the prophets, and stoned them, and cast them out from the beginning.
>
> Wherefore, *I, Moroni, am commanded to write these things that evil may be done away,* and that the time may come that Satan may have no power upon the hearts of the children of men, but that they may be persuaded to do good continually, that they may come unto the fountain of all righteousness and be saved.[1]

His prophecy was not only concerned with the danger from the secret combination, but was a warning that if a nation allowed the spread of such an organization in its midst, it would be so corrupt that God's justice would soon cause the fall and overthrow of that nation—a sobering thought!

Nephi's Warning: Satan Will Bind Secret Combinations With His Strong Cords Forever (2 Ne. 26:20-23)

Moroni wasn't alone in his prophetic warning of secret combinations among the latter-day Gentiles—Nephi also foresaw the last days existence of such combinations and the danger they would bring:

---

1. Eth. 8:23-26.

*And the Gentiles are lifted up in the pride of their eyes, and have
slumbled,* because of the greatness of their stumbling block, that they
have built up many churches; nevertheless, they put down the power
and miracles of God, and preach up unto themselves their own wisdom
and their own learning, that they may get gain and grind upon the face
of the poor.

And there are many churches built up which cause envyings, and
strifes, and malice.

And *there are also secret combinations, even as in times of old,
according to the combinations of the devil, for he is the foundation of
all these things; yea, the foundation of murder, and works of darkness;*
yea, and he leadeth them by the neck with a flaxen cord, until *he
bindeth them with his strong cords forever.*

For behold, my beloved brethren I say unto you that the Lord God
worketh not in darkness.[1]

Nephi's Warning: God Must Destroy Secret Works
of Darkness (2 Ne. 10:15)

Nephi had previously warned of the danger of secret combinations in a context that had international implications. After prophesying that God would "fortify this land against all other nations,"[2]
he warned that "he that fighteth against Zion shall perish, saith
God,"[3] and then cited the Lord's prophetic promise that *"I must
needs destroy the secret works of darkness, and of murders, and
of abominations."*[4]

Alma's Warning: Cursed Be the Land Forever to Secret Combina-
tions, Even Unto Destruction (Al. 37:28, 31)

Alma also warned that the land would be cursed and destroyed
unless the inhabitants repent of the influence of secret combinations. He was instructing his son, Helaman, concerning the secret
oaths and evil plans found in the twenty-four plates of the Jaredite
records. He reiterated that the Jaredites had been destroyed because they embraced the workings of the secret combinations,
asserted that such secret works would be brought to light, and told
his son not to pass on the details of the secret oaths, covenants,
and abominations:

And now, I will speak unto you concerning those twenty-four plates,
that ye keep them, that the mysteries and the works of darkness, and

1. 2 Ne. 26:20-23.
2. 2 Ne. 10:12.
3. 2 Ne. 10:13.
4. 2 Ne. 10:15.

their secret works, or the secret works of those people who have been destroyed, may be made manifest unto this people; yea, *all their murders, and robbings, and their plunderings, and all their wickedness and abominations, may be made manifest unto this people;* yea, and that ye preserve these interpreters.

For behold, the Lord saw that his people began to work in darkness, yea, work secret murders and abominations; therefore the Lord said, if they did not repent they should be destroyed from off the face of the earth.

And the Lord said: I will prepare unto my servant Gazelem, a stone, which shall shine forth in darkness unto light, that I may discover unto my people who serve me, that I may discover unto them the works of their brethren, yea, their secret works, their works of darkness, and their wickedness and abominations.

And now, my son, these interpreters were prepared that the word of God might be fulfilled, which he spake, saying:

I will bring forth out of darkness unto light all their secret works and their abominations; and except they repent I will destroy them from off the face of the earth, and I will bring to light all their secrets and abominations, unto every nation that shall hereafter possess the land.

And now, my son, we see that *they did not repent; therefore they have been destroyed,* and thus far the word of God has been fulfilled; yea, their secret abominations have been brought out of darkness and made known unto us.

And now, my son, I command you that ye retain all their oaths, and their covenants, and their agreements in their secret abominations; yea, and *all their signs and their wonders ye shall keep from this people, that they know them not,* lest peradventure they should fall into darkness also and be destroyed.[1]

Then Alma stated the first of his warnings of the curse that hangs over this land if the people embrace the works of secret combinations:

> *For behold, there is a curse upon all this land, that destruction shall come upon all those workers of darkness, according to the power of God, when they are fully ripe;* therefore I desire that this people might not be destroyed.[2]

He explained to Helaman what the people should be taught concerning secret combinations:

> Therefore ye shall *keep these secret plans of their oaths and their covenants from this people,* and only their wickedness and their murders and their abominations shall ye make known unto them; and ye shall

---

1. Al. 37:21-27.
2. Al. 37:28.

*teach them to abhor such wickedness and abominations and murders;
and ye shall also teach them that these people were destroyed on account
of their wickedness and abominations and their murders.*

*For behold, they murdered all the prophets of the Lord who came
among them to declare unto them concerning their iniquities;* and the
blood of those whom they murdered did cry unto the Lord their God
for vengeance upon those who were their murderers; and thus the judgments of God did come upon these workers of darkness and secret
combinations.[1]

And then Alma repeated his prophetic warning concerning
secret combinations in America that spans all eras of time:

Yea, and *cursed be the land forever and ever unto those workers of
darkness and secret combinations, even unto destruction,* except they
repent before they are fully ripe.[2]

Secret Combinations Prior to the Savior's Mortal Advent:
A Chronicle of the Rapid Growth of Evil in Government

The record of the rapid rise of secret combinations in Book
of Mormon days shows the great power which such groups can
rapidly acquire. One such combination was formed when Gadianton
became leader of a robber band about 50 B.C.[3] His network of evil
doers began to grow "in the more settled parts of the land."[4] At
that time they were *"not known unto those who were at the head
of government;* therefore they were not destroyed out of the land."[5]
In this era the Nephite society had become soft and corrupt,
"For behold, the Lord had blessed them so long with the riches of
the world that they had not been stirred up to anger, to wars, nor
to bloodshed; therefore they began to set their hearts upon their
riches; yea, *they began to seek to get gain that they might be lifted
up one above another; therefore they began to commit secret
murders, and to rob and to plunder, that they might get gain."[6]*
With the people in this condition, they were ripe for Satan's influence to be manifested on a national level, and

...behold, *Satan did stir up the hearts of the more part of the Nephites,
insomuch that they did unite with those bands of robbers, and did enter*

---

1. Al. 37:29-30.
2. Al. 37:31.
3. Hel. 2:2-11. This was in the 42nd year of the reign of the judges.
4. Hel. 3:23. This was in the 49th year of the reign of the judges.
5. *Ibid.*
6. Hel. 6:17.

into their covenants and their oaths, that they would protect and pre-
serve one another in whatsoever difficult circumstances they should be
placed, that they should not suffer for their murders, and their plunderings, and their stealings.

And it came to pass that *they did have their signs, yea, their secret*
signs, and their secret words; and this that they might distinguish a
brother who had entered into the covenant, that whatsoever wickedness
his brother should do he should not be injured by his brother, nor by
those who did belong to his band, who had taken this covenant.

And thus they might murder, and plunder, and steal, and commit
whoredoms and all manner of wickedness, contrary to the laws of their
country and also the laws of their God.

And whosoever of those who belonged to their band should reveal
unto the world of their wickedness and their abominations, should be
tried, not according to the laws of their country, but according to the
laws of their wickedness, which had been given by Gadianton and
Kishkumen.[1]

It wasn't long until Satan "got great hold upon the hearts of
the Nephites; yea, insomuch that they had become exceedingly
wicked; yea, *the more part of them had turned out of the way*
of righteousness."[2]

Only a short period transpired from the formation of the
secret combination to the day when the majority of the Nephite
population had joined it—only eighteen years.[3] In one more year
their infiltration was so extensive that "*they did obtain the sole*
management of the government."[4] When in full governmental control they began to persecute the righteous, "Insomuch that they did
trample under their feet and smite and rend and turn their backs
upon the poor and the meek, and the humble followers of God."[5]

These few verses not only chronicle the rise of a secret combination, but describe the characteristics which make them such
an abomination in the sight of God. Note them:

1. The members make covenants to protect each other so they
won't have to pay for their crimes.

2. They have signs and passwords.

---

1. Hel. 6:21-24.
2. Hel. 6:31.
3. Compare Hel. 3:22-24 [the 49th year...] when the people were righteous
   and only a handful of Gadiantons were functioning, still unknown to
   the government, and Hel. 6:31-32 [the 67th year...], when the majority
   had turned to wickedness.
4. Hel. 6:38-39.
5. Hel. 6:39.

3. They are willing to murder and steal to accomplish their ends.

4. If their members betray them, they are disciplined according to their own special code.

5. They flourish in a society which is dulled to the needs of social justice and which is devoted to seeking riches and power.

6. They strive to infiltrate and gain control of government, usurping the power and authority of the land.

7. They control the courts and judicial systems. Under their rule the righteous are condemned and the wicked go unpunished.

8. They grow rapidly and can gain control of a nation within two decades.

9. When in control, they persecute the poor and the righteous.

And then, with the people in such a wicked condition, the Lord revealed through Nephi the inevitable warning:

> And except ye repent ye shall perish; yea, even your lands shall be taken from you, and ye shall be destroyed from off the face of the earth.
>
> Behold now, I do not say that these things shall be, of myself, because it is not of myself that I know these things; but behold, *I know that these things are true because the Lord God has made them known unto me, therefore I testify that they shall be.*[1]

How did the people receive his prophetic warning in their wickedness? The judges raised their voices against Nephi, accusing him of reviling against the people and against their law:

> Therefore they did cry unto the people, saying: Why do you suffer this man to revile against us? For behold he doth condemn all this people, even unto destruction; yea, and also that these our cities shall be taken from us, that we shall have no place in them.
>
> And now we know that this is impossible, for behold, we are powerful, and our cities great, therefore our enemies can have no power over us.
>
> And it came to pass that *thus they did stir up the people to anger against Nephi....*[2]

Within three more years "the contentions did increase, insomuch that *there were wars throughout all the land among all the*

---

1. Hel. 7:28-29.
2. Hel. 8:5-7. See also verses 1-4. It was only Nephi's popularity among the people that saved him in this instance. Some of them recognized him as "a good man" and as a prophet. (See verses 7-10.)

people of Nephi. And it was this secret band of robbers who did carry on this work of destruction and wickedness."[1]

After three years of civil war the prophet Nephi pled with God that the people might not be completely destroyed by the sword. In answer to his prayer, God sent a famine to stir them up to repentance. Finally, after *"they did perish by thousands in the more wicked parts of the land,"*[2] they "began to remember the Lord their God."[3] The people repented and humbled themselves in sackcloth, and "swept away the band of Gadianton from among them" until the secret combination had "become extinct."[4]

But secret combinations, like pernicious weeds, keep springing up again and again, once they are established. How long did the newly-won period of freedom and righteousness last? Only five years! Then dissenters again united and formed the secret band, the robbers of Gadianton:

> And they did commit murder and plunder; and then they would retreat back into the mountains, and into the wilderness and secret places, hiding themselves that they could not be discovered, receiving daily an addition to their numbers, inasmuch as there were dissenters that went forth unto them.
> And thus in time, yea, even in the space of not many years, they became an exceeding great band of robbers; and they did search out all the secret plans of Gadianton; and thus they became robbers of Gadianton.
> Now behold, these robbers did make great havoc, yea, even great destruction among the people of Nephi, and also among the people of the Lamanites.[5]

The Gadianton forces grew so strong that even the whole armies of the Nephites and Lamanites could not stop them.[6] As the years passed, social unrest and discontent among the Nephites fed their ranks,[7] and they "had become so numerous, and *did slay so many of the people, and did lay waste so many cities, and did spread so much death and carnage throughout the land"*[8] that all the Nephites and Lamanites had to take up arms against them *"to maintain their rights, and the privileges of their church and of their worship, and*

---

1. Hel. 11:1-2. This was the 72nd year of the reign of the judges.
2. Hel. 11:6.
3. Hel. 11:7.
4. Hel. 11:10. This was the 75th year of the reign of the judges.
5. Hel. 11:25-27. The Gadianton band was reformed in the 80th year of the reign of the judges.
6. Hel. 11:28-33.
7. 3 Ne. 1:27-28.
8. 3 Ne. 2:11.

their freedom and their liberty."[1] It was only after eight years of war,[2] in which the Nephites and Lamanites were forced to abandon their homes and to unite in one central place, living for many months from stored provisions without being able to farm their lands, and enduring the most savage warfare that the Nephites had ever known, that they were finally able to conquer the secret combination after slaying its armies by the tens of thousands.[3]

But once again, like the recurring malignancy of cancer, the secret combinations were organized. In less than ten years of peace, Satan again extended his influence and, through secret combinations, brought about the assassination of the chief judge and the destruction of national government.[4] Through whom did Satan work this time? Through a combination of church leaders (high priests), judges, and lawyers who plotted to destroy the governor and establish a king in the land.[5]

It was not until the great destruction at the time of Christ's death that a lasting end came to the long series of secret combinations.

---

1. 3 Ne. 2:12. This was the 104th year since the beginning of the reign of the judges, which was called the 13th year (after the birth of Christ) in the new Nephite numbering system (see 3 Ne. 2:5-8).

2. 3 Ne. 2:13; 3 Ne. 4:16. During this era the pressure on the righteous Nephites and Lamanites to defect to the Gadianton band was intense. A letter from Giddianhi, leader of the secret combination, to the Nephite governor, Lachoneus, is evidence of this pressure:

   I write unto you, desiring that ye would yield up unto this my people, your cities, your lands, and your possessions, rather than that they should visit you with the sword and that destruction should come upon you.

   Or in other words, *yield yourselves up unto us, and unite with us and become acquainted with our secret works, and become our brethren that ye may be like unto us—not our slaves, but our brethren and partners of all our substance.*

   And behold, I swear unto you, if ye will do this, with an oath, ye shall not be destroyed; but *if ye will not do this, I swear unto you with an oath, that on the morrow month I will command that my armies shall come down against you, and they shall not stay their hand and shall spare not, but shall slay you, and shall let fall the sword upon you even until ye shall become extinct.*

   And behold, I am Giddianhi; and I am the governor of this the secret society of Gadianton; which society and the works thereof I know to be good; and they are of ancient date and they have been handed down unto us. (3 Ne. 3:6-9.)

3. 3 Ne. 4, 5:3-6.

4. 3 Ne. 7:1-2.

5. 3 Ne. 6:10-30.

Secret Combinations Caused Final Destruction of the Nephites

Two hundred years of peace and righteousness passed after the coming of the Savior to the Americas.[1] Then, as the Nephite society began to decay, secret combinations appeared once again. In just forty years, they "spread over all the face of the land:"

And it came to pass that the wicked part of the people began again to build up the secret oaths and combinations of Gadianton.

And also the people who were called *the people of Nephi began to be proud in their hearts, because of their exceeding riches, and become vain* like unto their brethren, the Lamanites.

And from this time the disciples began to sorrow for the sins of the world.

And it came to pass that when three hundred years had passed away, both the people of Nephi and the Lamanites had become exceeding wicked one like unto another.

And it came to pass that *the robbers of Gadianton did spread over all the face of the land; and there were none that were righteous save it were the disciples of Jesus.* And gold and silver did they lay up in store in abundance, and did traffic in all manner of traffic.[2]

As the final destruction of the Nephites approached,

...these Gadianton robbers, who were among the Lamanites, did infest the land, insomuch that *the inhabitants thereof began to hide up their treasures in the earth; and they became slippery, because the Lord had cursed the land, that they could not hold them, nor retain them again.*

And it came to pass that there were sorceries, and witchcrafts, and magics; and the power of the evil one was wrought upon all the face of the land....[3]

---

1. The Book of Mormon describes these choice years in this beautiful passage:

   And it came to pass that there was *no contention in the land, because of the love of God* which did dwell in the hearts of the people.

   And there were no envyings, nor strifes, nor tumults, nor whoredoms, not lyings, nor murders, nor any manner of lasciviousness; and *surely there could not be a happier people* among all the people who had been created by the hand of God.

   There were no robbers, nor murderers, neither were there Lamanites, not any manner of -ites; but *they were in one, the children of Christ, and heirs to the kingdom of God.*

   And how blessed were they! For the Lord did bless them in all their doings; yea, even they were blessed and prospered until an hundred and ten years had passed away; and the first generation from Christ had passed away, and there was no contention in all the land. (4 Ne. 15-18.)
2. 4 Ne. 42-46.
3. Morm. 1:18-19. The record says "...no man could keep that which was his own, for the thieves, and the robbers, and the murderers, and the magic art, and the witchcraft which was in the land." (Morm. 2:10.)

"The land was filled with robbers and with Lamanites...and it was one complete revolution throughout all the face of the land."[1] This great wickedness eventually led through a long succession of battles to the final destruction of the Nephites at the Hill Cumorah, when almost a quarter of a million Nephite men, plus their women and children, were slain in one day.[2]

Secret Combinations Among the Jaredites

The Jaredites, an earlier Book of Mormon culture, also knew the effect of secret combinations. Prince Jared and his daughter enticed Akish to begin a secret combination in order to assassinate Jared's father, Omer, and usurp the kingdom:

> And it came to pass that Akish gathered in unto the house of Jared all his kinsfolk, and said unto them: Will ye swear unto me that ye will be faithful unto me in the thing which I shall desire of you?
>
> And it came to pass that they all sware unto him, by the God of heaven, and also by the heavens, and also by the earth, and by their heads, that whoso should vary from the assistance which Akish desired should lose his head; and whoso should divulge whatsoever thing Akish made known unto them, the same should lose his life.
>
> And it came to pass that thus they did agree with Akish. And *Akish did administer unto them the oaths which were given by them of old who also sought power, which had been handed down even from Cain, who was a murderer from the beginning.*
>
> *And they were kept up by the power of the devil to administer these oaths unto the people, to keep them in darkness, to help such as sought power to gain power, and to murder, and to plunder, and to lie, and to commit all manner of wickedness and whoredoms.*
>
> And it was the daughter of Jared who put it into his heart to search up these things of old; and Jared put it into the heart of Akish; wherefore, Akish administered it unto his kindred and friends, leading them away by fair promises to do whatsoever thing he desired.
>
> And it came to pass that *they formed a secret combination, even as they of old; which combination is most abominable and wicked above all, in the sight of God.*
>
> *For the Lord worketh not in secret combinations,* neither doth he will that man should shed blood, but in all things hath forbidden it, from the beginning of man.[3]

In just one generation, *"So great had been the spreading of this wicked and secret society that it had corrupted the hearts of*

---

1. Morm. 2:8.
2. Morm. 6:1-15.
3. Eth. 8:13-19. See Eth. 9:1-6. It was this evil act which caused Moroni to write his prophetic warning cited at the beginning of this chapter.

all the people."[1] The wickedness soon led to war "which lasted for the space of many years, yea, unto the destruction of nearly all the people of the kingdom, yea, even all, save it were thirty souls."[2]

The Jaredite populace began to grow and multiply from this tiny remnant, but five generations later, "Heth began to embrace the secret plans again of old, to destroy his father."[3] Prophets were sent to warn of impending destruction from famine, and then many of the people died from that great dearth and from poisonous serpents, in fulfillment of their prophetic warnings.[4]

Generations later, near the end of the Jaredite civilization, secret combinations were again established. The Book of Mormon records that

> In the days of Com there began to be robbers in the land; and they adopted the old plans, and administered oaths after the manner of the ancients, and *sought again to destroy the kingdom.* [5]

These combinations caused the people to reject the word of God and to rise in rebellion:

> And they hearkened not unto the voice of the Lord, because of their wicked combinations; wherefore, there began to be wars and contentions in all the land, and also many famines and pestilences, insomuch that there was a great destruction, such as one as never had been known upon the face of the earth; and all this came to pass in the days of Shiblom....
>
> And it came to pass that *there arose a rebellion among the people, because of that secret combination which was built up to get power and gain;* and there arose a mighty man among them in iniquity, and gave battle unto Moron, in which he did overthrow the half of the kingdom; and he did maintain the half of the kingdom for many years.
>
> And in the days of Coriantor there also came many prophets, and prophesied of great and marvelous things, and cried repentance unto the people, and *except they should repent the Lord God would execute judgment against them to their utter destruction;*
>
> And that the Lord God would send or bring forth another people to possess the land, by his power, after the manner by which he brought their fathers.
>
> And *they did reject all the words of the prophets, because of their secret society and wicked abominations.* [6]

As the end of the Jaredite civilization drew near, the prophet, Ether, watched from his hiding place and saw that "there were

---

1. Eth. 9:6.   4. Eth. 9:28-32.
2. Eth. 9:12.   5. Eth. 10:33.
3. Eth. 9:26.   6. Eth. 11:7, 15, 20-22.

many people who were slain by the sword of these secret combinations, fighting against Coriantumr that they might obtain the kingdom."[1] Again, in that era, a curse was placed upon the land:

> And now there began to be *a great curse upon all the land because of the iniquity of the people, in which, if a man should lay his tool or his sword upon his shelf, or upon the place whither he would keep it, behold, upon the morrow, he could not find it, so great was the curse upon the land.*
>
> Wherefore every man did cleave unto that which was his own, with his hands, and would not borrow neither would he lend; and every man kept the hilt of his sword in his right hand, in the defence of his property and his own life and of his wives and children.[2]

As the ultimate conflict approached, members of the secret combinations committed murders in their own ranks as they sought to gain power and position.[3]

Lib became the leader of the secret combination and the final battle was fought between Lib (and Shiz, his brother), with his secret combination forces, and the legitimate Jaredite king, Coriantumr. Prior to that battle more than two million men, plus their wives and children, had already been slain.[4]

Summary

1. Secret combinations which are organized to obtain power and wealth through evil deeds are the most abominable and wicked above all in the sight of God. The Lord does not work in secret combinations.

2. Secret combinations caused the decline and collapse of two great Book of Mormon cultures: the Jaredites and the Nephites.

3. The Lord has warned that if a nation upholds secret combinations and allows them to spread over the nation, that nation shall be destroyed.

4. Prophetic warnings concerning secret combinations were given by

    A.   Moroni (Eth. 8:21).
    B.   Moroni (Eth. 8:23-26).

---

1. Eth. 13:18.
2. Eth. 14:1-2.

3. Eth. 14:8-10.
4. Eth. 15:2.

    C.   Nephi (2 Ne. 26:20-23).

    D.   Nephi (2 Ne. 10:15).

    E.   Alma (Al. 37:28, 31).

5. Moroni wrote to the American Gentiles of the last days, warning of a secret combination which will seek to overthrow the freedom of all nations and countries. He commanded the Gentiles to awake to a sense of their awful situation when they see the secret combination among them.

6. The Lord prepared the way so that the abominations of the secret combinations would be made manifest to other people.

7. Alma taught his son Helaman that the details of the secret oaths, signs, and plans of the wicked combinations should not be preserved in the histories or records of the people. He instructed that the people should be taught to abhor such wickedness and abominations, and that the members of evil combinations were destroyed because of their wickedness.

8. According to the prophet, Alma, there is a curse upon the Americas, that destruction will come upon workers of darkness when they are fully ripe, except they repent.

9. Nephi prophesied that there would be secret combinations among the latter-day Gentiles and warned that the Lord would destroy them.

10. An examination of secret combinations described in the Book of Mormon reveals some of their characteristics:

    A.   They make secret covenants to protect each other.

    B.   They have signs, passwords, and secret means of member identification.

    C.   They are willing to murder and steal to accomplish their ends.

    D.   They severely discipline members who betray them.

    E.   They flourish in societies dulled to social justice and devoted to seeking riches.

    F.   They strive to infiltrate and gain control of government and to usurp political power and authority.

    G.   They seek to control the courts and judicial systems.

H.   They condemn the righteous and let the wicked go unpunished.

I.   They grow rapidly and can gain control of a nation in two decades.

J.   When in control they persecute the poor and the righteous.

K.   When attacked or criticized, they seek to ostracize and condemn their critics.

11. A technique used by secret combinations to gain new members is to offer the individuals the alternatives of partnership and a share in the profits from their evil doings, or death.

12. The experiences of both the Nephites and the Jaredites indicate that secret combinations, once they are established, are not easily destroyed. Like a malignant cancer, they spread rapidly—if one portion of their evil doing is stopped, their evil activities break out in another direction. Even though the total secret combination would be defeated, new combinations would spring up within a few years.

13. Secret combinations can grow beyond the level of small, hidden crime activities. They can become large robber bands and full-fledged armies. In these latter stages, they attract dissenters, malcontents, and revolutionaries to their ranks.

Eighth Warning: XI
If The People Choose Iniquity, Judgments Will Come Upon Them

King Mosiah's Warning: If the Voice of the People Chooses Iniquity, God Will Visit Them With Great Destruction (Mos. 29:26-27)

King Mosiah, a righteous leader of the Nephites in the land of Zarahemla, reached the end of his long reign in 91 B.C. He had led his people in righteousness, as did his father, King Benjamin. In his wisdom, Mosiah recognized the danger of continuing their present form of government, and regarded the danger of an unjust king leading the people into unrighteousness as very real.[1] He wanted his people to continue to enjoy the benefits of freedom and peace, and expressed his wish forcefully to his people:

> *I desire that this land be a land of liberty, and every man may enjoy his rights and privileges alike, so long as the Lord sees fit that we may live and inherit the land,...*[2]

He proposed a new democratic form of government, in which the people would be ruled by judges whom they would elect:

> Let us appoint judges, to judge this people according to our law; and we will newly arrange the affairs of this people, for we will appoint wise men to be judges, that will judge this people according to the commandments of God.[3]

His plan contained checks and balances to control the judges who would rule. If necessary, higher judges would review the decisions of lower judges, while a group of lower judges would have power to evaluate the conduct of the higher judges.[4]

---

1. Mos. 29:31. See also verses 16-24.
2. Mos. 29:32.
3. Mos. 28:11. He continued with the observation that "it is better that a man should be judged of God than of man, for the judgments of God are always just, but the judgments of man are not always just." (Mos. 29:12)
4. Mos. 29:28-29.

Mosiah instructed his people to choose righteous judges who would rule by correct laws. Then he expressed his confidence that the majority of the people would choose the right, although a minority might seek improper ends. His observation was followed with a prophetic warning—if the majority of the people chooses wickedness, then is the time God will visit them with judgments and destruction:

> Now it is not common that the voice of the people desireth anything contrary to that which is right; but it is common for the lesser part of the people to desire that which is not right; therefore *this shall ye observe and make it your law—to do your business by the voice of the people.*
>
> *And if the time comes that the voice of the people doth choose iniquity, then is the time that the judgments of God will come upon you; yea, then is the time he will visit you with great destruction even as he has hitherto visited this land.*[1]

Thus King Mosiah stated a principle which has been proven true throughout Book of Mormon history, and which remains equally true today: if the majority of the populace of a nation chooses unrighteousness, that nation will soon be destroyed because of its wickedness.

Amulek's Warning: If the Righteous Are Cast Out, Destruction Comes by Famine, Pestilence and Sword (Al. 10:22-23)

Ten years later, Amulek, while performing his missionary labors, cited the prophetic warning of King Mosiah as a rebuke to wicked lawyers who were trying to entrap him:

> O ye wicked and perverse generation, ye lawyers and hypocrites, for ye are laying the foundations of the devil; for ye are laying traps and snares to catch the holy ones of God.
>
> Ye are laying plans to pervert the ways of the righteous, and *to bring down the wrath of God upon your heads, even to the utter destruction of this people.*
>
> Yea, well did Mosiah say, who was our last king, when he was about to deliver up the kingdom, having no one to confer it upon, causing that this people should be governed by their own voices—yea, well did he say that *if the time should come that the voice of this people should choose iniquity, that is, if the time should come that this people should fall into transgression, they would be ripe for destruction.*

---

1. Mos. 29:26-27.

And now I say unto you that well doth the Lord judge of your iniquities; well doth he cry unto this people, by the voice of his angels: *Repent ye, repent, for the kingdom of heaven is at hand.*[1]

Yea, well doth he cry, by the voice of his angels that:

I will come down among my people, with equity and justice in my hands.[2]

He taught that even when wickedness prevails in a land, the prayers of the remaining righteous inhabitants can stave off impending destruction. But if the righteous inhabitants are cast out, then the Lord will no longer stay his hand. This is his prophetic warning:

Yea, and I say unto you that *if it were not for the prayers of the righteous, who are now in the land, that ye would even now be visited with utter destruction;* yet it would not be by flood, as were the people in the days of Noah, but *it would be by famine, and by pestilence, and the sword.*

But it is by the prayers of the righteous that ye are spared; now therefore, *if ye will cast out the righteous from among you then will not the Lord stay his hand;* but in his fierce anger he will come out against you; then ye shall be smitten by famine, and by pestilence, and by the sword; and the time is soon at hand except ye repent.[3]

Just as the secret combinations later heaped epithets and abuse upon the prophet Nephi, who rebuked them,[4] Amulek's wicked audience accused him of speaking against their laws and the men they had chosen as their leaders. Amulek countered their hue and cry, however, showing that he had not spoken against their law. He reminded them that "I have spoken in favor of your law, to your condemnation."[5] And then he warned of what happens when the majority of the people choose unrighteous leaders:

---

1. Note the meaning of the phrase "the kingdom of heaven is at hand," as used in this context. It does not refer to available blessings but is a warning of impending destruction. It is used similarly in other passages. See Mt. 3:1-3; 4:17; 11:11-12.
2. Al. 10:17-21.
3. Al. 10:22-23. This principle was demonstrated early in Old Testament times at the destruction of Sodom. The Lord promised Abraham that the city wouldn't be destroyed if even ten righteous inhabitants remained (Gen. 18:20-32). But when Lot and his family, the remaining righteous, left the city, destruction sent by God was immediate (Gen. 19:1-25; see also 2 Pet. 2:6-9).
4. See Hel. 8:1-7.
5. Al. 10:26. See verses 24-30.

Behold, I say unto you, that *the foundation of the destruction of this people is beginning to be laid by the unrighteous of your lawyers and your judges.* [1]

Samuel's Warning: When You Cast Out the Righteous, You Are Ripe for Destruction (Hel. 13:12-14)

The theme that even a righteous minority of inhabitants of a city or nation can save it from destruction recurs several times throughout the ancient scriptures and appears to be a principle applicable to all times and places. Its corollary, that destruction is imminent when the righteous are cast out, also is found in these passages.

Samuel the Lamanite, for instance, sounded both concepts when he spoke of the impending destruction of Zarahemla:

Yea, wo unto this great city of Zarahemla; for behold, *it is because of those who are righteous that it is saved;* yea, wo unto this great city, for I perceive, saith the Lord, that there are many, yea, even the more part of this great city, that will harden their hearts against me, saith the Lord.

But blessed are they who will repent, for them will I spare. But behold, if it were not for the righteous who are in this great city, behold, I would cause that fire should come down out of heaven and destroy it.

But behold, it is for the righteous' sake that it is spared. But behold, *the time cometh, saith the Lord, that when ye shall cast out the righteous from among you, then shall ye be ripe for destruction;* yea, wo be unto this great city, because of the wickedness and abominations which are in her. [2]

Samuel the Lamanite warned the wicked Nephites that their land was already cursed because they had cast out the prophets and were willing to accept the words of evil men who spoke flattering words to them:

Yea, wo unto this people, because of this time which has arrived, that *ye do cast out the prophets, and do mock them, and cast stones at them, and do slay them, and do all manner of iniquity unto them,* even as they did of old time.

And now when ye talk, ye say: If our days had been in the days of our fathers of old, we would not have slain the prophets; we would not have stoned them, and cast them out.

Behold ye are worse than they; for as the Lord liveth, *if a prophet come among you and declareth unto you the word of the Lord, which*

---

1. Al. 10:27. The wicked practices of these lawyers and judges is explained in Al. 10:13-32.
2. Hel. 13:12-14.

testifieth of your sins and iniquities, ye are angry with him, and cast him out and seek all manner of ways to destroy him; yea, you will say that he is a false prophet, and that he is a sinner, and of the devil, because he testifieth that your deeds are evil.

But behold, if a man shall come among you and shall say: Do this, and there is no iniquity; do that and ye shall not suffer; yea, he will say: Walk after the pride of your own hearts; yea, walk after the pride of your eyes, and do whatsoever your heart desireth—and if a man shall come among you and say this, ye will receive him, and say that he is a prophet.

Yea, ye will lift him up, and ye will give unto him of your substance; ye will give unto him of your gold, and of your silver, and ye will clothe him with costly apparel; and because he speaketh flattering words unto you, and he saith that all is well, then ye will not find fault with him.

O ye wicked and ye perverse generation; ye hardened and ye stiff-necked people, how long will ye suppose that the Lord will suffer you? Yea, how long will ye suffer yourselves to be led by foolish and blind guides? Yea, how long will ye choose darkness rather than light?

Yea, behold, the anger of the Lord is already kindled against you; behold, he hath cursed the land because of your iniquity.

And behold, *the time cometh that he curseth your riches, that they become slippery, that ye cannot hold them; and in the days of your poverty ye cannot retain them.*

And in the days of your poverty ye shall cry unto the Lord; and *in vain shall ye cry, for your desolation is already come upon you, and your destruction is made sure;* and then shall ye weep and howl in that day, saith the Lord of Hosts.[1]

Nephi's Warning: Destruction Comes to Those Who Kill the Prophets and the Saints (2 Ne. 26:3-8)

Five-and-a-half centuries earlier, the prophet Nephi had foretold the destruction which would occur at the time of the Savior's death. In his prophecy he clearly foresaw that their casting out the prophets and the saints, and slaying them, would be the reason the people would reap God's wrath:

And after the Messiah shall come there shall be signs given unto my people of his birth, and also of his death and resurrection; and great and terrible shall that day be unto the wicked, for they shall perish; and *they perish because they cast out the prophets, and the saints, and stone them, and slay them; wherefore the cry of the blood of the saints shall ascend up to God from the ground against them.*

Wherefore, all those who are proud, and that do wickedly, the day that cometh shall burn them up, saith the Lord of Hosts, for they shall be as stubble.

---

1. Hel. 13:24-32. Casting out the prophets is a wicked practice frequently recorded in the Book of Mormon. See Mos. 17:3; Al. 8:13, 24-25, 29; 15:1; 26:29; Hel. 14:10; 3 Ne. 7:14; Eth. 13:13-15.

And they that kill the prophets, and the saints, the depths of the
earth shall swallow them up, saith the Lord of Hosts; and mountains
shall cover them, and whirlwinds shall carry them away, and buildings
shall fall upon them and crush them to pieces and grind them to powder.

And they shall be visited with thunderings, and lightnings, and earth-
quakes, and all manner of destructions, for the fire of the anger of the
Lord shall be kindled against them, and they shall be as stubble, and the
day that cometh shall consume them, saith the Lord of Hosts.

O the pain, and the anguish of my soul for the loss of the slain of
my people! For I, Nephi, have seen it, and it well nigh consumeth me
before the presence of the Lord; but I must cry unto my God: Thy
ways are just.

But behold, the *righteous that hearken unto the words of the proph-*
ets, and destroy them not, but look forward unto Christ with stead-
fastness for the signs which are given, notwithstanding all persecution—
behold, they are they which shall not perish. [1]

The scriptures tell the fulfillment of his prophecy, and record
the Savior's statement that casting out the righteous was the specific reason why the cities of Laman, Josh, Gad, and Kishkumen
were burned by fire at the time of his death:

And behold, the city of Laman, and the city of Josh, and the city of
Gad, and the city of Kishkumen, have I caused to be burned with fire,
and the inhabitants thereof, *because of their wickedness in casting out*
the prophets, and stoning those whom I did send to declare unto them
concerning their wickedness and their abominations.

And because they *did cast them all out, that there were none right-*
eous among them, I did send down fire and destroy them, that their
wickedness and abominations might be hid from before my face, that
the blood of the prophets and the saints whom I sent among them
might not cry unto me from the ground against them.

And many great destructions have I caused to come upon this land,
and upon this people, because of their wickedness and their abominations. [2]

Nephi's Warning: Speedy Destruction Comes to a People
If They Choose Darkness (2 Ne. 26:10-11)

Nephi also prophesied the final destruction of the Nephite
civilization, and stated the eternal principle that speedy destruction comes upon a people if they yield unto the devil and choose
works of darkness rather than light for that is the time the Spirit
ceases to strive with man. His prophecy begins with the appearance of the Savior to the Nephites following his resurrection:

---

1. 2 Ne. 26:3-8.
2. 3 Ne. 9:10-12.

But the Son of righteousness shall appear unto them; and he shall heal them, and they shall have peace with him, until three generations shall have passed away, and many of the fourth generation shall have passed away in righteousness.

And when these things have passed away *a speedy destruction cometh unto my people;* for, notwithstanding the pains of my soul, I have seen it; wherefore, I know that it shall come to pass; and they sell themselves for naught; for, for the reward of their pride and their foolishness they shall reap destruction; for because *they yield unto the devil and choose works of darkness rather than light, therefore they must go down to hell.*

For the Spirit of the Lord will not always strive with man. *And when the Spirit ceaseth to strive with man then cometh speedy destruction,* and this grieveth my soul.[1]

Jaredite History: Famine Because Prophets Were Cast Out (Eth. 9:28-30)

Many centuries before the time of Christ, the Jaredites suffered a destructive famine because they cast out the prophets. The nation had begun to turn to wickedness by adopting the evil plans of secret combinations:

And there came prophets in the land again, crying repentance unto them—that they must prepare the way of the Lord or there should come a curse upon the face of the land; yea, even *there should be a great famine, in which they should be destroyed if they did not repent.*

But the people believed not the words of the prophets, but they cast them out; and some of them they cast into pits and left them to perish. And it came to pass that they did all these things according to the commandment of the king, Heth.

And it came to pass that there began to be a great dearth upon the land, and the inhabitants began to be *destroyed exceeding fast because of the dearth, for there was no rain upon the face of the earth.*[2]

Their suffering continued until the people repented and humbled themselves:

...Now when the people saw that they must perish they began to repent of their iniquities and cry unto the Lord.

And it came to pass that *when they had humbled themselves sufficiently before the Lord he did send rain* upon the face of the earth;

---

1. 2 Ne. 26:9-11.
2. Eth. 9:28-30. Several generations earlier, when the people began to mock and revile against the prophets who were warning of an approaching curse upon the land, their righteous king protected the prophets by law, which caused the people to repent. "The Lord did spare them." (See Eth. 7:23-26.)

and the people began to revive again, and there began to be fruit in the
north countries, and in all the countries round about. *And the Lord did
show forth his power unto them in preserving them from famine.*[1]

Jaredite History: Wars, Famines and Pestilences When Prophets Are Slain (Eth. 11:1-7, 12-13)

Several generations after the above famine was abated, many
prophets were sent by the Lord to warn the Jaredites that ultimate destruction faced their civilization because of its great wickedness. They put some of the prophets to death, which brought famines and pestilences upon them, and caused the other prophets to
cease their labors among them:

> And there came also in the days of Com *many prophets, and proph-
> esied of the destruction of that great people except they should repent,*
> and turn unto the Lord, and forsake their murders and wickedness.
> And it came to pass that the prophets were rejected by the people,
> and they fled unto Com for protection, for the people sought to destroy
> them.
> And they prophesied unto Com many things; and he was blessed in
> all the remainder of his days.
> And he lived to a good old age, and begat Shiblom; and Shiblom
> reigned in his stead. And the brother of Shiblom rebelled against him,
> and there began to be an exceeding great war in all the land.
> And it came to pass that the brother of Shiblom caused that all the
> prophets who prophesied of the destruction of the people should be
> put to death;
> And there was *great calamity in all the land, for they had testified
> that a great curse should come upon the land, and also upon the people,
> and that there should be a great destruction among them, such an one as
> never had been upon the face of the earth, and their bones should be-
> come as heaps of earth upon the face of the land except they should
> repent of their wickedness.*
> And they hearkened not unto the voice of the Lord, because of their
> wicked combinations; wherefore, *there began to be wars and conten-
> tions in all the land, and also many famines and pestilences, insomuch
> that there was a great destruction,* such an one as never had been known
> upon the face of the earth; and all this came to pass in the days of
> Shiblom....
> And it came to pass that in the days of Ethem there came *many
> prophets, and prophesied again unto the people; yea, they did proph-
> esy that the Lord would utterly destroy them from off the face of the
> earth except they repented of their iniquities.*
> And it came to pass that the people hardened their hearts, and would
> not hearken unto their words; and the *prophets mourned and withdrew
> from among the people.*[2]

---

1. Eth. 9:34-35.
2. Eth. 11:1-7, 12-13.

While a wicked people may hasten their own destruction by casting out the righteous, they may also discover that the Lord can direct His followers to cease working among them, leaving them without the uplifting influence of the saints. In the days of Mormon, for instance,

> Wickedness did prevail upon the face of the whole land, insomuch that the Lord did take away His beloved disciples, and the work of miracles and of healing did cease because of all the iniquity of the people.
>
> And there were no gifts from the Lord, and the Holy Ghost did not come upon any, because of their wickedness and unbelief.[1]

Such will be the result when the saints are gathered out from among the wicked in anticipation of the great judgments which will be poured out[2]—there will be no leavening influence to lift and protect the wicked who remain.

The message of the scriptures is clear: God-sent destruction comes rapidly upon a people or nation if they reject and slay the prophets and the Lord's people.

Nephite History: Corrupt Laws and Political Leaders Bring Destruction (Helaman 5:2-3)

Nephi records another principle upon which the well-being of a nation depends: if the majority of a people choose to be governed by evil and corrupt laws, that nation will be ripening for destruction. He also stated a corollary to this principle: if the people refuse to be governed by law or by justice, their destruction is also near.

> For as their laws and their governments were established by the voice of the people, and *they who chose evil were more numerous than they who chose good, therefore they were ripening for destruction, for the laws had become corrupted.*
>
> Yea, and this was not all; they were a stiffnecked people, insomuch that *they could not be governed by the law nor justice,* save it were to their destruction.[3]

The people in Nephi's day, just three decades before the birth of the Savior, had allowed their laws to be corrupted. They found that governmental corruption was a sign of their general wicked-

---

1. Morm. 1:13-14. See also 2 Ne. 26:10-11.
2. See D & C 133:8-14, Rev. 18:4, etc.
3. Hel. 5:2-3.

ness, that the church was dwindling in their midst, that they no longer were being preserved by the Spirit of the Lord, and that judgments and destruction appeared imminent:

> They had altered and trampled under their feet the laws of Mosiah, or that which the Lord commanded him to give unto the people; and *they saw that their laws had become corrupted, and that they had become a wicked people,* insomuch that they were wicked even like unto the Lamanites.
>
> *And because of their iniquity the church had begun to dwindle;* and they began to disbelieve in the spirit of prophecy and in the spirit of revelation; and the judgments of God did stare them in the face.
>
> And they saw that they had become weak, like unto their brethren, the Lamanites, and that *the Spirit of the Lord did no more preserve them; yea, it had withdrawn from them* because the Spirit of the Lord doth not dwell in unholy temples—
>
> *Therefore the Lord did cease to preserve them by his miraculous and matchless power,* for they had fallen into a state of unbelief and awful wickedness; and they saw that the Lamanites were exceedingly more numerous than they, and *except they should cleave unto the Lord their God they must unavoidably perish.*[1]

Nephi saw that when men inspired from heaven came testifying boldly of the sins of the people,[2] these men were taken and "put to death secretly by the judges."[3] When these corrupt judges were brought to trial, the judicial leadership of the country formed a secret covenant to protect them, "And *they did set at defiance the law and the rights of their country; and they did covenant one with another to destroy the governor, and to establish a king over the land, that the land should no more be at liberty....*[4] And

> All this iniquity had come upon the people because they did yield themselves unto the power of Satan.
>
> And the regulations of the government were destroyed, because of the secret combination of the friends and kindreds of those who murdered the prophets.[5]

The problem of governmental corruption had existed among the Nephites a generation earlier. In that previous era, a righteous general gave vent to his displeasure concerning his nation's leadership: "Moroni was angry with the government, because of their indifference concerning the freedom of their country."[6] He chal-

---

1. Hel. 4:22-25.
2. 3 Ne. 6:20.
3. 3 Ne. 6:23.

4. 3 Ne. 6:30.
5. 3 Ne. 7:5-6.
6. Al. 59:13.

lenged the government, telling them that "it is because of your iniquity that we have suffered so much loss."[1]

And then Moroni warned that the Lord would not allow a corrupt government to destroy a righteous people, but would inspire the people to rise against them:

> The Lord will not suffer that ye shall live and wax strong in your iniquities to destroy his righteous people.
>
> Behold, can you suppose that the Lord will spare you and come out in judgment against the Lamanites, when it is the tradition of their fathers that has caused their hatred, yea, and it has been redoubled by those who have dissented from us, while your iniquity is for the cause of your love of glory and the vain things of the world?
>
> Ye know that ye do transgress the laws of God, and ye do know that ye do trample them under your feet. Behold, the Lord saith unto me: If those whom ye have appointed your governors do not repent of their sins and iniquities, ye shall go up to battle against them.[2]

The Lord summed up the danger of corrupt leaders and how they can be avoided with this modern revelation:

> When the wicked rule the people mourn.
>
> Wherefore, honest men and wise men should be sought for diligently, and good men and wise men ye should observe to uphold; whatsoever is less than these cometh of evil.[3]

Nephi's Warning: If People Forget God Because of Their Riches, He Will Chasten Them with Terror, Famine and Pestilence (Hel. 12:2-3)

In no area of human endeavor is the effect of choosing wickedness more apparent than in the deliberate choice of temporal riches over service to God. Nephi warned that when people who have been blessed by God harden their hearts because of their prosperity,

> ...We may see at the very time when he doth prosper his people, yea, in the increase of their fields, their flocks and their herds, and in gold, and

---

1. Al. 60:28.
2. Al. 60:31-33. Moroni received a reply to his threat from Pahoran, the chief governor, in which he learned that the government had become so weak that a corrupt faction had risen in rebellion against the free man and was attempting to overrun the nation from within while it was struggling to defend itself from outside attack. See Al. 61. Concerning the principle of rising up against wicked leaders and enemies, see D & C 98.
3. D & C 98:9-10.

in silver, and in all manner of precious things of every kind and art; *sparing their lives, and delivering them out of the hands of their enemies; softening the hearts of their enemies that they should not declare wars against them;* yea, and in fine, doing all things for the welfare and happiness of his people; yea, *then is the time that they do harden their hearts, and do forget the Lord their God,* and do trample under their feet the Holy One—yea, and this because of their ease, and their exceedingly great prosperity.

And thus we see that *except the Lord doth chasten his people with many afflictions, yea, except he doth visit them with death and with terror, and with famine and with all manner of pestilence, they will not remember him.* [1]

It can thus be clearly seen that Book of Mormon prophets warn that judgment will come upon a nation if its people choose iniquity and yield themselves to Satan's temptations. Well did the prophet Lehi say that

Men are free according to the flesh; and all things are given them which are expedient unto man. And they are *free to choose liberty and eternal life,* through the great mediation of all men, or to *choose captivity and death, according to the captivity and power of the devil;* for he seeketh that all men might be miserable like unto himself. [2]

Summary

1. Book of Mormon prophets have warned that if the people of a nation deliberately choose iniquity rather than righteousness, then they are ripe for destruction and the judgments of God will soon come upon them.

2. King Mosiah observed that it is not common that the majority of a people choose unrighteousness, though a minority commonly choose wickedness. Judgments come when the wicked minority grows to become the majority.

3. Prophetic and historical warnings concerning the danger of people choosing wickedness and/or casting out the righteous were given by

     A.   King Mosiah (Mos. 29:26-27)
     B.   Amulek (Al. 10:22-23)

---

1. Hel. 12:2-3.
2. 2 Ne. 2:27.

     C.   Samuel the Lamanite (Hel. 13:12-14)
     D.   Nephi (2 Ne. 26:3-8)
     E.   Nephi (2 Ne. 26:10-11)
     F.   Jaredite History (Eth. 9:28-30)
     G.   Jaredite History (Eth. 11:1-7, 12-13)
     H.   Nephi (Hel. 12:2-3)

4. The prayers of the righteous can save a land from being "visited with utter destruction," but if the righteous leave or are cast out, then the Lord will no longer stay his hand and withhold punishment.

5. Unrighteous laws, judges, and lawyers can lay the foundation for the destruction of a people. A nation cannot afford to allow or tolerate corruption in government.

6. The wicked cast out the prophets, mocking and slaying them. But if false prophets tell them their actions are not sinful and that they won't be held accountable for them, the wicked people receive those false prophets as their leaders.

7. The Lord promises to spare the righteous and repentant when he destroys the wicked. (2 Ne. 26:8)

8. The prophetic warnings indicate many ways in which God sends his judgments upon the wicked, including

     A.   famine (Al. 10:22-23; Eth. 9:28-30, 35; 11:7)
     B.   pestilence (Al. 10:22-23; Eth. 11:7)
     C.   war and the sword (Al. 10:22-23; Eth. 11:7)
     D.   fire coming down from heaven (Gen. 19:24; Hel. 13:13; 3 Ne. 9:11)
     E.   cursing their riches, so they become slippery (Hel. 13:31-32)
     F.   refusing to hear their cry (Hel. 13:32)
     G.   fire (2 Ne. 26:4)
     H.   earth swallow them up (2 Ne. 26:5)
     I.   mountains cover them (2 Ne. 26:5)
     J.   whirlwinds carry them away (2 Ne. 26:5)
     K.   buildings fall and crush them (2 Ne. 26:5)
     L.   thunder and lightning (2 Ne. 26:6)
     M.   earthquakes (2 Ne. 26:6)
     N.   no rain (Eth. 9:30)
     O.   terror (Hel. 12:3)

8. The Lord destroys the wicked to hide their wickedness and abominations from before his face, and to stop the blood of slain prophets and saints from crying from the ground unto him against them. (3 Ne. 9:11)

9. Righteous leaders have saved their people from destruction by passing laws protecting the prophets from harm and abuse. (Eth. 7:23-26; Al. 23:2. See also Al. 1:2-27)

10. When a wicked people repents and humbles itself, God moderates or ends the judgments which he is sending upon them.

11. When the wicked rule, the people mourn. Citizens should diligently seek for honest and wise leaders, and then uphold them in their leadership decisions.

12. Casting out the righteous and slaying the prophets brought destruction upon the Jaredites, and upon the Nephites both following the death of the Savior and three-and-a-half centuries later when the Nephite civilization was destroyed.

13. God blesses those who trust and serve him by prospering them, delivering them out of the hands of their enemies, and softening the hearts of their enemies so they won't declare war against them.

14. It is when people are living in ease and great prosperity that they tend to forget God and harden their hearts. When they forget him, God chastens them with death, terror, famine and pestilence.

15. Men are free to choose liberty and eternal life through obedience to Christ, or captivity and death according to the power of the devil.

XII

Ninth Warning:
Conflict and Apostasy

A final series of prophetic warnings found in the scriptures is related to the future of the Lord's church. These warnings are penetrating in their implications, for they indicate the far-reaching extent to which Satan will exert his influence in his efforts to thwart the Lord's work prior to the millennial era of the Savior's earthly reign. Most of these prophetic warnings appear to relate chronologically to the early period of the New Jerusalem.

Scriptural prophecies of future conflict within the church are not pleasant for Latter-day Saints to consider. Indeed, they are not pleasant to write about. The author would prefer to avoid them, but cannot do so with integrity, for they truly exist, and it is impossible to give an accurate portrayal of future events without giving them due consideration.

It is probable that some will attempt to explain them away, rationalizing that the prophecies refer to the "great apostasy" which commenced following the New Testament era. Such a rationalization would fly in the face of basic principles of scriptural interpretation, ignoring the many internal and contextual indications that the passages focus on a future era. Such rationalizations would also assume that the prophesied events have already come to pass, though no specific events can be cited as literal fulfillment.

There may also be some who would challenge the propriety of a "lay member" pointing out the existence of such a prophetic pattern, and somehow believe that their challenge would negate the scriptures cited. They, of course, would overlook the Lord's express commandment that

> ...*every man, both elder, priest, teacher, and also member*, go to with his might, with the labor of his hands, to prepare and accomplish the things which I have commanded.
> And *let your preaching be the warning voice, every man to his neighbor*, in mildness and in meekness.[1]

---

1. D & C 38:40-41.

Such individuals would also forget the scriptural admonition that "*every man* should take righteousness in his hands and faithfulness upon his loins, and *lift a warning voice* unto the inhabitants of the earth; and declare both by word and by flight that *desolation shall come upon the wicked.*"[1] Indeed, "it becometh *every man who hath been warned to warn his neighbor...and to prepare the saints* for the hour of judgment which is to come."[2]

Certainly I find no pleasure in these prophecies of future difficulties within the church. Nor do I want to see them come to pass, for I recognize the problems, sorrow, strife and confusion their fulfillment would inevitably bring. I write to avert or soften their fulfillment, in the spirit of a priesthood bearer functioning in the universal calling to "watch over the church always, and be with and strengthen them; and see there is no iniquity in the church."[3]

God's Kingdom Shall Never Be Destroyed

These prophetic warnings should be viewed, I believe, in the context of what God has revealed concerning His kingdom and authority in this last dispensation. Daniel prophesied of the permanent nature of the restored kingdom of God as he interpreted the prophetic dream received by the Babylonian king, Nebuchadnezzar. He foresaw that the God of heaven would

> ...set up a kingdom, which *shall never be destroyed:* and the *kingdom shall not be left to other people,* but it shall break in pieces and consume all these kingdoms, and *it shall stand for ever.* [4]

A modern revelation alludes to Daniel's interpretation of Nebuchadnezzar's vision, proclaiming that "the keys of the kingdom of God are committed unto man on the earth, and from thence shall the gospel roll forth unto the ends of the earth, as the stone which is cut out of the mountain without hands shall roll forth, *until it has filled the whole earth.*"[5]

---

1. D & C 63:37.
2. D & C 88:81, 84. See also D & C 84:87, 117.
3. D & C 20:53-54.
4. Dan. 2:44. For a discussion of Nebuchadnezzar's dream see the author's book, *The Prophecies of Joseph Smith,* pp. 197-199. Concerning other interpretational views of a political nature see *Prophecy—Key to the Future,* pp. 67-81.
5. D & C 65:2.

That this kingdom will endure was repeatedly emphasized by the Savior, who revealed to the Church in the days of Joseph Smith that "the kingdom is yours, and *the enemy shall not overcome,*"[1] and "Fear not, little flock, *the kingdom is yours until I come.*"[2] It was revealed to the saints that "the kingdom is given you of the Father, and *power to overcome all things which are not ordained of him—*"[3] The prophet Joseph was told by revelation that the "kingdom is coming forth *for the last time*"[4] and the saints believe that the Savior "shall deliver up the kingdom, and present it unto the Father, spotless," when "Christ shall have subdued all enemies under his feet, and shall have perfected his work."[5]

The priesthood power restored in the last days is also established with permanence, for John the Baptist proclaimed that the priesthood of Aaron *"shall never be taken again from the earth, until the sons of Levi do offer again an offering unto the Lord in righteousness."*[6] And the Lord has revealed that "the power of this priesthood [is] given, *for the last days and for the last time,* in the which is the dispensation of the fulness of times."[7]

Thus, though apostasy and strife may come among the saints in fulfillment of the prophecies, it is expected that the Church and priesthood will remain and fulfill the roles to which they have been called and appointed.

Though scriptural prophecies warn of difficult times ahead for the Lord's Church, the message of the scriptures is that the Church will survive the problems it must endure and will eventually come off victorious in the latter-days panorama.

Isaiah's Warning: The Earth Shall Be Left Desolate Because They Have Broken the Everlasting Covenant (Isaiah 24:5-6)

As has been seen, the scriptures speak repeatedly of a period in the last days called the "desolation of abomination"[8]—a time when the judgments of God will come upon the wicked and greatly reduce the population of the earth. Prophecies relating to this

---

1. D & C 38:9.
2. D & C 35:27. See also 62:9; 64:4; 78:18; 82:24.
3. D & C 50:35.
4. D & C 90:2.
5. D & C 76:106-107.
6. D & C 13:1. See D & C 84:18.
7. D & C 112:30.
8. See D & C 88:85, 84:117.

period refer to it as a time of "desolation," when the wicked will be destroyed "and their house shall be left unto them desolate."[1] The prophet Isaiah speaks of this future event. He prophesies that *"the Lord maketh the earth empty, and maketh it waste,* and turneth it upside down, and scattereth abroad the inhabitants thereof.... The land shall be utterly emptied, and utterly spoiled: for the Lord hath spoken this word."[2] As he prophesies of the future cleansing, Isaiah reveals the reason why it will come upon the earth—the earth's inhabitants will have "transgressed the laws, changed the ordinance, broken the everlasting covenant." This is his prophetic warning:

> The earth also is defiled under the inhabitants thereof: because *they have transgressed the laws, changed the ordinance, broken the everlasting covenant.*
> Therefore hath the curse devoured the earth and *they that dwell therein are desolate:* therefore the *inhabitants of the earth are burned, and few men left.*[3]

The prophecy continues by describing the people of the earth who will remain following this destruction:

> The new wine mourneth, the vine languisheth, all the merryhearted do sigh.
> The mirth of tabrets ceaseth, the noise of them that rejoice endeth, the joys of the harp ceaseth.
> They shall not drink wine with a song; strong drink shall be bitter to them that drink it.
> *The city of confusion is broken down: every house is shut up, that no man may come in.*
> There is a crying for wine in the streets; all joy is darkened, *the mirth of the land is gone.*
> *In the city is left desolation, and the gate is smitten with destruction.*[4]

It is the immediate cause of this desolating destruction that makes it appropriate for the prophecy to be cited in this context—

---

1. D & C 84:115.
2. Is. 24:1, 3.
3. Is. 24:5-6.
4. Is. 24:7-12. This description is indication that the burning of verse 6 is not the cleansing of the earth at Christ's coming in glory, for the prophesied situation differs markedly from the millennial era when "the former shall not be remembered, nor come into mind" and, as the Lord says, "I create Jerusalem a rejoicing, and her people a joy." See Is. 65:17-25.

Isaiah's warning that men will change the ordinance, and break the everlasting covenant. To do so would seem to require Church membership, for can one change something which he does not already have, or break a covenant which he has not made?

What is the everlasting covenant of which Isaiah speaks? It is the gospel of Jesus Christ. As a modern revelation states, "Blessed are you for receiving mine *everlasting covenant, even the fulness of my gospel,* sent forth unto the children of men, that they might have life and be made partakers of the glories which are to be revealed in the last days."[1] The Savior refers to the process of joining the Church "When men are *called unto mine everlasting gospel, and covenant with an everlasting covenant....*"[2] He speaks of "a new and everlasting covenant,..." and says that "I have caused *this last covenant and this church* to be built up unto me."[3] It is by making the everlasting covenant that saints are received into fellowship in the church.[4] Those who don't receive the gospel do not receive the everlasting covenant,[5] and he who enters into the new and everlasting covenant "must and shall abide the law, or he shall be damned."[6] The everlasting covenant, like the Church itself, is to be a standard for the nations.[7]

Isaiah's warning, then, is that judgments will come because Church members will transgress gospel laws, change gospel ordinances, and break the everlasting covenant by which they became members of the Church. His prophecy is very similar to a prophetic warning found in the Lord's "Preface" to the Doctrine and Covenants, which is considered next.

The Lord's Warning: Those Who Will Not Heed the Lord Nor His Prophets Shall Be Cut Off (D & C 1:14-16)

The Master has warned his people to prepare for the time to come when his anger shall fall upon the inhabitants of the earth.[8] It will come in a time when apostates who have strayed from his ordinances and broken his everlasting covenant will be cut off from among the people:

---

1. D & C 66:2.
2. D & C 101:39.
3. D & C 22:1-4.
4. D & C 88:133.
5. D & C 76:101.
6. D & C 132:6.
7. Compare D & C 45:9 with D & C 115:4-6.
8. D & C 1:12-13.

...The arm of the Lord shall be revealed; and the day cometh that they who will *not hear the voice of the Lord, neither the voice of his servants, neither give heed to the words of the prophets and apostles, shall be cut off from among the people;*

For they have strayed from mine ordinances, and have broken mine everlasting covenant;

They seek not the Lord to establish his righteousness, but every man walketh in his own way, and after the image of his own God, whose image is in the likeness of the world, and whose substance is that of an idol....[1]

Here, then, is one of a series of prophecies warning of a future time when saints will be "cut off." It has similarities to 3 Ne. 21:20, which talks about the unrepentant being cut off in the context of internal destruction in America at the time of the establishment of the New Jerusalem.[2] Other prophecies considered in this chapter will give greater insight into possible reasons for the future saints to refuse to heed the word of the Lord.

The Lord's Warning: The Rebellious Shall Be Cut Off from Zion and False Apostles and Prophets Shall Be Known (D & C 64:35-40)

A prophecy concerning the saints in the New Jerusalem indicates that there will be a rebellious faction in that day which will be cut off, and shows that the apostasy may even reach the highest councils, for the saints "will judge all things pertaining to Zion," and "they who are not apostles and prophets shall be known:"

...*The rebellious shall be cut off out of the land of Zion, and shall be sent away, and shall not inherit the land.*

For, verily I say that the rebellious are not of the blood of Ephraim, wherefore *they shall be plucked out.*

Behold, I, the Lord, have made my church in these last days like unto a judge sitting on a hill, or in a high place, to judge the nations.

For it shall come to pass that *the inhabitants of Zion shall judge all things pertaining to Zion.*

And liars and hypocrites shall be proved by them, and they who are not apostles and prophets shall be known.

---

1. D & C 1:14-16. Note the similarities to the wording of Isaiah's prophecy (compare Is. 24:5 with D & C 1:15), also that the D & C passage is future (the day *cometh....*). The Lord then says that he, *"Knowing the calamity which should come upon the inhabitants of the earth,"* called upon Joseph Smith and gave him commandments (D & C 1:17).
2. See 3 Ne. 21:12-24; D & C 63:63.

> And even the bishop, who is a judge, and his counselors, if they are not faithful in their stewardships *shall be condemned, and others shall be planted in their stead.* [1]

The Church has had to contend with false apostles and prophets in other dispensations. John the Revelator wrote to the saints in Ephesus, for instance, and commented that "I know thy works, and thy labour, and thy patience, and how thou canst not bear them which are evil: and *thou hast tried them which say they are apostles, and are not, and hast found them liars.* "[2] King Mosiah, in the Book of Mormon, alluded to prophets which had "fallen into transgression."[3] And many Old Testament passages tell of problems caused by false prophets who were the accepted leaders of the Church in their day.[4]

The Lord's Warning: False Christs and False Prophets Shall Deceive the Elect (Matthew 24:24)

In his great prophecy given on the Mount of Olives, Jesus warned of the last days "abomination of desolation"[5] which will come upon the earth. He described the period vividly, saying that

> ...*Then shall be great tribulation, such as was not since the beginning of the world to this time, no, nor ever shall be.*
> And except those days should be shortened, *there should no flesh be saved:* but for the elect's sake those days shall be shortened.[6]

At that juncture in the world's future will come false leaders who will seek to deceive the saints:

---

1. D & C 64:35-40. Note the context (verses 41-43) which indicates that the time of fulfillment for this passage is yet future, and not during the brief interlude in the first decade of the Church's existence when the saints lived in Jackson County, Missouri.
2. Rev. 2:2.
3. Mos. 15:13.
4. See, for instance, Zeph. 3:4; Jer. 2:8; 5:31; 10:21; 12:10-11; 14:13-16; 23:1-2, 11, 13, 16-17, 21-22, 25-40; 27:9-10, 14-18; 29:8-9; Ezek. 13:2-4; 22:25-28; 34:2-4; Zech. 10:2; Mal. 2:7-8; etc.
5. Mt. 24:15. See Dan. 9:26-27. Note that Mt. 24 speaks of two periods— shortly after the time of Christ (around 70 A.D., when the temple in Jerusalem was destroyed by the Romans), and the last days. The inspired translation of Mt. 24, found in the Writings of Joseph Smith 1, shows that there was to be two periods of "abomination of desolation": one in 70 A.D. and another in the last days (see J.S. 1:12 and 1:32).
6. Mt. 24:21-22. Compare Mk. 13:19-20.

> Then, if any man shall say unto you, Lo, here is Christ, or there;
> believe it not.
> *For there shall arise false Christs, and false prophets*, and shall shew
> great signs and wonders; insomuch that, if it were possible, *they shall
> deceive the very elect.*[1]

In his inspired translation of Matthew 24, Joseph Smith clar-
ifies the identity of the "elect," indicating that they are Church
members, or "the very elect, who are the elect according to the
covenant":

> ...If any man shall say unto you, Lo, here is Christ, or there, believe
> him not;
> For in those days there shall also arise *false Christs, and false proph-
> ets*, and shall show great signs and wonders, insomuch, that if possible,
> *they shall deceive the very elect, who are the elect according to the
> covenant.*[2]

Jesus, in his prophecy, describes his future coming to where
the saints [the eagles] will be assembled following the false Christ
experience:

> ...If they shall say unto you, Behold, he is in the desert; go not forth:
> behold, he is in the secret chambers; believe it not.
> For as the lightning cometh out of the east, and shineth even unto
> the west; so shall also the coming of the Son of man be.
> For wheresoever the carcass is, there will the eagles be gathered to-
> gether.[3]

He explains that his final coming in glory will be later than
this appearance, following other signs in the heavens.[4]

Another prophet, Nephi, also mentioned a false Christ situation in a last days context. In his explanation of future events,
Nephi alluded to a false Messiah who would work deception among
the unwary. He prophesied that the Jews, in the last days, will receive the words of Christ. These words are to convince them "that
they need not look forward any more for a Messiah to come, for
there should not any come, *save it should be a false Messiah which
should deceive the people....*"[5]

---

1. Mt. 24:23-24.
2. J.S. 1:21-22. See p. 231 concerning the "everlasting covenant."
3. Mt. 24:26-28. See Lk. 17:21-37.
4. Mt. 24:29-31.
5. 2 Ne. 25:18.

In Summary: Jesus, himself, warned of false Christs and false prophets who, if possible, will deceive the very elect, or members of the Church. This will precede an appearance he will make to where the saints are gathered together which will be prior to his final coming in glory. A Book of Mormon prophet, Nephi, was also aware of a false Christ who will appear. These prophetic warnings relate closely with D & C 64:35-40, which reveals that false apostles and prophets will be found in the early days of the New Jerusalem.

Paul's Warning: A Son of Perdition Will Show Himself As God in the Temple (2 Thess. 2:3-12)

The apostle Paul also prophesied of one who would attempt to deceive the saints and warned of a future "falling away." In his ministry he had taught the saints in Thessalonica about the coming of Christ. Some of them apparently misunderstood and believed that the second coming was imminent. To clarify his teachings, Paul wrote his epistle to them in which he gave them a sign. He carefully described a last days event which would precede Christ's coming, and taught them that the Savior would not appear until the event given as a sign had taken place. This is his prophetic warning:

> *Let no man deceive you by any means:* for that day [Christ's coming in glory] shall not come, except *there come a falling away first,* and that man of sin be revealed, *the son of perdition;*
> Who opposeth and exalteth himself above all that is called God, or that is worshipped; so that *he as God sitteth in the temple of God, shewing himself that he is God.*
> Remember ye not, that, when I was yet with you, I told you these things?
> And now ye know what withholdeth that he might be revealed in his time.
> For the mystery of iniquity doth already work: only he who now letteth will let, until he be taken out of the way.
> And then shall that Wicked be revealed, *whom the Lord shall consume with the spirit of his mouth, and shall destroy with the brightness of his coming:*
> Even him, *whose coming is after the workings of Satan* with all power and signs and lying wonders,
> And with all *deceivableness of unrighteousness* in them that perish, because they received not the love of the truth, that they might be saved.
> And for this cause God shall send them strong delusion, that they should believe a lie:

That all might be damned who believed not the truth, but had pleasure in unrighteousness. [1]

Paul's prophecy has several elements which require detailed comment:

1. There will be a falling away of unrighteous saints who will be deceived, before the coming of Christ (2:3, 10-12).

2. A son of perdition will be revealed whose coming is after the working of Satan (2:3, 9).

3. The son of perdition will sit in the temple of God, representing himself as being God (2:4).

4. Christ will destroy the son of perdition with the brightness of his coming (2:8).

1. *There will be a falling away of unrighteous saints who will be deceived, before the coming of Christ.* Other passages make reference to such an apostasy in the period of the New Jerusalem. 3 Ne. 21:20 describes a group of unrepentant individuals who will be cut off from among the Lord's people as the gathering to the New Jerusalem is taking place. [2] Nephi also tells of a group who will be "cut off" because they won't heed the words of Christ, while the righteous "shall not be confounded." This is to happen in the days of the New Jerusalem, for the passage speaks of those who will "fight against Zion" during this time. [3] D & C 64:35 tells how "the rebellious shall be cut off out of the land of Zion," [4] while D & C 85:11 proclaims that those who "have apostatized" or have been "cut off from the church" will be excluded from the New Jerusalem. [5] D & C 45:57 also alludes to those who will have been "deceived" among the church in the last days. [6] Thus there is a definite pattern of prophecy warning of apostasy and cleansing of the church in the last days, and specifically in the early days of the New Jerusalem period. This prophecy of Paul is a harmonious part of that pattern.

2. *A son of perdition will be revealed whose coming is after the working of Satan.* In the pre-mortal conflict in heaven, Satan

---

1. 2 Thess. 2:3-12.
2. See 3 Ne. 21:12-25.
3. 1 Ne. 22:14-22.
4. D & C 64:35. See 64:33-43.
5. D & C 85:11. See 85:3-12.
6. D & C 45:57. See 45:56-75.

stood in opposition to God. He was "thrust down from the presence of God and the Son, And *was called Perdition*, for the heavens wept over him—he was Lucifer, a son of the morning.[1] Members of the Church who succumb to Satan's temptations, after having full preparation and a firm testimony, become "sons of perdition":

> ...We beheld Satan, that old serpent, even the devil, who rebelled against God, and sought to take the kingdom of our God and his Christ—
>
> Wherefore, *he maketh war with the saints of God, and encompasseth them round about.*
>
> And we saw a vision of the sufferings of those with whom he made war and overcame, for thus came the voice of the Lord unto us:
>
> Thus saith the Lord concerning *all those who know my power, and have been made partakers thereof, and suffered themselves through the power of the devil to be overcome, and to deny the truth and defy my power—*
>
> *These are they who are the sons of perdition,* of whom I say that it had been better for them never to have been born;
>
> For they are vessels of wrath, doomed to suffer the wrath of God, with the devil and his angels in eternity;
>
> Concerning whom I have said there is no forgiveness in this world nor in the world to come—
>
> *Having denied the Holy Spirit after having received it, and having denied the Only Begotten Son of the Father, having crucified him unto themselves and put him to an open shame.*[2]

Latter-day Saint understanding has been that only members of The Church of Jesus Christ of Latter-day Saints can have sufficient preparation to become sons of perdition if they yield to Satan's wiles.[3] President Joseph Fielding Smith, for instance, taught the following in general conference:

> I think I am safe in saying that *no man can become a Son of Perdition until he has known the light: Those who have never received the light are not to become Sons of Perdition.* They will be punished if they rebel against God. They will have to pay the price of their sinning, but *it is only those who have the light through the priesthood and through the power of God and through their membership in the Church* who will be banished forever from his influence into outer darkness to dwell

---

1. D & C 76:25-26. Perdition means "Lost."
2. D & C 76:28-35. For further explanation on the sons of perdition—their sin and their fate—see the author's book *Life Everlasting*, pp. 289-308. D & C 76 also indicates that the sons of perdition are those who "deny the Son after the Father has revealed him" (76:43), and that there will be *many* who will suffer this fate (76:45-48).
3. See again D & C 76:29, 32.

with the devil and his angels. *That is a punishment that will not come to those who have never known the truth.* Bad as they may suffer, and awful as their punishment may be, they are not among that group which is to suffer the eternal death and banishment from all influence concerning the power of God.[1]

In the same conference, President Stephen L Richards alluded to President Smith's statement and said,

> I wish all of you—perhaps all did not—had heard what President Joseph Fielding Smith told us yesterday, something I have long believed, and I was glad to have sanction for my belief. He said in substance that *there will be no Sons of Perdition who do not hold the Priesthood.* I have believed that for years because I do not think that the Lord in his mercy would ever condemn a man to that indescribable penalty of being put out entirely from the Kingdom and from all grace *unless that man knew that Jesus was the Christ, unless he knew the power of the Christ, and he could only know that, I think, by holding the Priesthood.* I believe that in the main that can be said to be true—*that only men who hold the Priesthood of God stand in danger of that terrible penalty of being classed as outcasts.*[2]

If one must hold Church membership to be a son of perdition, then it becomes obvious that this false Christ cannot be a Catholic pope, nor a Protestant minister, nor some traveling evangelist. He will have to be an apostate Mormon, not some unknown outsider. This would explain how he may be able to "deceive the very elect," and how he will have temple access. He will appear to have priesthood power, and will perform "signs and lying wonders," but his power will be counterfeit, "after the working of Satan."[3]

---

1. Joseph Fielding Smith, President of the Council of the Twelve Apostles, *CR*, October, 1958, p. 21.
2. President Stephen L. Richards, First Counselor in the First Presidency, *CR*, October, 1958, p. 86.
3. 2 Thess. 2:9. Note that the false Christ will not be Satan himself—he will be a "son of perdition" and his power will be *"after the working of Satan."* He will be *"destroyed"* with the brightness of Christ's coming, but Satan will remain on the earth and finally be bound a thousand years. (See Rev. 20:2-3.) Concerning false apostles who function with Satanic power, the apostle Paul wrote:
   > But what I do, that will I do, that I may cut off occasion from them which desire occasion; that wherein they glory, they may be found even as we.
   > For such are *false apostles, deceitful workers, transforming themselves into the apostles of Christ.*

3. *The son of perdition will sit in the temple of God, presenting himself as being God.* The existence of a temple is an integral part of this prophetic warning, and the tangible existence of this building is a requisite for the literal fulfillment of the prophecy.

Paul visited Thessalonica during his second missionary journey,[1] then journeyed to Athens and on to Corinth. While in Corinth he wrote both his epistles to the Thessalonian saints. Bible scholars place the date of these epistles about 50 or 51 A.D. A temple existed at that time in Jerusalem. This temple, known as the temple of Herod, stood until 70 A.D., when it was destroyed by Roman legions under the command of Titus. No temple was then found on the earth until such sacred temples were again constructed in the last days, beginning with the Kirtland temple in the mid-1830s.

Since the son of perdition must sit in a temple to fulfill the prophecy, he would have to do so in a time when a temple exists upon the earth. This helps to determine the time of fulfillment of the prophecy. If it was fulfilled in ancient times, then the fulfillment would have had to take place in the two decades between the time of Paul's epistle and the fall of the temple, from 50 to 70 A.D.

But those who believe this prophecy was fulfilled in ancient times, as part of the "great apostasy," can offer no historical incident during that period which could be a possible fulfillment. Indeed, 70 A.D. would be an extremely early dating—an untenable dating—for the time of the "great apostasy" to have occurred.

If fulfillment wasn't accomplished before 70 A.D., then it must be in the last days era commencing with the Kirtland temple in 1836. Certainly no fulfillment is known from that date to the present, so it must be concluded that fulfillment is yet future.

The son of perdition will actually represent himself as being the Christ, exalting himself above all that is worshipped. He will occupy a place in God's temple (in the New Jerusalem?) and shew himself that he is God, deceiving the unrighteous who lack the spirit of discernment[2] through lying wonders, and causing their downfall.[3]

---

1. See Acts 17:1-14.
2. See D & C 50:1-34; 45:56-57.
3. 2 Thess. 2:9-12.

And no marvel; *for Satan himself is transformed into an angel of light. Therefore it is no great thing if his ministers also be transformed as the ministers of righteousness;* whose end shall be according to their works. (2 Cor. 11:12-15. See also Al. 30-53.)

4.   *Christ will destroy the son of perdition with the bright-ness of his coming.* Again, an element of the prophecy aids in its interpretation. Did Christ come in ancient times and destroy an apostate representing himself to be God, or is that event still future? The answer is obvious—history records no event that would fulfill the prophetic warning.[1] The event is yet future.

Here, then, is a prophecy of extreme importance to Latter-day Saints. It warns of a false Christ who will have profound influence upon the course of the Church in a future era, and will be able to deceive an unrighteous faction, leading them away into strong delusion and damnation. He must be a Church member to be able to be a son of perdition, and one who enjoys ready access to a temple in the last days. The ultimate message to future Church members was aptly stated by Paul: "Let no man deceive you by any means...."[2]

The Lord's Warning: Those Who Have Been Deceived Will Be Cast Into the Fire (D & C 45:56-57)

As part of his prophetic sermon on the Mount of Olives, Jesus told his disciples the parable of the ten virgins. The parable concerned ten virgins who went out to meet the bridegroom with their lamps. But the bridegroom tarried, and five of the virgins ran out of oil for their lamps. When the bridegroom came, he allowed only the five wise virgins who were properly prepared to enter into the marriage chamber with him.

Passages in the Doctrine and Covenants add insights to the interpretation of the parable, and indicate that the virgins represent the members of the Church in the last days. Some of the members, it is prophesied, will be wicked:

> These things are the things ye must look for; and, speaking after the manner of the Lord, they are nigh at hand, and in a time to come, even in the day of the coming of the Son of Man.

---

1. If there are those who would persist in the assertion that this prophecy was fulfilled long ago as part of the "great apostasy," they should be prepared to explain:
   A.   Who was the son of perdition?
   B.   In what temple did he manifest himself as God?
   C.   When and how Christ destroyed him by the brightness of his coming?
   D.   What historical records lend credence to such an interpretation?
2. 2 Thess. 2:3.

And until that hour there will be foolish virgins among the wise; and at that hour cometh an entire separation of the righteous and the wicked; and in that day will I send mine angels to pluck out the wicked and cast them into unquenchable fire.[1]

According to the Lord's prophetic warning, the saints will need to take the Holy Spirit for their guide or they will be deceived and cast into the fire:

And at that day, when I shall come in my glory, shall the parable be fulfilled which I spake concerning the ten virgins.

For they that are wise and have received the truth, and *have taken the Holy Spirit for their guide, and have not been deceived*—verily I say unto you they shall not be hewn down and cast into the fire, but shall abide the day.[2]

Nephi's Warning: Satan Will Lull the Inhabitants of Zion Into Carnal Security and Lead Them Down to Hell (2 Nephi 28:21-31)

The prophet Nephi warned of an event of serious consequence to the saints in the last days. He placed it in a future period when churches of men will deny the Holy Ghost[3] and revile against the just,[4] and in the era of the fall of the great and abominable church.[5] It was also linked with God's "marvelous work"[6] and the period in which God will set his hand to recover Israel.[7] He warned that in that period, Satan's work will have a double thrust—on one hand he will *"rage in the hearts of the children of men, and stir them up to anger against that which is good."*[8] The second part of his attack will be directed towards the saints themselves, whom he will attempt to lull into a false security.

It is clear that this second portion of his plan will actually concern the church members, both in the Americas and in Israel. Who else could be "at ease in Zion,"[9] have already "received the word

---

1. D & C 63:53-54. Concerning the things the saints are to look for, see 63:24-52.
2. D & C 45:56-57.
3. 2 Ne. 28:4.
4. 2 Ne. 28:16.
5. 2 Ne. 28:18.
6. See 2 Ne. 29:1.
7. *Ibid.*
8. 2 Ne. 28:20.
9. 2 Ne. 28:24.

of God,"[1] and have been taught "line upon line, precept upon precept"?[2]

This is Nephi's prophetic warning:

> And others will he pacify, and lull them away into carnal security, that they will say: All is well in Zion; yea, Zion prosperet.h, all is well— and thus the devil cheateth their souls, and leadeth them away carefully down to hell.
>
> And behold, others he flattereth away, and telleth them there is no hell; and he saith unto them: I am no devil, for there is none—and thus he whispereth in their ears, until he grasps them with his awful chains, from whence there is no deliverance.
>
> Yea, they are grasped with death, and hell; and death, and hell, and the devil, and all that have been seized therewith must stand before the throne of God, and be judged according to their works, from whence they must go into the place prepared for them, even a lake of fire and brimstone, which is endless torment.
>
> Therefore, wo be unto him that is at ease in Zion!
>
> Wo be unto him that crieth: All is well!
>
> Yea, wo be unto him that hearkeneth unto the precepts of men, and denieth the power of God, and the gift of the Holy Ghost!
>
> Yea, wo be unto him that saith: We have received, and we need no more!
>
> And in fine, wo unto all those who tremble, and are angry because of the truth of God! For behold, he that is built upon the rock receiveth it with gladness; and he that is built upon a sandy foundation trembleth lest he shall fall.
>
> Wo be unto him that shall say: We have received the word of God, and we need no more of the word of God, for we have enough!
>
> For behold, thus saith the Lord God: I will give unto the children of men line upon line, precept upon precept, here a little and there a little; and blessed are those who hearken unto my precepts, and lend an ear unto my counsel, for they shall learn wisdom; for unto him that receiveth I will give more; and from them that shall say, We have enough, from them shall be taken away even that which they have.
>
> Cursed is he that putteth his trust in man, or maketh flesh his arm, or shall hearken unto the precepts of men, save their precepts shall be given by the power of the Holy Ghost.[3]

What will be the nature of the conflict in that day? According to the prophetic warning, they will have received new revelation and be unwilling to accept it. Lacking the gift of the Holy Ghost, they will say, "We have received and we need no more!" "We have enough!" There will be "those who tremble, and are angry because of the truth of God!"

---

1. 2 Ne. 28:29.
2. 2 Ne. 28:30. See D & C 128:21, Is. 28:10, 13.
3. 2 Ne. 28:21-31.

As indicated in the prophecy, there will be those who will trust in man and hearken unto the precepts of man instead of following the promptings of the Holy Ghost. This indicates a conflict will exist in which the saints will be receiving direction from at least two different sources and will be uncertain who to follow. Will this be a result of the teachings of the false Christ?[1] Or of saints refusing to accept and heed the Savior when he appears?[2] Or of conflict between the "one mighty and strong" and the man who "putteth forth his hand to steady the ark of God"?[3]

The Lord's Warning: Those Who Won't Hear Christ When He Appears Shall Be Cut Off (3 Nephi 20:22-23)

The Savior himself, while ministering among the Nephites in the meridian of time, spoke of the future era of the New Jerusalem. He spoke of a time when the remnant of the house of Jacob will ravage the land and tread down their enemies,[4] and when the sword of God's justice will fall "upon all the nations of the Gentiles."[5] He will gather his people together,[6] establish the New Jerusalem,[7] and appear to his people there.[8] But he foresees that some will reject him and be cut off:

> And behold, this people will I establish in this land, unto the fulfilling of the covenant which I made with your father Jacob; and it shall be a *New Jerusalem. And the powers of heaven shall be in the midst of this people; yea, even I will be in the midst of you.*
>
> Behold, I am he of whom Moses spake, saying: A prophet shall the Lord your God rise up unto you of your brethen, like unto me; him shall ye hear in all things whatsoever he shall say unto you. *And it shall come to pass that every soul who will not hear that prophet shall be cut off from among the people.*[9]

He then spoke of the Gentile converts to the Church, saying that "when they shall have received the fulness of my gospel, *then*

---

1. See pp. 233-240.
2. See pp. 231-232, 244.
3. See pp. 244-247.
4. 3 Ne. 20:15-17. Compare with 3 Ne. 16:14-16 and 3 Ne. 21:14-25.
5. 3 Ne. 20:20.
6. 3 Ne. 20:18.
7. 3 Ne. 20-22.
8. 3 Ne. 20:22-23.
9. *Ibid.* Deut. 18:15, 18-19 is where Moses' original prophecy is recorded. Peter quoted the prophecy in Acts 3:22-23, and Moroni said that Christ would be the one to fulfill the prophecy in a time yet future (J.S. 2:40).

244 PROPHETIC WARNINGS TO MODERN AMERICA

if they shall harden their hearts against me I will return their iniquities upon their own heads,... "[1]

Here then, is prophetic indication that when the Savior appears to the saints in the New Jerusalem, some of them will harden their hearts and refuse to hear the Lord. According to the Master, they will be "cut off from among the people." Is it possible that they will have placed their confidence in the "arm of flesh"[2] of the false Christ[3] and will be deceived so they won't acknowledge the true Christ when he appears?

Nephi's Warning: Those Who Won't Hear the Prophet, Shall Be Cut Off (1 Nephi 22:20-22)

Nephi also cited the prophecy of Moses concerning the coming of Christ, which Jesus later explained. Like the Savior, he placed the prophecy in the chronological context of the gathering of Israel,[4] the fall of the great and abominable church,[5] the time of the New Jerusalem when men would be fighting against Zion,[6] and the pouring out of the wrath of God upon the wicked so they are destroyed by fire.[7] He said,

> ...The Lord will surely prepare a way for his people, unto the fulfilling of the words of Moses, which he spake, saying: A prophet shall the Lord your God raise up unto you, like unto me; him shall ye hear in all things whatsoever he shall say unto you. And it shall come to pass that *all those who will not hear that prophet shall be cut off from among the people.*
>
> And now I, Nephi, declare unto you, that this prophet of whom Moses spake was the Holy One of Israel; wherefore, *he shall execute judgment in righteousness.*
>
> And the righteous need not fear, for *they are those who shall not be confounded.*[8]

Once again the pattern emerges: when the Lord appears in the New Jerusalem, there will be confusion and apostasy. Some will be confounded and refuse to heed the Lord, and they will be cut off, or excommunicated.

The Lord's Warning: Apostates Will Be Cut Off When One Mighty and Strong Sets In Order the House of God (D & C 85:7-12)

Joseph Smith described the strong physical impact he felt when he received one particular revelation which is recorded in

---

1. 3 Ne. 20:28.
2. See 2 Ne. 28:31.
3. 2 Thess. 2:3-4.
4. See 1 Ne. 22:8-12.
5. See 1 Ne. 22:13.
6. See 1 Ne. 22:14, 19.
7. See 1 Ne. 22:15-17.
8. 1 Ne. 22:20-22.

the Doctrine and Covenants. His recording of his feelings was unusual, and not characteristic of other revelations he recorded. Yet it served to underscore the important prophecy which followed. He wrote,

> Yea, thus saith the still small voice, which whispereth through and pierceth all things, and *often times it maketh my bones to quake while it maketh manifest,* saying....[1]

The revelation he recorded is also unusual, for it tells of the coming of "one mighty and strong," who will come in the days of the New Jerusalem. He will set in order the house of God and arrange the inheritance of the righteous saints. At that time there will be apostates who will be cut off from the Church and denied a place to live among the saints:

> And it shall come to pass that I, the Lord God, *will send one mighty and strong,* holding the scepter of power in his hand, clothed with light for a covering, whose mouth shall utter words, eternal words; while his bowels shall be a fountain of truth, *to set in order the house of God, and to arrange by lot the inheritances of the saints* whose names are found, and the names of their fathers, and of their children, enrolled in the book of the law of God;
> *While that man, who was called of God and appointed, that putteth forth his hand to steady the ark of God, shall fall by the shaft of death, like as a tree that is smitten by the vivid shaft of lightning.*
> And all they who are not found written in the book of remembrance shall find none inheritance in that day, but they shall be cut asunder, and their portion shall be appointed them among unbelievers, where are wailing and gnashing of teeth.
> These things I say not of myself; therefore, as the Lord speaketh, he will also fulfil.
> *And they who are of the High Priesthood, whose names are not found written in the book of the law, or that are found to have apostatized, or to have been cut off from the church, as well as the lesser priesthood, or the members, in that day shall not find an inheritance among the saints of the Most High.*
> Therefore, it shall be done unto them as unto the children of the priest, as will be found recorded in the second chapter and sixty-first and second verses of Ezra.[2]

Several observations are appropriate concerning the prophecy. First, who is the "one mighty and strong"? It most probably is the Lord himself. Just as he is the prophet whom Moses said would

---

1. D & C 85:6. Joseph also emphasized that this is not his own statement but a message from the Lord which will certainly be fulfilled. (D & C 85:10.)
2. D & C 85:7-12.

come, can he not also be the fulfillment of this prophecy? That he will come in the days of the New Jerusalem has already been clearly established, as is the teaching that unrighteous saints will be cut off when the Lord makes his appearance. And note the phrases which describe the one mighty and strong, which are used in other contexts to describe the Lord Jehovah, who is Jesus Christ. He is *mighty*,[1] *strong*,[2] holds the *sceptre* of power,[3] and is clothed with *light*.[4]

Over the years, various apostates have claimed to be the one mighty and strong, yet they have not come in the time, nor the place, specified by the revelation; neither have they performed the dual mission of setting in order the house of God and arranging by lot the inheritances of the saints as stipulated in the revelation. Furthermore, they have not been opposed by one who was struck down, nor have they uttered "eternal words," nor have they shown themselves to have "bowels" that are "a fountain of truth." They have not functioned in a situation where there was a "book of the law of God" kept, nor in a situation when apostates have been prohibited from finding an inheritance among the saints. The prophecy refers to a time and situation which are yet future, and no "one mighty and strong" has been sent by the Lord to date.

The one mighty and strong is to set in order the house of God. Can this be action taken to correct the wrongs of the son of perdition who will sit in the temple?[5]

Note that the "one mighty and strong" will utter "eternal words." Are these the words that will cause those who are "at ease in Zion" to be "angry because of the truth of God" and say "we need no more of the word of God, for we have enough!" as prophesied in 2 Nephi 28?

1. Compare Ps. 24:8 (the Lord strong and mighty), Ps. 89:13 (Thou hast a mighty arm: strong is thy hand), Is. 63:1 (the greatness of his strength, mighty to save), Jer. 32:18-19 (the Mighty God, mighty in work), Is. 1:24 (the mighty One of Israel), Is. 49:26; 60:16 (the mighty One of Jacob), etc.
2. See again Ps. 24:8, 89:13; 1 Ki. 8:42, Neh. 1:10 (thy strong hand), Ps. 31:2 (be thou my strong rock), Ps. 71:7 (my strong refuge), Ps. 89:8 (who is a strong Lord like unto thee?), etc.
3. Ps. 45:6 (the sceptre of thy kingdom); Heb. 1:8 (a sceptre of righteousness); Num. 24:17 (a Sceptre shall rise out of Israel).
4. Ps. 4:6 (the light of thy countenance); Ps. 27:1 (the Lord is my light); Ps. 104:2 (coverest thyself with light as with a garment); Dan. 2:22 (light dwelleth with him); Hab. 3:4 (his brightness was as the light); etc.
5. 2 Thess. 2:3-4.

It appears that there will be conflict between the "one mighty and strong" and the man that "putteth forth his hand to steady the ark of God." Will this be the time in which "they who are not apostles and prophets shall be known," as prophesied in D & C 64?

According to the prophecy, people are to be cut off, and not allowed an inheritance with the saints. Is this the same "cutting off" as described in 3 Ne. 20:23 and 3 Ne. 21:20? And could this relationship indicate that the "one mighty and strong" is actually the Lord Jesus Christ himself?

Certainly the prophecy describes an important future event, and its message is one that cannot be ignored.

Isaiah's Warning: A Mighty and Strong One Shall Come, An Overflowing Scourge Shall Pass Through, and the Lord Will Bring to Pass His Strange Act (Isaiah 28:1-22)

An intriguing prophecy by Isaiah links key last days phrases that correlate with other prophetic warnings:

> Woe to the crown of pride, to the drunkards of Ephraim whose glorious beauty is a fading flower, which are on the head of the fat valleys of them that are overcome with wine!
>
> *Behold, the Lord hath a mighty and strong one, which as a tempest of hail and a destroying storm, as a flood of mighty waters overflowing, shall cast down to the earth with the hand.*
>
> The crown of pride, the drunkards of Ephraim, shall be trodden under feet:
>
> And the glorious beauty, which is on the head of the fat valley, shall be a fading flower, and as the hasty fruit before the summer; which when he that looketh upon it seeth, while it is yet in his hand he eateth it up.
>
> *In that day shall the Lord of hosts be for a crown of glory, and for a diadem of beauty, unto the residue of his people,*
>
> *And for a spirit of judgment to him that sitteth in judgment, and for strength to them that turn the battle to the gate.*
>
> But they also have erred through wine, and through strong drink are out of the way; *the priest and the prophet have erred through strong drink, they are swallowed up of wine, they are out of the way through strong drink; they err in vision, they stumble in judgment.*
>
> For all tables are full of vomit and filthiness, so that there is no place clean.
>
> Whom shall he teach knowledge? and whom shall he make to understand doctrine? them that are weaned from the milk, and drawn from the breasts.
>
> *For precept must be upon precept, precept upon precept; line upon line, line upon line; here a little, and there a little:*
>
> *For with stammering lips and another tongue will he speak to this people.*

To whom he said, This is the rest wherewith ye may cause the weary to rest; and this is the refreshing: yet they would not hear.

But the word of the Lord was unto them precept upon precept, precept upon precept; line upon line, line upon line; here a little, and there a little; that they might go, and fall backward, and be broken, and snared, and taken.

Wherewith hear the word of the Lord, ye scornful men, that rule this people which is in Jerusalem.

Because ye have said, We have made a covenant with death, and with hell are we at agreement; *when the overflowing scourge shall pass through, it shall not come unto us: for we have made lies our refuge, and under falsehood have we hid ourselves:*

Therefore thus saith the Lord God, *Behold, I lay in Zion for a foundation a stone, a tried stone, a precious corner stone, a sure foundation: he that believeth shall not make haste.*

Judgment also will I lay to the line, and righteousness to the plummet: and the *hail shall sweep away the refuge of lies, and the waters shall overflow the hiding place.*

And your covenant with death shall be disannulled, and your agreement with hell shall not stand; *when the overflowing scourge shall pass through, then ye shall be trodden down by it.*

From the time that it goeth forth it shall take you: for morning by morning shall it pass over, by day and by night: and it shall be a vexation only to understand the report.

For the bed is shorter than that a man can stretch himself on it: and the covering narrower than that he can wrap himself in it.

For the Lord shall rise up as in mount Perazim, he shall be wroth as in the valley of Gibeon, *that he may do his work, his strange work; and bring to pass his act, his strange act.*

Now therefore be ye not mockers, lest your bands be made strong: for I have heard from the Lord God of hosts *a consumption, even determined upon the whole earth.*[1]

The key phrases deserve special comment:

1.   *"The Lord hath a mighty and Strong One"* (Is. 28:2). Note the relationship with D & C 85:7, which foretells the coming of "one mighty and strong" to set in order the house of God and to arrange the inheritance of the saints in the New Jerusalem. His appearance is described as being accompanied by hail, a destroying storm, and a flood.[2] Does verse 5 ("In that day shall the Lord of hosts be for a crown of glory...") and verse 16 ("Behold, I lay in Zion for a foundation a stone, a tried stone, a precious corner

---

1. Is. 28:1-22.
2. Is. 28:2, 17. Is this prophecy linked to D & C 29:14-21, which associates a hailstorm, a terrible disease, and the fall of the great and abominable church?

stone,[1] a sure foundation...") indicate that Christ himself is the "mighty and strong one"?

2.   In that day the Lord will be a *"spirit of judgment to him that sitteth in judgment and for strength to them that turn the battle to the gate"* (Is. 28:6). This will be the era when the church will judge the nations (D & C 64:37-38) and during the period when those in Zion will be the only ones not as war (D & C 45:66-71).

3.   *"The overflowing scourge shall pass through"* (Is. 28:15, 18-19). Though the people think they will be able to escape this terrible last days plague (through a false "covenant with death"[2]), it will still come upon them. They will be "trodden down by it,"[3] and "it shall be a vexation only to understand the report."[4] This scourge is also prophesied in D & C 84:58, 96-97; 97:22-26, 5:19; and 45:31. Isaiah warns that there will be *"a consumption, even determined upon the whole earth"* (Is. 28:22).

4.   The Lord will *"do his work, his strange work; and bring to pass his act, his strange act"* (Is. 28:21). As prophesied in D & C 95:89-95, the Lord will vex the nation, and perform a strange act "that men may discern between the righteous and the wicked."[5] The relationship of this "strange act" and the "marvellous work and a wonder" were previously discussed.[6]

Yet the prophecy of Isaiah 28 does not appear to be directed only to the saints in America, but also to "scornful men, that rule this people which is in Jerusalem."[7] They are depicted as "the drunkards of Ephraim, whose glorious beauty is a fading flower,"[8] and they are described by Isaiah as erring in vision and being troubled by drunkenness:

> But they also have erred through wine, and through strong drink are out of the way; *the priest and the prophet have erred through strong*

---

1. Christ is the cornerstone and foundation. See Eph. 2:20, 1 Cor. 3:11, Ps. 118:22 and Mt. 21:42-44.
2. Is. 28:15, 18.
3. Is. 28:18.
4. Compare with D & C 97:23.
5. D & C 101:95.
6. See pp. 175-183. Note also the close proximity of Is. 28:21 and Is. 29:14, which links the two terms together. Both chapters of Isaiah are showing last days relationships between America and Israel.
7. Is. 28:14.
8. Is. 28:1.

drink, they are swallowed up of wine, they are out of the way through strong drink; they err in vision, they stumble in judgment.[1]

While the relationship of Isaiah 28 to the other prophetic warnings of the last days is not fully apparent, it is obvious that this prophecy makes pointed reference to key phrases found in modern scripture which can only be understood in a future context.

The Lord's Warning: A Scourge and Judgment Upon the Children of Zion Unless They Repent and Obey the Commandments (D & C 84:54-59)

In 1832 the Lord spoke with the voice of warning to the Church, and told them,

> And your minds in times past have been darkened because of unbelief, and because you have treated lightly the things you have received—
> *Which vanity and unbelief have brought the whole church under condemnation.*
> *And this condemnation resteth upon the children of Zion, even all.*
> And they shall remain under this condemnation until they *repent and remember the new covenant, even the Book of Mormon and the former commandments* which I have given them, not only to say, but to do according to that which I have written—
> That they may bring forth fruit meet for their Father's kingdom; *otherwise there remaineth a scourge and judgment to be poured out upon the children of Zion.*
> For shall the children of the kingdom pollute my holy land? Verily, I say unto you, Nay.[2]

The Master then instructed the Church members on how they should preach, saying, "Behold, I send you out to reprove the world of all their unrighteous deeds, and to teach them of a judgment which is to come."[3] And then he explained what that judgment would be:

> *...Wo unto that house, or that village or city that rejecteth you, or your words, or your testimony concerning me.*
> Wo, I say again, unto that house, or that village or city that rejecteth you, or your words, or your testimony of me;

---

1. Is. 28:7.
2. D & C 84:54-59. See D & C 63:63.
3. D & C 84:87. See also verse 117.

For I, the Almighty, have laid my hands upon the nations, to *scourge them for their wickedness.*

And plagues shall go forth, and they shall not be taken from the earth until I have completed my work, which shall be cut short in righteousness—

Until all shall know me, *who remain,* even from the least unto the greatest, and shall be filled with the knowledge of the Lord, and shall see eye to eye,...[1]

The Lord's Warning: Zion Will Be Visited With Scourge, Pestilence, Plague, Sword, and Fire If She Fails to Obey Commandments (D & C 97:21-26)

Another passage warns of the desolating scourge which will come upon the earth in the last days, and gives a conditional warning to the latter-day Zion and its inhabitants. The saints are promised that they can escape from the judgments *if* they do *"all things"* that God commands, but they are warned that severe judgments will come upon them if they fail to render complete obedience:

Therefore, verily, thus saith the Lord, *let Zion rejoice, for this is Zion—THE PURE IN HEART; therefore, let Zion rejoice, while all the wicked shall mourn.*

For behold, and lo, vengeance cometh speedily upon the ungodly as the whirlwind; and who shall escape it?

The Lord's scourge shall pass over by night and by day, and the report thereof shall vex all people; yea, it shall not be stayed until the Lord come;

For the indignation of the Lord is kindled against their abominations and all their wicked works.

Nevertheless, Zion shall escape *if* she observe to do all things whatsoever I have commanded her.

But if she observe not to do whatsoever I have commanded her, I will visit her according to all her works, with sore affliction, with pestilence, with plague, with sword, with vengeance, with devouring fire.[2]

---

1. D & C 84:94-98. Later in the revelation, speaking of Albany, Boston, and New York, the Savior alluded to *"the desolation and utter abolishment* which await them if they do reject these things. For if they do reject these things the hour of their judgment is nigh, and *their house shall be left unto them desolate."* (D & C 84:114-115.)

2. D & C 97:21-26. Yet the Lord emphasizes that he seeks to bless Zion rather than punish her, and promises that these judgments will be averted "if she sin no more":

    Nevertheless, let it be read this once to her ears, that I, the Lord, have accepted of her offering; and is she sin no more none of these things shall come upon her;

    And I will bless her with blessings, and multiply a multiplicity of blessings upon her and upon her generations forever and ever, saith the Lord your God. Amen. (D & C 97:27-28.)

252 PROPHETIC WARNINGS TO MODERN AMERICA

Coupled with this prophetic warning is a prophecy of the glory of the latter-day Zion, or New Jerusalem. But even that prophecy is conditioned upon righteousness, and expresses the danger that the New Jerusalem temple may be defiled:

> And inasmuch as my people build a house unto me in the name of the Lord, and *do not suffer any unclean thing to come into it, that it be not defiled,* my glory shall rest upon it;
>
> Yea, and my presence shall be there, for I will come into it, and all the pure in heart that shall come into it shall see God.
>
> *But if it be defiled I will not come into it, and my glory shall not be there; for I will not come into unholy temples.*
>
> And, now, behold, *if Zion do these things* she shall prosper, and spread herself and become very glorious, very great, and very terrible.
>
> And the nations of the earth shall honor her, and shall say: Surely Zion is the city of our God, and surely Zion cannot fall, neither be moved out of her place, for God is there, and the hand of the Lord is there;
>
> And he hath sworn by the power of his might to be her salvation and her high tower.[1]

The Lord's Warning: A Desolating Sickness, and Men Will Kill One Another With the Sword (D & C 45:31-33)

The Lord has spoken more concerning a future desolation of the earth in the 45th section of the Doctrine and Covenants. In the generation in which the time of the Gentiles are fulfilled,[2] God will pour out his "overflowing scourge"—a "desolating sickness." This will be the period that men will "harden their hearts" and "take up the sword, one against another":

> And there shall be men standing in that generation, that shall not pass until they shall *see an overflowing scourge; for a desolating sickness shall cover the land.*

---

1. D & C 97:15-20. Note again the prophetic pattern of scripture warning of false Christs and a son of perdition who will sit in the temple of God. The danger of the temple being defiled is real, and the subject of repeated scriptural warnings.

2. The "times of the Gentiles" are discussed in detail in the author's book *Prophecy—Key to the Future,* pp. 17-34. Briefly, the "times of the Gentiles" is the present era when the gospel is to be preached to the people of the Gentile (Caucasian) nations. The "fulfilling of the times of the Gentiles" is the end of the period of missionary labors to them. That end will be identified by the withdrawing of missionaries from among them and an increase in the judgments of God being poured out upon the world. The times of the Gentiles will be fulfilled before the saints return to establish the New Jerusalem in Jackson County, Missouri.

But my disciples shall stand in holy places, and shall not be moved; but among the wicked, men shall lift up their voices and curse God and die.

And there shall be earthquakes in divers places, and *many desolations; yet men will harden their hearts against me, and they will take up the sword, one against another, and they will kill one another.*[1]

The Savior has characterized this period (after the times of the Gentiles are fulfilled) as the time when the scattered remnant of Israel will be gathered[2] again to their promised land, and a time of world-wide wars and commotion:

And in that day shall be heard of wars and rumors of wars, and the whole earth shall be in commotion, and men's hearts shall fail them, and they shall say that Christ delayeth his coming until the end of the earth.

And the love of men shall wax cold, and iniquity shall abound.[3]

The Lord's Warning: A Desolating Scourge Shall Be Poured Out Until the Earth is Empty, If They Repent Not (D & C 5:18-19)

The warning of a last days desolation of the earth was revealed to Joseph Smith even before the Church was restored. Like so many of the other prophetic warnings, it was conditional. It describes what will happen *if* the people "harden their hearts" and *if* "they repent not":

And their testimony shall also go forth unto the condemnation of this generation if they harden their hearts against them;

For a desolating scourge shall go forth among the inhabitants of the earth, and shall continue to be poured out from time to time, if they repent not, until the *earth is empty, and the inhabitants thereof are consumed away and utterly destroyed by the brightness of my coming.*[4]

After giving the prophetic warning, the Master asserted the literal nature of the prophecy by comparing it with the destruction of Jerusalem (in 70 A.D.) and proclaiming that "my word *shall be verified* at this time as it hath hitherto been verified."[5]

---

1. D & C 45:31-33. Observe the pattern reported repeatedly throughout this book: people will clearly fall into two distinct categories at this time—the righteous (in this case the "disciples"), and the wicked who will reap God's judgments.
2. D & C 45:24-25. See also 3 Ne. 21:24-29.
3. D & C 45:26-27.
4. D & C 5:18-19.
5. D & C 5:20. See also D & C 1:7, 37-39.

The Lord's Warning: God's Wrath Will Begin Among Those
Who Blaspheme In His House (D & C 112:24-26)

Much has been said in this chapter about future problems which are to arise in the Church, primarily in the early days of the New Jerusalem. This final passage also focuses on that theme, and warns that there will be those who will blaspheme against God in his holy house. The Lord's vengeance will be poured out upon those apostates, and shall go forth from there:

> Behold, vengeance cometh speedily upon the inhabitants of the earth, *a day of wrath, a day of burning, a day of desolation, of weeping, of mourning, and of lamentation;* and as a whirlwind it shall come upon all the face of the earth, saith the Lord.
>
> *And upon my house shall it begin,* and from my house shall it go forth, saith the Lord;
>
> First among those among you, saith the Lord, *who have professed to know my name and have not known me, and have blasphemed against me in the midst of my house,* saith the Lord.[1]

That judgments would begin at the house of God was foreknown by the apostle Peter in Biblical days, and the passage in I Peter has important parallels[2] with D & C 112:24-26 and D & C 63:34. He saw that it would be a "fiery trial"[3] and warned that the righteous would "scarcely be saved."[4] This is his prophecy:

---

1. D & C 112:24-26. In the context of this prophecy the Lord describes the wickedness of the earth's inhabitants during this period with the observation that "darkness covereth the earth, and gross darkness the minds of the people, and all flesh has become corrupt before my face." (D & C 112:23.)

2. It is interesting to note how the time of fulfillment has been altered by translators' insertions in the I Peter passage. These insertions, rendered in italic type in the King James version, change the meaning of I Pet. 4:17 with the words *is come* and of I Pet. 4:18 with *begin.* These changes make the passage appear to have application only to that era, which is not clearly established as Peter's intent. Could it not be that he knew of the last days judgments which were to begin at the house of God? Was he attempting to compare that future event with circumstances in his day? (He made a comparison of this type in Acts 2:17-21. Compare that passage with Joel 2, which places this prophecy *afterward* [Joel 2:28] of the future Battle of Armageddon, and see Moroni's explanation that the event had not yet transpired in Joseph Smith's day [J.S. 2:41].)

3. Compare I Pet. 4:12 and I Pet.1:7 with D & C 112:24's day of burning and D & C 63:34's unquenchable fire.

4. Compare I Pet. 4:18 with D & C 63:34's "the saints also shall hardly escape."

> *For the time is come that judgment must begin at the house of God:* and if it first begin at us, what shall the end be of them that obey not the gospel of God?
> *And if the righteous scarcely be saved,* where shall the ungodly and sinner appear?
> Wherefore let them that suffer according to the will of God *commit the keeping of their souls to him in well doing, as unto a faithful Creator.*[1]

Both D & C 112:24-26 and Peter's prophecy are ominous warnings for ungodly sinners who will blaspheme against God. They will do well to heed Peter's counsel to *"commit the keeping of their souls to him in well doing,* as unto a faithful Creator."[2]

Summary

1. The scriptures contain numerous prophetic warnings of a future period of conflict and apostasy within the Church. Chronological clues in these passages and their contexts indicate that the apostasy will primarily occur in the early period of the New Jerusalem.

2. The Lord has revealed that it is the responsibility of every man and every Church member to warn others of coming judgments. They are to warn the inhabitants of the earth that "desolation shall come upon the wicked." They are also commanded to "prepare the saints for the hour of judgment which is to come."

3. Though the possibility of future difficulties within the Church is unpleasant to contemplate, discuss, or write about, it is a subject which cannot be avoided by those attempting to obey all the commandments. Priesthood bearers have the responsibility to "watch over the Church always, and be with and strengthen them; and see there is no iniquity in the Church."

4. Though it must endure future strife and apostasy, the kingdom of God shall "never be destroyed" nor "left to other people." It is to continue to grow, in spite of the difficulties it must endure, until "it has filled the whole earth." The kingdom has come forth "for the last time" and the saints have been given the divine promise that "the enemy shall not overcome."

---

1. I Pet. 4:17-19.
2. I Pet. 4:19.

5. Sixteen prophetic warnings are cited in this chapter. They are prophecies made by

    A.   Isaiah (Is. 24:5-6).
    B.   The Lord (D & C 1:14-16).
    C.   The Lord (D & C 64:35-40).
    D.   The Lord (Mt. 24:24).
    E.   Paul (2 Thess. 2:3-12).
    F.   The Lord (D & C 45:56-57).
    G.   Nephi (2 Ne. 28:21-31).
    H.   The Lord (3 Ne. 20:22-23).
    I.   Nephi (1 Ne. 20:20-22).
    J.   The Lord (D & C 85:7-12).
    K.   Isaiah (Is. 28:1-22).
    L.   The Lord (D & C 84:54-59).
    M.   The Lord (D & C 97:21-26).
    N.   The Lord (D & C 45:31-33).
    O.   The Lord (D & C 5:18-19).
    P.   The Lord (D & C 112:24-26).

6. Many of the prophecies are related to the last days period called the "desolation of abomination." This is a time when the judgments of God will come upon the wicked and greatly reduce the population of the earth, leaving portions of it desolate.

7. Isaiah prophesied that the Lord's curse will leave the earth desolate because the inhabitants will transgress the laws, change the ordinance, and break the everlasting covenant. The everlasting covenant is the fulness of the gospel. Since one can only break a covenant if he has made the covenant, and can only change an ordinance if he already has the ordinance, it appears that it will be transgression among the future saints which will occasion the judgments Isaiah foresees. This interpretation is reinforced by the Lord's prophecy concerning future saints who "shall be cut off"—he reveals that they will stray from his ordinances and break his everlasting covenant (D & C 1:14-16).

8. The saints to be "cut off" will "not hear the voice of the Lord, neither the voice of his servants." It appears that confusion will exist because of a false Christ, false prophets, false apostles, and other church leaders who will be unmasked in the days of the New Jerusalem. If possible, they will "deceive the very elect," or members of the Church. The inhabitants of Zion shall judge all things pertaining to Zion, and shall prove those who are liars and hypocrites.

9. The rebellious apostates shall be cut off out of the land of Zion, and shall be sent away, and shall not inherit the land.

10. There is to come a period of tribulation more severe than any the earth has ever seen or endured. Unless the period is shortened, no flesh shall be saved. The Lord has revealed the time will be shortened for the elect's sake.

11. A son of perdition will sit in the temple of God, showing himself to be God. He will show signs and wonders, and deceive the unrighteous. When Christ appears, he will destroy the son of perdition. (It is assumed that this will be Christ's appearance in the New Jerusalem, prior to his final coming in glory.)

12. Church leaders have taught that one must be a Church member to be able to be a son of perdition. Sons of perdition are those who know God's power and who have received the Holy Ghost, then denied the truth and defied God's power. According to D & C 76:45-48, there will be many sons of perdition.

13. Fire is repeatedly mentioned in the prophecies concerning the desolation of abomination. According to the prophecies, many of the wicked will be destroyed by fire. This is not the fire which will accompany Christ's final coming in glory.

14. In order to avoid being deceived during this period of apostasy, it will be necessary for the saints to take the Holy Spirit for their guide. That Spirit is the spirit of discernment.

15. Satan will lull some of the inhabitants of Zion into carnal security and will lead them down to hell. It appears they will trust in the precepts of men and will refuse to receive new revelation when it is given to them. Of specific concern are the prophetic warnings that they will refuse to accept and heed the Savior when he appears among the saints in the New Jerusalem. Those who refuse to hear him will be cut off.

16. "One mighty and strong," probably the Savior himself, will come to the New Jerusalem to set in order the house of God and to arrange by lot the inheritances of the saints. He may be counteracting the influence of the son of perdition who will sit in the temple of God. One called of God will put forth his hand "to steady the ark of God" and be struck down. Apostates will be denied

inheritances in the new Zion, which seems to indicate that these events will transpire relatively early in the New Jerusalem era.

17. God's vengeance in the last days shall begin at his house and from there it will go forth. It will begin with men who will have blasphemed in the midst of his house.

18. Repeated prophecies are recorded in the scriptures of an "overflowing scourge" or "desolating sickness" which will be poured out and will continue until the Lord comes. It will be "a consumption, even determined upon the whole earth." The children of Zion can escape it only if they repent, remember the new covenant (found in the Book of Mormon), live God's commandments, and bring forth fruit suitable for their Father's kingdom. Zion is specifically warned that if the saints fail to do "all things" the Lord has commanded, they will be visited with "sore affliction, with pestilence, with plague, with sword, with vengeance, with devouring fire."

19. The Lord has warned that if the New Jerusalem temple is defiled, he will not come into it, and his glory shall not be there, for he will not come to unholy temples.

20. As the overflowing scourge is poured out, the wicked will harden their hearts, then take up the sword and kill one another. God's disciples shall stand in holy places, and shall not be moved.

III

Famine, Sword and Pestilence-

Instruments of God's Judgments

XIII

Prophecies of Future Famine

Judgments by Famine, Sword, and Pestilence

On September 21, 1823, Joseph Smith received three visits from Moroni, an angelic representative of the Lord. Moroni taught the prophet, giving comment on a series of Biblical prophecies which foretell significant events of the last days. While relating the words of his angelic visitor, Joseph recorded that

> ...He informed me of *great judgments which were coming upon the earth, with great desolations by famine, sword, and pestilence;* and that these grievous judgments would come on the earth in this generation.[1]

Famine! Sword! Pestilence! These three terms have been used repeatedly in the scriptures to symbolize the full extent of God's judgments. Though they are used together, each represents a different aspect of the suffering which man can bring upon himself through disobedience to God's commandments.

Examples of these terms being used together in the scriptures are both numerous and varied. The Hebrews in the days of Moses pleaded with the Egyptian Pharoah to permit them to offer sacrifices to God so they wouldn't be smitten with pestilence or the sword.[2] When Israel sinned in King David's day, they were given the choice of seven years of famine, three months of war, or three days of pestilence. Pestilence was chosen and 70,000 men died before the pestilence abated.[3] King Solomon spoke of famine, pestilence, and enemies besieging Israel as he dedicated the great temple he had constructed.[4] Jehoshaphat, king of Judah, prayed God would prevent the evils of "the sword, judgment, or pestilence, or famine"[5] from coming upon his people. By the days of Jeremiah, Judah had become so wicked that God promised that his threefold judgments would come upon them, and even forbid Jeremiah from praying in their behalf:

---

1. J.S. 2:45.
2. Ex. 5:3.
3. 2 Sam. 24:13-16.

4. 1 Ki. 8:37-38; 2 Chron. 6:28-29.
5. 2 Chron. 20:9.

> Then said the Lord unto me, *Pray not for this people for their good.*
> *When they fast, I will not hear their cry;* and when they offer burnt
> offering and an oblation, I will not accept them: but *I will consume*
> *them by the sword, and by the famine, and by the pestilence.*[1]

Jeremiah warned repeatedly of the famine, sword, and pestilence which would come upon his people for their wickedness.[2]
The prophet Ezekiel issued numerous warnings concerning the people of Jerusalem, always linking the three aspects of God's judgments together.[3]

Famine, sword and pestilence are repeatedly linked in the
Book of Mormon also. Lehi warned his people that they would be
cursed for many generations, and that they would be "visited by
sword, and by famine, and are hated."[4] Abinadi cursed King Noah,
telling him his people would be driven by men and be smitten with
famine and pestilence.[5] Amulek warned the people of Ammonihah
of impending judgments by famine, pestilence, and sword.[6] Nephi
was given power to smite the earth with famine, pestilence, and
destruction a few years before the birth of the Savior.[7] Concerning
the final Nephite generation the Lord revealed, through Samuel the
Lamanite, that "I will visit them with the sword and with famine
and with pestilence."[8]

Both the Bible and the Book of Mormon, then, contain ample
evidence that famine, sword, and pestilence are combined tools of
God's judgments upon the wicked. Not only are they instruments
of divine retribution, they also serve as God's method for awaken-

---

1. Jer. 14:11-12. False prophets had been telling the people no famine nor
   war would come upon them. Concerning them the Lord warned,
   > ...Thus saith the Lord concerning the prophets that prophesy in my
   > name, and I sent them not, yet they say, Sword and famine shall not
   > be in this land; *By sword and famine shall those prophets be con-*
   > *sumed.*
   > *And the people to whom they prophesy shall be cast out in the*
   > *streets of Jerusalem because of the famine and the sword; and they*
   > *shall have none to bury them, them, their wives, nor their sons, nor*
   > *their daughters; for I will pour their wickedness upon them.* (Jer.
   > 14:15-16. See also verses 17-22.)
2. See Jer. 21:4-9; 24:10; 27:8, 13; 29:17-18; 32:24, 36; 34:17; 38:2.
3. See Ezek. 5:2, 12; 6:11-12; 7:15; 12:16. In Ezek. 14:21 a fourth judgment is added: "the noisome beast."
4. 2 Ne. 1:18.
5. Mos. 12:1-8.
6. Al. 10:22-23.
7. Hel. 10:6. Chapter 11 tells how he used this power.
8. Hel. 13:9.

ing his people to righteousness as it begins to slip away from them. As Nephi observed,

> ...We see that except the Lord doth chasten his people with many afflictions, yea, *except he doth visit them with death and with terror, and with famine and with all manner of pestilence, they will not remember him.*[1]

Future Judgments by Famine, Sword and Pestilence Predicted

The scriptures also speak of the future, and warn that famine, sword and pestilence will be combined in last days judgments which will be poured out upon the earth. The Lord has revealed his warning that

> ...*With the sword and by bloodshed the inhabitants of the earth shall mourn; and with famine, and plague,* and earthquake, and the thunder of heaven, and the fierce and vivid lightning also, shall the inhabitants of the earth be made to feel the wrath, and indignation, and chastening hand of an Almighty God, *until the consumption decreed hath made a full end of all nations;*
>
> That the cry of the saints, and of the blood of the saints, shall cease to come up into the ears of the Lord of Sabaoth, from the earth, to be avenged of their enemies.
>
> *Wherefore, stand ye in holy places, and be not moved,* until the day of the Lord come; for behold, *it cometh quickly,* saith the Lord.[2]

Christ, in his great panoramic prophecy on the Mount of Olives, taught that

> ...*Nation shall rise against nation, and kingdom against kingdom: and there shall be famines, and pestilences, and earthquakes, in diverse places.*
> All these are the *beginning* of sorrows.[3]

It is the intent of these next three chapters to examine each of these instruments of God's judgment as they pertain to the future.

Famine—Examples from the Past

Few people realize the number and severity of famines which have occurred in the earth's history. Most famines have taken place

---

1. Hel. 12:3.
2. D & C 87:6-8.
3. Mt. 24:7-8.

in areas lacking adequate communication with the outside world. Most have been poorly documented. The most complete published list includes 370 famines up to 1940,[1] but many local famines are excluded from it. The most serious famines include the following:

1333-37	China — a great famine, with 4,000,000 reported dead in one region only; it may have been the source of Europe's Black Death.
1600	Russia — 500,000 dead; also plague.
1769-70	India, Bengal — death estimates range from 3,000,000 (1/10 of population to 10,000,000 (1/3 of population).
1837-38	Northwest India — 800,000 dead.
1846-51	Ireland — great potato famines; 1,000,000 died from starvation and disease, even more immigrated.
1866	India, Bengal & Orissa — 1,500,000 deaths.
1876-78	India — over 36,000,000 affected; deaths estimated at 5,000,000.
1876-79	North China — 9,000,000-13,000,000 estimated deaths.
1892-94	China — 1,000,000 deaths estimated.
1896-97	India — 5,000,000 deaths estimated.
1899-1900	India — 3,250,000 affected, 1,250,000 deaths estimated.
1920-21	North China — 20,000,000 affected; 500,000 deaths.
1921-22	U.S.S.R. — 20,000,000-24,000,000 affected; death estimates 1,250,000-5,000,000.
1928-29	China, Shensi, Honan, & Kansu — in Shensi alone an estimated 3,000,000 died.
1932-34	U.S.S.R. — an estimated 5,000,000 died.
1941-43	Greece — losses estimated at 450,000.
1943-44	India, Bengal — 1,500,000 died.[2]

The most severe of the past famines have killed as much as one-third of the population of the affected areas.

What causes famines? Several reasons are given:

---

1. "Famine," *Encyclopaedia Britannica* (Chicago: Encyclopaedia Britannica, Inc., 1971), Vol. 9, p. 58A. To indicate the incompleteness of the above list the article adds:

   A detailed study by Ping-ti Ho of the local histories of Hupei Province of China indicates that 62 famines occurred between 1644 and 1911; not one is included in the list of 370. W. H. Mallory refers to a study made at the University of Nanking reporting 1,828 famines in China between 108 B.C. and A.D. 1911. *(Ibid.)*

2. Adapted from *Ibid.*, pp. 58-58A.

Crop Failure. Drought is the usual cause, with almost no rain falling in affected areas for from three to seven years. Other climatic factors include cold during the planting and early growing season; excess rain, often resulting in flooding; insects, plant diseases, and early frosts or snowfalls which shorten the growing season.

War and Civil Disturbances. Blockades and sieges of cities have caused many famines. Invading armies may prevent crops from being planted or harvested. Food has often been used as a weapon.

Natural Catastrophies. Hurricanes, floods, earthquakes, and volcanic eruptions can result in destruction of crops, food stores, and means of earning a living.

What happens to individuals when famine strikes? The immediate effect, of course, is a loss of body weight. After two to three months on a daily diet of 1,600 calories, weight loss will be about 25%. Activity will be reduced. General lethargy will occur. The mind becomes dominated by a desire for food. Other emotions are dulled. Birthrates fall and stillbirths increase. There is constant diarrhea, which often is the immediate cause of death. The belly becomes bloated, arms and legs become very thin, the hair turns grey, the eyes become piercing. Infectious diseases spread: cholera, malaria, smallpox, typhus, and influenza often accompany famine.

People search for food. They eat grass, sawdust, the bark of trees. They chew pieces of leather. Prices skyrocket, till food becomes impossible to buy. Moral values disintegrate. People rob and steal. Parents sell their children. Some turn to murder and cannibalism.

Consider the terrible effects of famine, as described in the Bible:

> And there was a great famine in *Samaria: and, behold, they besieged it, until an ass's head was sold for fourscore pieces of silver, and the fourth part of a cab of dove's dung for five pieces of silver.*
>
> And as the king of Israel was passing by upon the wall, there cried a woman unto him, saying, Help, my lord, O king.
>
> And he said, If the Lord do not help thee, whence shall I help thee? out of the barnfloor, or out of the winepress?
>
> And the king said unto her, What aileth thee? And she answered, *This woman said unto me, Give thy son, that we may eat him to day, and we will eat my son to morrow.*
>
> *So we boiled my son, and did eat him: and I said unto her on the next day, Give thy son, that we may eat him: and she hath hid her son.*

And it came to pass, when the king heard the words of the woman, that he rent his clothes; and he passed by upon the wall, and the people looked, and, behold, he had sackcloth within upon his flesh. [1]

The prophet Jeremiah described a famine in his day:

How is the gold become dim! how is the most fine gold changed! the stones of the sanctuary are poured out in the top of every street.

The precious sons of Zion, comparable to fine gold, how are they esteemed as earthen pitchers, the work of the hands of the potter!

Even the sea monsters draw out the breast, they give suck to their young ones: *the daughter of my people is become cruel, like the ostriches in the wilderness.*

The tongue of the sucking child cleaveth to the roof of his mouth for thirst: the young children ask bread, and no man breaketh it unto them.

They that did feed delicately are desolate in the streets: they that were brought up in scarlet embrace dunghills.

For the punishment of the iniquity of the daughter of my people is greater than the punishment of the sin of Sodom, that was overthrown as in a moment, and no hands stayed on her.

Her Nazarites were purer than snow, they were whiter than milk, they were more ruddy in body than rubies, their polishing was of sapphire:

Their visage is blacker than a coal; they are not known in the streets: *their skin cleaveth to their bones; it is withered, it is become like a stick.*

They that be slain with the sword are better than they that be slain with hunger: for *these pine away, stricken through for want of the fruits of the field.*

The hands of the pitiful women have sodden their own children: they were their meat in the destruction of the daughter of my people

The Lord hath accomplished his fury; he hath poured out his fierce anger, and hath kindled a fire in Zion, and it hath devoured the foundations thereof. [2]

But the degenerating morality that comes with widespread famine is perhaps best described by the historian Josephus, who related the events which took place in Jerusalem as that city was beseiged by the Romans in 70 A.D.:

...The madness of the seditious did also increase together with their famine, and both those miseries *were every day inflamed more and*

---

1. 2 Ki. 6:25-30. This famine occurred during the Syrian seige of Samaria. Fourscore pieces of silver, for purchasing an ass's head, amounted to about $50; a pint (the fourth part of a cab) of dove excrement cost about $3. 2 Ki. 7 tells how God brought a miraculous end to the famines. (See also Ezek. 5:10; Deut. 28:53-57.)
2. Lam. 4:1-11. This famine occurred as Jerusalem fell to Babylonia. See also Jer. 14:1-6.

more; for there was no corn which any where appeared publicly, *but the robbers came running into, and searched men's private houses; and then, if they found any, they tormented them, because they had denied they had any;* and if they found none, they tormented them worse, because they supposed they had more carefully concealed it. *The indication they made use of whether they had any or not was taken from the bodies of these miserable wretches; which, if they were in good case, they supposed they were in no want at all of food; but if they were wasted away, they walked off without searching any further;* nor did they think it proper to kill such as these, because they saw they would very soon die of themselves for want of food. *Many there were indeed who sold what they had for one measure; it was of wheat, if they were of the richer sort; but of barley, if they were poorer.* When these had so done, they shut themselves up in the inmost rooms of their houses, and ate the corn they had gotten; some did it without grinding it, by reason of the extremity of the want they were in, and others baked bread of it, according as necessity and fear dictated to them: a table was no where laid for a distinct meal, but they snatched the bread out of the fire, half-baked, and ate it very hastily.

It was not a miserable case, and a sight that would justly bring tears into our eyes, how men stood as to their food, while *the more powerful had more than enough, and the weaker were lamenting* [for want of it]. *But the famine was too hard for all other passions, and it is destructive to nothing so much as to modesty;* for what was otherwise worthy of reverence was in this case despised; insomuch that *children pulled the very morsels that their fathers were eating out of their very mouths, and what was still more to be pitied, so did the mothers do as to their infants; and when those that were most dear were perishing under their hands, they were not ashamed to take from them the very last drops that might preserve their lives:* and while they ate after this manner, yet were they not concealed in so doing; but the seditious every where came upon them immediately, and snatched away from them what they had gotten from others; for *when they saw any house shut up, this was to them a signal that the people within had gotten some food;* whereupon they broke open the doors, and ran in, and took pieces of what they were eating almost up out of their very throats, and this by force: the old men, who held their food fast, were beaten; and if the women hid what they had within their hands, their hair was torn for so doing; nor was there any commiseration shown either to the aged or to the infants, but they lifted up children from the ground as they hung upon the morsels they had gotten, and shook them down upon the floor. *But still they were more barbarously cruel to those that had prevented their coming in, and had actually swallowed down what they were going to seize upon, as if they had been unjustly defrauded of their right.* They also invented terrible methods of torments to discover where any food was, and they were these: to stop up the passages of the privy parts of the miserable wretches, and to drive sharp stakes up their fundaments; and a man was forced to bear what it is terrible even to hear, in order to make him confess that he had but one loaf of bread, or that he might discover a handful of barley-meal that was concealed; and this was done when these tormentors were not themselves hungry;

for the thing had been less barbarous had necessity forced them to it; but this was done to keep their madness in exercise, and as making preparation of provisions for themselves for the following days. These men went also to meet those that had crept out of the city by night, as far as the Roman guards, to gather some plants and herbs that grew wild; and *when those people thought they had got clear of the enemy, they snatched from them what they had brought with them*, even while they had frequently entreated them, and that by calling upon the tremendous name of God, to give them back some part of what they had brought; though these would not give them the least crumb, and they were to be well contented that they were only spoiled, and not slain at the same time. [1]

Seven Years of Famine

When God sends a famine, how long does it last? Though famines recorded in the scriptures and in secular history have continued for varying periods of time, one interval has been specified by scripture and modern-day prophets so many times that it cannot be overlooked. *Seven years* has been the duration proclaimed by God's prophets. That term is frightening, for it far exceeds the length of major famines which have claimed the lives of millions in years past. If a widespread famine of seven years' duration came upon the earth in the future, it would truly leave much of the earth desolate.

Probably the best-known instance of famine in the scriptures is the seven years of dearth that came in the days of Joseph, who was sold into Egypt. God favored the Egyptian Pharaoh with two prophetic dreams,[2] which warned that seven good years would be followed by seven years of famine. Joseph interpreted the dreams, telling the ruler that "God hath shewed Pharaoh what he is about to do:"

> The seven good kine are seven years; and the seven good ears are seven years; the dream is one.

---

1. Flavius Josephus, *The Life and Works of Flavius Josephus* (New York: Holt, Rinehart and Winston, n.d.), *Wars of the Jews*, Bk V, chpt. X, pp. 798-799.

2. See Gen. 41:1-7. Note that the revelation was given to a secular leader, not through God's prophet, as was also the case with King Nebuchadnezzar's visions of the future (see Dan. chpts. 2 & 4). These and other instances from the scriptures and religious history demonstrate that God, in his wisdom, grants valid prophetic insights to many others besides his prophets. Though such revelations do not constitute "doctrine" or "commandment" to God's church, they are nevertheless revealed truth.

And the seven thin and ill favoured kine that came up after them are seven years; and the seven empty ears blasted with the east wind shall be *seven years of famine.*[1]

With this prophetic warning as his guide, the Pharaoh established a vast food storage program in which sufficient food was made available when "the famine was over all the face of the earth"[2] and became "sore in the land."[3] Joseph, who was placed in charge of the storage program, played an inspired role. He later told his brothers that *"God did send me before you to preserve life."*[4]

Seven years of famine are mentioned in other scriptural instances. For instance, when the prophet Gad gave King David the choice between famine, war, or pestilence as the punishment to come upon Israel, his query was *"Shall seven years of famine come unto thee in thy land?"*[5]

Seven years of famine came to the Palestine area in the days of Elisha, and that prophet warned the Shunamite woman that *"the Lord hath called for a famine; and it shall also come upon the land seven years."*[6]

The Mormons endured severe famines during the early days of the Utah period. The saints have been continually counseled

---

1. Gen. 41:26-27. Joseph then told Pharaoh that "the thing is established by God, and God will shortly bring it to pass." (Gen. 41:32. For assurance that God brings famines see Hel. 12:1-3; Mos. 1:17; 9:3; Eth. 9:28; 11:7; 1 Ki. 17:1; Ezek. 5; Deut. 28; Ja. 5:17; etc.

2. Gen. 41:56. See Gen. 42-47. Note the economic conditions, in which money failed, during the famine (Gen. 47:15-26).

3. Gen. 43:1. A carving on an Egyptian tomb, now known as the "stele of famine," records another seven-year famine in Egypt:

    The tale is one of suffering and distress: "I am mourning on my high throne for the vast misfortune, because *the Nile flood in my time has not come for seven years!* Light is the grain; there is a lack of crops and of all kinds of food. Each man has become a thief to his neighbor. They desire to hasten and cannot walk. The child cries, the youth creeps along, and the old men; their souls are bowed down, their legs are bent together and drag along the ground, and their hands rest in their bosoms. The counsel of the great ones in the court is but emptiness. Torn open are the chests of provisions, but instead of contents there is air. Everything is exhausted." (From Ralph A. Graves, "Fearful Famines of the Past," *The National Geographic Magazine,* vol. xxxii, July 1917, p. 70.) (*Encyclopaedia Britannica, op. cit.,* vol. 9, pp. 58A.)

4. Gen. 45:5.

5. 2 Sam. 24:13.

6. 2 Ki. 8:1.

from that time forward to store for a time of future famine and hardship. What should be emphasized is that the counsel and instruction given was that the saints should store a *seven year supply of food.*

Heber C. Kimball, for instance, warned in an 1857 discourse that "after your testimony *cometh the testimony of earthquakes, of famine, of fire and of desolation:* it shall come upon the world, and it shall begin at my house, saith the Lord, that is, *with that portion who rebel against Him in the midst of His house....* These calamities are coming...." The following are excerpts from his discourse:

> Brethren and sisters, this is the time in which to prepare. If you are not saved temporally in these Valleys, I shall not be. If you will take a course to bring distress on this people, we shall have to be distressed....
>
> Brethren, go and build your storehouses before your grain is harvested, and lay it up, and *let us never cease until we have got a seven years' supply.* You may think that we shall not see times in which we shall need it. Do you not comprehend how comfortable it will be for us to know that we have *grain enough to last us seven years?...*
>
> Will you be slack, brethren, and let the evil come upon us, when we forewarn you of the future events that are coming;... We are telling of what the prophets have said—of what the Lord has said to Joseph. Wake up, now, wake up, O Israel, and lay up your grain and your stores. I tell you that there is trouble coming upon the world....
>
> Is it so in the United States? It is. They have got to eat that dish; *and when famine, pestilence, and starvation come upon us in a small degree, it will increase upon them fourfold,* packed down and running over, and they cannot help it.... *We will lay up the grain for seven years,* and thousands of them will worship us for a little johnny cake.[1]

Two months later, President Kimball again referred to the instruction to store up a seven years' supply:

> This is a part of our religion—to lay up stores and provide for ourselves and for the surrounding country; for the day is near when *they will come by thousands and by millions, with their fineries, to get a little bread.* That time is right by our door....
>
> Say I, wake up, ye Saints of Zion, while it is called to-day, lest trouble and sorrow come upon you, as a thief in the night.
>
> Suppose it is not coming, will it hurt you to *lay up the products of the earth for seven years?* Will it hurt you, if you have your guns, swords, and spears in good condition, according to the law of the United States?[2]

---

1. Heber C. Kimball, *JD* 4:336-339. June 7, 1857.
2. Heber C. Kimball, *JD* 5:163-164. August 30, 1857.

Elder George A. Smith reminded the saints of the counsel to lay up seven years' provisions, explained how it was to be done, and warned of the folly of selling it when it should have been stored to meet future needs:

> ...I wish to call the attention of the Conference to the text of President Young in relation to storing our wheat. This is a question of vast importance. A few years ago President Young gave counsel to the people of the Territory—most of whom agreed to it—*to lay by seven years provisions*. We were to have commenced three years ago, and were to have laid up one year's bread over and above the year's supply. The following year we were to add another year's supply, and so have continued until we had our seven years' supply laid up.... *I am aware that some of our brethren thought this counsel extravagant;* they considered that it could not be necessary to lay up such a quantity of bread; and some of them, instead of getting out lumber and making good substantial bins for the preservation of their wheat, turned out their means for teams, and freighted their bread to the north, to the east, and to the west; and not only so, but in many instances they gave it away, if they could only get half price for hauling it. Hundreds and thousands of sacks of flour have been hauled away, *when it should have been stored up here against a day of want.* [1]

President Brigham Young, while speaking about the exemplary role which should be played by bishops, commented on the instruction to store for seven years:

> We have said much to the people with regard to laying up provisions to last them a few years. This is our duty now; it has been our duty for years. How many of our bishops have provisions laid up for one year, two years, or *seven years?...* Each bishop should be an example to his ward. If the bishop of a ward lays up wheat to last his family a year, two years, *or seven years,* as the case may be, his neighbors on the right and on the left will be very apt to do the same; they will very likely build good bins and try to fill them. [2]

President Young reminded the saints of the counsel to store for as much as seven years, and warned that they cannot expect God to continue to give them abundant harvests if they do not store their food:

> *Years ago, Brother Kimball counseled the people to lay up two year's provisions, and then enough for four, for six and for seven years.* I have it now, and I am dealing it out. Some people have so much faith that

---

1. George A. Smith, *JD* 12:141. October 9, 1867.
2. Brigham Young, *JD* 12:106. November 3, 1867.

although the grasshoppers are around in such vast numbers, they are confident of an abundant harvest, because of the movements made to gather the poor this season. They say the Lord would not inspire His servants to bring the poor from the nations that they might starve. And so believing, they will go and sell the last bushel of wheat for comparatively nothing, trusting in God to provide for their wants. *My faith is not of this kind; it is reasonable. If the Lord gives good crops this season, and tells us to lay up from that abundance, I do not think He will increase His blessings upon us if we foolishly squander those He has already given us.* I believe He will bless the earth for His people's sake; and I will till it and try to get a crop from it; but *if I neglect to take advantage of the goodness of the Lord, or misuse or treat lightly His mercies, I need not expect that they will be continued upon me to the same extent.* Have not my sisters here, gleaned in the fields around for years past? And when they have had their gleanings thrashed out, *have they not taken the grain to the stores and sold it to our enemies, instead of laying it by?* And yet they will expect to be blessed continually with plenty! *I have not so much faith as this. I have a reasonable faith, a sustaining faith, one that I can build my hopes upon;* and I think I will not be disappointed. I labor and toil, but I do not waste my labor.[1]

While speaking of the need for the saints to provide for their own needs, Brigham Young commented on the need for an extensive supply of food, in preparation for a time when starving people will come to the saints for food. He warned that the saints must labor in their own behalf and bless themselves, not just expect God to supply their needs. Again, a seven year supply is mentioned:

...is it any more inconsistent than to throw away and waste the substance the Lord has given us, and when we come to want, crying to Him for what we have wasted and squandered? The Lord has been blessing us all the time, and *He asks us why we have not been blessing ourselves.*

Will this be instructive to you, my brethren, hereafter? *A great many have taken this counsel, and they are prepared. I had my seven years' breadstuffs on hand last year;* but I have to deal it out, and I will deal it out to the last bushel, and try my faith with my brethren. But are we deserving of praise from God or man? Who are deserving of praise? The persons who take care of themselves, or the ones who always trust in the great mercies of the Lord to take care of them? It is just as consistent to expect that the Lord will supply us with fruit when we do not plant the trees; or that, when we do not plow and sow and are saved the labor of harvesting, we should cry to the Lord to save us from want, as to ask Him to save us from the consequences of our own folly, disobedience and waste. It is said, by some, that the Lord is not going to tell His servants to gather His people here to starve. That is true; *but the Lord has said,* "Gather the poor from the nations;" and to the people

---

1. Brigham Young, *JD* 12:219. May 17, 1868.

here, *"Gather and save the produce I put within your reach, and prepare against a day of want."* *Suppose a hundred thousand or a million starving people were coming here, and we had only grain to last for a couple of years, with famine around; they would offer their gold and their silver and their plate and their precious things for bread to eat, and you would hand it out until all was gone. Then you could sit down and look at the riches you had got, until all would perish together with hunger. This would be so, unless the people act more wisely than they do now.*[1]

Most Saints Lack Adequate Food Storage

And how obedient are the saints to the counsel to store food which has been given to them for over a century? Statistics are not readily available to answer the question. However, results of a study of LDS people in Utah, made by Utah State University, was presented in the welfare meeting of October General Conference in 1975. Bishop H. Burke Peterson, first counselor in the Presiding Bishopric presented the statistics, which were regarded as a representative sampling:

> *Five percent of church members had a year's supply of meat products, three percent had a year's supply of dried or canned fruits or vegetables, about 18 percent had a year's supply of grains and only three families in a hundred had a year's supply of canned or powdered milk.*
> *"On the average, about 30 percent of the church had a two-month supply of food. The remainder had little or none,"* Bishop Peterson said.[2]

Reports from the meeting indicated that "just more than half of the Church's 5,000 wards around the world have welfare production projects."[3] The Church welfare program is designed to assist only the needy—about four percent of the Church, and would be insufficient to meet the needs of a large portion of the Church in time of widespread emergency.[4] The position of the

---

1. Brigham Young, *JD* 12:243-244. July 25, 1868.
2. "Most LDS Unprepared, Welfare Meeting Told," *Deseret News*, October 4, 1975.
3. *Ibid.*
4. The report stated:
   There are 78 bishop's storehouses in the church to distribute commodities to the needy. Most of these are concentrated in the western states, but bishops and stake presidents should be planning for such storehouses throughout the world, he said.
   Bishop Peterson showed a chart indicating that demands on the bishop's storehouses have reached as high as $600,000 in 1975 and the need is increasing at the rate of 25 percent a year.

Church is that the individual members are responsible for meeting their own needs in future emergencies. Again referring to Elder Peterson's report:

> He said it was "extremely important" that local leaders and members place greater emphasis on home storage for a year's supply of food, clothing, and where possible, fuel and to grow gardens and make their own clothes.
>
> "In general, become as self-sufficient as possible *to prepare against the days to come,*" he said.
>
> Bishop Peterson said the church has a total of 671 production projects, including 143,000 acres under cultivation, but this is only meeting current needs.
>
> "*Family preparedness, with home production and storage, must be the way the majority of our church families take care of themselves,*" he said.
>
> The ward, stake and multi-stake production projects are only a "backup system" for helping those who are unable to care for themselves, he said.[1]

Prophecies of Famine in a Time of Future Conflict

Prophets of the restored Church have repeatedly warned of famines that will come in the last days. They have focused, in particular, on famine that will be experienced in America during a period of internal conflict prior to the return to Jackson County. Several of these prophecies allude to the coming of many people to obtain food from the saints in the tops of the mountains. Joseph Smith warned, for instance, that

> I am prepared to say by the authority of Jesus Christ, that not many years shall pass away before *the United States shall present such a scene of bloodshed as has not a parallel in the history of your nation; pestilence, hail, famine, and earthquakes will sweep the wicked of this generation from off the face of the land, to open and prepare the way for the return of the lost tribes of Israel from the north country.*[2]

---

1. *Ibid.*
2. HC 1:315. Letter of Joseph Smith to editor N.E. Seaton, January 4, 1833.

> "*We must prepare now if we are to have adequate commodities stored to handle major economic problems of the future,*" he said.
>
> Despite the heavy volume, the *storehouses assisted only four percent of the church membership last year.*
>
> *One year's supply of commodities are on hand in the system* at the present time, Bishop Peterson said, but *this would be "quickly depleted by a major increase in demand." (Ibid.)*

In July, 1839, the prophet Joseph told of a vision which he had received which warned of serious internal conflict within the United States in which even family members would struggle to the death with each other. His allusion to famine at the end of the vision may be indication that the people will be struggling to obtain food in a time of extreme scarcity and may explain why family members would take the lives even of loved ones:

> There will be here and there a Stake [of Zion] for the gathering of the Saints. Some may have cried peace, but the Saints and the world will have little peace from henceforth. Let this not hinder us from going to the Stakes; for God has told us to flee, not dallying, or we shall be scattered, one here, and another there. There your children shall be blessed, and you in the midst of friends where you may be blessed. The Gospel net gathers of every kind.
>
> I prophesy, that that man who tarries after he has an opportunity of going, will be afflicted by the devil. Wars are at hand; we must not delay; but are not required to sacrifice. We ought to have the building up of Zion as our greatest object. When wars come, we shall have to flee to Zion. The cry is to make haste. The last revelation says, Ye shall not have time to have gone over the earth, until these things come. It will come as did the cholera, war, fires, and earthquakes; one pestilence after another, until the Ancient of Days comes, then judgment will be given to the Saints.
>
> Whatever you may hear about me or Kirtland, take no notice of it; for if it be a place of refuge, the devil will use his greatest efforts to trap the Saints. You must make yourselves acquainted with those men who like Daniel pray three times a day toward the House of the Lord. Look to the Presidency and receive instruction. Every man who is afraid, covetous, will be taken in a snare. The time is soon coming, when no man will have any peace but in Zion and her stakes.
>
> I saw men hunting the lives of their own sons, and brother murdering brother, women killing their own daughters, and daughters seeking the lives of their mothers. I saw armies arrayed against armies. I saw blood, desolation, fires. The Son of Man has said that the mother shall be against the daughter, and the daughter against the mother. These things are at our doors. They will follow the Saints of God from city to city. Satan will rage, and the spirit of the devil is now enraged. I know not how soon these things will take place; but with a view of them, shall I cry peace? No! I will lift up my voice and testify of them. How long you will have good crops, and the famine be kept off, I do not know; when the fig tree leaves, know then that the summer is nigh at hand.[1]

---

1. HC 3:390-391. July 1, 1839. This was a portion of the Prophet's address to the Twelve. Note pertinent aspects of his warning: 1. When wars come, the Saints will have to flee to the stakes of Zion so they won't be scattered, 2. the judgments will continue until the coming of the Ancient of Days [to the Council at Adam-ondi-Ahman, early in the New Jerusalem era. See HC 3:386-387, 389, 391], 3. his message was that one should testify of the vision when one receives such a warning.

A powerful prophecy made at the end of the Civil War by Elder Orson Hyde, then President of the Quorum of the Twelve, asserts that scarcity of food will be the reason for future conflict within the United States. The prophecy was made in 1865 at Nephi, Utah:

> The eagle of war will now take up his flight and perch on the banks of the river Rhine, returning to his native heath when it will not be the white man of the north fighting for the liberation of the colored man of the south, *but will be the white man of the north and the white man of the south fighting for bread for their wives and children!*[1]

Brigham Young warned of famine that would occur in America and throughout the world when the testimony of the Elders ceases to be given [the times of the Gentiles are fulfilled] and God pours out his judgments:

> "Do you think there is calamity abroad now among the people?" Not much. *All we have yet heard and all we have experienced is scarcely a preface to the sermon that is going to be preached. When the testimony of the Elders ceases to be given, and the Lord says to them, "Come home; I will now preach my own sermons to the nations of the earth,"* all you now know can scarcely be called a preface to the sermon that will be preached with fire and sword, tempests, earthquakes, hail, rain, thunders and lightnings, and fearful destruction. What matters the destruction of a few railway cars? You will hear of magnificent cities, now idolized by the people, sinking in the earth, entombing the inhabitants. The sea will heave itself beyond its bounds, engulphing mighty cities. *Famine will spread over the nations, and nation will rise up against nation, kingdom against kingdom, and states against states, in our own country and in foreign lands; and they will destroy each other, caring not for the blood and lives of their neighbours, of their families, or for their own lives.* They will be like the Jaredites who preceded the Nephites upon this continent, and will destroy each other to the last man, through the anger that the Devil will place in their hearts, because they have rejected the words of life and are given over to Satan to do whatever he listeth to do with them. You may think that the little you hear of now is grievous; yet *the faithful of God's people will see days that will cause them to close their eyes because of the sorrow that will come upon the wicked nations. The hearts of the faithful will be filled with pain and anguish for them.* [2]

---

1. This prophecy is contained in copies of personal papers of Elder Orson Hyde given to the author by Elder Hyde's granddaughter, Romania Woolley. Originals of these papers were contributed to the BYU library and copies were presented to the Church College of Hawaii.
2. *JD* 8:123. July 15, 1860.

Orson Pratt also warned of the future conflict which will take place in America, and said, concerning the food supply, that

> ...There will be too much bloodshed, too much mobocracy, too much going forth in bands and destroying and pillaging the land to suffer people to pursue any local vocation with any degree of safety. *What will become of millions of the farmers upon that land? They will leave their farms and they will remain uncultivated, and they will flee before the ravaging armies from place to place;* and thus will they go forth burning and pillaging the whole country;...[1]

In another discourse on the future period of internal conflict, Elder Pratt also spoke concerning the food supply:

> The time will come when *there will be no safety in carrying on the peaceable pursuits of farming or agriculture. But these will be neglected, and the people will think themselves well off if they can flee from city to city, from town to town and escape with their lives.* Thus will the Lord visit the people, if they will not repent.[2]

It takes little imagination to contemplate what would happen to the nation's food supply if this situation took place for even one season. To lose a national harvest would bring a famine of unprecedented proportions!

Elder Heber C. Kimball anticipated that the future famines, which will be part of the judgments to be poured out by God, "will be the most terrible and severe that have ever come upon the nations of the earth":

> ...Every man who has a farm needs a storehouse—one made of rock and lime, that will guard your grain against the mice, rats, and all other four-legged vermin; also against the two-legged ones. *I have more fears of the two-legged ones than I have of the four-legged ones.*
>
> Plan to build a good storehouse, every man who has a farm, and never cease until you have accomplished it. And do not forget to pay your tithing before you put the grain into the storehouse. *Lay up enough for seven years, at a calculation for from five to ten in each family; and then calculate that there will be in your families from five to ten persons to where you now have one, because you are on the increase....*
>
> When we have stored away our grain we are safe, independent of the world, in case of famine, are we not? Yes, we are; for, in that case, we will have the means for subsistence in our own hands. When the famines begin upon the earth, we shall be very apt to feel them first.

---

1. *JD* 20:151. March 9, 1879.
2. *JD* 12:344. December 27, 1868.

*If judgments must need begin at the house of God, and if the right-
eous scarcely are saved, how will it be with the wicked? Am I looking
for famines? Yes, the most terrible and severe that have ever come upon
the nations of the earth....*[1]

Elder Kimball prophesied that there will come a time when
the saints "will be obliged to depend upon our own resources,"
and the people of the U.S. will come to them for bread to eat:

Lay up your stores, and take your silks and fine things, and exchange them for grain and such things as you need, and *the time will
come when we will be obliged to depend upon our own resources; for
the time is not far distant when the curtain will be dropped between us
and the United States.* When that time comes, brethren and sisters, you
will wish you had commenced sooner to make your own clothing. I tell
you, God requires us to go into home manufacture; and, prolong it as
much as you like, you have got to do it.

*You will also see the day that you will wish you had laid up your
grain, if you do not do it now; for you will see the day, if you do not
take care of the blessings God has given to you, that you will become
servants, the same as the world will.*

We have told you this before. You have been exhorted, year after
year, to prepare for hard times: you have been told of this often enough.
We have told you that when hard times come again you won't have the
privilege that you had last time of having food dealt out to you gratui-
tously, but you will have to pay for all you get. This will come to pass.
I suppose there are many who don't believe it. To such it is like a tune
that strikes upon the drum of the ear, passes off, and is forgotten.

I will prove to you that I will put my faith with my works and *lay
up stores for my family and for my friends that are in the United States,
and I will be to them as Joseph was to the people in the land of Egypt.
Every man and woman will be a saviour if they will do as I say.* You may
write this down and send it to the States; for it will be published.

*...It behoves us to be saving and to prepare for the time to come. The
day will come when the people of the United States will come lugging
their bundles under their arms, coming to us for bread to eat....*

If you will do right—keep the commandments of God, I can say with
all the propriety that any man, prophet, or apostle ever did, *you shall
never want for food, or raiment, or houses, or lands; and no power on
the earth can injure you.* There is no power that shall prevent our prosperity; for we shall increase, while every other power upon the earth
that is opposed to this work and our God will go down. I just know it.
Amen.[2]

---

1. *JD* 5:20, April 6, 1857.
2. *JD* 5:10-11. July 5, 1857. Note the conditional nature of the last paragraph of his prophecy. Will the saints be able to claim this blessing if
   they do not maintain the food supply they have been commanded to
   have on hand?

And it was Elder Kimball who prophesied that *"The day will come that you (strangers) will have to come to us for bread to eat; and we will be your saviours here upon Mount Zion."*[1]

He also told how people would come to the tops of the mountains in this time of future peril. Speaking at the arrival of the second of the handcart companies, he prophesied that

> There will be *millions on millions* that will come much in the same way, only they will not have handcarts, for *they will take their bundles under their arms, and their children on their backs, and under their arms, and flee; and Zion's people will have to send out relief to them, for they will come when the judgments come on the nations.*[2]

Famine, then, has been clearly represented in prophecy as being an instrument of God's judgments upon the wicked in the last days. Though the saints have been repeatedly commanded to have extensive supplies on hand, it appears that most have failed to do so. Can they lay claim upon God's mercies when famines come if they have failed to obey the counsel they have been given? According to the prophetic warnings cited above, the famines will be severe, and the burdens placed upon the saints will be great. It may well be that possession of adequate food storage, in obedience to the commandment, will be the factor that separates the righteous and wicked saints—the wise and foolish virgins—in the last days.

Summary

1. The Angel Moroni warned Joseph Smith that judgments are coming upon the earth by famine, sword, and pestilence. These three terms have been used repeatedly in the scriptures to symbolize the full extent of God's judgments.

2. Examples from the Old Testament and Book of Mormon demonstrate the use of these terms. In many of the situations listed, divine retribution was both swift and complete, leaving destruction and desolation in its wake.

3. Famine, sword, and pestilence serve both as the instruments of God's retribution and as his method for awakening his people to obedience as righteousness begins to slip away from them.

---

1. *JD* 5:9. July 5, 1857.
2. *JD* 4:106. September 28, 1856.

4. God has warned that the inhabitants of the earth will mourn because of his chastening hand which will be manifested through sword, famine, and plague until the consumption he has decreed has made a full end of all nations. The saints are to stand in holy places as these events transpire.

5. Past famines have killed millions of people, sometimes slaying one-third of the population.

6. Causes of famine include crop failure, war and civil disturbances, and natural catastrophies.

7. The personal physical effects of famine include loss of body weight, lethargy, emotional dullness, diarrhea, the spread of infectious diseases as body resistance is reduced, bloated belly, and hair turning grey.

8. Examples of human behavior in other famines were cited from the Bible and from Josephus. They showed the economic problems caused by a scarcity of food, cannabalism, robbery and murder, and a general decline in moral values.

9. The duration of famines sent by God was seven years in several scriptural situations. Early LDS Church leaders instructed the saints to store food sufficient for seven years in order to be prepared for future famines. They warned that the saints cannot expect God to bless them with abundant harvests and adequate food supply if the saints don't work to supply their own needs and if they don't preserve a seven-year supply instead of selling all their produce.

10. A survey reported in a 1975 general conference showed that most Latter-day Saints have not obeyed the counsel given to them to store food. Only about 30% of the Church had a supply adequate for even two months. Approximately three percent had a one-year's supply.

11. Prophecies by early Church leaders warn of future famine during the period of internal conflict in the United States, and indicate that lack of food may be a major reason for the strife of that era. Future famines are prophesied to be the most severe that have ever come upon the earth.

12. According to the prophetic statements cited, the saints will be the suppliers of food to others when famines come. Millions are expected to flee to the saints in the tops of the mountains to obtain food in that future era.

13. Obedience to the commandment to store food may be the factor that separates the righteous from the wicked saints—the wise and foolish virgins—in the last days.

God Has Decreed Wars
Upon the Wicked

Freedom is a fragile state, and a blessing enjoyed by relatively few in the world today.[1] Peace is also fragile, and depends upon man's righteousness. Jesus Christ, the "Prince of Peace,"[2] has power to give peace to man and to remove it from him. He grants peace to the righteous, and denies it to the wicked. The Psalmist wrote that "Great peace have they which love thy law: and nothing shall offend them,"[3] and the wise author of Proverbs observed that "When a man's ways please the Lord, he maketh even his enemies to be at peace with him."[4] Unfortunately, it is the message of both the scriptures and of the prophets that man's iniquity in the last days will cause peace to be removed from the earth and fear to come upon all mankind.

War to be Poured Out Upon the Nations

Wars are to come upon the earth in the last days. This is the message God has repeatedly revealed through his prophets. In 1831 a revelation stated:

> I have sworn in my wrath, and decreed *wars* upon the face of the earth, and *the wicked shall slay the wicked, and fear shall come upon every man;*
> *And the saints also shall hardly escape;* nevertheless, I, the Lord, am with them, and will come down in heaven from the presence of my Father and consume the wicked with unquenchable fire.
> And behold, this is not yet, but by and by.[5]

---

1. Since the early 50's, a New York based organization named Freedom House has monitored the level of freedom enjoyed in each of the nations of the earth. Its findings show that freedom is declining:

   Freedom House concluded that *only 19.8 percent of the world's population lived in freedom, with 35.3 percent partly free and 44.9 not free.* One year ago, it stated, 35 percent of the world's people were free. ("World Freedom Plunges, Research Group Notes," *Salt Lake Tribune*, December 28, 1975.)

2. Is. 9:6.
3. Ps. 119:165.
4. Prov. 16:7.
5. D & C 63:33-35.

The 1832 "Prophecy on War" warned that wars would continue until there was "a full end of all nations:"

> Verily, thus saith the Lord concerning the *wars* that will shortly come to pass, beginning at the rebellion of South Carolina, which will eventually terminate in the death and misery of many souls;
> And the time will come that *war will be poured out upon all nations*, beginning at this place.[1]

The prophecy then foretold the difficulties of the U.S. Civil War and alluded to the role of Great Britain in World Wars I and II, then continued into the future:

> *Then war shall be poured out upon all nations.*
> And it shall come to pass, after many days, slaves shall rise up against their masters, who shall be marshaled and disciplined for war.
> And it shall come to pass also that the remnants who are left of the land will marshal themselves, and shall become exceedingly angry, and shall vex the Gentiles with a sore vexation.
> *And thus, with the sword and by bloodshed the inhabitants of the earth shall mourn;... until the consumption decreed hath made a full end of all nations.*[2]

The Lord warned the saints that

> Ye hear of wars in foreign lands; but, behold, I say unto you, they are nigh, even at your doors, and not many years hence ye shall hear of *wars* in your own lands.[3]

The same revelation spoke of the era when the "times of the Gentiles be fulfilled."[4] That future period of God's judgments will be a time of intense warfare:

> *And in that day shall be heard of wars and rumors of wars, and the whole earth shall be in commotion, and men's hearts shall fail them,* and they shall say that Christ delayeth his coming until the end of the earth.... Men will harden their hearts against me, and *they will take up the sword, one against another, and they will kill one another.*[5]

---

1. D & C 87:1-2.
2. D & C 87:3-5, 6.
3. D & C 45:63. Note that the passage speaks of wars in the plural. Clearly it encompasses more than the U.S. Civil War.
4. D & C 45:25.
5. D & C 45:26, 33.

Another revelation warned the saints that "ye hear of wars in far countries, and you say that there will soon be great wars in far countries, but *ye know not the hearts of men in your own land.*"[1]

Five Future Conflicts Prophesied

The prophecies speak of five major conflicts, or periods of warfare, which are still in the future:

1.   *A third world war,* in which Russia will be defeated and the United States will come off victorious after receiving divine aid.

2.   *Internal conflict in the Americas,* characterized by mob violence and an uprising of the Lamanites.

3.   *World War during the New Jerusalem period,* during which all nations except the saints will be at war.

4.   *World-wide conflict as the nations which are controlled by the great and abominable church war among themselves,* in which the great and abominable church will be destroyed.

5.   *Conflicts involving Israel,* which will culminate in the *Battle of Armageddon.*

These conflicts may tend to have a cause-and-effect relationship upon each other, and to merge chronologically. They may even overlap, with problems beginning in one part of the world as strife still rages elsewhere from a different conflict. They should be viewed as separate portions of the overall era when there will be "wars and rumors of wars among all the nations and kindreds of the earth."[2]

Two Types of War: Preparatory Wars and Wars of Complete Destruction

Early leaders of the Church explained that wars would occur during the last days, and that they would be of two different types:

Preparatory Wars — which would prepare the way for the preaching of the gospel, and

---

1. D & C 38:29.
2. 1 Ne. 14:15.

Wars of Complete Destruction — which will serve as punishment for the wicked and will result in great desolation.

These two types of warfare in the last days were discussed and documented in detail in *Prophecy—Key to the Future*[1] and will be considered here only briefly.

Orson Pratt contrasted the two types of war, stating that *"the one is a war preparatory to the proclamation of the Gospel; the other is a war of terrible destruction, which will not better the condition of those who escape."*[2]

The earliest period is the era of *Preparatory Wars.* In this period, the saints will still be scattered throughout the earth. Wars will serve to remove governments which are unreceptive to missionary labors and replace them with leaders which will allow the gospel message to be preached within their borders. World War II, the Korean War, and the war in Viet Nam, for instance, all served to open the way for the growth of the Church in Japan, Indo-China, and the Pacific area. The dividing line between the two periods will be the "fulfilling of the times of the Gentiles," when God will begin to gather out the saints and will commence pouring out his judgments upon the wicked in increased measure.

When the period of *Wars of Complete Destruction* commences, war will become God's instrument of terrible destruction and annihilation of the wicked as he cleanses the earth in preparation for his coming in glory. The Spirit will have withdrawn from the Gentile nations.

The third world war appears to take place during the period of preparatory wars. Though the other conflicts listed above may begin to develop during that era, it is anticipated that they will see their culmination as wars of complete destruction.

Prophecies of a Third World War

Joseph Smith made several prophetic statements which allude to future conflict which will apparently be of world war dimensions. In one of them, spoken on June 19, 1844, the prophet used the formation of a political unit known as the Independent Ameri-

---

1. See *Prophecy—Key to the Future,* pages 4-10. Those pages should be read in this context for full understanding to be gained of the explanation given herein.
2. *JD* 7:186. July 10, 1859.

can Party[1] to place the context of the prophecy in the twentieth century instead of his own era. He foresaw the time when other nations will attempt to "divide up the lands of the United States." He saw that the U.S. will be weakened militarily by having spent her strength and means warring in foreign lands, and that the army will be sufficiently demoralized that half will give up.[2] This is his prophecy:

> There will be two great political parties in this country. One will be called the Republican, and the other the Democrat party. These two parties will go to war and *out of these two parties will spring another party which will be the Independent American Party. The United States will spend her strength and means warring in foreign lands until other nations will say, "Let's divide up the lands of the United States,"* then the people of the U.S. will unite and swear by the blood of their forefathers, that the land shall not be divided. Then *the country will go to war, and they will fight until one half of the U.S. army will give up, and the rest will continue to struggle.* They will keep on until they are very ragged and discouraged, and almost ready to give up—when *the boys from the mountains will rush forth in time to save the American Army from defeat and ruin.* And they will say, 'Brethren, we are glad you have come; give us men, henceforth, who can talk with God.' Then you will

---

1. Considerable stir was caused by the creation of the American Independent Party during the 1960's to support the political ambitions of Governor George Wallace. The name of his party was not exactly the same as that prophesied by Joseph Smith, and was therefore probably not the fulfillment of the prophecy. Several political groups literally named the Independent American Party also were organized during that era.

   One, organized in 1955 in New Orleans, Louisiana, with editor Phoebe Courtney as its motivating force, publishes an anti-Communist newspaper known as "The Independent American." Mrs. Courtney claimed divine inspiration as the motivating force for her organizing efforts. (See "Who is Behind the Independent American and Its Activities?," a 4-page letter from Phoebe Courtney, P.O. Box 4223, New Orleans, La., 70118, March 28, 1969.) Perhaps fulfillment of Joseph Smith's prophecy lies in her work, or maybe the future will hold more literal fulfillment—it is not the author's prerogative to say.

   The importance of the Independent American Party spoken of by Joseph Smith is only that of a chronological guide, to identify the time of fulfillment of the remainder of the prophecy.

2. Certainly the tremendous outlays of the Korean and Vietnamese Wars could fulfill this portion of the prophecy, though further fulfillment may still be forthcoming. These "no-win" wars seriously demoralized the U.S. military, and saw many thousands of desertions by U.S. soldiers. They led to the formation of the all-volunteer army. Perhaps they set the stage for a situation when a large portion of the American army could "give up"—a situation previously unknown in U.S. military history.

have friends, but *you will save the country when it's [sic] liberty hangs by a hair, as it were.*[1]

Another prophecy by Joseph Smith alluding to future warfare was made to the father of President John Taylor. Joseph had been conversing with Father Taylor concerning the battle of Waterloo, in which Father Taylor had participated. Joseph turned to Brother Taylor and said,

> Father Taylor, you will live to see, though I will not, greater battles than that of Waterloo. The United States will go to war with Mexico, and thus gain an increase of territory. The slave question will cause a division between the North and the South, and in these wars greater battles than Waterloo will occur. *But...when the great bear lays her paw on the lion the winding up scene is not far distant.*[2]

A statement purportedly made by Joseph Smith on May 6, 1843, also sheds light on a third world war setting:

> The Lord took of the best blood of the nations and planted them on the small islands now called England and Great Britain, and gave them great power in the nations for a thousand years and *their power will continue with them, that they may keep the balance of power and keep Russia from usurping her power over all the world. England and France are now bitter enemies, but they will be allied together and be united to keep Russia from conquering the world.*[3]

Numerous other statements by various Church leaders concerning aspects of a Third World War are cited in *Prophecy—Key to the Future*, pp. 10-15, and need not be repeated here. The object of this section is to comment on other materials not generally available.

Patriarchs throughout the Church have been warning of a Third World War for several decades in the blessings they have pronounced upon the saints. These prophetic warnings are por-

---

1. Mosiah Lyman Hancock, *Life Story of Mosiah Lyman Hancock*, p. 29.
2. N.B. Lundwall, *Inspired Prophetic Warnings*, p. 75. The author was citing the *Juvenile Instructor*, March 15, 1890, p. 162. The traditional interpretation of this statement has been that the bear is the symbol for Russia and the lion is the symbol for England. See p. 287.
3. Prophecy recorded by Edwin Rushton as having been made on May 6, 1843. For comment on this prophecy see *Prophecy—Key to the Future*, pp. 301-322. Note that England and France are depicted as holding the "balance of power" rather than actually being the major power which will oppose Russia. See reference to this prophecy on page 290.

tions of patriarchal blessings which are personal in nature, and not intended for general distribution throughout the Church.[1] Yet the import of their combined message is great, and should at least be alluded to in this context.

During the past fifteen years, the author has frequently been sought out by others who have related prophetic insights which they have been granted. Hundreds have alluded to patriarchal blessings or personal revelations preparing them for personal roles they

---

1. Neither are patriarchal blessings official statements of Church doctrine. Doctrine, in the strictest and most specific sense, represents "official belief and position" of a religious organization. In this sense, among Latter-day Saints, it is the role of duly-constituted general authorities to annunciate doctrinal precepts which bind and command the Church. Such is the duty and prerogative of ordained general leadership who are to do so under the direction of revelation from on high.

But there are also other levels of doctrine. Passages exist in the revealed scriptures of the Church which, when shown to have specific patterns and relationships, take on new, more important meanings. The scriptures are canonized and regarded as doctrine, and such new insights, when properly demonstrated and documented, also stand as doctrine. Though they may not at first have been pronounced nor expounded by current Church authorities, yet those passages still constitute the revealed word of God, the highest authority of all. Man is obligated to search the scriptures, striving to understand their meaning completely, discovering in them the full meaning intended by God.

Yet another level exists. God has revealed that when men speak as they are moved upon by the Holy Ghost, then *"whatsoever they shall speak when moved upon by the Holy Ghost shall be scripture, shall be the will of the Lord, shall be the mind of the Lord, shall be the voice of the Lord, and the power of God unto salvation."* (D & C 68:4) The Lord made this promise unto "all the faithful elders" of his church (D & C 68:2, 7). Though individual revelations through the Spirit are not given as instructions or commandments to the entire church, and are not to be regarded as the official doctrine of the church unless annunciated by duly constituted general authorities, yet such manifestations undeniably constitute revealed truth. Certainly insights revealed through the Holy Ghost are not to be denied, nor criticized, nor disregarded. Revealed truth is truth, no matter to whom it is revealed.

When extensive patterns of private revelation emerge, especially on matters of such far-reaching import as a world war which will affect the life of every citizen and saint, there comes a time when such patterns should be brought to the attention of all. They should not be represented as official doctrine nor as the stated position of the church, but as information of value which individuals should evaluate by comparison with existing facts and doctrine, thoughtful logic, and supplication for revealed verification. In this context, especially, Paul's instruction should be observed: *"Quench not the Spirit. Despise not prophesyings. Prove all things; hold fast that which is good."* (1 Thess. 5:19-21.)

will play when God's judgments are poured out upon the earth. Dozens have told of patriarchal blessings which speak of a third world war. Frequently the Spirit has burned within us as these matters have been discussed. It has been right, and proper, that they bore testimony of these future events.[1]

Below are briefly summarized a few of these statements, regarded by the author as typical, relating to a future world war. For example, a blessing given in 1953 said,

> You will live to see the world go through *another world war*, where kingdom will rise against kingdom, and *Russia and her allies, in the due time of the Lord, will go down never to come up in such power again! And the United States, when and after the inside of the cup may be cleansed, will come off victorious*, and will after arise to great heights among the nations of the world.[2]

Another blessing prophesies the defeat of Russia and portrays the war as being typical of the period of preparatory wars, paving the way for missionary labors in that land:

> You will live to see the world go through *another world war, for the mother country will be attacked by a strong European power. This war will be largely in the air and under the surface of the ocean, and the waters will be unsafe for the ordinary traffic and the heavens will be unsafe, for deadly bombs will be sent to the affliction of the cities of this great country and, in turn we will afflict them with bombs* and you will live to see the mother country cleansed as the inside of a platter, for traitor after traitor will be suspicioned and detected and apprehended. You will live to see the *God of Heaven take over, as it were, and bring this war to a speedy victory to America and her allies. You will see Russia go down to defeat never to come up again as a major world power*, and you will live to see the *gospel go into that country after the war* has been brought to a termination, and a great and glorious work will be accomplished in that land.[3]

---

1. The author, for reasons not fully known to himself, has found himself cast in a role of receiving and analyzing information concerning future events. One sister, after sharing several prophetic dreams, later wrote that "It is strange, but I haven't had any more dreams on this subject since I spoke with you. It is almost as if the purpose has been filled by my telling you these things that day." (Letter dated October 16, 1967.)
2. It would appear, in the light of the events chronicled in this volume, that the rise of the United States to great heights which is mentioned in this context will be embodied in the work of the saints during the New Jerusalem era rather than the political scene as it is today.
3. Note the theme of divine intervention to bring the war to a victorious conclusion for America and her allies, which occurs repeatedly. Is this the same event as in Joseph Smith's prophecy recorded by Mosiah Hancock, cited earlier, when the "boys from the mountains will rush forth?"

In this day of nuclear armaments, is it not reasonable to assume that if the war reaches the level that Russia and the United States are bombing each other's homelands, these bombs will represent the latest in nuclear technology, with full atomic-bomb destructive power?

Another blessing, given in 1960, continues the "preparatory wars" theme of the way being opened for missionary labors in Russia:

> ...Many changes shall take place in your day and time. *Nations shall fall and rise again with barriers removed that missionaries may go freely to the nation of Russia* and that as Ephraim has been gathered from the far parts of the earth, so shall *the dispersed of Judah be gathered* as the Lord has decreed....[1]

Another blessing, given in 1956, warns of another world war. The theme of divine intervention is again mentioned:

> You will live upon the earth to see wars and commotions, and even much preparation for war, and you will see *bloodshed drench the earth* until your soul will be sick with seeing. You will live to see *another World War* and you may see service to your country before your passing, and *you will live to see the hand of providence come out on the side of free agency and the United States will be cleansed on the inside of the platter.... You will live to see the Russian Bear lay his heavy hand upon the British Lion, according to the prophecy of Joseph Smith.*[2]

And another:

> You will see nation rise against nation and kingdom against kingdom and see *a great and bloody war in which the U.S. and her forces will be arranged against Russia* and the God of Heaven will look on for awhile, apparently, and *then will take over and bring victory* to the side of the right, for the God of Heaven will never permit free agency to be trampled under foot and swept from the face of the earth.

And again:

> You will see *the nations of Europe torn into mighty fragments* and many of them uprooted, never again to come up as kingdoms. You will,

---

1. There are still far more Jews in Russia than there are in Israel. They must be gathered as part of the future gathering of Israel.
2. Similarities between several of the excerpts cited are readily apparent, for some of the blessings were pronounced by the same individual.

therefore, see wars and bloodshed in your day, for the unrest of men that exists at the present time will ultimately develop into *swords and deadly bombs. You will live to see terrible earthquakes and one of these will rock the continent from ocean to ocean.*

These excerpts should suffice to portray the pattern of prophetic warnings which exists from this source.

Other personal manifestations have contained insights which describe events of a future war. One such item, an account of future difficulties revealed to Elder Charles David Evans,[1] through an angelic visitor,[2] was printed in *The Contributor*. The manifestation describes what appears to be nuclear destruction, followed by radiation sickness. It tells of invasion by a foreign power, the sudden rise of a power in the west which counteracts the invasion,[3] and then gives the chronological indication that the war will precede the founding of the New Jerusalem:

> *...Dense clouds, blacker than midnight darkness, whose thunders reverberated with intonations which shook the earth, obscured the sunlight. Darkness reigned, unrivalled and supreme.*
>
> Again the light shone, revealing an *atmosphere tinged with a leaden hue, which was the precursor of an unparalleled plague* whose first symptoms were recognized by a *purple spot which appeared on the cheek, or on the back of the hand, and which, invariably, enlarged until it spread over the entire surface of the body, producing certain death.*

---

1. Charles David Evans joined the Church in England in 1848 and came to the United States and Utah in 1854. He was bishop of the Salem Ward for a decade, was ordained a High Councilor in 1889 and was called as a patriarch in 1895, in which position he served until his death on May 14, 1908 at Payson, Utah. (Information furnished by his great granddaughter, Mrs. Joyce Lindstrom, in personal correspondence with the author, September 8, 1969. His biographical sketch is contained in Andrew Jenson's *Latter-day Saint Biographical Encyclopedia*, Vol. 4, p. 568.)
2. Elder Evans vividly describes the angelic being and his entrance into his bedroom at a midnight hour. The angel greeted him with these words:
   Son, I perceive thou hast grave anxieties over the perilous state of thy country, that thy soul has felt deep sorrow for its future. I have therefore come to thy relief and to tell thee of the causes that have led to this peril. Hear me attentively. ("A Dream," *The Contributor, Representing the Young Men's Mutual Improvement Associations of the Latter-day Saints* (Salt Lake City, Utah: Deseret News Publishing Company, 1894), Vol. 15, p. 639.
3. Can this, again, be the time when "the boys from the mountains will rush forth," as foretold in the Joseph Smith prophecy recorded by Mosiah Lyman Hancock, cited earlier?

Mothers, on sight of it, cast away their children as if they were poisonous reptiles. This plague, in grown persons, rotted the eyes in their sockets and consumed the tongue as would a powerful acid or an intense heat. Wicked men, suffering under its writhing agonies, cursed God and died, as they stood on their feet, and the birds of prey feasted on their carcasses.

I saw in my dream the messenger again appear with a vial in his right hand, who addressing me said: "Thou knowest somewhat of the chemistry taught in the schools of human learning, behold now a chemistry sufficiently powerful to change the waters of the sea."

He then poured out his vial upon the sea and it became putrid as the blood of a dead man, and every living soul therein died. Other plagues followed I forbear to record.

A foreign power had invaded the nation which, from every human indication, it appeared would seize the government and supplant it with monarchy. I stood trembling at the aspect, when, lo, *a power arose in the west which declared itself in favor of the constitution in its original form; to this suddenly rising power every lover of constitutional rights and liberties throughout the nation gave hearty support. The struggle was fiercely contested,* but the stars and stripes floated in the breeze, and, bidding defiance to all opposition, waved proudly over the land. Among the many banners I saw, was one inscribed thus: "The government based on the Constitution, now and forever;" on another "Liberty of Conscience, social, religious, and political."

The light of the gospel which had but dimly shone because of abomination, now burst forth with a lustre that filled the earth. Cities appeared in every direction, *one of which, in the centre of the continent, was an embodiment of architectural science after the pattern of eternal perfections, whose towers glittered with a radiance emanating from the sparkling of emeralds, rubies, diamonds and other precious stones set in a canopy of gold* and so elaborately and skillfully arranged as to shed forth a brilliancy which dazzled and enchanted the eye, excited admiration and developed a taste for the beautiful, beyond anything man had ever conceived....[1]

---

1. "A Dream," *Ibid.,* pp. 640-641. Note the similarity of Elder Evan's description of the "plague" which comes from the dark clouds with the descriptions of survivors of the atomic bombing of Japan. Radiation breaks down the blood cells, causing people to bleed under the skin, in a manner similar to leukemia. Hence the purple spots like large bruises.

Elder Evan's manifestation also reported the internal strife which is prophesied to come upon the nation:

...At this juncture I saw a banner floating in air whereupon was written the words Bankruptcy, Famine, Floods, Fire, Cyclones, Blood, Plague. Mad with rage men and women rushed upon each other. *Blood flowed down the streets of cities like water. The demon of bloody hate had enthroned itself on the citadel of reason; the thirst for blood was intenser than that of the parched tongue for water. Thousands of bodies lay untombed in the streets.* Men and women fell dead from the terror inspired by fear. Rest was but the precursor of the bloody work of the morrow. All around lay the mournfulness

Prophecies Showing Relationships Between World War III and Internal Conflict in the United States

The prophetic panorama seems to indicate that there will be a third world war, followed by internal strife in the United States, and then the return to Jackson County for the establishing of the New Jerusalem. Some prophetic warnings show chronological relationships between these events.

A vision granted to President Wilford Woodruff in 1878 seems to vividly depict this time period. He was shown that great desolation would come upon the land from a terrible disease which would kill many people;[1] that Independence, Missouri [Jackson County] would be destroyed; internal strife [from lack of food?] and people struggling to come to the mountains; and finally the beginning of construction of the New Jerusalem; which establishes the chronological relationship and identifies the time of fulfillment.

President Woodruff recorded the vision in his personal journal,[2] which also contained numerous other prophetic insights. This is what he recorded:

1. Is this the same plague described by Charles David Evans? It appears to be. Is it radiation sickness? (Note characteristics which would seem to support that possibility: extreme thirst, sudden death leaving thousands unburied, the streets vacant but people using basements for refuge, world-wide devastation.) Is it the Lord's desolating scourge? Are the two the same?
2. Apostle Matthias F. Cowley, who prepared a biography of President Woodruff, based on his journals and other personal papers, cited the last

of a past in ruins. Monuments erected to perpetuate the names of the noble and brave were ruthlessly destroyed by combustibles. A voice now sounded aloud these words, "Yet once again I shake not the earth only, but also heaven. And this word yet once again signifies the removing of things that are shaken, as of things that are made; that those things that cannot be shaken may remain."

Earthquakes rent the earth in vast chasms, which engulfed multitudes; terrible groanings and wailings filled the air; the shrieks of the suffering were indescribably awful. Water wildly rushed in from the tumultuous ocean whose very roaring under the mad rage of the fierce cyclone, was unendurable to the ear. Cities were swept away in an instant, missiles were hurled through the atmosphere at a terrible velocity and people were carried upward only to descend an unrecognized mass. Islands appeared where ocean waves once tossed the gigantic steamer. In other parts *voluminous flames, emanating from vast fires,* rolled with fearful velocity destroying life and property in their destructive course. The seal of the dread menace of despair was stamped on every human visage; men fell exhausted, appalled and trembling. Every element of agitated nature seemed a demon of wrathful fury.... (*Ibid.*, p. 640)

I went to bed at the usual hour, half past nine o'clock. *I had been reading the Revelations in the French language.* My mind was calm, more so than usual if that were possible. I composed myself for sleep, but felt a strange stupor come over me and I apparently became partially unconscious. Still I was not asleep nor awake, but had a strange far-away dreaming feeling.

The first thing I recognized was that I was in the Tabernacle at Ogden, Utah, sitting in the corner for fear they would call on me to preach;—which, after singing the second song, they did by calling me to the stand. I arose to speak and said that I did not know that I had anything special to say except to bear my testimony of the truth of this work—when all at once it seemed I was lifted out of myself. I said, "Yes, I have something to say, it is this: Some of my brethren present have been asking me what is coming to pass. *I will tell you what will shortly come to pass—*"

Then I was in Salt Lake City walking through the streets. In parts of the city and upon the door of every house, I saw a badge of mourning, and I could not find a house but what was in mourning. I passed my own home and saw the same sign there. I asked the question, "Is that me who is dead?"

Something gave the answer, "No."

It seemed strange to me that *I saw no person on the streets in my wandering around the city. They seemed to be in their houses with their sick and dead.* I saw no funeral processions or anything of this kind, but the city was very still and quiet as if the people were praying. *It seemed as though the people had control over the disease, whatever it was,* I do not know, that was not shown to me.

I then looked in all directions over the territory,—east, west, north and south, and *found the same mourning in every place throughout the land.*

The next I knew I was *this side of Omaha.* It seemed I was above the earth looking down upon it as I passed along on my way east. *I saw the roads full of people, principally women, with just what they could carry in bundles on their backs, traveling to the mountains on foot.* And I wondered how they would get there with nothing but a small pack on their backs. It was remarkable to me that *there were so few men among them.* It did not seem as though trains were running; *the rails looked rusty and the roads abandoned.* In deed, I have no conception of how I traveled myself as I looked down upon the people.

I continued east through *Omaha and Council Bluffs, which were full of disease, and women were everywhere. The streets of Missouri and Illinois were in turmoil and strife. Men were killing one another, and women joined in the fighting. Family against family were cutting each other to pieces in the most horrible manner imaginable.*

---

portion of the vision in his book *Wilford Woodruff—History of His Life and Labors* (Salt Lake City, Utah: Bookcraft, 1964), p. 505. It is noted that the account published in *Wilford Woodruff* differs slightly in wording, though not in message, from the account printed herein, a possible indication that various copies, or "versions," of this manifestation now exist.

Next I saw *Washington, D.C., and found the city a desolation. The White House was empty and the Halls of Congress likewise.* Everything was in ruin and the people seemed to have fled from the city and left it to take care of itself.

I was next in the city of *Baltimore,* in the square where the monument of 1812 stands in front of the St. Charles and other hotels. *The dead were everywhere. I saw their bodies piled up, filling the square. I saw women cut the throats of their own children for the sake of their blood. I saw them suck it from their veins to quench their own thirst, and then lie down in the streets and die.*

The waters of the city and the *Chesapeake Bay* were so stagnant, and such a stench arose from them on account of the putrefaction of the dead carcasses in them, that the very smell carried death with it.

Singularly again, I saw no men, except they were dead or dying in the streets. There were but very few women, and they were crazy and mad, or in a dying condition. Everywhere I went I saw the same all over the city. It was horrible beyond conception to behold.

I thought this was the end; but not so. Seemingly in an instant I was in *Philadelphia* where everything was still. No living soul was to be seen to greet me. It seemed as though the whole city was without inhabitants. In Arch and Chestnut streets, in fact, everywhere I looked the putrefaction of the dead bodies created such a stench that it was impossible for any creature to remain alive.

I next found myself on Broadway in *New York.* There it seemed as if the people had done all they could to overcome the disease. But in wandering down Broadway, I saw the bodies of beautiful women lying, some dead, and others in a dying condition, on the sidewalks. I saw men crawl out of the basements and violate the persons of some that were alive, then kill them and rob their dead bodies of the valuables they had on them. Then, before they could return to their basements, they themselves rolled over a time or two in agony and died.

On some of the streets *I saw mothers kill their own offspring and eat their flesh,* and then in a few minutes die themselves. And wherever I looked, I saw the same sights,—horror and desolation, rapine and death. *No horses, nor carriages, nor omnibusses, nor streetcars,—nothing but death and destruction everywhere.*

I then went to Central Park, and looking back, I saw a fire start, and just at that moment a mighty east wind sprang up and carried the flames west over the great city. And *it burned until there was not a single building left standing whole;* even down to the water's edge. —Warves and shipping—all seemed to be burned and swallowed up in common destruction. Nothing was left but desolation where a great city stood a short time before. Stench from the bodies that were burned was so great that it was carried a great distance across the Hudson River, and it spread disease and death wherever the fumes penetrated.

I cannot paint in words the horrors that seemed to encompass me about, it was beyond description or thought for me to conceive.

I supposed this was the end, *but I was given to understand that the same horrors that were here inacted were all over the world, east, west, north, and south.—That few were left alive,—still there were some.*

Immediately after, I seemed to be standing on the left bank of the Missouri River, opposite the city of *Independence;—but I saw no city. I saw the whole states of Illinois and Missouri and part of Iowa, a complete wilderness of desert with no living human being there.*

I then saw a short distance from the river, twelve men draped in the robes of the Temple, standing in a square, or nearly so. I understood it to represent the twelve gates of the *New Jerusalem.* And *they with uplifted hands, were consecrating the ground and laying the cornerstone of the Temple.*

And while they were thus employed, I saw myriads of angels hovering over them and around them. And I heard the angels singing the most heavenly music. The words were: *"Now is established the Kingdom of God and His Christ, and He shall reign forever and ever! And the Kingdom shall never be thrown down, for the Saints have overcome!"*

I saw people coming from the river and from distant places to help build the Temple and the City. It seemed as though *there were hosts of angels helping to bring material for the construction of that building. Some were in Temple robes,* and the pillar-like cloud continued to hover over the spot.

Later, I found myself in the Ogden Tabernacle, where I was calling upon the people to listen to the beautiful strains of music from the angels, as the building seemed to be filled with them, and they were singing the words I heard before: "Now is the Kingdom of our God and His Christ established forever and ever!"

I rolled over on my bed and the clock struck twelve. The vision had occurred between 9:30 P.M. and midnight.

Even outside the Church many people have claimed manifestations and/or made prophecies of a third world war.[1] One such item, recorded by Mrs. Sols Guardisto, is of particular interest because it appears to show chronological and geographical relationships between the world war, the beginning of renewed religious persecution against the saints, disease and famine throughout the continent, and the gathering of the saints to places of refuge. Mrs. Guardisto visited the site of the Cardston Temple on two occasions in 1922, prior to the completion and dedication of the building. According to her account, each time she visited the site she received "powerful impressions" about the building and its role in the future. These she wrote in a letter which was placed in the possession of President Edward James Wood, the first president of that temple. He preserved the letter in his family file, and also made it available to others. A BYU masters thesis on the life of President Wood, written by Melvin S. Tagg, a student in the

---

1. A discussion of such materials and an analysis of their validity and merits is beyond the scope of this volume. What is important, however, is the reader's realization that many such prophecies exist.

College of Religious Instruction, records the manifestation in an appendix. In her[1] account, she told how she observed former Church

---

1. Little is documented on the identity of Mrs. Guardisto. Though the author of the thesis which preserved her manifestation asserts that she later joined the Church, a check with the Church membership department yields no record of her membership. A letter to this author from J. Forrest Wood, a descendant of Edward Wood, states

   It is a remarkable experience she seemed to have had and she does tell of things which have come about and other things which could come about. But any person who studies world conditions and the surrounding country about the temple could see its possibilities. I have asked our temple president here and also the wife of our former president; both of whom grew up here and remember well the story of her visit and experience. Both say they never knew of it being called a prophecy.

   I do not know her exact name. It is not shown on my copy. We have a copy here at the temple where I am recorder. It was given before the dedication of the temple. Melvin Tagg does not give the complete story; but his main facts are correct. All those directly connected with the story have passed away. I well remember of it and heard father speak many times about it. I have access to the records here in the temple but have never found anything more than I have given above. (Letter from Cardston, Canada dated 5 May, 1971.)

   In an L.D.S.S.A. forum at the University of Utah Institute of Religion, October 10, 1969, the author queried President Hugh B. Brown about the manifestation and its author. He replied, "I knew the woman quite well and went through the temple with her. She claimed to have quite a remarkable manifestation but she didn't follow through. She ran off with another woman's husband. *That doesn't disqualify the validity of the manifestation, but she didn't follow through.*" (The author recorded his statement immediately after it was made.) Attempts to learn more of the woman through the avenues of genealogical research have not met with success.

   The beginning of her letter indicates that the impressions she received were a new type of experience for her, yet she found them strong and compelling:

   We have been to the temple erected by your church, wherein the sacred rites are to be performed in accordance with your faith. *The first time I was strongly impelled to describe to you my impressions.* I did so, but before the completion of the letter I received some news which so affected me that, acting upon the spur of the moment, I destroyed the document in its entirety.

   The continued feeling within me of dissatisfaction as of something left undone, coupled with the desire upon the part of members of my household, who had not visited the temple, led to our second visit to Cardston, in which you so kindly consented to accompany us; notwithstanding the inclement weather and personal inconveniences to yourselves, which the journey necessarily entailed.

leaders, then dead, who instructed her there in the temple and showed her future events. Then she recorded the impressions

---

It is because of this and many other evidences of your friendship that has given me the priviledge to presume to bother you with what, after all, may be only the foolish fantasies of a too impressionable mentality. *To me it does not seem so, for never before in my lifetime has such powerful impressions been impinged upon my inner consciousness as during my visits thru the temple. Especially was this so at our second visit; the impressions of our first visit were repeated with such overwhelming intensity and variety of detail that I must positively inform you of my experiences.*

It seems to me it is a sacred duty on my part to do this, and knowing as I do that your friends will not lightly ridicule to outsiders what to me is a personal matter, I am going to give you in detail my experiences in the hope that if, *as it may well be, it is something more than imagination, that you or others of your faith may wisely analyze and correctly use whatever may be gleaned from this letter.*

(Melvin Tagg, "A Remarkable Occurrence in the Cardston Temple," *The Life of Edward James Wood* [A Thesis Presented to the College of Religious Instruction, Brigham Young University, July 1959], p. 148.)

Note that the author, Mrs. Guardisto, had no ulterior motive in recording the manifestation; she did so only because she received the impression that it was her "sacred duty" to do so.

This is how she described the revelatory experience and her observance of former Church leaders:

Time and again as I listened to the speaker explaining some phase of the building or its meaning, *I would be seeing beyond him some illustration of a kaleidoscopic nature depicting what he was describing, only more completely and more vividly.* The characters were so plain to me that I required all my self-control to keep silence from room to room. This continued and only ceased when we emerged into the frost and snow once more.

There was no set plan for presenting these pictures or expressions to me. *It seemed as if when I thought of something mental a picture instantly presented itself in explanation of some word of the conductor, which would have the same effect.* I was not afraid, only awed by the wonder of it all and the fearful impressive feeling I received, which seemed to imbed every little detailed scene into my brain, from which I feel it will never be erased. Every now and again I would seem to receive a command, observe, remember and record, and vivid as all of it was, these incidents herein related are the ones upon which I received the instructions.

The scenes which I observed of an historical character seemed chiefly to verify and amplify the speaker's outline of past history and so I do not feel impressed to record such, except to state that the same patriarchal characters whom I observed directing and influencing the early movements of the church, were the same down through every age and epoch and as the scene advanced to more modern times, *I saw among these spiritual counsellors persons whose*

granted to her concerning future international war and internal conflict in America:

I can give no time as to the happenings except that the impressions I received was of actual present or immediate future.

I saw first a brief but comprehensive sketch of the present state of the world, or, as you would term it, the Gentile Kingdoms. Each country in turn was shown, its anarchy, hunger, ambitions, distrusts and warlike activities, etc., and in my mind was formed from some source the words, "As it is today with the Gentiles."

I saw next international war again break out with its centre upon the Pacific Ocean, but sweeping and encircling the whole globe. I saw that the *opposing forces were roughly divided by so-called Christianity on the one side, and by the so-called followers of Mohammed and Budda upon the other.* I saw that the great driving power within these so-called Christian Nations was the *Great Apostacy of Rome* in all its political, social and religious aspects. *I saw the world-wide dislocation and devastation of production and slaughter of people occur more swiftly and upon a larger scale than ever before. I saw an antagonism begin to express itself from those so-called Christian nations against your people. I saw those of a similar faith to yours in the Far-East begin to look toward Palestine for safety.*

I saw the international world war automatically break down, and national revolutions occur in every country and complete the work of chaos and desolation. I saw *geological disturbances occur,* which helped in this work as if it were intended to do so. I saw the Cardston Temple preserved from all of this geological upheaval. *I saw the international boundary line disappear as these two governments broke up and dissolved into chaos. I saw race rioting upon this American continent on a vast scale.*

I saw hunger and starvation in this world granary of the American Continent sweep off vast numbers of these conflicting elements. I saw disease produced by hunger, strife and chaos complete the end of this present order or epoch. How long these events were in reaching this consummation, I do not know. But, my impression was *from the outbreak of the international war, these things developed in a continuous*

---

features I had previously observed as being in the material body on other historical occasions.

It seemed as though the Temple was filled with the actual spiritual bodies of these previous leaders of the Church, each seeming to have a definite work to do, automatically taking up in the spirit world the work that person was engaged in whilst in the flesh. In that Temple I saw persons who were leaders of your Church during its march across the American Desert, now engaged in helping those patriarchs under whose orders they seemed to be working. *It was these leaders of your Church, or spiritual leaders, if I may use that term, who seemed instructed to show me the scenes here recorded.* (*Ibid.*, pp. 150-151)

procession, and almost ran concurrently, as it is with a sickness, the various symptoms are all in evidence at one and the same time, but in different stages of development.

My intensified thought was, "What of the Church, if such is to become the kingdom of the earth?" The thought was immediately answered by a subconscious statement, "As it is in the Church today," and I saw these higher spiritual beings throughout the length and breadth of the air, marshalling their spiritual forces and concentrating them upon the high officials of your Church on earth. I saw these spiritual forces working upon these officers, impressing and moving them, influencing and warning them. I saw these spiritual forces begin to unfold these things into the minds of your elders and other high officials, especially during their spiritual devotions and official duties, and those activities which exalt the mind of the individual or groups. I saw the impressions take hold and inspire the more receptive and spiritual men, until it was all clearly revealed to them in the way the spiritual patriarchs desired.

Again I seemed to hear the words, "As it will be." I saw the high officials in council, and under inspired guidance issue instructions to your people, *to reconsecrate their lives and energies to their faith.* To voluntarily discipline themselves by abstaining from all those forms of indulgence which weaken the body, sap the mentality, and deaden the spirit or waste their incomes. I saw further on, instructions given whereby the *places of refuge were prepared, quietly, but efficiently by inspired elders. I saw Cardston and the surrounding foothills—especially west and north—for miles being prepared for a refuge for your people, quietly but quickly.*

I saw artesian wells bored and other wells dug all over that territory, so that *when the open waters were polluted and poisoned* that the people of the Church and their cattle would be provided for. I saw the fuel resources of the district developed in many places, and vast piles of coal and timber stored for future use and building.

I saw the elders, still under Divine guidance, counselling and encouraging *the planting of every available acre of soil in this district, so that large supplies could be near the refuge.* I saw the Church property under cultivation of an intensified character, not for sale or profit, but for the use of the people. I saw the inspired officers giving instructions as to what would be the best crops to plant and cultivate, not for profit but *for use in storage at the time of chaos.* I saw the territory carefully surveyed and *mapped out for the camping of a great body of people* of the Church. I saw provisions also made for *a big influx of people who at present do not belong to the Church, but who will gather in their tribulation.* I saw vast quantities of surgical appliances, medicines, disinfectants, etc., stored in the Temple basement. I saw inspiration given the elders whereby the quality, quantity, and kind of things to be stored were judged, which might not be attainable in this territory during the time of chaos. I saw *defensive preparations made and stored as suggested by the power of inspiration.* I saw the elders working out the organizations of the camps upon maps. I saw the mining corridors used as places of storage underground; I saw the hills surveyed and corrals built in sequestered places for cattle, sheep, etc., quietly but quickly.

I saw the plans for the organization of the single men, and their duties, the scouts, the guards, the nurses, the cooks, the messengers, the children, the herders, the Temple guards, etc., etc., I saw all these preparations going on practically unknown to the Gentile world, except to the Great Apostacy, whose knowledge and hatred is far-reaching in this day of its temporary power. This was going on piece by piece as the elders were instructed so to do for the refuge.

I saw other officials obeying the inspired instructions carrying their messages and exhorting your people to follow out from time to time, the revelations given them. Whilst *all around throughout the Gentile world the chaos developed in its varying stages—faction against faction, nation against nation, but all in open or secret hostility to your people and their faith.* I saw your people draw closer and closer together as this became more intense and as the spiritual forces warned them through the mouth of your elders and other officers. I saw the spiritual forces influencing these members who had drifted away to reenter the fold. I saw a greater thing than ever before. *I saw vast quantities of necessaries supplied by members* whose spiritual eyes had been opened. I saw a *liquidation of properties and effects disposed of* quietly and quickly by members of the Church, as the spiritual influences directed them.

I saw the inspired call sent forth to all the Church to gather to the refuges of Zion. I saw the stream of your people quietly moving in the direction of their refuge. I saw your people moving more quickly and in larger numbers until all the stragglers were housed. I saw the wireless messages flashed from Zion's refuge to Zion's refuge in their several places, that all was well in the world. *And then the darkness of chaos closed around the boundaries of your people, and the last days of tribulations had begun.*[1]

Like other prophetic warnings recorded in this chapter, the above is not presented as "doctrine." The reader is invited to

---

1. Lest some might confuse the international war she observed with World War II, some of the identifying characteristics of the future conflict should be identified which were not typical of World War II:

    1. The forces tend to divide along religious lines—Christians vs. Moslems and Buddists. (Would this tend to identify those who will ally themselves with the Communists?)

    2. The church in Rome will be a driving power behind the Christian forces.

    3. Antagonism develops among the Christian nations against the Mormons.

    4. People in the Far East with a faith similar to Latter-day Saint belief will begin to look toward Palestine, or Israel for safety.

    5. The international war will break down, and national revolutions occur in every country.

    6. The international boundary line between the U.S. and Canada will disappear as the two governments break up and dissolve into chaos.

    None of these aspects characterize the scenario of World War II.

determine its validity for himself by seeking revealed confirmation, as should be done with any spiritual manifestation.

In summary concerning prophecies of a third world war, it should be observed that numerous prophetic warnings foretell its reality. They assert that America will be attacked by Russia and her allies, and that the war will have an extremely high casualty rate. Bombs will be dropped on both homelands, and it is reasonable to expect that nuclear warheads will be used. Some of the manifestations cited appear to describe the vast nationwide effects of radiation sickness and destruction. Many spies and traitors will be detected within the United States. The war will go badly for America, then God will intervene and bring the war to a victorious conclusion for America and her allies, while Russia and her allies will go down to defeat, never to rise in such power again. The way will be opened for missionary work to begin in Russia, which indicates that the war will be a "Preparatory War," before the "times of the Gentiles" are fulfilled. The war will be followed by a period of chaos in which governments will fall and anarchy will prevail, both in the United States and throughout the world.

Russia Rapidly Preparing for War

For more than a decade, Russia has been preparing for future war. Its rush for military superiority has made it increasingly obvious that mere protection of the Russian homeland is not its goal. There will come a time when its massive forces will be employed for conquest, not just for defense.

Yet many Americans refuse to accept the indications of Russia's intentions. Former U.S. Secretary of Defense James Schlesinger described the apathetic attitude which is prevalent in the nation:

> *We as a nation are indulging in an ostrich syndrome, in burying our heads in the sand and not observing what is going on.*
>
> The Soviets have increased their military establishment to over four million men.... They have, in recent years, *produced four times as many subs and surface combatants as we have. They are producing 70 percent more tactical aircraft. In ground forces equipment, it is a production ratio of seven and eight to one....*
>
> *What we have is a flight from reality.*[1]

---

1. Jack Anderson, "America's Flight From Reality," *Deseret News*, January 1, 1976.

Yet knowledgeable sources are deeply concerned about Russia's military growth, and are increasingly vocal about the growing danger to the nation. Before leaving his office as Secretary of Defense in January, 1977, Donald Rumsfeld said

> ...*The power balance trends of the last 10 to 15 years have been "decidedly adverse" to the United States.*
>
> Rumsfeld said expanded Soviet nuclear and conventional force strength has increased Soviet options. He suggested that continuation of these trends could tempt the Soviets to challenge the United States in an area of American national interest.
>
> Intelligence reports made public at that time said that though *the Soviet military budget had grown by a third between 1965 and 1975, U.S. arms spending had dropped by a similar amount from the 1968 wartime high.*[1]

A report by the National Strategy Information Center has warned that there has never been greater military danger to the nation than at the present:

> "*In terms of explicit Soviet military capabilities...the over-all military threat to the United States has never been greater in this century....*"
>
> "*The current and projected U.S. defense posture is inadequate to meet the threat posed by the Soviet Union,*" the report says. It estimated that *Russian military spending has risen dramatically to the equivalent of at least $130 billion a year.*
>
> Meanwhile, the report says, "the United States has been disinvesting in defense through a subtle process of congressional budget cuts, inflation...and inadequate administration requests for defense expenditure."
>
> Since 1971, the center study says, *congressional budget cuts and inflation have reduced real U.S. defense resources by $45 billion.*[2]

Russia's annual percent of expenditure for armaments now exceeds Germany's peak when Adolf Hitler was preparing for the Nazi invasion of Europe:

> *For the past decade, Russia has been spending 20 percent of its gross national product annually on arms,* the former head of Defense Intelligence said this week.
>
> By contrast, Lt. Gen. Daniel O. Graham, who retired November 3, told reporters this is well over three times as much as has been previously estimated by U.S. intelligence.

---

1. George Gedda, "Russians Gaining Power Balance?" *Salt Lake Tribune*, July 10, 1977.
2. "Defense Funds To Fall Short?" *Deseret News*, June 16, 1976.

Adolf Hitler's peak arms expenditure in his pre-World War II program of "guns, not butter," only came to 19 percent of Germany's GNP. The United States this year is budgeting defense at a mere 5.4 percent.[1]

The Institute for Strategic Studies, in a "Strategic Survey, 1975," reported that

The numerical balance has moved against the West over the years and (the West's) qualitative edge could be eroded if present trends in Soviet weapons procurement continue. "The momentum of the Soviet arms buildup presents a major risk for detente and a cause for the *growing skepticism...over Soviet longer-term intentions."*[2]

Others around the world are warning that Russia's intentions are to wage war. China, particularly, has expressed this fear:

Russia is, for all practical purposes, on a war footing. The army has been increased to 4.3 million men. The crash naval building program has been accelerated.

Terrified Peking insists *the Russian military buildup is not primarily for diplomatic bargaining purposes and that Russia intends to make war.*

The Chinese, indeed, state that Leonid Breztnev is already waging war through small surrogate nations and that, moreover, he is winning them.[3]

From London comes this warning concerning the accelerated growth of the Russian navy, from the prestigious naval annual, "Jane's Fighting Ships:"

Russia has outspent and outbuilt the United States by 50 percent or more in warship construction for the past decade and now has an offensive navy which, in the judgment of an internationally authoritative handbook, *"has outrun the legitimate requirements of national defense...."*

Warning that a navy of the scale Russia is now building can only be for "aggressive action," Capt. Moore contrasted the difficulties of the U.S. Navy in face of "the very vocal and sometimes downright dishonest efforts of a number of influential people who see their mission in life as the emasculation of America's defenses."[4]

1. Col. Robert D. Heinl Jr., "Russia Is Spending 20 Pct. On Military, General Says," *Deseret News*, March 4, 1976.
2. "Both U.S., Russ 'Losing Influence,' " *Deseret News*, May 7, 1976.
3. Ernest Cuneo, "Russia Is On A War Footing," *Deseret News*, May 3, 1976.
4. "Ominous New Russ Navy," *Deseret News*, September 20, 1975.

Editorial voices are also warning that Russia is rapidly outstripping the U.S. in the arms race. A decade ago the U.S. held
clear superiority, now the two forces are regarded as on approximately equal par. But within a few short years Russia will have
gained clear and undisputed superiority. A typical editorial gives
the following warning:

> It shouldn't have taken a change in defense chiefs to impress on Con-
> gress and the nation that *the U.S. is slipping behind Russia in military
> power.*
> Secretary of Defense Donald Rumsfeld sounded that warning this
> week, but declared the U.S. still has a "rough equivalence" with Russia.
> He warned, however, that *if present trends continue, the U.S. would
> definitely slip to No. 2 among world powers, with dangerous implica-
> tions for international stability.*
> That's the same thing James R. Schlesinger was saying last year when
> he was fired by President Ford, apparently for being too strident in his
> opposition to deep cuts in the defense budget.
> That concern also has been voiced by Air Force Gen. George S.
> Brown, chairman of the Joint Chiefs of Staff. "We believe that U.S.
> military strength...is sufficient today," says Gen. Brown. *"But we are
> greatly concerned about adverse military trends and what they portend
> for the future."*
> Those concerns are buttressed by a recent study done by the Library
> of Congress on request of Iowa's Sen. John Culver, a liberal Democrat.
> *It showed the U.S. and Russia roughly equal in overall strategic nuclear
> power. But Russia is significantly ahead in conventional arms like tanks,
> attack submarines, and overall armed forces....*
> Critics have pointed out—and rightfully—that overall defense isn't
> just a matter of comparing gun for gun and man for man. *The U.S., for
> example, has tremendous economic power and technological expertise
> which must be figured into the balance.*
> *The drawback here is that while such advantages may be brought to
> bear in a conventional war, they would be almost insignificant in a
> nuclear war.*
> *With Russia spending an estimated 40% more than the U.S. on
> defense expenditures,* now seems a poor time to try to cut U.S. spend-
> ing for preparedness.[1]

Numerous comparisons of Russian and America military capacities are published, in an effort to warn of the nation's increasingly perilous position. The assessments change every few months,
as the gaps in the arms race continue to widen, but this is a typical
example:

---

1. "Is America Already No. 2 In Military Power Race?" *Deseret News,*
   March 9, 1976.

If you're convinced the Soviet Union isn't going to attack the United States no matter what, read no further.

If, on the other hand, you are concerned about the viability of our deterent posture compared to the Soviet Union's growing military strength, the following may give you pause.

Item: *The United States, for the first time in history, now lies virtually naked to both bomber and missile attack.*

All U.S. antiaircraft missiles (the Nikes and Bomarc rockets that guarded our cities for nearly two decades) have been removed. All U.S. antiballistic missile missiles (ABMs) are being dismantled.

In contrast, the Russians currently have about 12,000 antiaircraft missiles, along with one "Galosh" ABM site around Moscow.

The United States today has a mere 33 jet interceptors, and almost all are 10 to 20 years old. The Soviet Union reportedly has 2,600 jet interceptors, all first-line, modern craft.

Item: *The Soviet Union surpassed the U.S. in the number of missile launchers in 1971, and now leads by about 500.* The USSR surpassed the U.S. in the number of intercontinental ballistic missiles in 1969, and now is about 500 ahead. It attained virtual equality in the number of submarine-launched ballistic missiles last year.

The Russian missiles are substantially bigger and capable of carrying much larger, vastly more destructive warheads. The Soviet SS-9 ICBM, for example, carries a nuclear warhead equal to 25 million tons of TNT. And the new SS-18 can deliver an even bigger warhead or several smaller ones at once.

Together, Soviet missiles can deliver about 7.5 times the destructive force on American targets that U.S. missiles can deliver.

Moreover, the Russians have developed *a Fractional Orbital Bombardment System in which their ICBMs first are put in orbit, then brought down at will over a target.* The system gives the missiles virtually unlimited range. The U.S. has no similar capability.

Item: *New Soviet launch silos have a so-called "cold launch" capability.* This means the missiles can be blasted from their silos by compressed gas (the way American Polaris missiles are launched from their submarine tubes) and their rocket engines ignited only after the missiles clear the silo.

This technique leaves a missile silo unaffected by the flame and heat of the rocket exhaust, thus ready for instant reuse. Thus, the Soviet Union may give every appearance of adhering to the Strategic Arms Limitation Talks (SALT) restrictions, and still store additional missiles, ready for instant reloading.

American Minuteman and Titan II silos are damaged by a launching and have no such quick reload capability.

Item: *The Soviet Union now has an unsurpassed capability to conduct chemical warfare.* Secretary of Defense Donald Rumsfeld has termed this capability *"particularly worrisome since we do not possess a similar capability."*

Item: *The Soviet Union has 4.4 million active members in its armed forces* and 6.8 million reservists for a total of 11.2 million. The U.S. has 2.1 million active members of the armed services and 1.8 million reservists, including National Guardsmen for a total of 3.9 million.

The Russians also have 42,000 tanks against our 9,000; at least 15,000 artillery pieces against our 6,000, and at least 35,000 armored and other fighting vehicles against our 22,000.

According to the Defense Department and other sources, *the Soviet Union is ahead of the U.S. in virtually every major area of military strength, though some American weapons remain technologically superior.*[1]

The concept of "overkill," or MAD ("mutual assured destruction," an assumption that neither major nuclear power can afford to initiate a nuclear war because the losses which both sides would ultimately sustain would be too devastating) is being challenged.[2] Observers are pointing out that the Russians have not accepted the validity of that theory, only the Americans believe it:

The essential and dangerous difference between American and Soviet response to the terrifying possibility of nuclear war is that *Americans really believe no exchange will ever occur,* because neither nation will risk its own destruction; but *the Soviets "have never accepted the 'overkill' concept or the concept of 'mutual assured destruction'.... The Soviet emphasis has rather been on survivability and indeed on the possibility of victory in a nuclear war."*[3]

A report received by the House Armed Services Committee in 1976, based on estimates of current Soviet civil defense capabilities and the present U.S. defense inadequacy, presented seriously lopsided differences:

The panel received truly alarming estimates...about the comparative casualties in the event of nuclear attack if the Soviets had evacuated their people during the crisis period and we were unable to do so: *the*

1. Peter Reich, "Russ Outstripping U.S. Defenses," *Salt Lake Tribune,* April 10, 1976.
2. One article defined "overkill" in this manner:
   Russia controls 5.3 billion tons of strategic nuclear firepower with intercontinental range. America controls 4.2 billion tons.
   These figures, from the Brookings Institution, mean that the Soviets could destroy every American man, woman and a child with a personal force equal to 23½ tons of TNT. The Americans have 16 tons for each Russian.
   But it takes only a few ounces of TNT to kill a person.
   This is what the experts mean when they talk about "overkill."
   (Arthur L. Gavshon, "Technology Is Outpacing Politicians in N-Arms Race," *Deseret News,* August 5, 1977.)
3. Rowland Evans and Robert Novak, "Russian Roulette and Civil Defense," *Deseret News,* May 26, 1976.

Soviets would lose about 10½ million people; the United States would lose about 90 million people.[1]

Military leaders have now recognized that "the Soviet Union has improved its civil defense to the point where it could receive very little damage in a nuclear war.... *Russian civil defense capabilities are so extensive the nation could cut its deaths in a nuclear war to about 10 million people—less than the number of dead in World War II.... The United States has virtually no civil defense capability and would take 10 times as many casualties in an attack.*"[2]

A study released in mid-1977 refined the casualty estimates for a nuclear holocaust, and emphasizes the folly of relying on a strategy that assumes each side is capable of virtually destroying the other. The Jones study measured potential fatalities under an arbitrary scenario in which the Soviets make a first-strike nuclear attack against U.S. strategic launchers and the U.S. immediately retaliates with an all-out nuclear strike specifically designed as a population killer. It predicts only 4 million Russian fatalities. In a reverse situation, however, U.S. losses are estimated at 72 million:

> The study claims that under "a full evacuation in accordance with Soviet Civil defense principles" *the number of fatalities from the American retaliatory attack would be as low as 4 million*—even lower, if the 24-hour walking time for evacuation is lengthened.

---

1. *Ibid.* The article noted that

     Soviet survival is based on *rapid evacuation of the cities*, on vast *subterranean fallout shelters* in the evacuated areas and on war plants capable of continuing operations after a nuclear exchange by virtue of *"hardened" sites or geographic dispersal* in remote areas.

     Lacking even skeleton programs for these "war-survival" measures (often called passive defense), the U.S. could find itself prohibitively out-psyched if deadlock between Moscow and Washington became the prelude to a possible nuclear exchange. Rather than risk such an exchange from a position of proven inferiority in terms of the ability to withstand it, the U.S. might be forced to yield. *(Ibid.)*

   It also expressed concern that the U.S. civil defense program was funded with less than 10% of the $1 billion spent by the Soviets each year.

2. "Is Russia Bomb-proof?" *Deseret News*, July 20, 1976. The article then observed that

     The asymmetry in war survival capability is one of the factors which influence the Soviet belief that the correlation of world forces is shifting in favor of the USSR and hence one that bears importantly on Moscow's strategic and risk calculations and on assessments of the probable outcome of a nuclear war.

But the U.S. today has no plan whatever for "expedient shelters."
Indeed civil defense has been lost under the liturgy of MAD, the concept of deterrence and the mythology of "overkill" (superfluous nuclear power).

Accordingly, in the reverse case—an American first strike against Soviet launchers, and Soviet retaliation designed only to kill people— the study predicts 72 million dead in the U.S. What is worse—if anything could be—is that even if the American people had access to "expedient shelters," the study predicts there would still be 20 million dead.

The catastrophic results both assume that 90 percent of the urban population has 24 hours to get out of town; that the evacuees take maximum advantage of residential housing for fall-out protection; and that the 10 percent left in the cities make "optimum use" of designated fall-out shelters (such as subways)—in tragic short supply here.

One reason for these ghoulishly high estimates is the *size of Soviet nuclear weapons, with much higher yields in both explosive force and in radiation than U.S. long-range missiles.*

The arithmetic is startling. A shelter that would protect a Soviet citizen one mile from the point of impact of an average-size American warhead (a Poseidon submarine-launched weapon) would give protection only at three miles from the point of impact of an average one-megaton (million tons of TNT equivalent) Soviet warhead.

The study correctly suggests this conclusion: *"If this highly exaggerated model...cannot produce casualty levels far greater than those of past wars, then the 'population hostage' concept of mutual deterrence loses much of its credibility."* The Soviet Union suffered 20 million fatalities in World War II, five times more than it suffered in the theoretical American nuclear strike aimed solely at Soviet people.[1]

Russia, then, is rapidly preparing for war, both through accelerated weapons production and through an intensive civil defense program. The balance of power is rapidly shifting in favor of the Soviets, and it appears that the Russians could hold their casualties to levels they would regard as acceptable if they initiated a nuclear conflict (and past internal persecutions of the Russian citizenry indicate that the lives of their people are not held in high regard by the government).

If Russia gains a clear-cut military superiority, the stage may well be set for the fulfillment of the many prophecies cited earlier in this chapter.

Prophecies of Internal Conflict in the Americas

The scriptures speak expressly of a period of internal strife and conflict in the United States and the rest of the Americas.

1. Rowland Evans and Robert Novak, "In Nuclear Holocaust, How Many Deaths?" *Deseret News*, July 6, 1977.

Interestingly enough, the major scriptural prophecies of this future conflict were all spoken by the Savior himself as he visited the Nephites and Lamanites in America following his resurrection. Though they have been considered previously in this work,[1] yet they merit renewed attention with different emphasis, for the Lord gave in these prophecies an explanation of how the Lamanites would regain much of the Americas as the land for their inheritance. This is the Savior's prophetic message:

> But wo, saith the Father, unto the unbelieving of the Gentiles—for notwithstanding they have come forth upon the face of this land, and have scattered my people who are of the house of Israel; and my people who are of the house of Israel have been cast out from among them, and have been trodden under feet by them;
>
> And because of the mercies of the Father unto the Gentiles, and also the judgments of the Father upon my people who are of the house of Israel, verily, verily, I say unto you, that after all this, and I have caused my people who are of the house of Israel to be smitten, and to be afflicted, and to be slain, and to be cast out from among them, and to become hated by them, and to become a hiss and a byword among them—
>
> And thus commandeth the Father that I should say unto you: *At that day when the Gentiles shall sin against my gospel, and shall be lifted up in the pride of their hearts above all nations, and above all the people of the whole earth, and shall be filled with all manner of lyings, and of deceits, and of mischiefs, and all manner of hypocrisy, and murders, and priestcrafts, and whoredoms, and of secret abominations; and if they shall do all those things, and shall reject the fulness of my gospel, behold, saith the Father, I will bring the fulness of my gospel from among them.*
>
> And *then* will I remember my covenant which I have made unto my people, O house of Israel, and *I will bring my gospel unto them.*
>
> And I will show unto thee, O house of Israel, that *the Gentiles shall not have power over you; but I will remember my covenant unto you, O house of Israel, and ye shall come unto the knowledge of the fulness of my gospel.*
>
> But if the Gentiles will repent and return unto me, saith the Father, behold they shall be numbered among my people, O house of Israel.
>
> *And I will not suffer my people, who are of the house of Israel, to go through among them, and tread them down, saith the Father.*
>
> *But if they will not turn unto me, and hearken unto my voice, I will suffer them, yea, I will suffer my people, O house of Israel, that they shall go through among them, and shall tread them down, and they shall be as salt that hath lost its savor, which is thenceforth good for nothing but to be cast out, and to be trodden under foot of my people, O house of Israel.*

---

1. See pp. 129-131, 152-154.

*Verily, verily, I say unto you, thus hath the Father commanded me—
that I should give unto this people this land for their inheritance.*[1]

Again, in 3rd Nephi 20, the Savior spoke of the internal strife
in America which would serve to restore the Americas to the
Lamanites as the land of their inheritance. It will be in the same
era that the sword of God's justice will fall on "all the nations of
the Gentiles."[2] He said that it was to occur in the era when God
would complete the "fulfilling of the covenant" he has made to
the House of Israel.[3] This was his prophecy:

And *then* shall the remnants, which shall be scattered abroad upon
the face of the earth, be *gathered in from the east and from the west,
and from the south and from the north;* and they shall be brought to
the knowledge of the Lord their God, who hath redeemed them.

And the Father hath commanded me that *I should give unto you
this land, for your inheritance.*

And I say unto you, that if the Gentiles do not repent after the
blessing which they shall receive, after they have scattered my people—

*Then shall ye, who are a remnant of the house of Jacob, go forth
among them; and ye shall be in the midst of them who shall be many;
and ye shall be among them as a lion among the beasts of the forest,
and as a young lion among the flocks of sheep, who, if he goeth through
both treadeth down and teareth in pieces, and none can deliver.*

*Thy hand shall be lifted up upon thine adversaries, and all thine
enemies shall be cut off.*

And I will *gather my people together as a man gathereth his sheaves
into the floor.*

For I will make my people with whom the Father hath covenanted,
yea, I will make thy horn iron, and I will make thy hoofs brass. And
thou shalt beat in pieces many people; and I will consecrate their gain
unto the Lord, and their substance unto the Lord of the whole earth.
And behold, I am he who doeth it.

And it shall come to pass, saith the Father, that *the sword of my
justice shall hang over them at that day; and except they repent it shall
fall upon them, saith the Father, yea, even upon all the nations of the
Gentiles.*

And it shall come to pass that I will establish my people, O house of
Israel.

And behold, this people will I establish in this land, unto the fulfilling of the covenant which I made with your father Jacob; and *it shall*

---

1. 3 Ne. 16:8-16.
2. Recall the observation, reported earlier, that "I saw the international
   world war automatically break down, and *national revolutions occur in
   every country and complete the work of chaos and desolation.*" See
   p. 299.
3. See 3 Ne. 20:11-12.

be a New Jerusalem. And the powers of heaven shall be in the midst of this people; yea, even I will be in the midst of you.[1]

A third prophetic statement made by the Master during his appearance in the Americas describes the future conflict in more vivid detail. It shows the Lamanites as conquering their enemies, destroying the transportation, military strongholds, and also the cities:

> *And my people who are a remnant of Jacob shall be among the Gentiles, yea, in the midst of them as a lion among the beasts of the forest, as a young lion among the flocks of sheep, who, if he go through both treadeth down and teareth in pieces, and none can deliver.*
>
> Their hand shall be lifted up upon their adversaries, and all *their enemies shall be cut off.*
>
> Yea, wo be unto the Gentiles except they repent; for it shall come to pass in that day, saith the Father, that *I will cut off thy horses out of the midst of thee, and I will destroy thy chariots;*
>
> *And I will cut off the cities of thy land, and throw down all thy strongholds;*
>
> And I will cut off *witchcrafts* out of thy land, and thou shalt have no more soothsayers;
>
> Thy graven *images* I will also cut off, and thy standing *images* out of the midst of thee, and thou shalt no more worship the works of thy hands;
>
> And I will pluck up thy *groves* out of the midst of thee; *so will I destroy thy cities.*
>
> And it shall come to pass that all lyings, and deceivings, and envyings, and strifes, and priestcrafts, and whoredoms, shall be done away.
>
> For it shall come to pass, saith the Father, that at that day whosoever will not repent and come unto my Beloved Son, them will I cut off from among my people, O house of Israel;
>
> *And I will execute vengeance and fury upon them, even as upon the heathen, such as they have not heard.*[2]

The prophet Mormon, while recording the final destruction of the Nephites, suddenly looked ahead in time to the last days, and warned the Gentiles of that era that they must repent or be attacked by "a remnant of the seed of Jacob." He foresaw that if such occurs, "there is none to deliver."

> And then, O ye Gentiles, how can ye stand before the power of God, *except ye shall repent and turn from your evil ways?*

---

1. 3 Ne. 20:13-22. Note that the final verse establishes the time of the conflict as prior to the establishing of the New Jerusalem.
2. 3 Ne. 21:12-21. Note verses 22-23, of the context, which again establish the events as preceding the establishment of the New Jerusalem.

> Know ye not that ye are in the hands of God? Know ye not that he hath all power, and at his great command the earth shall be rolled together as a scroll?
>
> Therefore, repent ye, and humble yourselves before him, *lest he shall come out in justice against you—lest a remnant of the seed of Jacob shall go forth among you as a lion, and tear you in pieces, and there is none to deliver.*[1]

The "Prophecy on War," given through Joseph Smith in 1832, alludes to this period, and warns that *"the remnants who are left of the land will marshal themselves, and shall become exceedingly angry, and shall vex the Gentiles with a sore vexation."*[2]

The unworthy saints who pollute their inheritances in the last days during the era of the New Jerusalem, may also feel the wrath of the returning Lamanites if they do not live worthily. The Lord has warned that

> ...They were set to be a light unto the world, and to be the saviors of men;
>
> And inasmuch as they are not the saviors of men, they are as salt that has lost its savor, and is thenceforth *good for nothing but to be cast out and trodden under foot of men.*
>
> But verily I say unto you, *I have decreed that your brethren which have been scattered shall return to the lands of their inheritances, and shall build up the waste places of Zion.*
>
> For after much tribulation, as I have said unto you in a former commandment, cometh the blessing.
>
> Behold, this is the blessing which I have promised *after your tribulations, and the tribulations of your brethren*—your redemption, and the redemption of your brethren, even *their restoration to the land of Zion,* to be established, no more to be thrown down.
>
> Nevertheless, *if they pollute their inheritances they shall be thrown down; for I will not spare them if they pollute their inheritances.*[3]

Modern prophets have said much about this period of internal conflict, indicating that it be a scene of local conflicts, mobocracy, and anarchy that will fill the land. Lack of food and the breakdown

---

1. Morm. 5:22-24. Concerning the remnant of the seed of Jacob see Al. 46:23-27; also D & C 109:65 and 113:10.
2. D & C 87:5.
3. D & C 103:9-14. See again D & C 85:7-12. Is it, then, apostate saints whom the Lord is referring to as the "Gentiles who shall *sin against my gospel,*" and who "shall *reject the fulness of my gospel?*" Will they cause the remnant of Jacob to go through and tread them down? (See 3 Ne. 16:10, 14-15.)

of local manufacture, with resulting economic chaos, have been linked to this period. Already cited is Joseph Smith's vision in which he *"saw men hunting the lives of their own sons, and brother murdering brother, women killing their own daughters, and daughters seeking the lives of their own mothers. I saw armies arrayed against armies. I saw blood, desolation, fires."*[1]

Reference was also made to Orson Hyde's warning that it *"will be the white man of the north and the white man of the south fighting for bread for their wives and children!"*[2]

Orson Pratt said, concerning the internal conflict, that

> *It will be a war of neighborhood against neighborhood, city against city, town against town, county against county, state against state,* and they will go forth, destroying and being destroyed and *manufacturing will, in a great measure, cease, for a time among the American nation.* Why? Because in these terrible wars, they will not be privileged to manufacture, there will be *too much bloodshed, too much mobocracy, too much going forth in bands and destroying and pillaging the land* to suffer people to pursue any local vocation with any degree of safety. *What will become of millions of the farmers upon that land? They will leave their farms and they will remain uncultivated, and they will flee before the ravaging armies from place to place;...*[3]

He also warned,

> "What! This great and powerful nation of ours to be divided one part against the other and *many hundreds of thousands of souls to be destroyed by civil wars!"* Not a word of it would they believe. They do not believe *what is still in the future....* The time will come when there will be *no safety in carrying on the peaceable pursuits of farming or agriculture. But these will be neglected, and the people will think themselves well off if they can flee from city to city, from town to town and escape with their lives.*[4]

Brigham Young taught that he heard Joseph Smith say,

> They shall have mobbing to their hearts content, if they do not redress the wrongs of the Latter-day Saints. *Mobs will not decrease, but will increase until the whole government becomes a mob, and eventually it will be state against state, city against city, neighborhood against neighborhood.*

---

1. *HC* 3:390-391. See p. 275.
2. Prophecy made at Nephi, Utah by Elder Orson Hyde. See p. 276.
3. *JD* 20:151. March 9, 1879.
4. *JD* 12:344. December 27, 1868.

He then amplified the statement, saying that "it will be Christian against Christian, and man against man, and *those who will not take up the sword against their neighbors, must flee to Zion.*"[1] President John Taylor warned that

> ...God will lay his hand upon this nation, and they will feel it *more terribly* than ever they have done before. *There will be more bloodshed, more ruin, more devastation than ever they have seen before....* There is yet to come a sound of war, trouble and distress, in which *brother will be arrayed against brother, father against son, son against father, a scene of desolation and destruction that will permeate our land* until it will be a vexation to hear the report thereof.[2]

Thus it is evident that the modern prophets have been fully aware of the coming internal conflict and have warned repeatedly of its devastating effect upon the nation.

Though their insights will not be repeated here, it should be noted that there are many Latter-day Saints today who have received prophetic indications of roles they will perform in this era. These indications have come in patriarchal blessings, personal manifestations, or both. It has been the author's privilege to talk with some of these individuals, at times interviewing them in depth. It is obvious that God is directing his people at many levels as this tumultuous period approaches.

The New Jerusalem Saints Will Assume Political Power as U.S. Government Ceases

The question is often asked if the nation of America will endure. The answer set forth by the prophets is yes! Political power and unity following the era of internal conflicts will eventually be restored, and the American nation will be again pre-eminent among the nations of the earth.

However, the prophets have clearly taught that there will be a complete change of government. Washington, D.C. will cease to be the capital. The present national bureaucracy will have its end. The internal conflict will sweep away the current system of governments and will pave the way for the political kingdom of God[3]

---

1. *Deseret News*, Vol. II, No. 9. May 1, 1861.
2. *JD* 20:318. October 6, 1879.
3. A full treatment of statements concerning this political entity is beyond the scope of this work. See "The Establishment of the Kingdom of God," *Prophecy—Key to the Future*, pp. 67-81, for greater detail.

and the millennial kingdom through which Jesus Christ will rule and reign. The New Jerusalem will take its prophesied place as the dominant center of national and world affairs.

The loss of our national government is not a pleasant concept for patriotic Americans imbued with a love of their country, and we do not seek to hasten that day. Yet an eventual time of transition must come. Certainly the anticipation of righteous rule by inspired men of God, and eventually by the Saviour himself, outshines the predicted loss of our government as it is known today.

Prophetic statements by early Church leaders were repeatedly made to the effect that United States government will cease as the hand of God moves over the nation in judgment.

Joseph Smith, on several occasions, foretold the collapse of the federal government. On March 4, 1840, shortly after returning from a visit to Washington, D.C., Joseph wrote:

> ...My heart faints within me when *I see, by the visions of the Almighty, the end of this nation,* if she continues to disregard the cries and petitions of her virtuous citizens, as she has done, and is now doing.[1]

Another such prophecy was uttered by Joseph as part of an amazing prediction concerning American politics which has since seen literal fulfillment.[2] On May 18, 1843, Joseph prophesied the following to Judge Stephen A. Douglas:

> *I prophesy in the name of the Lord God of Israel,* unless the United States redress the wrongs committed upon the Saints in the state of Missouri and punish the crimes committed by her officers that *in a few*

---

1. *HC* 4:89. March 4, 1840. The government continued to disregard the petitions of the Saints, leaving the conditional aspects of the prophecy unfulfilled.

2. On May 18, 1843, Joseph prophesied to a judge of the Illinois court, Stepehn A. Douglas, that he (Douglas) would aspire to the presidency of the United States, warning him that if he ever turned against the Latter-day Saints, he would "feel the weight of the hand of the Almighty." Douglas became the presidential candidate of the Independent Democratic Party, the predominant party of the day, in 1860. He espoused a position critical of the saints. Though it appeared that Douglas would gain an easy presidential victory, his party was suddenly split and he lost to the little-known Republican candidate, Abraham Lincoln.

   For further details on the remarkable prophecy made by Joseph Smith and its literal fulfillment, see the author's book, *The Prophecies of Joseph Smith,* pp. 336-338.

years the government will be utterly overthrown and wasted, and there will not be so much as a potsherd left. [1]

On December 16, 1843, Joseph Smith again prophesied the destruction of the national government, as follows:

> While discussing the petition to Congress, *I prophesied, by virtue of the holy Priesthood vested in me, and in the name of the Lord Jesus Christ,* that, if Congress will not hear our petition and grant us protection, *they shall be broken up as a government.* [2]

Other Church leaders also warned that the U.S. Government would come to an end. President Brigham Young, for instance, said:

> *The nations will consume each other,* and the Lord will suffer them to bring it about. It does not require much talent or tact to get up opposition in these days. You see it rife in communities, in meetings, in neighborhoods, and in cities. *That is the knife that will cut down this government. The axe is laid at the root of the tree, and every tree that bringeth not forth good fruit will be hewn down.* [3]

Orson Pratt, while describing the future conflict within the United States, said,

> If a war of this description should take place, who could carry on his business in safety? Who would feel safe to put his crops in the ground,

1. *HC* 5:394. May 18, 1843. The prophecy was a conditional one, with the conditions remaining unfulfilled. The saints were never redressed for their losses in Missouri, nor were the Missourians punished for their offenses. With the conditions unmet, it appears that the judgments upon the government can still be expected to take place.
2. *HC* 6:116. December 16, 1843. An interpretation that Joseph "doubtless had reference to the party in power," the Democratic party, rather than the national government, is set forth in an editorial comment on that page of the History of the Church. While it gives interesting comment on the politics of the day, it in no way documents the unjustified assumption that Joseph meant other than what he actually said, that *"Congress...* shall be broken up as a government." In the light of Joseph's other statements cited herein and the statements by other Church leaders also cited, the validity of the footnote with its assumption, is doubtful.
   Again, the prophecy is a conditional one in which the conditions were not met. Congress did not grant protection to the saints, who so desperately needed it.
3. *JD* 8:143. August 12, 1860.

or to carry on any enterprise? *There would be fleeing from one State to another, and general confusion would exist throughout the whole Republic.* Such eventually is to be the condition of this whole nation, if the people do not repent of their wickedness; and *such a state of affairs means no more or less than the complete overthrow of the nation, and not only of this nation, but the nations of Europe.* [1]

Elder Pratt aptly described the transition of rule from the U.S. Government to the saints, depicting the saints as maintaining stability when present government ceases:

God has sent forth his warning message in the midst of this nation, but they have rejected it and treated his servants with contempt; the Lord has gathered out his people from their midst, and has planted them here in these mountains; and *he will speedily fulfill the prophecy in relation to the overthrow of this nation, and their destruction. We shall be obliged to have a government to preserve ourselves in unity and peace; for they, through being wasted away, will not have the power to govern;* for state will be divided against state, city against city, town against town, and the whole country will be in terror and confusion; mobocracy will prevail and their [sic] will be no security, through this great Republic, for the lives or property of the people. *When that time shall arrive, we shall necessarily want to carry out the principles of our great constitution and as the people of God, we shall want to see those principles magnified, according to the order of union and oneness which prevails among the people of God.* We can magnify it, and all will be united without having democrats or republicans and all kinds of religions; we can magnify it according to the spirit and letter of the constitution, though we are united in politics, religion, and everything else. [2]

President Wilford Woodruff also foresaw and foretold the eventual fall of U.S. Government. He wrote that

The American nation will be broken in pieces like a potter's vessel and will be cast down to hell if it does not repent,—and this, because of murders, whoredoms, wickedness, and all manner of abominations, *for the Lord has spoken it.* [3]

---

1. *JD* 18:341. February 25, 1877.
2. *DEN,* Vol. 8, No. 265. October 2, 1875.
3. Matthias F. Cowley, *Wilford Woodruff—History of His Life and Labors* (Salt Lake City, Utah: Bookcraft, 1964), p. 500. Summer, 1877. While closing his journal for the previous year, Elder Woodruff wrote his observation that "To a great extent, *virtue has departed from the land, and honesty has been driven from the various departments of government.* Men seek to aggrandize themselves rather than to serve the interests of the people. *Death and destruction are sown in the land which is ripening for the harvest.*" (*Ibid.,* p. 490.)

In an epistle to the world, written by Wilford Woodruff on February 22, 1879, he prophesied,

> *...I will say, in the name of Jesus Christ,* the Son of the living God, that "Mormonism" will live and prosper, Zion will flourish, and the Kingdom of God will stand in power and glory and dominion as Daniel saw it, *when this nation is broken to pieces as a potter's vessel and laid in the dust, and brought to judgment,* or God never spoke by my mouth.[1]

In the same epistle he warned that the period would be a time of international anarchy, when legal barriers would fall and laws would not be observed:

> ...I wish to warn all nations of the judgments of God which are at their doors. *Thrones will be cast down, nations will be overturned, anarchy will reign, all legal barriers will be broken down, and the laws will be trampled in the dust. You are about to be visited with war, the sword, famine, pestilence, plague, earthquakes, whirlwinds, tempests, and with the flame* of devouring fire; by fire and with the sword will God plead with all flesh, and *the slain of the Lord will be many.* The anger of the Lord is kindled and His sword is bathed in heaven, and is about to fall upon Idumea, or the world. And who is able to abide these things? And who will stand when He appeareth? The fig trees are leaving, and the signs of all heaven and earth indicate the coming of the Son of Man. *The seals are about to be opened, the plagues to be poured forth. Your rivers and seas will be turned to blood and to gall. And the inhabitants of the earth will die of plagues.* And the unbelief of great Babylon, with the whole Christian world, will not make the truths of God without effect....[2]

In a letter to the leaders of the Church, written from Arizona on September 15, 1879, Elder Woodruff wrote that *"the lawyers, judges, and the nation are hastening to their doom as fast as time will permit, and they are sure of their fate."*[3]

---

1. *Ibid.,* p. 508.
2. *Ibid.,* p. 511.
3. *Ibid.,* p. 528. Elder Woodruff knew well the future events which will transpire in America, having seen them in vision. As early as October 18, 1848, he wrote:

   > ...the visions of my mind have been opened so that I saw clearly my duty to my God, to my wife, to my children, to the Saints, and to the world at large. *I have also seen the awful and certain judgments of God, which like a gathering storm are ready to burst upon the whole Gentile world, especially this nation which has heard the sound of the gospel but rejected it,* together with the testimony of the servants of God; has stoned and killed the prophets; has become drunk with the blood of martyrs and Saints; and finally has driven the entire Church with the priesthood and keys of eternal life out of its midst into the wilderness and mountains of Israel." (*Ibid.,* p. 333. See also pp. 152-153.)

On January 26, 1880, a vision to Elder Woodruff again showed him the destruction of the nation. He wept, as would anyone who loves his country:

> I went to bed filled with prayer and meditation. I fell asleep and remained in slumber until about midnight, when I awoke. The Lord then poured out His spirit upon me and opened the vision of my mind so that I could comprehend in a great measure the mind and will of God concerning the nation and concerning the inhabitants of Zion. *I saw the wickedness of the nation, its abominations and corruptions and the judgments of God and the destruction that awaited it.* Then I also comprehended the great responsibility which rested upon the Quorum of the Apostles. My head became a fountain of tears, and my pillow was wet with the dews of heaven. Sleep departed from me. The Lord revealed unto me the duty of the Apostles and of all the faithful elders of Israel. [1]

In a discourse delivered in 1880, Elder Woodruff asserted that the destruction of the American nation, together with other nations of the world, "is sure":

> When I contemplate the condition of our nation, and see that wickedness and abominations are increasing, so much so that the whole heavens groan and weep over the abominations of this nation and the nations of the earth, *I ask myself the question, can the American nation escape? The answer comes, No; its destruction, as well as the destruction of the world, is sure;* just as sure as the Lord cut off and destroyed the two great and prosperous nations that once inhabited this continent of North and South America, because of their wickedness, so will he them destroy, and *sooner or later they will reap the fruits of their own wicked acts, and be numbered among the past.* [2]

---

1. *Ibid.*, pp. 530-531. The account records that "The revelation was submitted to the Quorum of the Twelve Apostles just prior to the April conference of that year. It was accepted by that body as the word of the Lord, according to Elder Woodruff's journal, under date of April 4th, 1880." (*Ibid.*, p. 531.)

   Two days after the vision, on January 28, 1880, another vision was granted to him:

   > "On January 28th I was again given a vision. It concerned the destiny of our nation and of Zion. My pillow was again wet by a fountain of tears as I beheld the judgments of God upon the wicked. I was strongly impressed that the Apostles and elders should warn the inhabitants of the earth." *(Ibid.)*

2. *JD* 21:301. August 1, 1880. Wilford Woodruff's prophecy of December 16, 1878, should be recalled in this context. He saw terrible destruction throughout the world, with Washington, D.C. a desolation. Congress and the White House were empty, and the people had fled from the city. (See pp. 294-296.)

Others also have seen the end of the American nation in vision. One was apostle Moses Thatcher, who told a congregation in 1882, "I have seen the *end of this nation,* and it is terrible."[1]

But as the present political system crumbles under the prophesied chaos and anarchy, both law and order, and Constitutional government are expected to be preserved among the saints.

Brigham Young taught that the saints would save the Constitution at a "critical juncture":

> Will the Constitution be destroyed? No: it will be held inviolate by this people; and, as Joseph Smith said, "The time will come when *the destiny of the nation will hang upon a single thread. At that critical juncture, this people will step forth and save it from the threatened destruction."* It will be so.[2]

The following year he taught that

> ...When the Constitution of the United States hangs, as it were, upon a single thread, *they will have to call for the "Mormon Elders to save it from utter destruction; and they will step forth and do it.*[3]

President Young taught that the maintaining of Constitutional principles by the saints would be under their own government, the Kingdom of God, not under U.S. Government as it is known today:

> *When the day comes in which the Kingdom of God will bear rule,* the flag of the United States will proudly flutter unsullied on the flag staff of liberty and equal rights, without a spot to sully its fair surface; the glorious flag our fathers have bequeathed to us will then be unfurled to the breeze *by those who have power to hoist it aloft and defend its sanctity.*[4]

President John Taylor observed in 1879,

> ...And then *the day is not far distant when this nation will be shaken from centre to circumference.* And now, you may write it down, any of

---

1. *Franklin Ward Historical Record,* Franklin, Idaho, June 16, 1882.
2. *JD* 7:15. July 4, 1854.
3. *JD* 2:182. February 18, 1855.
4. *JD* 2:317. July 8, 1855. See D & C 105:32-34. Though some have interpreted these statements as having been fulfilled in the U.S. Civil War, Brigham Young made it clear that such was not a proper interpretation. Following that war he said, "How long will it be before the words of the prophet Joseph will be fulfilled? *He said if the Constitution of the United States were saved at all it must be done by these people.* It will not be many years before these words come to pass." (*JD* 12:204. April 8, 1868.)

you, and *I will prophesy it in the name of God.* And then will be fulfilled that prediction to be found in one of the revelations given through
the Prophet Joseph Smith. *Those who will not take up their sword to
fight against their neighbor must needs flee to Zion for safety.... When
the people shall have torn to shreds the Constitution of the United States
the Elders of Israel will be found holding it up to the nations of the earth
and proclaiming liberty and equal rights to all men,* and extending the
hand of fellowship to the oppressed of all nations. This is part of the
programme, and as long as we do what is right and fear God, he will
help us and stand by us under all circumstances.[1]

George Q. Cannon also asserted that the time will come when
liberty and Constitutional government will only be found among
the saints:

> ...the day will come—and this is another prediction of Joseph Smith's—
> I want to remind you of it, my brethren and sisters, *when good govern-
> ment, constitutional government—liberty—will be found among the
> Latter-day Saints, and it will be sought for in vain elsewhere;* when the
> Constitution of this land and republican government and institutions
> will be upheld by this people who are now so oppressed and whose
> destruction is now sought so diligently. *The day will come when the
> Constitution, and free government under it, will be sustained and pre-
> served by this people....*[2]

The scenario is drawn, then, with the numerous statements
cited above, of a future time of internal conflict in which lawless-
ness and anarchy will reach such devastating proportions that national and local government will fail. There will be greater stability
among the saints during this era, and people will be drawn to it to
escape the chaos of other areas. A new government will be established among the saints and that political Kingdom of God will
espouse and uphold the principles of Constitutional government.
Eventually it will be the only governing power with stability in the
nation, and it will grow in power and influence as the New Jerusalem rises to unparalleled pre-eminence.

Will this nation, then, endure? Yes, but only after a tragic
reduction of population, complete economic disruption and upheaval, disintegration of governmental control and finally of the
government itself. There will be much suffering, much fear, much
sorrow, and much chastening. The nation which will emerge will

---

1. *JD* 21:8. August 31, 1879.
2. *JD* 23:104. November 20, 1881. For other statements on this subject
   see the author's book, *Prophecy—Key to the Future,* "Appendix 1, The
   United States Constitution Will Hang By A Thread," pp. 297-300.

be as the butterfly which has struggled to emerge from its cocoon. It will become a thing of beauty, leaving behind the withered shell which once housed and encompassed it.

International Conflict During the New Jerusalem Era—A Fourth World War

It is expected that the period of internal conflict will mark the time for the saints to wend their way back to Jackson County, Missouri to establish the New Jerusalem. Orson Pratt expressed the expectation held by the saints concerning the future time of return:

> *When the time shall come that the Lord shall waste away this nation, he will give commandment to this people to return and possess their own inheritance* which they purchased some forty-four years ago in the state of Missouri.[1]

The area is expected to have been swept clean in the destruction of the world war or internal conflicts which will precede the return. As he related his vision of future judgments he received in 1878, Wilford Woodruff related that "I seemed to be standing on the left bank of the Missouri River, opposite the city of *Independence,—but I saw no city. I saw the whole states of Illinois and Missouri and part of Iowa, a complete wilderness of desert with no living human being there.*[2]

Heber C. Kimball, in his extended prophecy to Amanda H. Wilcox, said that Jackson County "will be swept so clean of its inhabitants that...there will not be left so much as a yellow dog to wag his tail."[3]

---

1. *DEN*, Vol. 8, No. 265, October 2, 1875. For a broader description of the return to and establishment of the New Jerusalem, and events to take place therein, see *Prophecy—Key to the Future*, pp. 84-126.
2. Revelation to Wilford Woodruff, December 16, 1878. See pp. 293-296.
3. *Prophetic Sayings of Heber C. Kimball to Amanda H. Wilcox.* The "yellow dog" statement, it appears, was originally made by Joseph Smith, as identified in the following letter written by George Burkett to his children in December, 1870, from Eden City (Ogden Valley, Weber County), Utah. Earlier in the letter, Elder Burkett indicated that members of Zion's Camp went to his home when cholera broke out among them [see *HC* 2:112]. It was probably at that time that the statement was made by Joseph Smith, which Elder Burkett quotes:
   > Do not be in a hurry of going to Jackson County for the land has to be cleared and the power of God to rest upon it before we think of returning there.

Indeed, the Lord has revealed that he will clear the way for the returning saints by removing their enemies:

> For behold, *I do not require at their hands to fight the battles of Zion;* for, as I said in a former commandment, even so will I fulfil—*I will fight your battles.*
> Behold, the destroyer I have sent forth to destroy and lay waste mine enemies; and not many years hence they shall not be left to pollute mine heritage, and to *blaspheme my name upon the lands which I have consecrated for the gathering together of my saints.*[1]

Yet it appears that the saints will still have to be prepared militarily, and to function as an army in their return:

> And after these lands are purchased, *I will hold the armies of Israel guiltless in taking possession of their own lands, which they have previously purchased with their moneys, and of throwing down the towers of mine enemies that may be upon them, and scattering their watchmen, and avenging me of mine enemies* unto the third and fourth generation of them that hate me.
> *But first let my army become very great, and let it be sanctified before me, that it may become fair as the sun, and clear as the moon, and that her banners may be terrible unto all nations:*
> That the kingdoms of this world may be constrained to acknowledge that the kingdom of Zion is in very deed the kingdom of our God and his Christ; therefore, let us become subject unto her laws.[2]

There will be other cities and towns in nearby areas which will be standing, but desolate, and as the tribes of Israel gather to the New Jerusalem area they will inherit them. They will outnumber the church members, "for more are the children of the deso-

---

1. D & C 105:14-15.
2. D & C 105:30-32.

> *I heard Joseph Smith say in my house when in Clay Co. that when we returned there, there would not be a dog to wag its tail, or move its tongue against us,* none but the pure in heart will go up there and the Lord will prepare the people. They shall be clear as the sun, fair as the moon and terribly valiant as an army with banners; there are virgins and hundred and forty four thousand that shall stand on Mount Zion, these are the bride the Lamb's wife.

A copy of this portion of the letter was given to the author February 11, 1965 by Geraldine Nelson (Mrs. Merrell Nelson), of Logan, Utah. She is a third great-granddaughter of George Burkett.

late than the children of the married wife, saith the Lord."[1] The
Saviour has promised them that

> ...thou shalt break forth on the right hand and on the left, and *thy seed
> shall inherit the Gentiles and make the desolate cities to be inhabited.*[2]

The New Jerusalem will be a place of refuge for people from
throughout the world, who will come to escape the warfare that
will be raging around them. Indeed, the Lord has revealed that its
inhabitants "shall be the only people that shall not be at war one
with another":

> And with one heart and with one mind, gather up your riches that
> ye may purchase an inheritance which shall hereafter be appointed unto
> you.
> And it shall be called the New Jerusalem, a land of peace, *a city of
> refuge, a place of safety for the saints of the Most High God;*

---

1. 3 Ne. 22:1. See also D & C 133:26-34; 2 Ne. 29:12-14. Orson Pratt
supported this interpretation when he said,

   The city of Zion, with its Sanctuary and Priesthood, and the
   glorious fulness of the Gospel, will constitute a standard which will
   put an end to jarring creeds and political wranglings, by *uniting the
   republics, states, provinces, territories, nations, tribes, kindreds,
   tongues, people, and sects of North and South America in one great
   and common bond of brotherhood;* while truth and knowledge shall
   make them free, and love cement their union. (*JD* 24:31-32. October
   26, 1879.)

2. 3 Ne. 22:3. Note the important chronological sequence outlined in the
preceding verses:

   1. The remnant of Jacob will tread down the cities of the Gentiles
   (3 Ne. 21:12-19).

   2. The wicked (apostate) will be cut off from among the Lord's people (3 Ne. 21:20-21).

   3. The church will help the remnant of Jacob build the New Jerusalem (3 Ne. 21:23).

   4. The Lord's people, scattered across the land, will gather to the
   New Jerusalem (3 Ne. 21:24).

   5. The Lord will appear to them (3 Ne. 21:25).

   6. The gospel will be preached to the (Lamanite) remnant (3 Ne.
   21:26).

   7. The work will commence among the lost tribes of Israel (3 Ne.
   21:26).

   8. The major period of gathering scattered Israel will commence,
   among all nations (3 Ne. 21:27-29).

   9. Those gathering will inhabit the desolate cities (3 Ne. 22:1-3).

And the glory of the Lord shall be there, and *the terror of the Lord also shall be there, insomuch that the wicked will not come unto it,* and it shall be called Zion.

And it shall come to pass among the wicked, that *every man that will not take his sword against his neighbor must needs flee unto Zion for safety.*

And there shall be gathered unto it out of every nation under heaven; *and it shall be the only people that shall not be at war one with another.*

And it shall be said among the wicked: *Let us not go up to battle against Zion, for the inhabitants of Zion are terrible; wherefore we cannot stand.*

And it shall come to pass that the righteous shall be gathered out from among all nations, and shall come to Zion, singing with songs of everlasting joy....

For when the Lord shall appear he shall be terrible unto them, that *fear may seize upon them, and they shall stand afar off and tremble.*

And all nations shall be afraid because of the terror of the Lord, and the power of his might. Even so. Amen.[1]

Here then, is a significant prophecy of international conflict—not a third world war, for that war will have ended previously. Is it not, then, a fourth world war—a devastating conflagration which only the New Jerusalem will escape because the power of God is there?

Other revelations speak of it. The Lord spoke of *wars* which were to come upon the earth, then warned of one specific war during which the saints will be assembled on the land of Zion and desolation comes upon the wicked:

I, the Lord, am angry with the wicked; I am holding my Spirit from the inhabitants of the earth.

I have sworn in my wrath, and decreed wars upon the face of the earth, and the wicked shall slay the wicked, and fear shall come upon every man;

And the saints also shall hardly escape; nevertheless, I, the Lord, am with them, and will come down in heaven from the presence of my Father and consume the wicked with unquenchable fire.

And behold, this is not yet, but by and by.

Wherefore, seeing that I, the Lord, have decreed all these things upon the face of the earth, *I will that my saints should be assembled upon the land of Zion;*

And that every man should take righteousness in his hands and faithfulness upon his loins, and lift a warning voice unto the inhabitants of the earth; and *declare both by word and by flight that desolation shall come upon the wicked.*[2]

---

1. D & C 45:65-71, 74-75.
2. D & C 63:32-37. Note that this description in no way matches the events of the Third World War. It is in a different geographical and chronological setting.

The Savior, after telling how the New Jerusalem would be cleansed of apostates and false prophets and apostles,[1] foretold the flight of people from all nations to the New Jerusalem and the fear the nations of the earth will have of the New Zion:

> For, behold, I say unto you that Zion shall flourish, and the glory of the Lord shall be upon her;
>
> And she shall be an ensign unto the people, and *there shall come unto her out of every nation under heaven.*
>
> And the day shall come when *the nations of the earth shall tremble because of her, and shall fear because of her terrible ones.* The Lord hath spoken it. Amen.[2]

Again, a later revelation depicts the New Jerusalem as a place of defense when God's wrath is poured out upon the whole earth:

> Verily I say unto you all: Arise and shine forth, that thy light may be a standard for the nations;
>
> And that the gathering together upon the land of Zion, and upon her stakes, *may be for a defense, and for a refuge from the storm, and from wrath when it shall be poured out without mixture upon the whole earth.*[3]

A prophecy in the Book of Revelation appears to refer to this Fourth World War, when every nation except the New Jerusalem will be at war. John foresaw war emanate from near the River Euphrates, in which a terrible army uses fire and smoke and brimstone[4] which slays a third of mankind:

> And the sixth angel sounded, and I heard a voice from the four horns of the golden altar which is before God,
>
> Saying to the sixth angel which had the trumpet, *Loose the four angels which are bound in the great river Euphrates.*
>
> *And the four angels were loosed, which were prepared for an hour, and a day, and a month, and a year, for to slay the third part of men.*
>
> *And the number of the army of the horsemen were two hundred thousand thousand: and I heard the number of them.*

---

1. See D & C 64:35-40.
2. D & C 64:41-43. Note again the world-wide scope of the warning.
3. D & C 115:5-6. Note again the world-wide implications of the prophecy.
4. Rev. 9:17-18. Nuclear weapons again? Imagine what terrible weaponry is required to slay one-third of mankind! See the commentary on the chronological relationship of this war, followed by the gathering of Israel to Palestine, then followed by the Battle of Armageddon in *Prophecy—Key to the Future,* p. 185. The commentary is related to Rev. 9:13-11:19.

And thus I saw the horses in the vision, and them that sat on them, having breastplates of fire, and of jacinth, and brimstone: and the heads of the horses were as the heads of lions; and out of their mouths issued fire and smoke and brimstone.

By these three was the third part of men killed, by the fire, and by the smoke, and by the brimstone, which issued out of their mouths.[1]

Orson Pratt, that great student and expounder of prophecy, was fully aware of this period of warfare which will come upon the earth during the New Jerusalem era. He spoke of it on several occasions. Characteristic of his comments is the following:

By-and-by the Spirit of God will entirely withdraw from those Gentile nations, and leave them to themselves. *Then they will find something else to do besides warring against the Saints in their midst—besides raising their sword and fighting against the Lamb of God; for then war will commence in earnest,* and such a war as probably never entered into the hearts of men in our age to conceive of. *No nation of the Gentiles upon the face of the whole earth but what will be engaged in deadly war, except the Latter-day Kingdom.* They will be fighting one against another. And when that day comes, *the Jews will flee to Jerusalem, and those nations will almost use one another up,* and those of them who are left will be burned; for that will be the last sweeping judgment that is to go over the earth to cleanse it from wickedness.[2]

He also taught,

It is not only a Gospel to be preached to all the nations of the earth, but in connection with it *you will have to make proclamation connected with it, to all people, to fear God and give glory to him, for the hour of his judgment is come.* And as these judgments come, *kingdoms and thrones will be cast down and overturned. Empire will war with empire, kingdom with kingdom, and city with city, and there will be one general revolution throughout the earth, the Jews fleeing to their own country,* desolation coming upon the wicked, with the swiftness of whirlwinds and fury poured out.[3]

And also:

When that day shall come [when the missionaries will be called home] there shall be wars, not such wars as have come in centuries and years

---

1. Rev. 9:13-18.
2. *JD* 7:188. July 10, 1859. For additional exposition of the theme of a Fourth World War, and other statements by Elder Pratt, see *Prophecy—Key to the Future,* "Universal Conflict and the Fall of the Christian Nations," pp. 159-166.
3. *JD* 14:65-66. March 26, 1871.

that are past and gone, but *a desolating war.* When I say desolating, I mean that *it will lay these European nations in waste. Cities will be left vacated, without inhabitants. The people will be destroyed by the sword of their own hands. Not only this but many other cities will be burned;* for when contending armies are wrought up with the terrible anger, without the Spirit of God upon them, when they have not that spirit of humanity that now characterizes many of the wars amongst the nations, when they are left to themselves, there will be no quarter given, no prisoners taken, but *a war of destruction, of desolation, of the burning of the cities and villages, until the land is laid desolate.*[1]

Thus it is seen that a pattern of scripture and modern exposition indicates there will be a period of world-wide warfare at the day the New Jerusalem has been established in Jackson County, Missouri. Indeed, the inhabitants there "shall be the only people that shall not be at war one with another." In that era, the New Jerusalem will be "a city of refuge, a place of safety," and "every man that will not take his sword against his neighbor must needs flee unto Zion for safety." This gathering will be "out of every nation under heaven." Truly this future event—a fourth world war— is one of the most significant signs of the times which will precede the Savior's glorious return.

Conflict as the Great and Abominable Church Collapses—Part of Fourth World War

A previous chapter[2] has discussed in detail the extensive persecution which is to be experienced by the saints at the hands of a "great and abominable church." As was recorded therein, that persecution will continue until nations embracing that church war among themselves and bring about the collapse of that Satan-inspired entity. That broad panorama of prophecy need not be repeated in this context. What is important here is some comment on the chronological relationships of these events.

Comment was made on the "great and marvelous work" and the Lord's "strange act" which will cause men to join either the church of God or the church of the devil.[3] That devisive event was prophesied in several Book of Mormon passages, which also indicate its chronological relationships to other future events. 1 Ne. 22:8-12

---

1. *JD* 20:150-151. March 9, 1879.
2. See "Sixth Warning: The Great and Abominable Church Will Persecute the Saints," pp. 171-197.
3. See pp. 175-183.

indicates that the devisive event will precede the gathering of Israel
to the lands of their inheritance (which 3 Ne. 21:22-29 shows will
be after the construction of the New Jerusalem). 2 Ne. 25:15-18
also speaks of the devisive event in a context preceding the gathering of Israel, but linking it with the coming of a false Messiah.[1]

2 Ne. 27:26 speaks of "a marvelous work and a wonder," and
the chapter places it in the context of the era when "the multitude
of all the nations" shall "fight against Mount Zion"[2] but early
enough that the Gentiles of "this land" will still be "drunken with
iniquity and all manner of abominations."[3] 2 Ne. 28:32-29:14
again shows that the "marvelous work" will precede the time when
the house of Israel "shall be gathered home to the lands of their
possessions."[4] 3 Ne. 21:9-23 also places the "marvelous work"
prior to the uprising of the remnant of Jacob and the building of
the New Jerusalem. The Lord's "strange act" is to precede the
fall of the U.S. Government, for the Lord in his fury shall "vex the
nation."[5] The Canadian manifestation of Sols Guardisto tells of
the religious animosity and persecution which will arise against the
Church during the Third World War.

All of these allusions combine to show that the persecutions
of the saints by the great and abominable church will begin early
in the future series of last days events—prior to the internal conflict in the United States and before the return to Jackson County,
Missouri. Animosity will continue against the Church during the
New Jerusalem period, and "the nations of the earth shall tremble
because of her, and shall fear because of her terrible ones."[6] The
wicked will want to war against the New Jerusalem but will be
afraid to do so,[7] and the Lord will fight battles for the saints.[8]

But there is to come a time when the persecution will cease,
and the great and abominable church will be destroyed in a period
of intense international warfare. That warfare will involve the

---

1. See pp. 233-240. These pages and the balance of Chapter XII give strong
   indication that there will be difficulty with the coming of a false Messiah
   in the early days of the New Jerusalem.
2. 2 Ne. 27:3.
3. 2 Ne. 27:1.
4. 2 Ne. 29:14. This gathering, presumably, includes the uprising of the
   remnant of Jacob in which the Lamanites will reclaim the Americas as
   the land of their inheritance. See 3 Ne. 16:15-16; 20:14-18; 21:12-22.
5. D & C 101:89-95.
6. D & C 64:43.
7. D & C 45:67, 70.
8. D & C 105:14.

Church, for John prophesied of ten kings that *"shall make war with the Lamb, and the Lamb shall overcome them."*[1]

Nephi saw that the wrath of God would come upon the great and abominable church, resulting in international warfare, while the saints will still be scattered throughout the earth:

> And it came to pass that I looked and beheld the whore of all the earth, and she sat upon many waters; and she had dominion over all the earth, *among all nations, kindreds, tongues, and people.*
>
> And it came to pass that *I beheld the church of the Lamb of God, and its numbers were few, because of the wickedness and abominations of the whore who sat upon many waters; nevertheless, I beheld that the church of the Lamb, who were the saints of God, were also upon all the face of the earth; and their dominions upon the face of the earth were small, because of the wickedness of the great whore whom I saw.*
>
> And it came to pass that I beheld that the great mother of abominations *did gather together multitudes upon the face of all the earth, among all the nations of the Gentiles, to fight against the Lamb of God.*
>
> And it came to pass that I, Nephi, beheld the power of the Lamb of God, that it descended upon the saints of the church of the Lamb, and *upon the covenant people of the Lord, who were scattered upon all the face of the earth;* and they were armed with righteousness and with the power of God in great glory.
>
> And it came to pass that I beheld that the *wrath of God was poured out upon the great and abominable church, insomuch that there were wars and rumors of wars among all the nations and kindreds of the earth.*[2]

Then he described the fall of the great and abominable church as the nations under its power war among themselves:

> *And the blood of that great and abominable church, which is the whore of all the earth, shall turn upon their own heads; for they shall war among themselves, and the sword of their own hands shall fall upon their own heads, and they shall be drunken with their own blood.*
>
> *And every nation which shall war against thee, O house of Israel, shall be turned one against another,* and they shall fall into the pit which they digged to ensnare the people of the Lord. *And all that fight against Zion shall be destroyed, and that great whore, who hath perverted the right ways of the Lord, yea, that great and abominable church, shall tumble to the dust* and great shall be the fall of it.
>
> For behold, saith the prophet, the time cometh speedily that Satan shall have no more power over the hearts of the children of men; for the day soon cometh that all the proud and they who do wickedly shall be as stubble; and the day cometh that they must be burned.

---

1. Rev. 17:12-14.
2. 1 Ne. 14:11-15.

> For the time soon cometh that the fulness of the wrath of God shall be poured out upon all the children of men; for *he will not suffer that the wicked shall destroy the righteous.*
>
> Wherefore, he will preserve the righteous by his power, even if it so be that the fulness of his wrath must come, and *the righteous be preserved, even unto the destruction of their enemies by fire.* Wherefore, the righteous need not fear; for thus saith the prophet, they shall be saved, even if it so be as by fire.
>
> Behold, my brethren, I say unto you, that these things must shortly come; yea, even *blood, and fire, and vapor of smoke must come;* and it must needs be upon the face of this earth; and it cometh unto men according to the flesh if it so be that they will harden their hearts against the Holy One of Israel.
>
> For behold, *the righteous shall not perish; for the time surely must come that all they who fight against Zion shall be cut off.*[1]

Its demise will be an event of major proportions, for Nephi prophesies that *"great must be the fall thereof."*[2] He also prophesied that *"all that fight against Zion shall be destroyed,* and that great whore, who hath perverted the right ways of the Lord, yea, *that great and abominable church, shall tumble to the dust and great shall be the fall of it.*[3]

According to John's prophecy, the ten kings who will fight against the church will turn upon the capital city of the abominable church "and shall make her desolate and naked, and shall eat her flesh, and burn her with fire."[4]

Nephi learned from an angel the time of this terrible destruction of the great and abominable church, and indicated that it would still precede the major period of Israel's gathering:

> ...When the day cometh that the wrath of God is poured out upon the mother of harlots, which is the great and abominable church of all the earth, whose foundation is the devil, *then, at that day, the work of the Father shall commence, in preparing the way for the fulfilling of his covenants, which he hath made to his people who are of the house of Israel.*[5]

The prophet clearly linked the gathering of Israel to the lands of their inheritance, the warring of the nations of the great and abominable church, and fighting against Zion by the nations into one chronological era as he expounded the prophecies.[6]

---

1. 1 Ne. 22:13-19.
2. 2 Ne. 28:18.
3. 1 Ne. 22:14.

4. Rev. 17:16.
5. 1 Ne. 14:17.
6. 1 Ne. 22:8-14.

The conclusion becomes inevitable, then: the conflict which brings the fall of the great and abominable church is the same which will rage in the days of the New Jerusalem, when every nation will be at war except the inhabitants of that protected city. Though two separate patterns of prophecy seem to speak of these conflicts, the chronological relationships show that both are the same period of international conflict, and both represent important aspects of the Fourth World War.

The Battle of Armageddon

This momentous conflict, the most prophesied event in all scripture, will take place in Israel in the last days. It draws its name from Megiddo,[1] a mountain located in the plain of Esdraelon, a triangular valley about sixty miles northwest of Jerusalem. This mountain is a strong defensive position which dominates the valley and commands the north-south route through Palestine. It has been the site of innumerable battles in the past, and the archaeological remains of several fortresses dating back to Old Testament times are still very much in evidence there.

John the Revelator foretold this great future conflict. He spoke of three "unclean spirits" that will "come out of the mouth of the dragon, and out of the mouth of the beast, and out of the mouth of the false prophet."[2] He then described their mission:

> ...They are the spirits of devils, working miracles, which go forth unto the kings of the earth and of the whole world, *to gather them to the battle of that great day of God Almighty....*
>
> And he gathered them together into a place called in the Hebrew tongue *Armageddon.*[3]

Israel has lived its precarious existence for more than two decades, fighting several wars, and the world has talked continuously about the approaching conflict of Armageddon, often assuming that the conflict at hand was the beginning of that battle. Though Israel will probably endure continued conflict and tension with its neighbors in the years to come,[4] those who are well acquainted with the message of the scriptures recognize that numer-

---

1. Har-Magedon is the Greek transliteration of the Hebrew for "mountain of Megiddon."
2. Rev. 16:13.
3. Rev. 16:14, 16.
4. See "Prophecies Concerning Israel's Political Affairs," *Prophecy—Key to the Future,* pp. 192-194.

ous major events (plus a host of minor events which have been prophesied) must precede that final conflict. These include:

1. A third World War.[1]
2. The fulfilling of the times of the Gentiles.[2]
3. Internal conflict in the United States and other nations.[3]
4. The establishment of the New Jerusalem and the political kingdom of God.[4]
5. The appearance of Christ in the New Jerusalem.[5]
6. A fourth World War.[6]
7. The return of the Ten Tribes from the north.[7]
8. The calling of 144,000 high priests.[8]
9. Christ's appearance at the council at Adam-ondi-Ahman.[9]
10. The gathering of all the tribes of Israel to the land of Israel.[10]
11. The rule of David the Prince.[11]
12. The construction of the temple in Jerusalem.[12]

Then, and not until then, will the Battle of Armageddon be waged.

This book focuses on America's future, rather than events in Israel and elsewhere, and will not attempt to describe the Battle of Armageddon in detail (a project which could be a complete book). Yet that prophesied conflict is of such major import that it deserves at least summary consideration in this chapter on wars which have been prophesied.

Greed will be the motive for the war, and Ezekiel prophesied that Israel's enemies will come

> To take a spoil, and to take a prey; to turn thine hand upon the desolate places that are now inhabited, and upon the people that are

---

1. See pp. 285-309, *Prophecy—Key to the Future*, pp. 1-16.
2. See *Prophecy—Key to the Future*, pp. 17-34.
3. See pp. 293-302, 309-315, *Prophecy—Key to the Future*, pp. 49-66.
4. See pp. 315-323, *Prophecy—Key to the Future*, pp. 67-105.
5. See *Prophecy—Key to the Future*, pp. 112-117.
6. See pp. 323-333, *Prophecy—Key to the Future*, pp. 159-166.
7. See *Prophecy—Key to the Future*, pp. 117-121.
8. See *Prophecy—Key to the Future*, pp. 121-125.
9. See *Prophecy—Key to the Future*, pp. 167-176.
10. See *Prophecy—Key to the Future*, pp. 127-139, 177-179, 182-189.
11. See *Prophecy—Key to the Future*, pp. 179-182.
12. See *Prophecy—Key to the Future*, pp. 189-192.

gathered out of the nations, which have gotten cattle and goods, that dwell in the midst of the land.[1]

The leader of the attacking army is to be "God, the chief prince of Meshech and Tubal."[2] His army will be called "Magog";[3] and will be comprised primarily of people from countries surrounding Israel.[4]

The war, which will continue for three-and-a-half years,[5] will take a heavy toll. Two-thirds of the people of Israel will be slain,[6] and five-sixth's of the attacking army, including its leader, Gog, will fall on the mountains of Israel.[7] The battle will rage in Jerusalem. Zechariah prophesies that "the city shall be taken, and the houses rifled, and the woman ravished; and half of the city shall go forth into captivity, and the residue of the people shall not be cut off from the city."[8] Even a portion of the temple will be overrun by the invaders.[9] Two prophets in Jerusalem will prophesy during the 3½ years, and will have power to withhold rain from the earth and smite with plagues. They will be killed in the conflict. Their bodies will lie unattended in the streets for 3½ days, then life will return to them and they will be caught up to heaven.[10]

During the battle great judgments will be poured out. Not only will the rain be withheld by the two prophets, but God will send pestilence, an over-flowing rain, great hailstones, fire and

---

1. Ezek. 38:12.
2. Ezek. 38:2-3. These geographical terms date back to the "table of nations" found in Genesis 10, and refer to the settling places of the descendants of Noah, who spread across the face of the land following the flood. Meshech and Tubal appear to refer to portions of modern Turkey and southern Russia near the Caspian Sea. It should be remembered that two world wars will transpire before the Battle of Armageddon which will greatly alter the boundaries and stature of the nations of the earth. Present-day attempts to assert that Gog will be of a certain nationality are of little value.
3. Ezek. 39:6.
4. See "Nations Which Will Attack Palestine," *Prophecy—Key to the Future,* pp. 198-202.
5. Rev. 11:2. Note that the time for the Battle of Armageddon is to be longer than that of the fourth World War, or universal conflict, which John prophesies will last for about thirteen months (Rev. 9:15).
6. Zech. 13:7-9.
7. Ezek. 39:1-6.
8. Zech. 14:2.
9. Rev. 11:1-2.
10. Rev. 11:3-12.

brimstone.[1] A great earthquake will level a tenth of the city of Jerusalem, and destroy the cities of other nations at the same time.[2]

Israel will fare poorly in the struggle, and will appear doomed to defeat, when Christ will suddenly appear on the Mount of Olives. The mountain will cleave in two, allowing an avenue of escape for the beleagered Israelites.[3] They will rally as God lends his strength in the fray.[4]

Ezekiel prophesied the eventual fall of the invading army:

> Therefore, thou son of man, prophesy against Gog, and say, Thus saith the Lord God; Behold, I am against thee, O Gog, the chief prince of Meshech and Tubal:
>
> And I will turn thee back, and *leave but the sixth part of thee*, and will cause thee to come up from the north parts, and will bring thee upon the mountains of Israel:
>
> And I will smite thy bow out of thy left hand, and will cause thine arrows to fall out of thy right hand.
>
> *Thou shalt fall upon the mountains of Israel, thou, and all thy bands, and the people that is with thee: I will give thee unto the ravenous birds of every sort, and to the beasts of the field to be devoured.*
>
> Thou shalt fall upon the open field: for I have spoken it, saith the Lord God.[5]

Birds of prey will eat the flesh of the fallen armies,[6] and seven months will be required to bury the dead.[7] It will be a time of great mourning in Israel.[8]

The great Battle of Armageddon, tragic as it will be, will still serve to lead man to the knowledge and acceptance of God's great power. They will see the miraculous aid God will grant unto Israel, and know of his glorious appearance on the Mount of Olives. As the Savior said, after revealing the great judgments that will come upon the invaders,

> Thus will I magnify myself, and sanctify myself; and I will be known in the eyes of many nations, and they shall know that I am the Lord.[9]

---

1. Ezek. 38:22; Rev. 16:21; Zech. 14:12, 15.
2. Rev. 11:13; 16:19.
3. Zech. 14:4-5, D & C 45:47-50.
4. Zech. 12:8.
5. Ezek. 39:1-5.
6. Ezek. 39:17-20; Rev. 19:17-18.
7. Ezek. 39:9-16.
8. Zech. 12:10-14.
9. Ezek. 38:23. This concept, that God will "magnify himself" or "make bare his arm" in the eyes of all nations, is frequently expressed in connection with the Battle of Armageddon and at times becomes a "code word" for that event in scriptural allusions.

And also:

> And I will set my glory among the heathen, and *all the heathen shall see my judgment that I have executed,* and my hand that I have laid upon them.
>
> So the house of Israel shall know that I am the Lord their God from that day and forward.
>
> *And the heathen shall know* that the house of Israel went into captivity for their iniquity; because they trespassed against me, therefore hid I my face from them, and gave them into the hand of their enemies: so fell they all by the sword.
>
> According to their uncleanness and according to their transgressions have I done unto them, and hid my face from them.
>
> Therefore thus saith the Lord God; Now will I bring again the captivity of Jacob, and have mercy upon the whole house of Israel, and will be jealous of my holy name;
>
> After that they have borne their shame, and all their trespasses whereby they have trespassed against me, when they dwelt safely in their land, and none made them afraid.
>
> *When I have brought them again from the people, and gathered them out of their enemies' lands, and am sanctified in them in the sight of many nations;*
>
> *Then shall they know that I am the Lord their God,* which caused them to be led into captivity among the heathen: but I have gathered them unto their own land, and have left none of them any more there.
>
> *Neither will I hide my face any more from them:* for I have poured out my spirit upon the house of Israel, saith the Lord God.[1]

Summary

1. God has sworn to send wars upon the earth in the last days "until the consumption decreed hath made a full end of all nations." These conflicts will serve as judgments upon those who do evil and who harden their hearts. "The wicked shall slay the wicked, and fear shall come upon every man."

2. The scriptures and the prophets have warned of five future major conflicts, or periods of warfare:

    A.   A Third World War.
    B.   Internal conflict in the Americas.
    C.   A Fourth World War during the New Jerusalem period.
    D.   World-wide conflict related to the fall of the great and abominable church.
    E.   The Battle of Armageddon.

---

1. Ezek. 39:21-29.

3. There are to be two types of warfare in the last days:
- A. Preparatory Wars, which prepare the way for the preaching of the gospel, and
- B. Wars of Complete Destruction, which punish the wicked and result in great desolation.

4. A Third World War, between Russia and her allies and America and her allies has been repeatedly prophesied. Prophesied characteristics of this future war are to include the following:
- A. An initial attack by Russia.
- B. Each of the major powers will bomb the other's homeland.
- C. Much of the war will be fought in the air and in the sea.
- D. The war will be a great and bloody war.
- E. The United States will appear to be losing the war in its initial stages.
- F. Many spies and traitors will be apprehended in the United States.
- G. A major portion of the U.S. army will give up.
- H. God will intervene and enter the conflict, helping America to achieve the victory.
- I. A major force will suddenly rise in America's west to counteract enemy invasion.
- J. Russia will go down to defeat, never to rise in such power again.
- K. Missionaries will go into Russia, preaching the gospel to the house of Israel there.

5. The probability of nuclear warfare during this conflict, as the major powers bomb their enemy's homelands, is great. Some of the prophetic warnings describe scenes and events which appear to be atomic warfare with the resulting effects of radiation.

6. Russia is presently on a war footing and has developed a major military force. The balance of military power is rapidly shifting in Russia's favor, and she has established momentum which military experts assert will give her definite superiority within a few years.

7. Of particular concern is Russia's extensive civil defense preparations, as compared to very limited civil defense capability in the United States. According to recent studies, a Russian nuclear

attack on America might be reasonably expected to produce 72,000,000 casualties, while losses in an American attack on Russia could be limited to as few as 4,000,000. The strategic assumption that Russia would not risk a nuclear attack on the U.S. because of losses she would suffer in retaliatory strikes is being abandoned.

8. Some prophetic warnings establish the relationship between World War III and later internal conflict in the United States, indicating that national revolutions will result as the international war breaks down, and that the strife and destruction of the world war will establish conditions of shortages, famine, economic instability, and antagonism which will lead to the internal conflict.

9. Chronological relationships in the prophetic warnings indicate that internal conflict in the United States (and hence World War III which will precede the internal conflict) will occur prior to the return to the New Jerusalem.

10. The Savior prophesied that the remnant of Jacob [the Lamanites] will reclaim much of the Americas as the land of their inheritance as they rise up to destroy transportation, military strongholds, and cities.

11. The internal conflict in the United States has been depicted as local strife and anarchy, with mob rule and pillaging bands making it impossible for the nation to continue the pursuit of manufacturing, farming, and commerce effectively. Even family members will slay one another. The spectre of widespread famine is clearly raised in the prophetic warnings, and may explain the reason for much of the strife.

12. Early Church leaders repeatedly prophesied the complete destruction of U.S. Government and the end of this nation as it presently exists. As the internal conflict brings government control to an end, it is prophesied that the saints will be able to maintain a higher level of stability. They will form a government, a political "Kingdom of God," which will maintain liberty and constitutional principles, and will increase in influence as people rally to its standard. There will be a transfer of rule to the saints, in preparation for Christ's millennial rule.

13. During the period of third World War and/or internal conflicts, areas will be swept clean of their populations, leaving them

desolate. Independence, Missouri is prophesied to be one such area. The saints will return and there build a great city, the New Jerusalem. Desolate areas nearby will also be inhabited.

14. The saints will be organized in military fashion during the return to Jackson County. Their army will become very great, and will be regarded with fear and terror by the other nations.

15. The New Jerusalem will serve as a place of refuge to which people from throughout the world will flee to escape the destruction of a fourth World War. God's power will be upon the city protecting it, but it will be the only place that is not at war as a fourth World War rages.

16. John the Revelator prophesied of a war which would last for thirteen months and which would slay the third part of men. His prophecy indicates some type of geographical link with the River Euphrates.

17. The saints will be persecuted by the great and abominable church, even prior to the return to Jackson County. The wrath of God will finally be turned against that wicked organization during the fourth World War. Nations assembled to fight against the saints will turn on each other and wage war, causing the great church to collapse. Ten kings who had previously warred against the saints will destroy the capitol city of the great and abominable church.

18. The Battle of Armageddon is a conflict which will take place in the land of Israel following the fourth World War, the return of the Jews and Ten Tribes to their homeland, and the construction of the Jerusalem temple. It will take place during the rule of David the Prince. The battle draws its prophetic name from Megiddo, a fortress in the plain of Esdraelon. This war is the most prophesied event in all scripture.

19. The enemy army, Magog, will be led by a general named Gog. His army will advance on Jerusalem and capture most of the city. A sudden appearance by the Savior on the Mount of Olives will aid the Israelites, enabling them to rally and win the war. Two-thirds of Israel will be slain while Gog and five-sixths of his army will fall on the mountains of Israel.

20. The Battle of Armageddon will show the heathen nations that the Lord is God. They will be receptive to missionary work after learning of the Lord's divine intervention during the conflict.

XV

Pestilence and the Lord's Desolating Scourge

The two preceding chapters, with this one, examine the three major instruments of God's judgments upon the wicked: famine, sword, and pestilence. Less is said of the third of these instruments than of the other two, but the prophesied impact of the ravages of pestilence upon the wicked nations of the world obviously will be tremendous.

The Lord has said unto the nations of the earth,

> *How oft have I called upon you* by the mouth of my servants, and by the ministering of angels, and by mine own voice, and by the voice of thunderings, and by the voice of lightnings, and by the voice of tempests, and by the voice of earthquakes, and great hailstorms, *and by the voice of famines and pestilences of every kind,* and by the great sound of a trump, and by the voice of judgment, and by the voice of mercy all the day long, and by the voice of glory and honor and the riches of eternal life, and would have saved you with an everlasting salvation, but ye would not?
>
> *Behold, the day has come, when the cup of the wrath of mine indignation is full.*[1]

Sickness and pestilence, then, are tools with which God chastens his people and chastizes the wicked of the earth.

Warnings of Pestilence in the Last Days

The Lord has revealed that pestilence is to be expected in the last days:

> Behold, I speak for mine elect's sake; for nation shall rise against nation, and kingdom against kingdom; *there shall be famines, and pestilences, and earthquakes, in divers places.*
>
> And again, *because iniquity shall abound, the love of many shall wax cold;* but he that shall not be overcome, the same shall be saved.[2]

---

1. D & C 43:25-26.
2. JS 1:29-30.

Repeated warnings of future disease and pestilence have been given in numerous private manifestations and through patriarchs of the Church. Such warnings are intended as private counsel and not as official Church doctrine. Yet here again, as with prophetic warnings of a third World War and of internal conflict within the United States, the saints should certainly be aware that this widespread pattern of personal revelation exists. The following brief excerpts from patriarchal blessings are typical of the pattern:

> You will live upon the earth to see scourge after scourge of sickness poured out upon the world, and *the saints will hardly escape, for many will fall by the plague*—even on your right hand and on your left.

Also:

> You will see the scourge of sickness poured out from time to time and you will *see the wicked swept from under Heaven in the twinkling of an eye, time and time again.*

And again:

> ...you will live as long as life is desirable, and the scourges of the day in which you live will pass by you, as the scourge did in the days of the Israelites in Egypt, and not slay you. *You will see famines stalk abroad on the land. You will see the pestilence of earthquakes and upheavals in the earth.*

Another warns,

> You will live to see the nations of the earth scourged for their sins. You will *live to see epidemics go forth that will baffle the skill of doctors and will sweep the inhabitants of the earth into the spirit world by thousands....* You will have the blessings of the earth through your long life and hunger will never be forced upon you by *the scourge or the scourges of hunger that will afflict man.*

Yet another tells of the Ten Tribes coming from the north to Zion, and says, "You will see the *earth cleansed by a scourge of sickness before their coming* to make room for a dwelling place for them."

These brief excerpts should suffice as an indication that a broad pattern of personal warnings exists. God is moving at many levels and in many ways to prepare his people for the days of trouble and distress which are coming.

The Lord's Desolating Scourge

A scriptural pattern of prophecy exists which warns of a specific disease identified in modern revelation as "the Lord's desolating scourge." One revelation, given even before the restoration of the Church, warns of the judgment that will go forth upon the earth if men harden their hearts against the gospel:

> ...*A desolating scourge shall go forth* among the inhabitants of the earth, and *shall continue to be poured out from time to time,* if they repent not, *until the earth is empty, and the inhabitants thereof are consumed away* and utterly destroyed by the brightness of my coming.[1]

An 1831 revelation spoke of sickness that will come after the time of the Gentiles have been fulfilled:

> ...There shall be men standing in that generation, that shall not pass until *they shall see an overflowing scourge, for a desolating sickness shall cover the land.*
> But my disciples shall stand in holy places, and shall not be moved; but *among the wicked, men shall lift up their voices and curse God and die.*[2]

A year later, in September, 1832, the Lord revealed that

> ...I, the Almighty, have laid my hands upon the nations, *to scourge them* for their wickedness.
> And plagues shall go forth, and they shall not be taken from the earth until I have completed my work, which shall be cut short in righteousness—[3]

Of particular concern to Church members is the realization that several revelations warn of the possibility of this terrible scourge being visited upon the saints because of disobedience. A warning to the Church in 1832 was sobering:

> ...Your minds in times past have been darkened because of unbelief, and because you have treated lightly the things you have received—
> *Which vanity and unbelief have brought the whole church under condemnation.*
> *And this condemnation resteth upon the children of Zion, even all.*

---

1. D & C 5:19. Concerning this warning, the Lord promised that "my word shall be verified at this time as it hath hitherto been verified." (D & C 5:20)
2. D & C 45:31-32.
3. D & C 84:96-97.

> *And they shall remain under this condemnation until they repent and remember the new covenant, even the Book of Mormon and the former commandments which I have given them, not only to say, but to do according to that which I have written—*
>
> That they may bring forth fruit meet for their Father's kingdom; *otherwise there remaineth a scourge and judgment to be poured out upon the children of Zion.*
>
> For shall the children of the kingdom pollute my holy land? Verily, I say unto you, Nay.[1]

A year later, the Lord warned the saints that his scourge would come upon the world, and cautioned the saints that if they were not obedient, they would be afflicted with pestilence and plague:

> For behold, and lo, vengeance cometh speedily upon the ungodly as the whirlwind; and who shall escape it?
>
> *The Lord's scourge shall pass over by night and by day, and the report thereof shall vex all people; yea, it shall not be stayed until the Lord come;*
>
> For the indignation of the Lord is kindled against their abominations and all their wicked works.
>
> Nevertheless, Zion shall escape *if* she observe to do all things whatsoever I have commanded her.
>
> But *if* she observe not to do whatsoever I have commanded her, *I will visit her according to all her works, with sore affliction, with pestilence, with plague, with sword, with vengeance, with devouring fire.*[2]

A remark made by President Heber C. Kimball is significant in this context:

> If the Saints will repent, the Lord's wrath will be turned away, but *they will not repent until it is too late.*[3]

Biblical passages also speak of this terrible desolating scourge. Reference has previously been made to Isaiah's prophecy,[4] in which he speaks of men who will think to escape the scourge by making a "covenant" with death and hell. But he warns,

> And your covenant with death shall be disannulled, and your agreement with hell shall not stand; *when the overflowing scourge shall pass through, then ye shall be trodden down by it.*

---

1. D & C 84:54-59. See also D & C 112:24-26, 1 Pet. 4:17. Note that the last two verses allude to Zion, possibly associating the time of the scourge to the return to that land.
2. D & C 97:22-26.
3. Orson F. Whitney, *Life of Heber C. Kimball* (Salt Lake City, Utah: Bookcraft, 1967), p. 446.
4. See pp. 247-250.

> From the time that it goeth forth it shall take you: for morning by morning shall it pass over, by day and by night: and *it shall be a vexation only to understand the report.* [1]

Isaiah concludes his reference to the scourge with the observation that "I have heard from the Lord God of hosts *a consumption, even determined upon the whole earth.*"[2]

Another chapter of Isaiah pronounces a "woe" to "the land shadowing with wings," a reference Church commentators have ascribed to America because of important illusions in the context.[3] In his prophecy, the population is compared to a grapevine. Isaiah pronounces this warning of destruction to come upon the land in the era people are to be gathered[4] to Mount Zion:

> For afore the harvest, when the bud is perfect, and the sour grape is ripening in the flower, *he shall both cut off the sprigs with pruning hooks, and take away and cut down the branches.*
> *They shall be left together unto the fowls of the mountains, and to the beasts of the earth: and the fowls shall summer upon them, and all the beasts of the earth shall winter upon them.* [5]

Elder Orson Pratt, while expounding Isaiah's prophecy, said that God will visit the American continents

> ...with judgments that are terribly severe that will cause them to *lie by hundreds and thousands unberied* [sic], *from one end of the land to the other,* to be meat for the fowls of the air and the beasts of the earth. Why? Because *the judgments will be swift, giving no time for burial.*
> Inquires one—"Do you really believe that such judgments are coming upon our nation?" I do not merely believe, but I know it. [6]

The devastating effects of the terrible disease(s) which will be poured out will not be felt just in America. It should be recalled

---

1. Is. 28:18-19. Note the strong parallel in the wording between this passage and D & C 97:23.
2. Is. 28:22.
3. See *JD* 17:318-319, *JD* 2:295. Note characteristics of the land in the prophecy: it sends out messengers [missionaries] to "a nation scattered and peeled" [scattered Israel], it lifts an ensign on the mountains, and it has a Mount Zion. Yet it is not Palestine, but "beyond the rivers of Ethiopia." What other nation but America could this be? No other possibility even presents itself.
4. See Is. 18:7. This verse, then, helps to fix the time of the prophetic fulfillment.
5. Is. 18:5-6.
6. *JD* 17:319. February 28, 1875.

that Wilford Woodruff, when he saw the scene in vision, "Was given to understand that *the same horrors that were here enacted were all over the world, east, west, north, and south.—That few were left alive,—still there were some.*[1]

John the Revelator prophesied a series of plagues which are to come upon the earth in the beginning of the seventh thousand years of the earth's existence.[2] They will constitute the first of three "woes" which he pronounced:

> The first angel sounded, and there followed hail and fire mingled with blood, and they were cast upon the earth: and the *third part of trees was burnt up, and all green grass was burnt up.*
>
> And the second angel sounded, and as it were a great mountain burning with fire was cast into the *sea: and the third part of the sea became blood;*
>
> *And the third part of the creatures which were in the sea, and had* life, died; and the third part of the ships were destroyed.
>
> And the third angel sounded, and there fell a great star from heaven, burning as it were a lamp, and *it fell upon the third part of the rivers, and upon the fountains of waters;*
>
> And the name of the star is called Wormwood: and the third part of the waters became wormwood; and many men died of the waters, *because they were made bitter.*
>
> And the fourth angel sounded, and the third part of the sun was smitten, and the third part of the moon, and the third part of the stars; so as *the third part of them was darkened,* and the day shone not for a third part of it, and the night likewise.
>
> And I beheld, and heard an angel flying through the midst of heaven, saying with a loud voice, Woe, woe, woe, to the inhabiters of the earth by reason of the other voices of the trumpet of the three angels, which are yet to sound!
>
> And the fifth angel sounded, and I saw a star fall from heaven unto the earth: and to him was given the key of the bottomless pit.
>
> And he opened the bottomless pit; and there arose a smoke out of the pit, as the smoke of a great furnace; and the *sun and the air were darkened by reason of the smoke of the pit.*
>
> *And there came out of the smoke locusts upon the earth: and unto them was given power,* as the scorpions of the earth have power.
>
> And it was commanded them that they should not hurt the grass of the earth, neither any green thing, neither any tree; but *only those men which have not the seal of God in their foreheads.*
>
> And to them it was given that they should not kill them, but that *they should be tormented five months: and their torment was as the torment of a scorpion, when he striketh a man.*

---

1. Revelation to Wilford Woodruff December 16, 1878. See pp. 294-296.
2. See D & C 77:12-13. These plagues are to follow the sealing of the 144,000 (see Rev. 7:2-8) and hence, the return of the Ten Tribes.

And in those days shall men seek death, and shall not find it; and shall desire to die, and death shall flee from them.

And the shapes of the locusts were like unto horses prepared unto battle; and on their heads were as it were crowns like gold, and their faces were as the faces of men.

And they had hair as the hair of women, and their teeth were as the teeth of lions.

And they had breastplates, as it were breastplates of iron; and the sound of their wings was as the sound of chariots of many horses running to battle.

And they had tails like unto scorpions, and there were stings in their tails: and *their power was to hurt men five months.*

And they had a king over them, which is the angel of the bottomless pit, whose name in the Hebrew tongue is Abaddon, but in the Greek tongue hath his name Apollyon.

One woe is past; and, behold, there come two woes more hereafter.[1]

Descriptions of the Scourge

Various new diseases may be poured out upon the earth in the last days. For instance, the possibility of radiation sickness from nuclear war is also very real.[2] There remain, however, several descriptions in the scriptures and other manifestations which allude to a horrible disease which cannot at present be identified. One such description is in the Doctrine and Covenants, Section 29, which is linked with the fall of the great and abominable church:

But, behold, I say unto you that before this great day shall come the sun shall be darkened, and the moon shall be turned into blood, and the stars shall fall from heaven, and there shall be greater signs in heaven above and in the earth beneath;

And there shall be weeping and wailing among the hosts of men;

And there shall be a great hailstorm sent forth to destroy the crops of the earth.

And it shall come to pass, because of the wickedness of the world, that I will take vengeance upon the wicked, for they will not repent; for the cup of mine indignation is full; for behold, my blood shall not cleanse them if they hear me not.

Wherefore, I the Lord God will send forth flies upon the face of the earth, which shall take hold of the inhabitants thereof, and shall eat their flesh, and shall cause maggots to come in upon them;

And their tongues shall be stayed that they shall not utter against me; and their flesh shall fall from off their bones, and their eyes from their sockets;

---

1. Rev. 8:7-9:12.
2. See pp. 291-293.

And it shall come to pass that the beasts of the forest and the fowls of the air shall devour them up.

And the great and abominable church, which is the whore of all the earth, shall be cast down by devouring fire, according as it is spoken by the mouth of Ezekiel the prophet, who spoke of these things, which have not come to pass but surely must, as I live, for abominations shall not reign.[1]

A similar description, of flesh falling from the bones and eyes falling from their sockets, is found in Zechariah's prophecy of the judgment that will come upon nations which fight against Jerusalem during the Battle of Armageddon:

...This shall be the plague wherewith the Lord will smite all the people that have fought against Jerusalem; *Their flesh shall consume away while they stand upon their feet, and their eyes shall consume away in their holes,* and their tongue shall consume away in their mouth....

And so shall be the plague of the horse, of the mule, of the camel, and of the ass, and *of all the beasts* that shall be in these tents, as this plague.[2]

The prophet Isaiah also describes the period of the Battle of Armageddon, as does Zechariah. He warns that "by fire and by his sword will the Lord plead with all flesh: and the slain of the Lord shall be many."[3] Then, like Zechariah's 14th chapter, he tells how people will go up to Jerusalem following that battle. In doing so, he apparently alludes to the aftermath of the plague, saying:

...They shall go forth, and look upon the carcases of the men that have transgressed against me: *for their worm shall not die, neither shall their fire be quenched;* and they shall be an abhorring unto all flesh.[4]

In the manifestation shown to Charles D. Evans, he was shown a disease with similar symptoms. He saw that

This plague in grown persons *robbed the eyes in their sockets and consumed the tongue as would a powerful acid or an intense heat.* Wicked men suffering under its writhing agonies cursed God and died, or they stood on their feet and birds of prey feasted on their carcasses.[5]

Past Manifestations of the Disease

It appears that the same terrible disease, or one similar to it, has been manifested in past situations in which it was regarded as

1. D & C 29:14-21.
2. Zech. 14:12, 15.
3. Is. 66:16.
4. Is. 66:24.
5. Charles D. Evans, *op. cit.* See p. 292.

the result of God's judgments upon the wicked. Specifically, various cases of the affliction have been reported through the years in connection with the mobocrats who assassinated Joseph Smith. One such account was left by Martha James Cragun, who encountered one of the mobocrats, Jack Reed, in August, 1881:

> About the last of September I heard that Jack Reed was very sick of a strange ailment. He was taken ill in a few days after having made the statement that he took part in the affair at Carthage—but no one had told me of his sickness until I heard it from one of my Indian friends who said he had worms in his flesh. I determined to see him if I could and try to get him to verify the statement he had made at the meeting. The man had no family and Mr. McGuire was his attendant. I asked Mr. McGuire if he would allow Mrs. Whitmore and myself to visit Mr. Reed. *He said that Mr. Reed was a sight that no white woman could be allowed to look upon. He was literally eaten alive by worms. His eye balls had fallen out, the flesh on his cheeks and neck had fallen off and though he could breathe he could take nourishment only through an opening in his throat,* and said McGuire, *"Pieces of flesh as large as my two hands have fallen off from different parts of his body...."* One called "Jack Longstreet" became Reed's first attendant in company with McGuire. To these men Reed confessed that his participation in the murder of the Prophets was the cause of his affliction. *He said to Longstreet: "It is the Mormon curse that is upon me. I cannot live—I must utterly rot before I die."* He said that Brigham Young had pronounced *that curse upon all that mob, and he had known thirteen of them to die just as he was dying.*[1]

Parley P. Pratt, an early apostle, also recorded a similar fate for some of the mobocrats. He wrote of several examples:

> A colonel of the Missouri mob, who helped to drive, plunder and murder the Mormons, died in the hospital at Sacramento, 1849. Beckwith had the care of him; *he was eaten with worms—a large black headed kind of maggot—which passed through him by myriads, seemingly a half pint at a time!* Before he died these maggots were crawling out of his mouth and nose! He literally rotted alive! Even the flesh on his legs burst open and fell from the bones! They gathered up the rotten mass in a blanket and buried him, without awaiting a coffin!
>
> A Mr. ——, one of Missouri mob, died in the same hospital about the same time, and under the care of Mr. Beckwith. *His face and jaw on one side literally rotted, and half of his face actually fell off! One eye rotted out, and half of his nose, mouth and jaw fell from the bones!* The doctor scraped the bones, and unlocked and took out his jaw from

---

1. N.B. Lundwall, comp., "Thirteen Mobocrats Meet a Common Fate," *The Fate of the Persecutors of the Prophet Joseph Smith* (Salt Lake City, Utah: Bookcraft, 1952), pp. 295-296. See also pp. 298, 304, 334-335, 337, which cite other examples.

the joint round to the centre of the chin. *The rot and maggots continued to eat till they ate through the large or jugular vein of his neck, and
he bled to death!* He, as well as Townsend, stank so previous to their
death that they had to be placed in rooms by themselves, and it was
almost impossible to endure their presence, and the flies could not be
kept from blowing them while alive![1]

Even in ancient times, a similar fate was recorded as coming
upon the wicked. The historian Josephus recorded the fatal sickness of the evil King Herod (son of Antipater), as follows:

But now Herod's distemper greatly increased upon him after a severe
manner, and *this by God's judgment upon him for his sins;* for a fire
glowed in him slowly, which did not so much appear to the touch out-
wardly, as it augmented his pains inwardly; for it brought upon him a
vehement appetite to eating, which he could not avoid to supply with
one sort of food or other. *His entrails were also exulcerated, and the
chief violence of his pain lay on his colon; an aqueous and transparent
liquor also had settled itself about his feet, and a like matter afflicted
him at the bottom of his belly. Nay, further, his privy-member was
putrified, and produced worms;* and when he sat upright, he had a difficulty of breathing, which was very loathsome, on account of the stench
of his breath, and the quickness of its returns; he had also convulsions
in all parts of his body, which increased his strength to an insufferable
degree.[2]

With the limited descriptions available, it is impossible to
determine if these examples from the past are the same as those
prophesied for the future judgments. Yet one broad principle is
evident: disease and pestilence are used as instruments of God's
retribution upon the wicked. The record of the past shows that

---

1. *Autobiography of Parley P. Pratt* (Salt Lake City, Utah: Deseret Book
   Company, sixth edition, 1966), p. 425.
2. *The Life and Works of Flavius Josephus* (New York: Holt, Rinehart
   and Winston, n.d.), "Antiquities of the Jews," Book XVII, paragraph
   5, p. 514. In his "Wars of the Jews," Bk. I, paragraph 5, p. 664, he gave
   a similar description:
   After this, *the distemper seized upon his whole body, and greatly
   disordered all its parts with various symptoms;* for there was a gentle
   fever upon him, and an *intolerable itching* over all the surface of his
   body, and *continual pains in his colon, and dropsical tumours about
   his feet, and an inflammation of the abdomen, and a putrefaction
   of his privy member, that produced worms.* Besides which he had a
   difficulty of breathing upon him, and *could not breathe* but when he
   sat upright, and had a convulsion of all his members, insomuch that
   *the diviners said those diseases were a punishment upon him for
   what he had done to the Rabbins.*

they have been used on a limited basis, but prophecies of the future warn that their effect will be widespread as increased wickedness prevails.

Summary

1. The Lord has called the people of the earth by many methods, including preaching, angels, earthquakes, famines, and pestilence, offering the people everlasting salvation, but they would not receive it. The day has now come when the cup of his wrath and indignation is full.

2. The Lord has warned that there shall be wars, famines, pestilences, and earthquakes in the last days. Because iniquity shall abound, the love of many shall grow cold.

3. Many private manifestations and patriarchal blessings warn of future plagues and pestilences which will occur, taking a heavy toll of casualties. Some of these manifestations link the sicknesses to famines.

4. The Lord has warned repeatedly of a terrible last days' disease called the "Lord's desolating scourge." It will cover the land, and will continue to be poured out from time to time until the Lord comes in glory.

5. The Lord has warned his Church that if the members do not repent and obey his commandments, he will scourge them with pestilence, plague, the sword, and with devouring fire.

6. In his vision of the terrible plague which would come upon America, Wilford Woodruff saw that "few were left alive," and that the horrors he saw were to happen all over the world.

7. Isaiah prophesied that destruction will come to America in the era people are to be gathered to Mount Zion. John the Revelator also prophesied a series of plagues which are to come upon the earth in the beginning of the seventh thousand years of the earth's existence.

8. John prophesied that
   A.   A third part of the trees and grass will be burned.
   B.   One-third of the animals of the sea will be destroyed.

C.   One-third of the fresh waters will become bitter, and many men will die from them.

D.   Locusts [or other entities depicted as locusts] will torment those who are not God's servants for five months.

E.   The affliction in those days will be so severe that men will seek death and desire to die.

9. Scriptural descriptions of a terrible last days' disease depict a sickness in which the flesh will fall from men's bones and eyeballs fall from their sockets, while maggots infest them. The disease described is linked chronologically with the third world war, with the fall of the great and abominable church and also with the Battle of Armageddon. Thus it appears to be a constantly-recurring plague.

10. Descriptions of deaths of some of the men who participated in the assassination of Joseph Smith seem to fit the pattern of the prophesied disease, as does Josephus' account of the death of wicked King Herod. It is possible there is a specific disease which God visits upon the wicked. It may be the same plague that will be manifested in the last days.

IV

PERSONAL PREPARATION FOR THE LAST DAYS

XVI

Choosing a Course
For the Future

America stands at the crossroads! Though the last fifteen years was a period of serious moral decay for the nation, it is still possible to cause changes that will bring blessings, rather than cursing, upon the land. But now is the time for action, for if the national rush towards sin and corruption continues at the previous pace, wickedness will soon abound to the degree that the judgments of the last days will be poured out without measure upon us all.

Questions such as these are frequently asked:

"What should *my* attitude be towards the future?"

"What can *I* do to help America escape the terrible judgments which have been prophesied?"

"What should *I* do to protect myself and my family from the suffering which will accompany the judgments?"

"How can *I* prepare for the cataclysmic events which lie ahead?"

This final chapter is written to suggest specific actions that citizens of America and faithful Latter-day Saints can undertake to prepare for the future. It should be observed that every principle suggested is based on counsel and insight God has revealed in the scriptures. He has foreseen, forewarned, and revealed the course his saints should follow in the last days. The principles suggested will be presented in a numbered list, designed to serve as a tangible summary which can be taken and literally applied.

Adopt Attitudes Based on Gospel Principles

The gospel of Jesus Christ provides instruction and insight, telling man how he should conduct himself during the perilous era of the last days. If he will adopt the eternal perspectives revealed in the gospel plan, he will "build his house upon a rock," rather than upon sand,[1] and have stability and meaning to life as the

---

1. See Mt. 7:24-27.

355

judgments are poured out. This section will suggest attitudes and understandings which should prove beneficial.

1. Gain eternal perspective: God directs the affairs of man. There is comfort in the knowledge that God, who created the earth and made man after his own image,[1] sees and knows all things.[2] "All things are before him,"[3] and he "governeth and executeth all things."[4] Though he allows man to exercise his free agency,[5] he maintains ultimate control over the actions and fate of both individuals and nations.[6] He has promised to guide and shape the course of those who live righteously, and has instructed the saints to "let your hearts be comforted; *for all things shall work together for good to them that walk uprightly.*"[7]

2. Gain eternal perspective: God desires to bless and reward man. God seeks the eternal progress and well-being of his people. He has revealed that "this is my work and my glory—to bring to pass the immortality and eternal life of man."[8] The Savior has told the saints they are *"ye whom I delight to bless with the greatest of all blessings, ye that hear me;"*[9] and he has said:

> I, the Lord, am merciful and gracious unto those who fear me, and *delight to honor those who serve me* in righteousness and in truth unto the end.
> *Great shall be their reward and eternal shall be their glory.*[10]

He has said to his people that the fulness of the earth is theirs to use and enjoy, and that "it pleaseth God that he hath given all these things unto man."[11] He would extend his richest blessings to all mankind if they would only accept his overtures:

---

1. D & C 20:17-18.
2. D & C 38:1-3.
3. D & C 88:41.
4. D & C 88:40.
5. D & C 58:28; 104:17.
6. For extensive listings of examples concerning this principle, see the author's book *Prophets and Prophecies of the Old Testament,* p. 91.
7. D & C 100:15. As Paul taught, "All things work together for good to them that love God." (Ro. 8:28) See also D & C 90:24; 105:40; 111:11.
8. Moses 1:39.
9. D & C 41:1. But the same verse contains a strong warning to the saints: saying that *"Ye that hear me not will I curse,* that have professed my name, with the heaviest of all cursings."
10. D & C 76:5-6. Verses 7-10 promise choice blessings to these individuals.
11. D & C 59:16-21.

O, ye nations of the earth, how often would I have gathered you together as a hen gathereth her chickens under her wings, but ye would not!

How oft have I called upon you...by the voice of mercy all the day long, and by the voice of glory and honor and the riches of eternal life, and *would have saved you with an everlasting salvation, but ye would not!*[1]

3. Gain eternal perspective: Last days' judgments are part of man's mortal probation. The prophet Alma explained the probationary nature of mortal life, saying that

...There was a space granted unto man in which he might repent; therefore *this life became a probationary state; a time to prepare to meet God;* a time to prepare for that endless state which has been spoken of by us, which is after the resurrection of the dead.[2]

God has revealed to the saints that they must be tested and refined through that testing process:

...I have decreed in my heart, saith the Lord, that *I will prove you in all things, whether you will abide in my covenant, even unto death, that you may be found worthy.*

For if ye will not abide in my covenant ye are not worthy of me.[3]

Indeed, remaining faithful in tribulation appears to be a necessary requirement for gaining the highest of eternal rewards. A revelation from the Lord teaches that

...Blessed is he that keepeth my commandments, whether in life or in death; and *he that is faithful in tribulation, the reward of the same is greater in the kingdom of heaven.*

Ye cannot behold with your natural eyes, for the present time, the design of your God concerning those things which shall come hereafter, and *the glory which shall follow after much tribulation.*

For after much tribulation come the blessings. Wherefore the day cometh that ye shall be crowned with much glory; the hour is not yet, but is nigh at hand.[4]

4. Gain eternal perspective: God chastens those he loves. Our Heavenly Father loves his children who are here on earth. His son,

1. D & C 43:24-25. See Mt. 23:37.
2. Al. 12:24. See also 2 Ne. 2:21; 9:27; 33:9; Al. 42:4; Hel. 13:38; D & C 29:42-44.
3. D & C 98:14-15.
4. D & C 58:2-4. See also D & C 103:11-14.

Jesus Christ, also loves his people—those who are "children of Christ" through the gospel covenant.[1] Like any loving parent, they seek to teach and encourage man, sometimes correcting his conduct and directing him towards the proper course of behavior.

This correcting process will be a part of the judgments of the last days and will ultimately prove to be a blessing for the saints who heed the warning message. The Master has revealed,

> Verily, thus saith the Lord unto you whom I love, and *whom I love I also chasten that their sins may be forgiven,* for with the chastisement *I prepare a way for their deliverance* in all things out of temptation....[2]

He has said that

> *My people must be tried in all things,* that they may be prepared to receive the glory that I have for them, even the glory of Zion; and *he that will not bear chastisement is not worthy of my kingdom.*[3]

The chastening process has previously been experienced in the Church in connection with the failure to properly establish the New Jerusalem. Yet "Zion shall be redeemed, although she is chastened for a little season."[4] The early problem concerning Jackson County, in which the saints were driven out by their enemies, provided the basis for a revelation in which the Lord explained the relationship between chastening and the sanctification process:

> Verily I say unto you, concerning your brethren who have been afflicted, and persecuted, and cast out from the land of their inheritance—
> *I, the Lord, have suffered the affliction to come upon them, wherewith they have been afflicted, in consequence of their transgressions;*
> Yet I will own them, and they shall be mine in that day when I shall come to make up my jewels.
> Therefore, they must needs be chastened and tried, even as Abraham, who was commanded to offer up his only son.
> *For all those who will not endure chastening, but deny me, cannot be sanctified.*[5]

The saints must obtain confidence that the chastening which will come will ultimately bless them if they endure it in faith. As the Lord told Joseph Smith concerning the great tribulations he suffered:

---

1. See Mos. 5:5-7.
2. D & C 95:1.
3. D & C 136:31.
4. D & C 100:13. See D & C 103:4.
5. D & C 101:1-5.

...Know thou, my son, that all these things shall give thee experience, and shall be for thy good.

The Son of Man hath descended below them all. Art thou greater than he?[1]

5. Gain eternal perspective: Death is sweet to those who die in the Lord. All men must die. Death is an essential element of the eternal plan of salvation, for it is also birth into the next phase of man's probationary existence, the spirit world. For the righteous, it constitutes entrance into Paradise, where man can progress more rapidly than in mortality, and where he will experience greater joy than here on earth. Yes, man should make it his goal to live his mortal life well and fulfill his life's mission with honor, but his more advanced goal is to leave this "frail existence" and to partake of the increased blessings available in the spirit world.

As the time approaches for the earth to end its temporal existence, God will increase the pace of entrance into the next phase of life, sweeping millions of mortals, both righteous[2] and wicked, into the spirit existence through the varied judgments of the last days. For the righteous, death will be a blessing and a much-desired release from sorrow and tribulation as these events occur. The wicked will also seek death, but will be without hope and will fear it.[3]

The saints can bless and prepare themselves by learning about death and life after death. Joseph Smith taught that "it is important that we should understand...our departure hence...and *it is a subject we ought to study more than any other*."[4]

Concerning those who die, the Lord has revealed that

...If they die they shall die unto me, and if they live they shall live unto me.

Thou shalt live together in love, insomuch that thou shalt weep for the loss of them that die, and more especially for those that have not hope of a glorious resurrection.

---

1. D & C 122:7-8. See verses 1-7.
2. The belief that the righteous will be completely spared from the judgments of the last days is incorrect, and in direct contradiction to dozens of the scriptural passages previously cited in this book. God alluded to the death of many of the righteous when he revealed that "the day of my visitation cometh speedily, in an hour when ye think not of; and where shall be the safety of my people, and refuge for those *who shall be left of them?*" (D & C 124:10.)
3. Rev. 9:6. See also Morm. 2:13-15; 6:7.
4. *HC* 6:50. October 9, 1843.

> And it shall come to pass that *those that die in me shall not taste of death, for it shall be sweet unto them;*
> *And they that die not in me, wo unto them, for their death is bitter.*[1]

God has promised that

> ...All they who suffer persecution for my name, and endure in faith, though they are called to lay down their lives for my sake yet they shall partake of all this glory.
> Wherefore, *fear not even unto death;* for in this world your joy is not full, but in me your joy is full.
> Therefore, *care not for the body, neither the life of the body; but care for the soul, and for the life of the soul.*
> And seek the face of the Lord always, that in patience ye may possess your souls, and ye shall have eternal life.[2]

His instruction has been to

> Let no man be afraid to lay down his life for my sake; for whoso layeth down his life for my sake shall find it again.
> And whoso is not willing to lay down his life for my sake is not my disciple.[3]

6. Gain eternal perspective: There must be a transition to Christ's millennial kingdom. While the prospect of upheaval and chaos in America is extremely unpleasant to contemplate, yet the realization that it will serve as the transition to the Savior's personal rule on earth places it in the necessary perspective. Jesus has revealed,

> Wherefore, hear my voice and follow me, and *you shall be a free people, and ye shall have no laws but my laws when I come,* for I am your lawgiver, and what can stay my hand?[4]

His promise is that "I will be your ruler when I come; and behold, I come quickly, and ye shall see that my law is kept."[5] Concerning the saints, he has promised that "the Lord shall be in their midst, and his glory shall be upon them, and *he will be their*

---

1. D & C 42:44-47.
2. D & C 101:35-38. See Al. 24:7-27.
3. D & C 103:27-28. See also D & C 101:10-16; 63:2-4; 49-51; 84:80-84; Mt. 6:25-34; 10:38-39; 16:24-27; 3 Ne. 12:30.
4. D & C 38:22.
5. D & C 41:4.

king and their lawgiver."[1] "The Lord, even the Savior, shall stand in the midst of his people, and shall reign over all flesh."[2]

The judgments which will come upon America will serve to cleanse her, eliminating much of the wicked and criminal element which would not abide by the Savior's rule. The ultimate result will be a change from the present telestrial level to the blessings of the terrestrial level which the earth will enjoy during the millennium.[3]

7. **Gain eternal perspective: The earth is approaching the end of its temporal existence.** It is difficult to understand the events of the last days unless those events are viewed in the light of God's eternal plan. The Lord has revealed that the earth only is to exist under present mortal conditions for a very short period, for he has referred to "the seven thousand years of its continuance, or its temporal existence."[4] Sometime in the beginning of the final thousand years, Christ is to come in glory and rule for a millennium in righteousness.[5] The earth will then undergo a dramatic change,[6] passing away[7] and then being recreated, or resurrected, as a celestial earth.[8] It will be removed from its present location and "placed in the cluster of the celestial kingdoms,"[9] and there complete its eternal mission, serving as an everlasting home for exalted, celestialized beings.[10]

---

1. D & C 45:59.
2. D & C 133:25.
3. "The earth will be renewed and receive its paradisiacal glory." (Article of Faith 10)
4. D & C 77:6.
5. D & C 29:11.
6. As Elder Orson Pratt explained,
   Not only will the elements melt with fervent heat, but *the great globe itself will pass away. It will cease to exist as an organized world.* It will cease to exist as one of the worlds that are capable of being inhabited. Fire devours all things, converting the earth into its original elements; it passes away into space.
   But not one particle of the elements which compose the earth will be destroyed or annihilated. They will all exist and be brought together again by a greater organizing power than is known to man. *The earth must be resurrected again,* as well as our bodies; *its elements will be re-united,* and they will be brought together by the power of God's word. (*JD* 18:346-347. February 25, 1877.)
7. D & C 29:26; 88:25-26.
8. D & C 88:18-19.
9. Brigham Young, *JD* 17:117. June 28, 1874.
10. D & C 88:19-20.

Seen from this perspective, mortal existence upon the earth is a transitory experience—only a brief but important interlude in God's eternal plan. Problems of the world today, such as the "population explosion," the danger of exhausting world food and mineral supplies, and similar concerns, take on a different perspective when viewed with the realization that God's plan does not call for this earth to continue as a mortal habitation much longer than another thousand years. We can have confidence in the Lord's indication that "the earth is full, and *there is enough and to spare;* yea, I have prepared all things."[1]

8. Gain eternal perspective: Look forward to the blessings of the millennial era. As the sorrows of last days' tribulation approach, there is comfort in looking past them to the glorious blessings of the millennial era. The revelations teach that *"he that liveth when the Lord shall come, and hath kept the faith, blessed is he."*[2] It will be a time of peace and harmonious living, and God has revealed that *"they shall not hurt nor destroy* in all my holy mountain; for the earth shall be full of the knowledge of the Lord."[3] Satan will be bound,[4] and men "shall *not labour in vain,* nor bring forth for trouble."[5] After the Savior comes "that same *sociality* which exists among us here will exist among us there, only it will be coupled with eternal glory."[6] The Lord has promised that "you shall be a *free people,* and ye shall have no laws but my laws."[7] The great Jehovah has sworn that in that era "I will pour out my *spirit upon all flesh,"*[8] and "in that day when the Lord shall come, he shall *reveal all things.*"[9] Indeed, it will be the "time to come in the which nothing shall be withheld."[10] During the millennial era "there shall be *no sorrow because there is no death,"*[11] and "for the space of a thousand years the *earth shall rest.*"[12]

Look forward, past the strife and sorrow of the days of chastisement and cleansing. Focus on the joys of the millennial era, live to be worthy to partake of them, and kindle a hope that the glorious day will soon come.

---

1. D & C 104:17.
2. D & C 63:50.
3. Is. 11:9; 65:25.
4. Rev. 20:1-3. See D & C 101:28.
5. Is. 65:23.
6. D & C 130:2.
7. D & C 38:22.
8. Joel 2:28.
9. D & C 101:32.
10. D & C 121:28.
11. D & C 101:29.
12. Moses 7:64.

Spiritual Preparations for Survival

It must be remembered that the cataclysmic events of the last days are God's judgments upon the wicked. He will send them upon men, and the inhabitants of the earth shall *"be made to feel the wrath, and indignation, and chastening hand of an Almighty God"*[1] in *"the day when the wrath of God shall be poured out upon the wicked without measure."*[2]

Man's wickedness will bring the judgments. Individual righteousness is the only valid shield against them. National righteousness is the only deterent that will prevent their being poured out upon the land.

Personal preparedness through righteous living, being obedient to God's commandments, and being attuned to receive guidance from the Holy Ghost hold the key to survival during the troubled times to come. In these areas the Lord has given much counsel in the scriptures.

9. Cleanse yourself from sins which will bring judgments: Repent. Counsel given by revelation has a vital message for God's people today. The Lord has commanded the saints to

> *Cleanse your hearts and your garments, lest the blood of this generation be required at your hands.*
> Be faithful until I come, for I come quickly; and my reward is with me to recompense every man according as his work shall be.[3]

His commandment has been emphatic:

> *...I command you to repent—repent, lest I smite you* by the rod of my mouth, and by my wrath, and by my anger, *and your sufferings be sore*—how sore you know not, how exquisite you know not, yea, how hard to bear you know not.[4]

His warning is that the judgments will extend to every man who fails to cleanse his life:

> ...Surely *every man must repent or suffer,* for I, God, am endless.
> Wherefore I revoke not the judgments which I shall pass, but woes shall go forth, weeping, wailing and gnashing of teeth, yea, to those who are found on my left hand.[5]

---

1. D & C 87:6.

2. D & C 1:9.

3. D & C 112:33-34.

4. D & C 19:15.

5. D & C 19:4-5.

The commandment to repent is given especially to the saints, with the admonition, "Wherefore, *let the church repent of their sins*, and I, the Lord, will own them, otherwise they shall be cut off."[1] The unrepentant saints will lack the inspiration and strength of testimony needed to sustain them when the trials come, for the Lord has warned that "he that repents not, from him shall be taken even the light which he has received; for my Spirit shall not always strive with man...."[2] But for those who will repent of all their sins, his promise is that "I will go before you and be your rearward; and I will be in your midst, and you shall not be confounded."[3]

Here, then, is the grand key to survival—those who will not repent will reap God's judgments, but those who will repent will receive God's guidance and protection in the perilous period ahead. But even the repentant must maintain themselves beyond sin, for the Lord has commanded,

> Abide ye in the liberty wherewith ye are made free; *entangle not yourselves in sin, but let your hands be clean, until the Lord comes.*[4]

10. Escape judgments through obedience: Keep God's commandments. Obedience to God's commandments will also provide the avenue for escape from the judgments to come. A revelation warns that

> ...The indignation of the Lord is kindled against their abominations and all their wicked works.
>
> Nevertheless, *Zion shall escape if she observe to do all things whatsoever I have commanded her.*[5]

While warning of sin, pride, covetousness, and detestable things among the saints, the Lord stressed that repentance and obedience are the keys to escaping his judgments:

> Verily I say unto you, that *I, the Lord, will chasten them and will do whatsoever I list, if they do not repent and observe all things whatsoever I have said unto them.*
>
> And again I say unto you, *if ye observe to do whatsoever I command you, I, the Lord, will turn away all wrath and indignation from you,* and the gates of hell shall not prevail against you.[6]

---

1. D & C 63:63. See D & C 84:55-59.
2. D & C 1:33.
3. D & C 49:26-27.
4. D & C 88:86.
5. D & C 97:24-25.
6. D & C 98:21-22.

Obedience to every commandment God reveals will be the test which the saints must meet, as the Lord proves them with the trials of the last days:

> ...I give unto you a commandment, that ye shall forsake all evil and cleave unto all good, that *ye shall live by every word which proceedeth forth out of the mouth of God.*
>
> For he will give unto the faithful line upon line, precept upon precept; and *I will try you and prove you herewith.*
>
> And whoso layeth down his life in my cause, for my name's sake, shall find it again, even life eternal.[1]

Just as God's guidance is pledged for the repentant, he has promised to shape events for the benefit of the obedient in the last days:

> Keep all the commandments and covenants by which ye are bound; and *I will cause the heavens to shake for your good,* and Satan shall tremble and Zion shall rejoice upon the hills and flourish.[2]

But loss of the faith and the triumph of their enemies await those who fail to render obedience:

> Be diligent in keeping all my commandments, *lest judgments come upon you, and your faith fail you, and your enemies triumph over you.*[3]

11. Be free from the sins of the generation: Sanctify yourselves. Sanctification is the process whereby men "yield their hearts unto God,"[4] so that the Holy Ghost helps them to deny themselves of all ungodliness and thus become holy individuals[5] able to stand spotless before God.[6] Their garments are "washed white through the blood of the Lamb" and sin becomes abhorrent to them.[7]

In the last days context, the Lord has warned that "all those who will not endure chastening, but deny me, cannot be sanctified."[8] Concerning the day of his coming in glory, he has revealed that "the day soon cometh that ye shall see me, and know that I am; for the veil of darkness shall soon be rent, and *he that is not purified shall not abide the day.*[9]

---

1. D & C 98:11-13. See D & C 45:2, 6.
2. D & C 35:24.
3. D & C 136:42.
4. Hel. 3:35.
5. Moro. 10:32-33.
6. 3 Ne. 27:20.
7. Al. 13:11-12.
8. D & C 101:5.
9. D & C 38:8.

Their being sanctified will enable the saints to be found free from the blood and sins of this wicked generation. The Lord has revealed,

> *Behold, I will hasten my work in its time.*
> And I give unto you, who are the first laborers in this last kingdom, a commandment that you assemble yourselves together, and organize yourselves, and prepare yourselves, and *sanctify yourselves; yea, purify your hearts, and cleanse your hands and your feet before me, that I may make you clean;*
> *That I may testify unto your Father, and your God, and my God, that you are clean from the blood of this wicked generation;...*[1]

The sanctification process causes an actual change and renewing of the body.[2] John the Revelator has told of 144,000 men who will be called from the tribes of Israel and "sealed...in their foreheads."[3] These men will labor during the judgments of the last days to bring converts into the church.[4] As Elder Orson Pratt explained, God "will purify their bodies until they shall be quickened, and renewed and strengthened, and they will be partially changed.... This will prepare them for further ministrations among the nations of the earth,...they can stand forth in the midst of these desolations and plagues and not be overcome by them."[5]

Attaining sanctification, then, will shield the saints from the judgments, allow them to be accounted free from the blood and sins of the generations, and prepare them to receive the full eternal benefits of the Lord's atoning sacrifice.

12. Prepare Spiritually: Be guided by the Holy Ghost. Ability to receive inspiration and guidance of the Spirit will be necessary for survival of the saints during the judgments of the last days. The Lord has revealed that

> ...At that day, when I shall come in my glory, shall the parable be fulfilled which I spake concerning the ten virgins.
> *For they that are wise and have received the truth, and have taken the Holy Spirit for their guide, and have not been deceived—verily I say*

---

1. D & C 88:73-75. See verses 85, 138; 109:42; 112:33.
2. See D & C 84:33; 88:67-68.
3. Rev. 7:3.
4. For more detailed information on the 144,000 see the author's book, *Prophecy—Key to the Future*, pp. 121-125, 141-142.
5. *JD* 15:365-366. March 9, 1873.

unto you they shall not be hewn down and cast into the fire, but shall abide the day.[1]

Recognizing promptings of approaching danger; receiving guidance on methods of obtaining food and other necessary items; being directed in where to live and travel; discerning between friends and enemies, truth and error, true and false prophets—all these abilities will be indispensible when the period of "the desolation of abomination" begins. But being continually receptive to the Spirit does not come easily. It requires a conditioning of the mind and will—a humbling and cleansing of the self:

> Let him that is ignorant *learn wisdom by humbling himself and calling upon the Lord his God,* that his eyes may be opened that he may see, and his ears opened that he may hear;
> *For my Spirit is sent forth into the world to enlighten the humble and contrite, and to the condemnation of the ungodly.*[2]

"Ye receive the Spirit through prayer,"[3] drawing near unto God so that he in turn draws near unto you.[4] The power of the Holy Spirit is then bestowed by God "on those who love him, and purify themselves before him."[5] There is the need to develop a relationship of faith and trust in the promptings which come:

> *...Put your trust in that Spirit which leadeth to do good*—yea, to do justly, to walk humbly, to judge righteously; and this is my Spirit.
> Verily, verily, I say unto you, *I will impart unto you of my Spirit, which shall enlighten your mind, which shall fill your soul with joy;*
> *And then shall ye know, or by this shall you know, all things whatsoever you desire of me,* which are pertaining unto things of righteousness, in faith believing in me that you shall receive.[6]

The Holy Ghost is a comforter,[7] who will teach and bring necessary things to remembrance.[8] He will testify of the Christ,[9] guide into all truth,[10] and will reveal things to come[11]—all of which are blessings which will be sorely needed by the saints during the era of future strife and chaos.

---

1. D & C 45:56-57.
2. D & C 136:32-33.
3. D & C 63:64. See 14:8.
4. D & C 88:63-65.
5. D & C 76:116.
6. D & C 11:12-14.

7. Jn. 14:26.
8. *Ibid.*
9. Jn. 15:26.
10. Jn. 16:13.
11. *Ibid.*

13. Recognize last days events: Watch for signs of the times.
The Lord instructed his people to be alert to signs that prophesied
events are about to take place. After giving his great prophecy of
last days events to his disciples on the Mount of Olives, he told
them,

> Now learn a parable of the fig tree; when his branch is yet tender,
> and putteth forth leaves, ye know that summer is nigh:
> So likewise ye, when ye shall see all these things, know that it is
> near, even at the doors.[1]

One of the identifying characteristics of those who fear and
serve the Lord is their awareness of the signs of the times. As the
Savior observed,

> ...He that feareth me shall be looking forth for the great day of the
> Lord to come, *even for the signs of the coming of the Son of Man....*
> And he that watches not for me shall be cut off.[2]

An understanding of the signs of the times is promised to the
saints:

> And he that believeth shall be blest with signs following, even as it
> is written.
> *And unto you it shall be given to know the signs of the times, and
> the signs of the coming of the Son of Man;...*[3]

The Lord's instruction is to

> Gird up your loins and be watchful and be sober, *looking forth for
> the coming of the Son of Man,* for he cometh in an hour you think not.[4]

The purposes of knowing the prophesied signs of the times,
and then being aware of their fulfillment as the events transpire,
are fourfold. First, that knowledge prevents deception and confusion:

> Wherefore, *be not deceived,* but continue in steadfastness, looking
> forth for the heavens to be shaken, and the earth to tremble and to reel
> to and fro as a drunken man, and for the valleys to be exalted, and for

---

1. Mt. 24:32-33. See D & C 35:16.
2. D & C 45:39, 44.
3. D & C 68:10-11.
4. D & C 61:38.

the mountains to be made low, and for the rough places to become smooth—[1]

Second, observing the fulfillment of the signs of the times reminds the saints of their need to maintain personal worthiness:

> ...*Take heed to yourselves*, lest at any time your hearts be overcharged with surfeiting, and drunkenness, and cares of this life, and so that day come upon you unawares.
>
> For as a snare shall it come on all them that dwell on the face of the whole earth.
>
> *Watch ye therefore, and pray always, that ye may be accounted worthy to escape all these things that shall come to pass, and to stand before the Son of Man.*[2]

Third, knowing the prophesied events and the order in which they will transpire allows one to prepare for them and to accept them when they take place. The Lord, speaking of the tribulations of the last days, has told the saints to "remember this, *which I tell you before*, that you may lay it to heart, and *receive that which is to follow.*"[3]

Finally, knowing the prophecies and recognizing the signs of the times allows the saints to bear witness of God's hand in future events:

> Behold, verily I say unto you, for this cause I have sent you—that you might be obedient, and *that your hearts might be prepared to bear testimony of the things which are to come;...*[4]

The author has observed "the ostrich syndrome" among the saints from time to time. There are those who say "I don't want to know about the prophecies of last days—they frighten me." Others have said, "The prophecies are negative in their approach. We should 'think positive'—let's only talk about happy things." Their philosophies are not the Lord's way, and are in direct opposition to his oft-repeated instructions. They neither prepare themselves, nor fulfill the commandments that they should warn and prepare others. They would do well to heed the Lord's warning that "*he that watches not for me shall be cut off.*"[5]

---

1. D & C 49:23.
2. Lk. 21:34-36. See also Mt. 24:42; 25:13; Mk. 13:35-37; Lk. 12:37-40; Eph. 6:18; 1 Thess. 5:6; 1 Pet. 4:7; Rev. 16:15.
3. D & C 58:5. See D & C 106:4-5.
4. D & C 58:6.
5. D & C 45:44.

14. Teach doctrines of the last days: Seek knowledge for protection. A major element in the spiritual preparation of the saints is the necessity of their being properly informed concerning the prophecies of the last days. The Lord has emphasized that this people need to understand what is prophesied to come to pass, and they need to be able to discern the signs of the times by recognizing the preparations for these events among the nations of the earth. This instruction was given by revealed commandment:

> And I give unto you a commandment that you shall teach one another the doctrine of the kingdom.
>
> Teach ye diligently and my grace shall attend you, that you may be instructed more perfectly in *theory*, in *principle*, in *doctrine*, in the *law of the gospel*, in *all things that pertain unto the kingdom of God*, that are expedient for you to understand;
>
> Of things both in heaven and in the earth, and under the earth; *things which have been, things which are, things which must shortly come to pass; things which are at home, things which are abroad; the wars and the perplexities of the nations, and the judgments which are on the land; and a knowledge also of countries and of kingdoms—*
>
> *That ye may be prepared in all things* when I shall send you again to magnify the calling whereunto I have called you, and the mission with which I have commissioned you.[1]

Not only are the saints commanded to teach each other about the things which are to come to pass, they are also commanded to personally "treasure up wisdom" to protect themselves against the wickedness of men in the last days:

> And again, I say unto you that the *enemy in the secret chambers seeketh your lives.*
>
> Ye hear of wars in far countries, and you say that there will soon be great wars in far countries, but ye know not the hearts of men in your own land.
>
> I tell you these things because of your prayers; wherefore, *treasure up wisdom in your bosoms, lest the wickedness of men reveal these things unto you by their wickedness*, in a manner which shall speak in your ears with a voice louder than that which shall shake the earth; but *if ye are prepared ye shall not fear.*
>
> And that ye might *escape the power of the enemy, and be gathered unto me a righteous people*, without spot and blameless—[2]

15. Prepare the saints for the hour of judgment: Warn your neighbor. After commanding the saints to teach one another about

---

1. D & C 88:77-80. See also D & C 88:118; 97:12-14.
2. D & C 38:28-31.

"things which must shortly come to pass" and about the "judgments which are on the land,"[1] the Lord specified the warning
duty required of all his people:

> Behold, I sent you out to *testify and warn the people,* and *it be-
> cometh every man who hath been warned to warn his neighbor.*[2]

The context of this passage clearly indicates that the warning
spoken of by the Savior is not merely the preaching of general
gospel principles. That warning is

> *...to prepare the saints for the hour of judgment which is to come;* that
> their souls may *escape the wrath of God, the desolation of abomination*
> which awaits the wicked, both in this world and in the world to come.[3]

In the dedicatory prayer for the Kirtland Temple, which was
given to the Prophet Joseph Smith by revelation, deep concern is
expressed for the need to prepare the saints against coming judgments:

> Put upon thy servants the testimony of the covenant, that when they
> go out and proclaim thy word they may seal up the law, and *prepare
> the hearts of thy saints for all those judgments thou art about to send,*
> in thy wrath, upon the inhabitants of the earth, because of their trans-
> gressions, *that thy people may not faint in the day of trouble.*[4]

And also:

> We know that thou hast spoken by the mouth of thy prophets ter-
> rible things concerning the wicked, in the last days—that thou wilt pour
> out thy judgments, without measure;
> Therefore, O Lord, *deliver thy people from the calamity of the
> wicked;* enable thy servants to seal up the law, and bind up the testi-
> mony, that *they may be prepared against the day of burning.*[5]

The Lord has commanded the saints repeatedly to

> *Prepare ye, prepare ye for that which is to come,* for the Lord is nigh;
> And the anger of the Lord is kindled, and his sword is bathed in
> heaven, and it shall fall upon the inhabitants of the earth.[6]

---

1. See again D & C 88:79.
2. D & C 88:81.
3. D & C 88:84-85.
4. D & C 109:38.
5. D & C 109:45-46.
6. D & C 1:12-13. See also D & C 31:8; 33:10; 65:1-3; 85:3; 88:92;
133:4-5, 10, 19.

He has told them that

> ...I give unto you a commandment, that *every man*, both elder, priest, teacher, and also member, go to with his might, with the labor of his hands, *to prepare and accomplish the things which I have commanded.*
> And let your preaching be the warning voice, every man to his neighbor, in mildness and in meekness.[1]

The commandment of the Lord, then, is that the saints admonish and warn one another, helping each other to prepare for the difficult times to come. This, obviously, is the motive for *Prophetic Warnings to Modern America.*

16. Preach repentance to non-members: Warn of coming judgments. The Lord has commanded that warning of coming judgments be a major part of the missionary message to the world at large in the last days. Two messages, repentance and the warning of coming judgments, are to go hand in hand as the major themes of missionary labor. The Lord told the elders, for instance, *"Behold, I sent you out to reprove the world of all their unrighteous deeds, and to teach them of a judgment which is to come."*[2] He commanded that all the church should preach that two-fold message:

> And verily I say unto you, the rest of my servants, go ye forth as your circumstances shall permit, in your several callings, unto the great and notable cities and villages, *reproving the world in righteousness of all their unrighteous and ungodly deeds, setting forth clearly and understandingly the desolation of abomination in the last days.*[3]

The Lord has instructed those laboring in the missionary effort to "open your mouths and they shall be filled, saying: *Repent, repent, and prepare ye the way of the Lord,* and make his paths straight; for the kingdom of heaven is at hand;..."[4] Another revelation instructs those who are called to preach the gospel to

> ...*Cry repentance* unto a crooked and perverse generation, *preparing the way of the Lord* for his second coming.
> For behold, verily, verily, I say unto you, the time is soon at hand that I shall come in a cloud with power and great glory.

---

1. D & C 38:40-41.
2. D & C 84:87.
3. D & C 84:117. The same dual message, of calling to repentance and prophesying of future judgments, characterized the work even in the days of Enoch. See Moses 6:27.
4. D & C 33:10.

And it shall be a great day at the time of my coming, for all nations shall tremble.

But before that great day shall come, the sun shall be darkened, and the moon be turned into blood; and the stars shall refuse their shining, and some shall fall, and *great destructions await the wicked.*

Wherefore, *lift up your voice and spare not,* for the Lord God hath spoken; therefore *prophesy,* and it shall be given by the power of the Holy Ghost.[1]

And also:

Lift up your voices and spare not. *Call upon the nations to repent,* both old and young, both bond and free, *saying: Prepare yourselves for the great day of the Lord;*

For if I, who am a man, do lift up my voice and call upon you to repent, and ye hate me, what will ye say when the day cometh when the thunders shall utter their voices from the ends of the earth, speaking to the ears of all that live, saying—Repent, and prepare for the great day of the Lord?[2]

Thus the two-fold message of latter-day missionaries is clearly set forth by the Lord. They are to call to repentance, and prepare the people for the Lord's coming by warning of the judgments of the last days.

Warning of future events is required of those who are obedient to the Lord, and is not to be omitted from the missionary message:

Behold, verily I say unto you, for this cause I have sent you, that you might *be obedient,* and that your hearts might be prepared *to bear testimony of the things which are to come;...*[3]

And that requirement extends to "every man":

Wherefore, seeing that I, the Lord, have decreed all these things upon the face of the earth, I will that my saints should be assembled upon the land of Zion;

And that *every man* should take righteousness in his hands and faithfulness upon his loins, and *lift a warning voice unto the inhabitants of the earth;* and declare both by word and by flight that desolation shall come upon the wicked.[4]

17. Bind the law and seal the testimony: Testify against the wicked. The Lord has revealed that this wicked generation has

---

1. D & C 34:6-10.   3. D & C 58:6.
2. D & C 43:20-21.   4. D & C 63:36-37.

ripened in iniquity until it is now *"white already to be burned."*[1]
It is now the eleventh hour, and the last time missionaries will be
called:

> ...Ye are called to lift up your voices as with the sound of a trump, to
> *declare my gospel unto a crooked and perverse generation.*
>   For behold, the field is white already to harvest; and it is the *eleventh
> hour,* and the *last time* that I shall call laborers into my vineyard.
>   *And my vineyard has become corrupted every whit; and there is none
> which doeth good save it be a few;* and they err in many instances be-
> cause of priestcrafts, all having corrupt minds.[2]

This "crooked and perverse generation"[3] has become so
wicked the Lord is withholding his spirit from the inhabitants of
the earth.[4] The saints have been instructed to

> ...Watch, for the adversary spreadeth his dominions, and darkness reign-
> eth;
>   And the anger of God kindleth against the inhabitants of the earth;
> *and none doeth good, for all have gone out of the way.*[5]

Concerning the rest of the world besides the saints, the Lord has
revealed that

> ...*All flesh is corrupted before me; and the powers of darkness prevail
> upon the earth,* among the children of men, in the presence of all the
> hosts of heaven—
>   Which causeth silence to reign, and all eternity is pained, and *the
> angels are waiting the great command to reap down the earth,* to gather
> the tares that they may be burned; and, behold, *the enemy is combined.*[6]

God has decreed that "this gospel of the kingdom shall be
preached in all the world *for a witness unto all nations;* and then
shall the end come."[7] The Lord has said that the missionaries are
"called to prune my vineyard with a *mighty pruning,* yea, even for
the last time."[8] This witness, or "pruning," will serve to convert
and gather out the righteous who remain, but it will also condemn
the wicked. Speaking of those who will have believed on his words
and will have been born again, the Lord said, "Their testimony
shall also go forth *unto the condemnation of this generation* if
they harden their hearts against them."[9]

---

1. D & C 31:4.
2. D & C 33:2-4.
3. D & C 34:6.
4. D & C 63:32.
5. D & C 82:5-6.

6. D & C 38:11-12.
7. Mt. 24:14.
8. D & C 24:19.
9. D & C 5:18.

The Lord's servants are to seal up the righteous to partake of the blessings of eternal life and to be protected against Satan's power in the last days.[1] They have a similar responsibility to seal up the wicked unto judgment and condemnation. A revelation from the Savior states that

> ...They who go forth, bearing these tidings unto the inhabitants of the earth, *to them is power given to seal both on earth and in heaven, the unbelieving and rebellious;*
> Yea, verily, *to seal them up unto the day when the wrath of God shall be poured out upon the wicked without measure—*[2]

This "sealing up" process is a fundamental aspect of the labor of the missionaries in the last days. The Lord has commanded,

> ...Tarry ye, and labor diligently, that you may be perfected in your ministry to go forth among the Gentiles for the last time, as many as the mouth of the Lord shall name, *to bind up the law and seal up the testimony,...*[3]

Then the Lord's answer to the wicked at the last day shall be that they have been sealed up unto darkness by the Lord's servants:

> Behold, and lo, there are none to deliver you; for ye obeyed not my voice when I called to you out of the heavens; ye believed not my servants, and when they were sent unto you ye received them not.
> Wherefore, *they sealed up the testimony and bound up the law,* and ye were delivered over unto darkness.[4]

Thus the Lord's servants have been commanded to leave a witness against those who reject them by shaking off the dust from their feet,[5] and they eventually stand as witnesses of the house, village or city which cast them out.[6] The Lord has said, concerning enemies who come against the saints to drive them out,

> ...*Ye shall curse them;*
> *And whomsoever ye curse, I will curse, and ye shall avenge me of mine enemies.*
> And my presence shall be with you even in avenging me of mine enemies, unto the third and fourth generation of them that hate me.[7]

---

1. See D & C 68:11-12; 109:38; 124:124; 131:5.
2. D & C 1:8-9. See D & C 124:93; 128:8-11.
3. D & C 88:84.
4. D & C 133:71-72.
5. D & C 24:15-17; 60:15; 99:4-5.
6. D & C 75:18-22; 84:92-97.
7. D & C 103:24-26.

Bearing testimony against the wicked is an awesome responsibility, and one not to be taken lightly, nor used indiscriminately without careful restraint! Yet it is a duty commanded of God, and an integral part of his plan. It is necessary in the last days, just as it was in Alma's time[1] and in the era of the New Testament church.[2] As the gap between righteousness and iniquity widens, the necessity for testimony against the wicked will rapidly increase.

18. Go ye out from Babylon: Be separate from the wicked. The Lord has commanded, "Prepare ye, prepare ye, O my people,"[3] and then has told the saints to *"go ye out from Babylon. Be ye clean that bear the vessels of the Lord."*[4] In another revelation his counsel is to *"go ye out from among the wicked. Save yourselves."*[5] Another warning proclaims the Lord's message that "all the proud and they that do wickedly shall be as stubble; and I will burn them up, for I am the Lord of Hosts; and *I will not spare any that remain in Babylon."*[6] The Lord's instruction has been given to *"Go ye out from among the nations, even from Babylon, from the midst of wickedness, which is spiritual Babylon."*[7]

That saint who wishes to be spiritually and temporally prepared would do well to examine the environment in which he lives and works. He should evaluate his situation, prayerfully assessing whether his surroundings and associates are conducive to his living the gospel, or whether his environment is leading him and his family away from that which is righteous and good. It would be to his benefit, also, to evaluate what the situation would be if difficult conditions were to arise such as severe food shortages, international war or internal conflict, or persecution of the Church. In such extreme situations, would he be able to continue in his present surroundings, or would he be subjected to severe pressures, and perhaps even have to "take his sword against his neighbor"[8] in defense of his family, his home, his supplies, and his liberty? Every Latter-day Saint who is in tune with the Holy Spirit is entitled to revealed guidance concerning where he should work and reside. Such promptings come to many. Indeed, over the past decade the author has conversed with numerous individuals who had moved to new environments because of personal inspiration which they have received.

---

1. Al. 14:11.
2. Lk. 11:49-51.
3. D & C 133:4.
4. D & C 133:5.

5. D & C 38:42.
6. D & C 64:24.
7. D & C 133:14.
8. D & C 45:68.

The present activity and direction of the Church, however, should be considered when making a decision concerning where to live. In this day of "lengthened stride" towards missionary work, the gospel message is being taught world-wide. The place where the saints are most needed is in the outlying stakes and missions, where they can be most actively involved with the rapid growth, rather than being clustered in the center of the Church. No general "gathering" call has been given, and it still appears *necessary that ye should remain for the present time in your places of abode*, as it shall be suitable to your circumstances."[1] It is still a time of preparation prior to the gathering, but a time to assist the saints and to *strengthen them and prepare them* against the time when they shall be gathered."[2]

Even at the height of the future difficulties, when the Church will be the subject of intense persecution, the saints will still be scattered throughout the world. In his vision of that future era, Nephi saw that "the church of the Lamb, who were the saints of God, were also *upon all the face of the earth;...*"[3]

The scriptures indicate that there will be two times, and types, of gathering. The first will be to various places of refuge among the stakes of Zion, as the nation endures the agonies of world war and internal conflict. Then, after the Missouri area has been swept clean,[4] the New Jerusalem will be built. The scriptures reveal that there will be a general assemblying to that area. No advantage is to be gained by undirected moves which are out of chronological synchronization with these periods. To move to the New Jerusalem area, prior to its cleansing, for instance, could be disasterous.

In the first gathering period, the saints will have need to assemble in various places of refuge[5] throughout the Americas, the "land of Zion,"[6] among the stakes:

---

1. D & C 48:1.
2. D & C 31:8.
3. 1 Ne. 14:12. Nephi added, however, that "their dominions upon the face of the earth were small, because of the wickedness of the great whore whom I saw." *(Ibid.)*
4. See Wilford Woodruff's vision, p. 296, also pp. 323-325.
5. See pp. 300-301.
6. In this passage the term "Zion" appears to be used in the broad sense, as expressed by Joseph Smith in the April, 1844 conference: ..."I will make a proclamation that will cover a broader ground. *The whole of America is Zion itself from north to south,* and is described by the prophets, who declare that it is the Zion where the mountain of the Lord should be, and that it should be in the center of the land." (*HC* 6:318-319. April 8, 1844.)

...That the gathering together upon *the land of Zion, and upon her stakes, may be for a defense, and for a refuge from the storm,* and from wrath when it shall be poured out without mixture upon the whole earth.[1]

The Lord speaks of *"Zion, and in her stakes, and in Jerusalem"* as "those places which I have appointed for refuge."[2] He revealed that his will is that the saints "gather together, and stand in holy places."[3] The Savior says that as the overflowing scourge of sickness is poured out, "My disciples shall stand in holy places, and shall not be moved."[4] The Lord has cautioned that this gathering should be accomplished *"not in haste, lest there should be confusion, which bringeth pestilence."*[5] His caution to the saints is to "let not your gathering be in haste, nor by flight; but *let all things be prepared before you.*"[6] It appears that the saints will need to be alert to this approaching time of gathering to places of refuge, and not tarry or procrastinate when the need arises.

A prophetic statement made by President Heber C. Kimball seems to indicate that the separation, or "sifting time," will even involve the saints of the Utah area. In 1856 he said,

> We think we are secure here in the chambers of the everlasting hills, where we can close those few doors of the canyons against mobs and persecutors, the wicked and the vile, who have always beset us with violence and robbery, but I want to say to you, my brethren, the time is coming when *we will be mixed up in these now peaceful valleys to that extent that it will be difficult to tell the face of a Saint from the face of an enemy to the people of God. Then, brethren, look out for the great sieve, for there will be a great sifting time, and many will fall;* for I say unto you there is a *test,* a *TEST,* a TEST coming, and who will be able to stand?[7]

The scriptures also speak of a second gathering, a later assembling of the saints, at the site of the New Jerusalem in Missouri:

1. D & C 115:6.
2. D & C 124:36.
3. D & C 101:22. Verses 20-22 allude to the stakes as being the "holy places." See also verses 64-68.
4. D & C 45:32. See 87:8.
5. D & C 63:24.
6. D & C 101:68.
7. Orson F. Whitney, *Life of Heber C. Kimball* (Salt Lake City, Utah: Bookcraft, 1967), p. 446. This statement was preserved by Elder Edward Stevenson. President A.F. McDonald recorded, concerning Heber C. Kimball, that "he clearly foreshadowed the time of trial the Saints are now passing through, *and to a period still before us. He often used the language, 'A test, a test is coming.'* " (*Ibid.* p. 447.)

...The decree hath gone forth from the Father that they shall be gathered in unto *one place upon the face of this land,* to prepare their hearts and be prepared in all things against the day when *tribulation and desolation are sent forth upon the wicked.*[1]

The Lord has revealed his desire "that my covenant people may be *gathered in one* in that day when I shall come to my temple."[2] He described the New Jerusalem as a "city of refuge, a place of safety for the saints of the Most High God,"[3] and said that

...It shall come to pass among the wicked, that *every man that will not take his sword against his neighbor must needs flee unto Zion for safety.*
And there shall be gathered unto it out of every nation under heaven; and it shall be the only people that shall not be at war one with another.[4]

Yet even in that day, when world-wide conflict will make it imperative that the saints be "gathered in one," there will still be those who will have been "commanded to tarry"[5] who will be scattered throughout the world.[6]

To be prepared to gather to appropriate places of refuge as the difficulties come upon the world will require individual alertness to personal promptings and responsiveness to Church directions, plus adequate preparation for mobility, coupled with the realization that many saints will find it necessary to *"declare both by word and by flight that desolation shall come upon the wicked."*[7] It will be necessary to grasp and accept the implications of a separation of the obedient from the disobedient and unjust. It will also place tremendous responsibility upon Church authorities to properly prepare the saints and to help them develop adequate places of refuge, and also to be sufficiently responsive to divine guidance that they can give proper and timely directives in a time when many lives are at stake and the potential for human suffering is enormous.

19. Seek divine strength, guidance and protection: Pray always. There is tremendous strength and power gained through effective

---

1. D & C 29:8.
2. D & C 42:36.
3. D & C 45:66.
4. D & C 45:68-69.
5. D & C 133:4.
6. See again 1 Ne. 14:12. Also *Prophecy—Key to the Future,* pp. 90-91.
7. D & C 63:37.

prayer and the Lord has commanded that his people utilize that strength for their own benefit during the difficult events of the last days.

Elder Heber C. Kimball spoke of the importance of each individual being personally receptive to divine guidance and possessing a firm testimony in connection with the events of the last days. He said,

> This Church has before it many close places through which it will have to pass before the work of God is crowned with victory. To meet the difficulties that are coming, *it will be necessary for you to have a knowledge of the truth of this work for yourselves. The difficulties will be of such a character that the man or woman who does not possess this personal knowledge or witness will fall.* If you have not got the testimony, live right and call upon the Lord and cease not till you obtain it. If you do not you will not stand.
>
> Remember these sayings, for many of you will live to see them fulfilled. *The time will come when no man nor woman will be able to endure on borrowed light. Each will have to be guided by the light within himself. If you do not have it, how can you stand?* Do you believe it?...
>
> *You will have all the persecution you want and more too,* and all the opportunity to show your integrity to God and truth that you could desire.[1]

On another occasion he remarked, *"Unless a man knew that Jesus was the Christ, he could not stand in this Church.* He said

---

1. Orson F. Whitney, *Life of Heber C. Kimball, op. cit.,* pp. 449-450, 451. In this same discourse, delivered in 1867, he said:

> You have the First Presidency, from whom you can get counsel to guide you, and you rely on them. The time will come when they will not be with you. Why? Because *they will have to flee and hide up to keep out of the hands of their enemies.* You have the Twelve now. You will not always have them, for *they too will be hunted and will have to keep out of the way of their enemies.* You have other men to whom you look for counsel and advice. Many of them will not be amongst you, for the same reason. *You will be left to the light within yourselves. If you don't have it you will not stand; therefore seek for the testimony of Jesus and cleave to it, that when the trying time comes you may not stumble and fall.* (*Ibid.,* p. 450.)

The saints endured this type of experience during the anti-Mormon persecutions of the 1880's. Whether a similar situation will occur in connection with the persecutions prophesied for the future remains to be seen. The fulfillment of Heber C. Kimball's prophecy that *"the time would come when the government would stop the Saints from holding meetings. When this was done the Lord would pour out His judgments,"* (*Ibid.,* p. 442) has not yet been realized. Does it imply future persecution from Governmental sources, and foreshadow a similar situation to the 1880's period?

that the Lord would allow all manner of abominations to come to Zion, in order to purify His people."[1]

The Savior has commanded that Divine supplication be made for many things, but foremost is individual prayer for protection and strength so that one can endure till Christ comes. The revealed instruction has been given to *"Pray always that you enter not into temptation*, that you may abide the day of his coming, whether in life or in death."[2] A similar revelation conveyed the Savior's admonition to *"Pray always, that ye may not faint, until I come.* Behold, and lo, I will come quickly, and receive you unto myself."[3]

Diligent obedience is required if the saints are to be able to rely on prayer to assist them when troubled times come. Said the Lord concerning earlier saints,

> They were slow to hearken unto the voice of the Lord their God; therefore, the *Lord their God is slow to hearken unto their prayers, to answer them in the day of their trouble.*[4]

The Lord had delivered the same warning to the people of King Noah in Book of Mormon times:

> ...Except this people repent and turn unto the Lord their God, they shall be brought into bondage; and none shall deliver them, except it be the Lord the Almighty God.
>
> Yea, and it shall come to pass that *when they shall cry unto me I will be slow to hear their cries; yea, and I will suffer them that they be smitten by their enemies.*
>
> And except they repent in sackcloth and ashes, and cry mightily to the Lord their God, *I will not hear their prayers, neither will I deliver them out of their afflictions;...*[5]

Truly no course but righteous obedience can safely be followed in the perilous times to come.

Another scriptural warning speaks of prayer being made ineffective because of unwillingness to share with the needy. As the shortages and famines of the last days occur, this may become a matter of serious import, affecting both the temporal and spiritual salvation of many:

---

1. *Ibid.*, p. 441. This statement was made in 1856.
2. D & C 61:39.
3. D & C 88:126.
4. D & C 101:7.
5. Mos. 11:23-25. See also Mos. 7:29, 33; 9:3, 17-18; 21:14-15.

> *...If ye turn away the needy, and the naked, and visit not the sick and afflicted, and impart of your substance, if ye have, to those who stand in need*—I say unto you, if ye do not any of these things, behold, *your prayer is vain, and availeth you nothing,* and ye are as hypocrites who do deny the faith.[1]

The saints would do well to pray for the nation and its leaders, seeking that it might follow a course of righteousness, and making supplication that impending judgments be delayed until the Lord's work of gleaning the righteous is accomplished. As in Book of Mormon times, such prayers can delay the judgments, a process which may presently be happening:

> Yea, and I say unto you that *if it were not for the prayers of the righteous, who are now in the land, that ye would even now be visited with utter destruction;* yet it would not be by flood as were the people in the days of Noah, but it would be by famine, and by pestilence, and the sword.
> *But it is by the prayers of the righteous that ye are spared;* now therefore, if ye will *cast out the righteous from among you then will not the Lord stay his hand;* but in his fierce anger he will come out against you; then ye shall be smitten by famine, and by pestilence, and by the sword; and the time is soon at hand except ye repent.[2]

Yet prayer alone cannot save the nations—only their repentance and acceptance of the gospel can avert the judgments. The Lord has said,

> Behold, verily, verily, I say unto you, that the people in Ohio call upon me in much faith, *thinking I will stay my hand in judgment upon the nations, but I cannot deny my word.*
> Wherefore lay to with your might and call faithful laborers into my vineyard, that it may be pruned for the last time.
> *And inasmuch as they do repent and receive the fulness of my gospel, and become sanctified, I will stay mine hand in judgment.*[3]

Like the prophets and disciples of old, the saints should seek to "leave a blessing upon this land in their prayers."[4] Yet there

---

1. Al. 34:28.
2. Al. 10:22-23. See pp. 214-221. Concerning the time in the last days when the Lord will "in his fury vex the nation," the Lord has instructed the saints to "Pray ye, therefore, *that their ears may be opened unto your cries,* that I may be merciful unto them, that these things may not come upon them." (D & C 101:92.)
3. D & C 39:16-18.
4. See D & C 10:46-52.

will come a time, when the persecution against the saints becomes intense, that they may be

> Calling upon the name of the Lord day and night, saying: *O that thou wouldst rend the heavens,* that thou wouldst come down, that the mountains might flow down at thy presence....
> O Lord, *thou shalt come down to make thy name known to thine adversaries,* and all nations shall tremble at thy presence—
> When thou doest terrible things,...[1]

20. Prepare for return of the united order: Be ready to share. With the strong prophetic warnings concerning future famine which have been given, there is reason to ponder how the needs of large portions of the population can be met. Surely there is need for the saints to "warn their neighbor," encouraging those around them to anticipate the possibility of future shortages. But the question "Must I share in a time of extreme need?" often arises.

The third world war and internal conflict within the United States will serve as a transition period, in preparation for the return of the saints to establish the New Jerusalem. The Lord has revealed that by the time of that return, the saints must again be living the united order, for that unity is a

> ...Union required by the law of the celestial kingdom;
> And *Zion cannot be built up unless it is by the principles of the law of the celestial kingdom;* otherwise I cannot receive her unto myself.[2]

Just how, and when, the principle of consecration under the united order is to be reinstated is not known by the author, but it is obvious that a major need may arise if famine and extreme shortages come upon the saints. Such a scenario might set the stage, creating sufficient need that the saints might overcome the obstacle of selfishness which prevented the united order from becoming their way of life in the past.[3]

The Lord has said that the united order is to be "for the benefit of my church, and *for the salvation of men until I come.*"[4] While speaking of the united order, he revealed that it was to serve to make the church independent in the time of tribulation:

---

1. D & C 133:40, 42-43. See Al. 33:10; D & C 109:50-52.
2. D & C 105:4-5.
3. See D & C 105:1-10.
4. D & C 104:1.

Behold, this is the preparation wherewith I prepare you, and the foundation, and the ensample which I give unto you, whereby you may accomplish the commandments which are given you;

That through my providence, *notwithstanding the tribulation which shall descend upon you, that the church may stand independent* above all other creatures beneath the celestial world;...[1]

And he also said,

...*It is my purpose to provide for my saints,* for all things are mine.

But it must needs be done in mine own way; and behold *this is the way that I, the Lord, have decreed to provide for my saints,* ...[2]

Sometime in the future, then, the saints can expect the Lord to again command them, saying, "I require all their surplus property to be put into the hands of the bishop of my church in Zion."[3] And they will again be instructed that

...*Inasmuch as they receive more than is needful for their necessities and their wants, it shall be given into my storehouse;*

And the benefits shall be consecrated unto the inhabitants of Zion, and unto their generations, inasmuch as they become heirs according to the laws of the kingdom.

Behold, *this is what the Lord requires of every man in his stewardship,* even as I, the Lord, have appointed *or shall hereafter appoint* unto any man.

And behold, *none are exempt from this law who belong to the church of the living God.*[4]

They can anticipate the instruction that

...Zion must arise and put on her beautiful garments.

Therefore I give unto you this commandment, that ye *bind yourselves by this covenant,* and it shall be done according to the laws of the land.

Behold, here is wisdom also in me for your good.

And you are to be equal, or in other words, *you are to have equal claims on the properties,* for the benefit of managing the concerns of your stewardships, *every man according to his wants and his needs,* inasmuch as his wants are just—

And all this for the benefit of the church of the living God, that every man may improve upon his talent, that every man may gain other talents, yea, even an hundred fold, to be cast into the Lord's storehouse, to become the common property of the whole church—[5]

---

1. D & C 78:13-14.   4. D & C 70:7-10.
2. D & C 104:15-16.   5. D & C 82:14-18.
3. D & C 119:1.

The Lord has stressed the attitude with which the saints must function when the principles of the united order are restored, emphasizing that every man must be "seeking the interest of his neighbor, and doing all things with an eye single to the glory of God,"[1] and warning that "in your temporal things you shall be equal, *and this not grudgingly*, otherwise the abundance of the manifestations of the Spirit shall be withheld."[2]

When this eternal principle[3] is restored, the Lord has warned of severe penalties which will come upon those who harden their hearts against it. His instruction is that they "shall be dealt with according to the laws of my church, and shall be delivered over to the buffetings of Satan until the day of redemption."[4] The person who breaks the covenant of the united order, according to the Lord, "shall be cursed in his life, and shall be trodden down by whom I will,"[5] and shall eventually "lift up his eyes in hell, being in torment."[6] Those who won't abide by the law of the united order in the days of the New Jerusalem "shall not be found worthy to abide among you."[7]

Thus a vital aspect of the spiritual preparation of the saints is that they condition themselves to the future acceptance of the principles of the united order. Their willingness to share for the common good may hold the key to both spiritual and temporal salvation in the days to come.

21. Resolve to attain eternal goals: Endure to the end. Much has been written about the judgments God will pour out in the last days. Comment has been made about the testing of the saints, and concerning the possibility of the saints receiving chastening from the Almighty. It appears that there will be many trials to be endured, and that the future will not be easy. In the face of such a possibility, it is imperative that the Lord's people fix their sights clearly upon the attaining of their eternal goals. They must commit to themselves, to their families, and to their Father in Heaven that no matter what comes, they will endure to the end, overcoming their trials and obstacles. They will set a course to obtain their

---

1. D & C 82:19.
2. D & C 70:14.
3. See D & C 82:20; 104:1; 119:4.
4. D & C 82:21. See 104:9.
5. D & C 104:5. See verses 2-9; 105:6.
6. D & C 104:18.
7. D & C 119:5. See also verse 6.

salvation and exaltation, and not be swayed from it by the trials of the last days.

The Lord has promised that *"if you keep my commandments and endure to the end you shall have eternal life*, which gift is the greatest of all the gifts of God."[1]

He has warned of the condemnation that will await the fearful and unbelieving,[2] while promising that *"he that endureth in faith and doeth my will, the same shall overcome,* and shall receive an inheritance upon the earth when the day of transfiguration shall come."[3]

"The Lord giveth no commandments unto the children of men, save *he shall prepare a way for them* that they may accomplish the thing which he commandeth them."[4] The Father has given the saints *"power to overcome all things* which are not ordained of him—"[5] The saints have been instructed to "pray continually, that ye may not be tempted above that which ye can bear."[6] There is power granted to every man, then, to fulfill the commandments, overcome the challenges and resist the temptations which may come.

The hardships may become intense. The saints may have to "endure" in the fullest sense of the word. They may cry out in sorrow, as did the prophet Alma, "How long shall we suffer these great afflictions, O Lord? O Lord, give us strength according to our faith which is in Christ, even unto deliverance."[7] They may feel God has abandoned them, and cry out to him in anguish, as did the prophet Joseph:

> O God, where art thou? And where is the pavilion that covereth thy hiding place?
> How long shall thy hand be stayed, and thine eye, yea thy pure eye, behold from the eternal heavens the wrongs of thy people and of thy servants, and thine ear be penetrated with their cries?
> Yea, O Lord, how long shall they suffer these wrongs and unlawful oppressions, before thine heart shall be softened toward them, and thy bowels be moved with compassion toward them?[8]

Yet the eternal goal cannot be abandoned, and "blessed are they who are faithful and endure, whether in life or in death, for they shall inherit eternal life."[9] They must be like the Lamanite

---

1. D & C 14:7.
2. D & C 63:17-18.
3. D & C 63:20.
4. 1 Ne. 3:7. See 1 Ne. 17:3, 50-51.
5. D & C 50:35.
6. Al. 13:28.
7. Al. 14:26.
8. D & C 121:1-3.
9. D & C 50:5.

converts of old: "They never did look upon death with any degree of terror, for their hope and views of Christ and the resurrection; therefore, *death was swallowed up to them by the victory of Christ over it.*"[1] And they must be like the missionaries who labored in Book of Mormon times, whose afflictions "were swallowed up in the joy of Christ."[2] As one prophet expressed his confidence in prayer, *"I will cry unto thee in all mine afflictions, for in thee is my joy."*[3]

Yes, the saints would do well to fix their path upon the eternal goal, and resolve that they will endure to the end, no matter what trials they must overcome.

Temporal Preparations for Survival

22. Anticipate physical needs: Store food, clothing, fuel. The saints have been counseled repeatedly to store the supplies needed to preserve life in times of shortage and want.[4] Theirs is the responsibility to prepare for their own personal and family needs, and also to anticipate the needs of many who will gather together in times of future distress. As Heber C. Kimball explained, *"This is a part of our religion—to lay up stores and provide for ourselves and for the surrounding country;* for the day is near when they will come by thousands and by millions, with their fineries, to get a little bread."[5]

Many events can cause shortages and scarcity of necessary commodities. Besides the obvious dangers of crop failure and war, consider other possibilities: strikes, transportation breakdown, economic upheaval, energy shortages, disruption of farming, quarantine against pestilence, etc. The supply of basic commodities is directly dependent upon manpower, equipment, and profit. If it becomes unprofitable to manufacture, distribute, or sell commodities, the items will either disappear from the stores or exorbitantly increase in price until the average family cannot afford to purchase them.

Serious difficulties can develop overnight. Food stores were suddenly left bare in many parts of the nation, for instance, as the "Cuban crisis" developed. The "great depression" erupted in a matter of hours as the stock market collapsed. The "energy crisis"

1. Al. 27:28.
2. Al. 31:38.
3. Al. 33:11.
4. See pages 269-274.
5. *JD* 5:163-164. August 30, 1857.

emerged abruptly, with no meaningful advance warning to the general public.

Because of the possibility of rapid changes, and because of the prophetic warnings of future hardships, it is vital that an effective preparedness program be established in every family unit.

Several brief suggestions might prove helpful:

A.   *Anticipate emergency situations.* Think what would happen in a variety of situations such as a prolonged power failure, an extended transportation strike which would leave stores bare, a major disaster such as an earthquake, etc. What would you need if you were unable to buy anything from local merchants? Record your observations and analyze them in terms of preparatory actions required.

B.   *Inventory present needs and supplies.* No meaningful storage program can be developed without proper assessment of needs and the setting of realistic goals and timetables. No comprehensive, long-range storage program can be maintained without a record-keeping system. The inventory should include food, clothing, fuel, and household necessities. Anticipate family growth and needs for years to come.

C.   *Store medical and sanitation supplies.* If severe shortages occurred, people would soon feel particular need for basic medicinal goods to ward off the typical minor ailments with which families are beset. There would also be need for disinfectants, first aid supplies, home pesticides, etc.

D.   *Buy home maintenance supplies.* If difficult times come, there is a definite possibility of extended periods in which basic services such as power and fuel supply are maintained, but in which many necessary items are unavailable from merchants. There is wisdom in storing a basic supply of nuts and bolts, nails, faucet washers, toilet parts, electrical switches, light bulbs, etc. Every home should have basic tools for repair and construction available.

E.   *Involve the neighborhood in storage activities.* Latter-day Saints have been commanded to warn their neighbors and to prepare them for coming judgments.[1] In no situation is this command more imperative than in the area of storage of survival commodities. In a time of real shortage, unprepared neighbors could cause serious dilemmas of both a moral and temporal nature.

F.   *Avoid the "hoarding" mentality.* In times of scarcity, the "have nots" tend to accuse the "haves" of hoarding. The pub-

---

1. D & C 88:81, 84.

licity they generate can sometimes place a viable storage program in an unfavorable light, causing discouragement and even persecution. Systematically-spaced buying, rather than "panic buying," tends to dispel this attitude. Prior emphasis and community publicity on the advantages of food storage and preparedness will help place the practice in better prospective.

G.   *Plant a garden.* Prepare to be self-supporting to as great a degree as possible. Successful gardening requires skill and experience which cannot be learned overnight, and it often requires long-range soil development. Tools should be acquired. Seeds should be stored. Records should be kept.

H.   *Obtain a survival library.* Many books explain helpful techniques for self-sufficient living. Building a basic library on food storage and preservation, gardening, home repair, and outdoor survival is a wise precaution.

I.   *Provide emergency heating and cooling facilities.* Emergency ability to maintain warmth in even one room could be the means of averting severe discomfort and suffering in a fuel shortage or power outage. There should also be provision for emergency cooking on the stove or fireplace. A supply of wood or coal should be on hand. There should be some provision for the emergency refrigeration of foodstuffs in case of prolonged power failure.

J.   *Insulate homes.* Advance effort to properly insulate homes would be of particular value in times of fuel shortages. Adding insulation, upgrading window quality, installing weather stripping and storm doors—all are effective preparedness measures as well as hedges against rapidly-rising fuel costs.

K.   *Repair, paint homes.* A vital aspect of preparedness is having the home in good repair. Plumbing, heating, electrical items, the roof, exterior surfaces—every aspect of a home should be maintained in good condition. Homes should be painted. Once hard times come, it is difficult to meet the costs of such repairs.

L.   *Replace worn appliances.* Old stoves, refrigerators, toilets, and other necessary appliances should be upgraded while supplies are plentiful.

M.   *Provide for home security from theft.* Scarcity of food and other necessary supplies would cause a serious increase in the danger of theft. Preparation should be made to maintain the security of the home.

N.   *Safe storage of important records.* In the event of major disruptions or emergencies, there might be increased need for ready access to vital family records. Such records should be cataloged and preserved in a safe place, protected from fire and water damage and from theft. There might also be a need for ready access to addresses of family members and other important directions for distant geographical areas.

O. *Maintain mobility and travel potential.* In case of serious emergency, families might find it necessary to travel relatively long distances to reach shelter in the homes of other family members or acquaintances. An automobile should be maintained in good working order, and an adequate supply of gas should be safely stored in portable containers. An emergency travel kit should be planned and prepared. Maps should be on hand.

P. *Pre-arranged emergency travel plan.* The chance of having to rapidly leave one area and travel to another increases as the possibility of future war increases. Contingency decisions should be made, and all family members should be made aware of them.

23. Anticipate the reality of nuclear war: Strengthen civil defense. Chapter XIV discussed the possibility of a Third World War, and included detailed prophecies which asserted that such a conflict would come to pass.[1] Evidence of Russia's rapid increase in offensive weaponry, on a scale which indicates the intent of ''aggressive action,'' was also cited.[2] Of particular concern were the reports indicating America's vulnerability to attack,[3] which indicated the probable destruction of over a third of the population should a sudden nuclear assault occur.

In the author's opinion, there is vital need to strengthen the nation's civil defense program, making greatly increased provision for protection from nuclear attack. The fallout shelter program should be re-emphasized, with renewed effort to locate new shelters, restock existing shelters, and inform and educate the public. It is the author's belief that thoughtful citizens should exert their influence at the local, the state, and the national level, calling for immediate action to strengthen the land against attack.

Much has been said about America's offensive capability, and there are those who monitor it closely. In the light of Russia's rapid increase in military might, it is imperative that a strong offensive force be maintained. But that offensive force will not prevent attack on America's homeland, nor preserve the people if an attack occurs. There is immediate need to strengthen the nation's defense capability as well as offensive capacity.

1. See pp. 285-302.   3. See pp. 308-309.
2. See pp. 302-309.

On an individual level, it would be wise for families to carefully consider the need for a family fallout shelter. With many federal shelters now unstocked, citizens are increasingly vulnerable and often have no alternative but to make personal provision for protection against fallout. They need to re-educate themselves concerning the dangers of nuclear radiation, and discover that a two-week shelter stay would be far less than adequate protection against radiation sickness if one of Russia's huge new warheads were exploded nearby, with its larger radiation output and resulting extended period of radioactive decay.

Remember, the warning of prophecy is that a Third World War will occur, and that it will include the bombing of America's homeland, with severe loss resulting.

24. Anticipate the danger of economic upheaval: Be free from debt. As the world enters the trauma of the last days, economic stability may become increasingly fragile. Shortages of supplies may occur. Production may cease. Transportation and distribution systems may become inoperative. There continues to be the dual dangers of inflation and depression. War always influences the economy.

With the potential for economic instability looming ever more ominous as perilous times approach, there is wisdom in proceeding cautiously in matters of personal finance. These suggestions are offered:

A.   *Be free from debt.* This counsel has been given to Latter-day Saints by their leaders on many occasions. It is wise instruction. In times of difficulty, indebtedness becomes financial bondage, and those who are in debt are not in full control of either their lives or their property. Set a course which will repay all indebtedness as soon as possible. That may not be the most profitable course for "good" times, but the freedom and security it offers for troubled times far outweighs the profit lost.

B.   *Place preparation for security before pleasure and profit.* In establishing personal priorities, recognize the value of proper food storage, home care, and other basics of personal security over the many luxury items which are available. Preparation for future family well-being should take precedence over boats, campers, and speculative financial ventures.

C.   *Be self-sustaining.* Every effort should be made for able-bodied individuals to provide for their own needs, and to resist the temptation to draw from government welfare programs. Those who do not provide for their own needs are not free, and are locked into unproductive situations which will not allow them to make adequate preparations for the future, nor enjoy life fully in the present. There is no effective substitute for personal effort and the development of individual skills and abilities.

D.   *Provide for financial emergencies.* A family needs a cushion of readily-available capital to serve as protection against sudden emergencies. An amount equal to six month's income is often recommended. There is also need for the protection available through insurance programs.

E.   *Recognize that money has value only in a working economy.* Money is only a means of exchange and has no value in and of itself. It can be used to obtain goods and services in normal times, but may be worthless in times of economic distress. There is wisdom in obtaining needed and desired items before periods of instability arise.

24. Anticipate communication disruption: Make long range emergency plans. Communication and transportation networks could be seriously disrupted or destroyed in the event of war or internal strife. Many of today's families are scattered across the nation. There is wisdom in establishing a family emergency plan, specifying what steps the family would take to be reunited or maintain family ties in the event of major problems in the nation, fixing dates and places for future meetings, proposing alternate communication systems, etc. A formal family organization would strengthen the emergency plans.

Interacting with Others in the Last Days Environment

The duties of the American citizen are many, and require diligent service and loyalty to the principles of freedom if liberty is to be preserved. A present role of the saints is to be a stabilizing influence in the many communities in which they reside across the land.

25. Fulfill the responsibilities of citizenship: Obey the laws of the land. As the perilous days of the "Saturday night of time" draw closer, it is vital that obedience be rendered to the laws of the land and that governmental stability be maintained. The Lord has revealed his counsel on this matter, instructing his people to

> Let no man break the laws of the land, for *he that keepeth the laws of God hath no need to break the laws of the land.*

> Wherefore, *be subject to the powers that be*, until he reigns whose right it is to reign, and subdues all enemies under his feet.[1]

He has commanded the saints to support laws which maintain man's freedom, rights and privileges:

> ...Verily I say unto you concerning the laws of the land, it is my will that my people should observe to do all things whatever I command them.
>
> *And that law of the land which is constitutional, supporting that principle of freedom in maintaining rights and privileges,* belongs to all mankind, and is justifiable before me.
>
> Therefore, I, the Lord, justify you, and your brethren of my church, in befriending that law which is the constitutional law of the land;
>
> And as pertaining to law of man, whatever is more or less than this, cometh of evil.
>
> *I, the Lord God, make you free, therefore ye are free indeed, and the law also maketh you free.*[2]

A declaration of belief regarding governments and laws was adopted by the Church in 1835, which asserts that "we believe that governments were instituted of God for the benefit of man; and that he holds men accountable for their acts in relation to them,..."[3] That declaration holds that governments should make and administer laws "for the good and safety of society,"[4] and that governments are to frame and hold inviolate laws which accomplish three purposes:

1.   secure to each individual the free exercise of conscience,[5]
2.   secure to each individual the right and control of property, and
3.   secure to each individual the protection of life.[6]

That declaration also holds that "*to the laws all men owe respect and deference, as without them peace and harmony would*

---

1.   D & C 58:21-22.
2.   D & C 98:4-8.
3.   D & C 134:1.
4.   *Ibid.*
5.   Note that the Lord said this was his purpose in establishing the U.S. Constitution, "That every man may act in doctrine and principle pertaining to futurity, *according to the moral agency which I have given unto him, that every man may be accountable for his own sins in the day of judgment.*" (D & C 101:78. See verses 79-80.)
6.   D & C 134:2.

be supplanted by anarchy and terror;..."[1] Such a period of anarchy, or internal conflict, is clearly indicated by many prophetic warnings concerning America's future.[2] It appears obvious that anarchy will be averted, in that future period, only to the degree that America's citizens maintain peace and stability through obedience to law and loyal allegiance to existing governments.

What can each individual do to support his country and render obedience to the laws of the land? The author listed the following suggestions in the program to a patriotic bicentennial pageant which he wrote and directed. They were presented under the title, "What Can *I* Do To Preserve My Freedoms?"

1.   I'll study the Constitution and the basic documents of America with my family.

2.   I'll fly the flag, and respect it as the symbol of our country.

3.   I'll make national holidays a special time to teach my children their national heritage.

4.   I'll pledge to keep myself and my family free from sin and the evils of the land.

5.   I'll have respect for law and order, and for those who administer the law.

6.   I'll know what my children are studying in school, and encourage school officials to promote patriotism and loyalty.

7.   I'll work to keep our community and country clean and beautiful.

8.   I'll do an honest day's work, and be honest and above reproach in all my dealings.

9.   I'll study the scriptures and know the prophetic promises and warnings revealed concerning this great land.

10.   I'll teach my children the value of work, and strengthen their qualities of self-reliance and personal initiative.

11.   I'll support clubs and organizations which are working to build character and establish positive values.

12.   I'll actively resist crime and corruption, and be alert to dangers such as vandalism, drugs, and pornography.

13.   I'll strengthen my family relationships and make my family unit a solid building block of society.

14.   I'll prepare for the possibility of difficult times ahead by having an emergency supply of food and clothing and being free from debt.

---

1. D & C 134:6.
2. See pp. 293-302, 309-323; also *Prophecy—Key to the Future*, pp. 49-66.

15. I'll speak out for what I believe, but be sure my statements are characterized by dignity, decency, maturity of thought, and knowledge of the facts.

16. I'll study and properly prepare myself for a vocation so I can be a productive member of the community.

17. I'll be aware of the rising strength of potential enemies to our freedom, and be alert to changes in the international balance of power.

18. I'll work to help good men be elected, and seek to have governmental officials accountable for their actions.

19. I'll read and learn what actually happens when people fall into bondage, so I can understand the freedoms we sometimes take for granted.

20. I'll know the political candidates who can shape my way of life, and support only those I feel will serve competently and righteously.

21. I'll support programs and policies which make government the servant of the people, rather than people the servants of government.

22. I'll study the effects of opposing ideologies on our peace and liberty so I can recognize these theories and those who teach them.

23. I'll list the principles and policies which I believe will help preserve our freedom, and then work to support them.

24. I'll subscribe to a patriotic publication and try to be well-informed on current events.

25. I'll study the major local, state, and national political issues, and know where I stand concerning them.

26. I'll be aware of our national defense capabilities, and work to keep my country prepared.

27. I'll obey the scriptural commandments to warn others of the judgments that are coming if the people of this nation allow wickedness to prevail.

28. I'll preach the gospel by word and by example, for I know that the righteousness of the people is the key to this nation's destiny.

29. I'll pray each day for our country and for its leaders, asking God to let His blessings and protection continue with us.[1]

---

1. Program, *This Is My Country,* presented by the Bountiful, Utah Stake, March 12 and 13, 1976, in the Bountiful Regional Center.

26. Elect good leaders: Uphold honest and wise men. In this era when the nation has plunged rapidly towards wickedness which may bring God's judgments, it is essential that the tide be stemmed, by choosing men of integrity for positions of governmental leadership. God has revealed that

> ...*When the wicked rule the people mourn.*
> Wherefore, honest men and wise men should be sought for diligently, and good men and wise men ye should observe to uphold; otherwise whatsoever is less than these cometh of evil.[1]

The declaration of belief regarding governments and laws states that

> We believe that all governments necessarily require civil officers and magistrates to enforce the laws of the same; and that *such as will administer the law in equity and justice should be sought for and upheld* by the voice of the people if a republic, or the will of the sovereign.[2]

Latter-day Saints believe they should work within the governmental system to accomplish necessary ends. Criminals should be "delivered up and dealt with according to the laws of the land."[3] Those who have been wronged should "importune for redress, and redemption, by the hands of those who are placed as rulers and are in authority over you—according to the laws and constitution of the people,..."[4] The saints are to be tolerant of others, and even of imperfections in the actions of their elected leaders, remembering the Lord's counsel:

> ...Verily I say unto you, and this is wisdom, make unto yourselves friends with the mammon of unrighteousness and they will not destroy you.
> *Leave judgment alone with me,* for it is mine and I will repay.[5]

27. Prepare for future persecutions: Learn how to deal with enemies. Another major message of prophecy is that the saints must endure severe persecution in a time yet future.[6] The Lord has seen fit to give very specific instructions concerning how the saints should deal with those who oppose them. His people should be aware of these instructions and be prepared to abide by them if the need arises. He has told them to

---

1. D & C 98:9-11.
2. D & C 134:3.
3. D & C 42:79. See verses 84-86.
4. D & C 101:76-77. See verses 81-92.
5. D & C 82:22-23. See 58:20.
6. See pp. 171-195.

...Organize yourselves according to the laws of man; That your enemies may not have power over you; that you may be preserved in all things; that you may be enabled to keep my laws; that every bond may be broken wherewith the enemy seeketh to destroy my people.[1]

Revealed counsel has been given to "Be patient in afflictions, *revile not against those that revile.* Govern your house in meekness, and be steadfast."[2] The Lord has also commanded, "Behold, it is said in my laws, or forbidden, to get in debt to thine enemies."

Zion's Camp was taught other principles to help them be safe from their enemies. The Lord instructed them to "Talk not of judgments, neither boast of faith nor of mighty works, but *carefully gather together,* as much in one region as can be, consistently with the feelings of the people;..."[3] They were also told to

...Sue for peace, not only to the people that have smitten you, but also to all people:

And lift up an ensign of peace, and make a proclamation of peace unto the ends of the earth;

And make proposals for peace unto those who have smitten you, according to the voice of the Spirit which is in you, and all things shall work together for your good.[4]

While he was a prisoner in Liberty Jail, the prophet Joseph Smith set forth the duties of the saints in relation to their persecutors. He said it was their "imperative duty" to

1.   Be sure all the saints were informed and given knowledge of the sufferings and abuses which had been endured.[5]

2.   Be sure a record was kept of all damages sustained, both of character, personal injuries, and real property.[6]

3.   Be sure a record was kept of the names of all persons involved in instances of oppression.[7]

4.   Be sure to obtain evidence in the form of statements and affidavits.[8]

5.   Be sure to gather copies of all libelous publications.[9]

6.   Publish the above to all the world and present them to heads of government.[10]

---

1. D & C 44:4-5.
2. D & C 31:9.
3. D & C 105:24.
4. D & C 105:38-40.
5. D & C 123:1.

6. D & C 123:2.
7. D & C 123:3.
8. D & C 123:4.
9. D & C 123:4-5.
10. D & C 123:6.

All of the preceding is

> ...Enjoined on us by our Heavenly Father, before we can fully and com-
> pletely claim that promise which shall call him forth from his hiding
> place; and also that *the whole nation may be left without excuse before
> he can send forth the power of his mighty arm.*[1]

Doctrine and Covenants section 98 contains a comprehensive explanation of how to deal with enemies who persecute the
saints. The Lord has said,

> Now, I speak unto you concerning your families—*if men will smite
> you, or your families, once,* and ye bear it patiently and revile not
> against them, neither seek revenge, ye shall be rewarded;
> But if ye bear it not patiently, it shall be accounted unto you as be-
> ing meted out as a just measure unto you.
> And again, *if your enemy shall smite you the second time,* and you
> revile not against your enemy, and bear it patiently, your reward shall
> be an hundred-fold.
> And again, *if he shall smite you the third time,* and ye bear it pa-
> tiently, your reward shall be doubled unto you four-fold;
> *And these three testimonies shall stand against your enemy if he re-
> pent not, and shall not be blotted out.*
> And now, verily I say unto you, if that enemy shall escape my
> vengeance, that he be not brought into judgment before me, then *ye
> shall see to it that ye warn him in my name, that he come no more
> upon you, neither upon your family,* even your children's children unto
> the third and fourth generation.
> And then, if he shall come upon you or your children, or your chil-
> dren's children unto the third and fourth generation, *I have delivered
> thine enemy into thine hands;*
> And then if thou wilt spare him, thou shalt be rewarded for thy
> righteousness; and also thy children and thy children's children unto
> the third and fourth generation.
> *Nevertheless, thine enemy is in thine hands;* and if thou rewardest
> him according to his works thou art justified; *if he has sought thy life,
> and thy life is endangered by him, thine enemy is in thine hands and
> thou art justified.*[2]

The declaration of belief regarding governments and laws
states that

> *We believe that men should appeal to the civil law for redress of all
> wrongs and grievances,* where personal abuse is inflicted or the right of

---

1. *Ibid.* He added that "there is much which lieth in futurity, pertaining
   to the saints, which depends upon these things." (D & C 123:15.)
2. D & C 98:23-31.

property or character infringed, where such laws exist as will protect the same; but we believe that *all men are justified in defending themselves, their friends, and property, and the government, from the unlawful assaults and encroachments of all persons in times of exigency,* where immediate appeal cannot be made to the laws, and relief afforded.[1]

Two passages from the Book of Mormon explain the motives under which it is appropriate to engage in combat with enemies. The first deals with the Nephites as they united to resist the Lamanites who were attacking under the leadership of their wicked chief captain, Zerahemnah:

> Nevertheless, the Nephites were inspired by a better cause, for *they were not fighting for monarchy nor power but they were fighting for their homes and their liberties, their wives and their children, and their all, yea, for their rites of worship and their church.*
>
> And they were doing that which they felt was the *duty which they owed to their God;* for the Lord had said unto them, and also unto their fathers, that: *Inasmuch as ye are not guilty of the first offense, neither the second, ye shall not suffer yourselves to be slain by the hands of your enemies.*
>
> And again, the Lord has said that: *Ye shall defend your families even unto bloodshed.* Therefore for this cause were the Nephites contending with the Lamanites, *to defend themselves, and their families, and their lands, their country, and their rights, and their religion.*[2]

The second describes the motives of the Nephites as they united under the leadership of General Moroni:

> *Now the Nephites were taught to defend themselves against their enemies, even to the shedding of blood if it were necessary;* yea, and they were also taught *never to give an offense,* yea, and *never to raise the sword except it were against an enemy, except it were to preserve their lives.*
>
> *And this was their faith, that by so doing God would prosper them in the land,* or in other words, if they were faithful in keeping the commandments of God that *he would prosper them in the land; yea, warn them to flee, or to prepare for war, according to their danger;*
>
> And also, that *God would make it known unto them whither they should go to defend themselves against their enemies,* and by so doing, the Lord would deliver them; and this was the faith of Moroni, and his heart did glory in it; not in the shedding of blood but *in doing good, in preserving his people, yea, in keeping the commandments of God, yea, and resisting iniquity.*[3]

---

1. D & C 134:11.
2. Al. 43:45-47.

3. Al. 48:14-16.

If enemies attempt to drive the saints from the land of Zion,[1] the Lord has instructed his people that

> ... *Ye shall curse them;*
> *And whomsoever ye curse, I will curse* and ye shall avenge me of mine enemies.
> And my presence shall be with you even in avenging me of mine enemies, unto the third and fourth generation of them that hate me.[2]

During all the events of the future, the saints should remember the Lord's decree that they will prevail against their enemies so long as they keep his commandments:

> Behold, *they shall,* for I have decreed it, *begin to prevail against mine enemies from this very hour.*
> And by hearkening to observe all the words which I, the Lord their God, shall speak unto them, *they shall never cease to prevail* until the kingdoms of the world are subdued under my feet, and the earth is given unto the saints, to possess it forever and ever.
> *But inasmuch as they keep not my commandments, and hearken not to observe all my words, the kingdoms of the world shall prevail against them.*[3]

In Conclusion

Thus ends this account of God's message concerning the events of the last days. It is scriptural. It is accurate in its interpretation. It is true. It is written in partial fulfillment of the inspired prayer of Joseph Smith, in which he asked the Savior to

> *Put upon thy servants the testimony of the covenant,* that when they go out and proclaim thy word they may *seal up the law, and prepare the hearts of thy saints for all those judgments thou art about to send,* in thy wrath, upon the earth, because of their transgressions, *that thy people may not faint in the day of trouble.*[4]

---

1. See D & C 64:41-43; 45:66-75.
2. D & C 103:24-26. See verses 2-3. This commandment differs from the Savior's instruction to "love your enemies" (see Mt. 5:38-45), but is in accordance with other passages of scripture: Al. 33:10; D & C 109: 50-53; 133:40, 42-43. It conforms to the Lord's commandment that the saints should leave a witness against the wicked in the last days. (See pp. 373-376.)
3. D & C 103:6-8.
4. D & C 109:38.

It has not been an easy book to write. Neither has it been a pleasant one, for it speaks of tragic events which will bring much sorrow and suffering upon the land and people I love. But the Spirit gave repeated instruction that it come forth, and I have sought to obey. If it were in my power to turn away the prophesied calamities, I would do so, and save the nation from the impending judgments. I recognize that deliverance will only be granted to the Lord's people who live in righteousness, and I seek to be numbered among them. My sentiments were well expressed in the prayer of dedication offered by the prophet Joseph:

> O Lord, *we delight not in the destruction of our fellow man;* their souls are precious before thee;
> *But thy word must be fulfilled.* Help thy servants to say, with thy grace assisting them: Thy will be done, O Lord, and not ours.
> We know that thou hast spoken by the mouth of thy prophets *terrible things concerning the wicked, in the last days—that thou wilt pour out thy judgments, without measure;*
> Therefore, O Lord, *deliver thy people from the calamity of the wicked;* enable thy servants to seal up the law, and bind up the testimony, that they may be prepared against the day of burning.[1]

Ye saints, remember that "All victory and glory is brought to pass unto you through your diligence, faithfulness, and prayers of faith."[2] Put on the whole armor of God, "That ye may be able to withstand the evil day,"[3] and look forward to the day when the Church will arise and "Shine forth fair as the moon, clear as the sun, and terrible as an army with banners; and be adorned as a bride...."[4] "Fear not to do good,"[5] and trust in the Lord as he brings about the establishment of his Zion and prepares the pure in heart. Find joy in the anticipation of his peaceable kingdom, and remember that he has instructed the saints to

> ...Let your hearts be comforted concerning Zion; for all flesh is in mine hands; *be still and know that I am God.*[6]

Summary

1.   This chapter has been written to assist those desiring to adopt an effective course for the future. It summarizes scriptural

---

1. D & C 109:43-46.
2. D & C 103:36.
3. D & C 27:15-18. See Eph. 6:10-17.
4. D & C 109:73-74.
5. D & C 6:33-34.
6. D & C 101:16.

counsel for proper attitudes and conduct, and attempts to point out a viable path that will safely lead through the perilous times to come.

    2.   It is wise to adopt attitudes concerning the last days which are based on eternal perspective. Attempting to envision the events to come from God's point of view can help man to properly orient his life. Eight observations were made:

    A.   God directs the affairs of man.
    B.   God desires to bless and reward man.
    C.   Last day's judgments are part of man's mortal probation.
    D.   God chastens those he loves.
    E.   Death is sweet to those who die in the Lord.
    F.   There must be a transition to Christ's millennial kingdom.
    G.   The earth is approaching the end of its temporal existence.
    H.   Look forward to the blessings of the millennial era.

    3.   Scriptural counsel was cited concerning spiritual preparations for survival. The saints have been instructed to

    A.   Cleanse themselves from sins which bring judgments: Repent.
    B.   Escape judgments through obedience: Keep God's commandments.
    C.   Be free from the sins of the generation: Sanctify themselves.
    D.   Prepare spiritually: Be guided by the Holy Ghost.
    E.   Recognize last day's events: Watch for signs of the times.
    F.   Teach doctrines of the last days: Seek knowledge for protection.
    G.   Prepare the saints for the hour of judgment: Warn their neighbor.
    H.   Preach repentance to non-members: Warn of coming judgments.
    I.   Bind the law and seal the testimony: Testify against the wicked.
    J.   Go ye out from Babylon: Be separate from the wicked.
    K.   Seek divine strength, guidance and protection: Pray always.

      L.   Prepare for return of the united order: Be ready to share.

      M.   Resolve to attain eternal goals: Endure to the end.

    4.   Temporal preparations for survival were also recommended, which included the following principles and instructions:

      A.   Anticipate physical needs: Store food, clothing, fuel.

      B.   Anticipate the reality of nuclear war: Strengthen civil defense.

      C.   Anticipate the danger of economic upheaval: Be free from debt.

      D.   Anticipate communication disruption: Make long-range emergency plans.

    5.   Scriptural counsel for interacting with others in the last days was presented, together with many suggestions for being an effective citizen. This counsel was summarized under the following categories:

      A.   Fulfill the responsibilities of citizenship: Obey the laws of the land.

      B.   Elect good leaders: Uphold honest and wise men.

      C.   Prepare for future persecution: Learn how to deal with enemies.

    6.   As the events of the last days unfold, the saints must be willing to say "Thy will be done, O Lord, and not ours," and then "be still and know" that God is governing the affairs of men.

List of Quotations

D & C (Cont.)		D & C (Cont.)		D & C (Cont.)		D & C (Cont.)	
19:15	363	45:44	369	63:32-37	326	82:24	229
20:17-18	356	45:47-50	336	63:33-35	282	84:2-5	163
20:53-54	228	45:56-57	239	63:34	254	84:18	229
22:1-4	231	45:56-57	240	63:35-40	256	84:33	366
24:15-17	375	45:56-57	241	63:36-37	373	84:54-59	250
24:19	374	45:56-57	256	63:37	228	84:54-59	256
27:15-18	401	45:56-57	367	63:37	379	84:54-59	344
29:8	379	45:56-75	236	63:50	362	84:55-59	364
29:11	361	45:57	236	63:53-54	241	84:80-84	360
29:14-21	348	45:59	361	63:63	232	84:87	3
29:26	361	45:63	283	63:63	250	84:87	250
29:42-44	357	45:65-71,		63:63	364	84:87	372
31:4	374	74-75	326	63:64	367	84:87, 117	228
31:8	371	45:66	169	64	247	84:92-97	375
31:8	377	45:66	379	64:4	229	84:94-98	251
31:9	397	45:66-67	163	64:33-43	236	84:96-97	343
33:2-4	374	45:66-67	400	64:35	236	84:114-115	251
33:10	371	45:67	169	64:35-40	232	84:117	3
33:10	372	45:67, 70	330	64:35-40	233	84:117	229
34:6	374	45:68	169	64:35-40	235	84:117	372
34:6-10	373	45:68-69	168	64:35-40	327	85:3	371
35:16	368	45:68-69	379	64:37-39	185	85:3-12	236
35:24	365	45:68-71,		64:41-43	400	85:6	245
35:27	229	74-75	164	64:41-43	327	85:7	248
38:1-3	356	45:69	168	64:43	330	85:7-12	245
38:8	365	45:69	169	65:1-3	371	85:7-12	256
38:9	229	45:69, 71	169	65:2	228	85:10	245
38:11-12	374	45:70, 74-75	169	66:2	231	85:11	236
38:18-22	19	45:74-75	168	68:2, 7	288	87:1-2	283
38:22	360	48:1	377	68:4	288	87:3-5, 6	283
38:22	362	49:23	369	68:10-11	368	87:5	313
38:28-31	370	49:26-27	364	68:11-12	375	87:6	363
38:29	284	50:1-34	239	70:7-10	384	87:6-8	263
38:29-31	19	50:5	386	70:14	385	87:8	378
38:40-41	227	50:35	229	75:18-22	375	88:2	184
38:40-41	372	50:35	386	76:5-6, 7-10	356	88:18-19	361
39:16-18	382	57:1-5	163	76:25-26	237	88:19-20	361
41:1	356	58:2-4	357	76:28-35	237	88:25-26	361
41:4	360	58:5	369	76:29, 32	237	88:40	356
42:36	379	58:6	369	76:43	237	88:41	356
42:44-47	360	58:6	373	76:45-48	237	88:63-65	367
42:79, 84-86	396	58:20	396	76:45-48	257	88:67-68	366
43:20-21	373	58:21-22	393	76:68	184	88:73-75,	
43:24-25	357	58:26-28	5	76:101	231	85, 138	366
43:25-26	341	58:28	356	76:106-107	229	88:77-80	370
44:4-5	397	59:16-21	356	76:116	367	88:79	371
45:2, 6	365	60:2-3	3	77	183	88:81	3
45:9	231	60:12-13	3	77:6	361	88:81	371
45:24-25	253	60:15	375	77:12	184	88:81	385
45:25	283	61:38	368	77:12-13	346	88:81, 84	228
45:26-27	253	61:39	381	78:13-14	384	88:84	375
45:26-33	283	62:9	229	78:18	229	88:84-85	3
45:31-32	343	63:2-4, 49-51	360	82:5-6	374	88:84-85	371
45:31-33	252	63:17-18	386	82:14-18	384	88:85	229
45:31-33	253	63:20	386	82:19	385	88:86	364
45:31-33	256	63:24	378	82:20	385	88:87-89	3
45:32	378	63:24-52	241	82:21	385	88:92	371
45:39, 44	368	63:32	374	82:22-23	396	88:118	370

Index

411